Listen up, Clay.
If you ever find yourself alone in a dungeon ...
just one misstep will mean certain doom.
Don't slip up.
Okay!
1
For example.
?!!

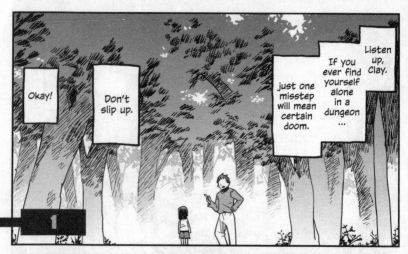

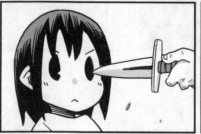

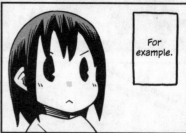

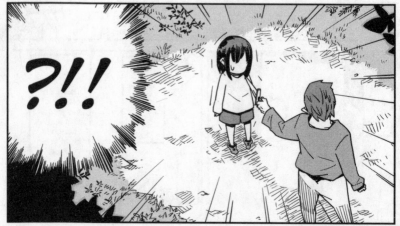

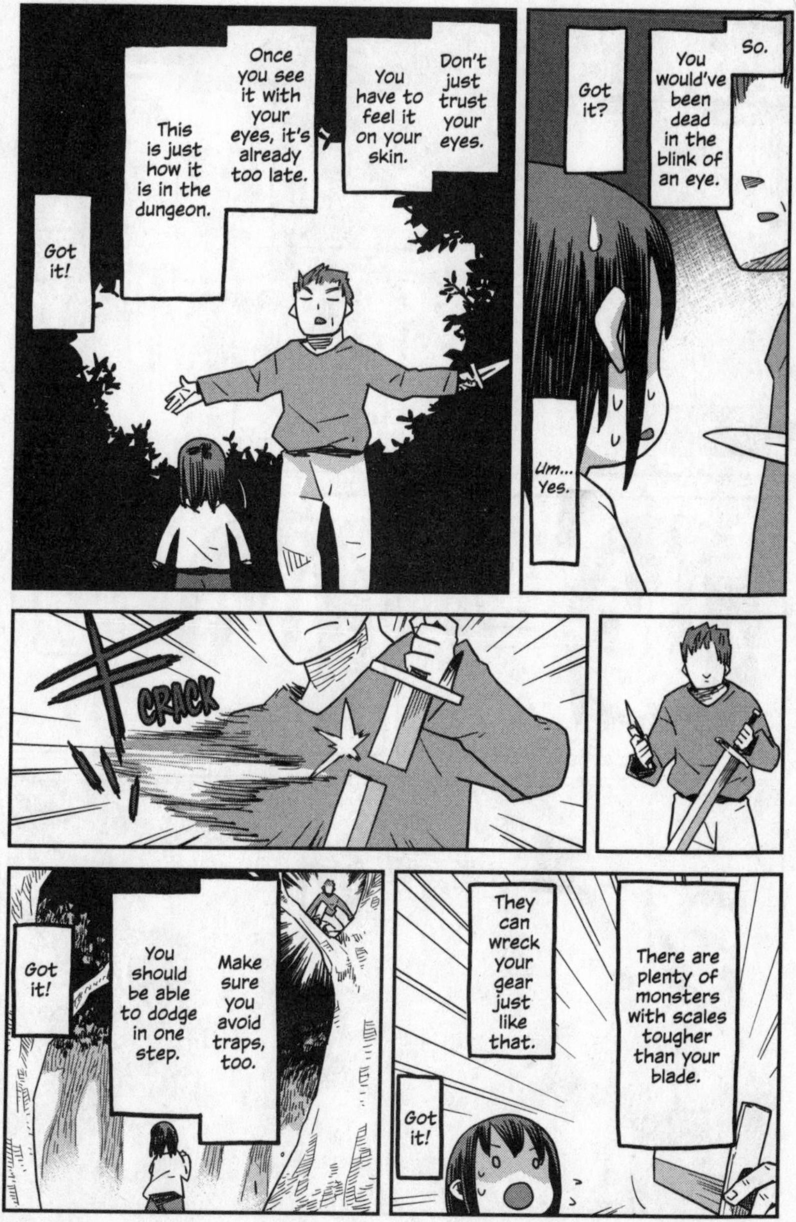
So.
You would've been dead in the blink of an eye.
Got it?
Um... Yes.
Don't just trust your eyes.
You have to feel it on your skin.
Once you see it with your eyes, it's already too late.
This is just how it is in the dungeon.
Got it!
CRACK
There are plenty of monsters with scales tougher than your blade.
They can wreck your gear just like that.
Got it!
Make sure you avoid traps, too.
You should be able to dodge in one step.
Got it!

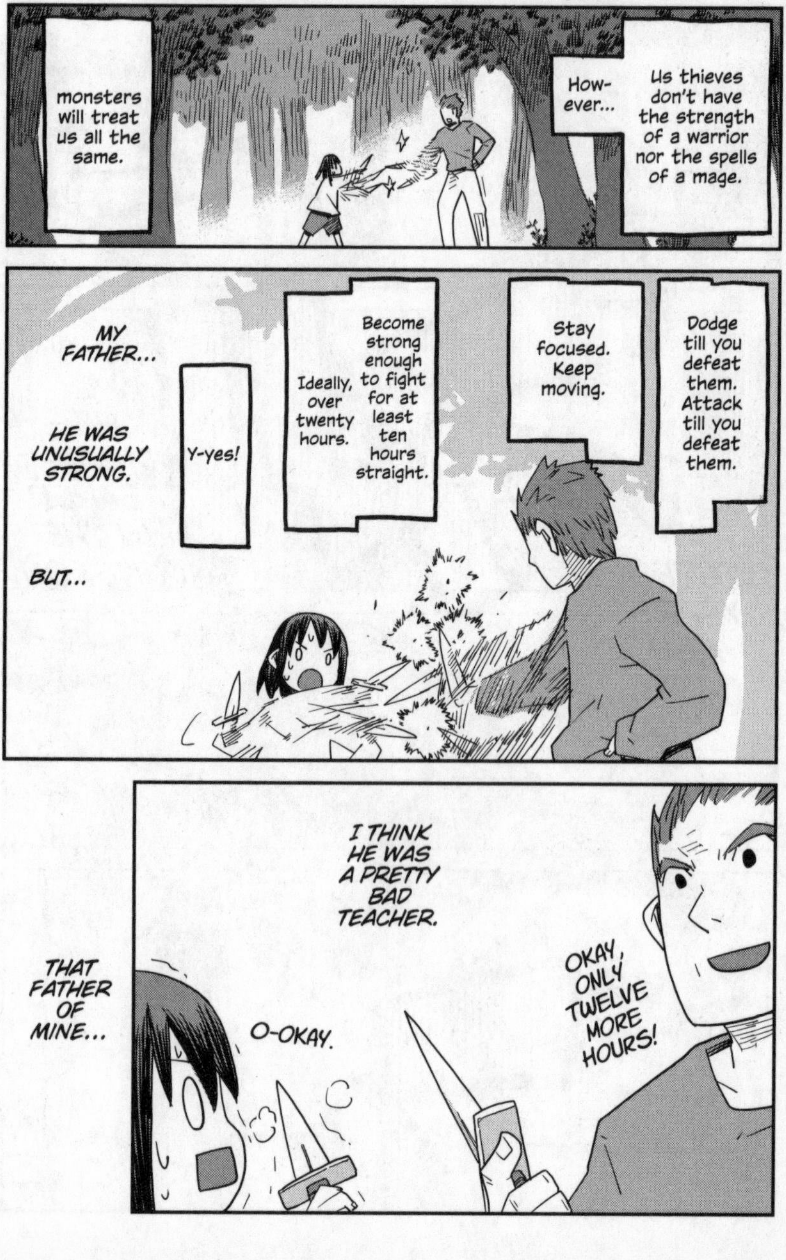
Us thieves don't have the strength of a warrior nor the spells of a mage.
How-ever...
monsters will treat us all the same.
Dodge till you defeat them. Attack till you defeat them.
Stay focused. Keep moving.
Become strong enough to fight for at least ten hours straight.
Ideally, over twenty hours.
Y-yes!
MY FATHER...
HE WAS UNUSUALLY STRONG.
BUT...
OKAY, ONLY TWELVE MORE HOURS!
I THINK HE WAS A PRETTY BAD TEACHER.
O-OKAY.
THAT FATHER OF MINE...

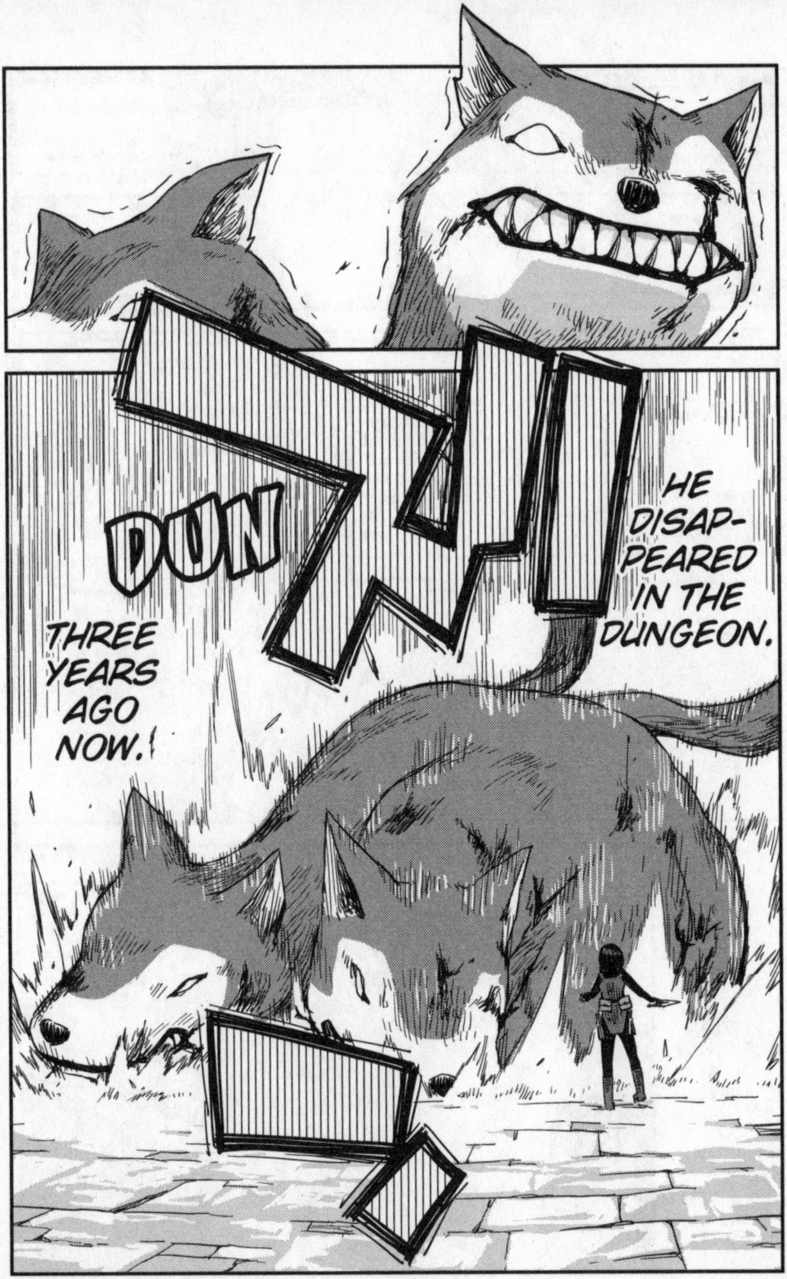
HE DISAP-
PEARED
IN THE
DUNGEON.
DUN
THREE
YEARS
AGO
NOW.

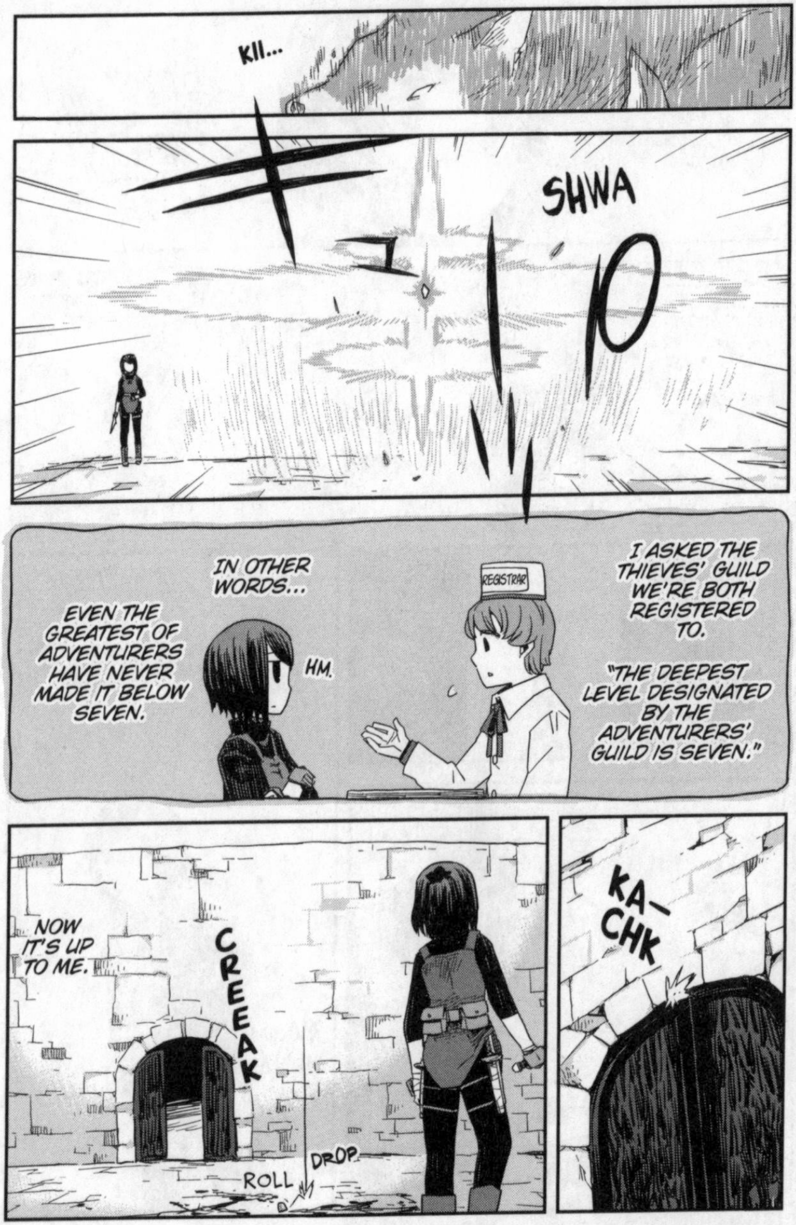
KII...
SHWA
I ASKED THE THIEVES' GUILD WE'RE BOTH REGISTERED TO.
"THE DEEPEST LEVEL DESIGNATED BY THE ADVENTURERS' GUILD IS SEVEN."
IN OTHER WORDS...
HM.
EVEN THE GREATEST OF ADVENTURERS HAVE NEVER MADE IT BELOW SEVEN.
KA-CHK
CREEAK
NOW IT'S UP TO ME.
DROP
ROLL

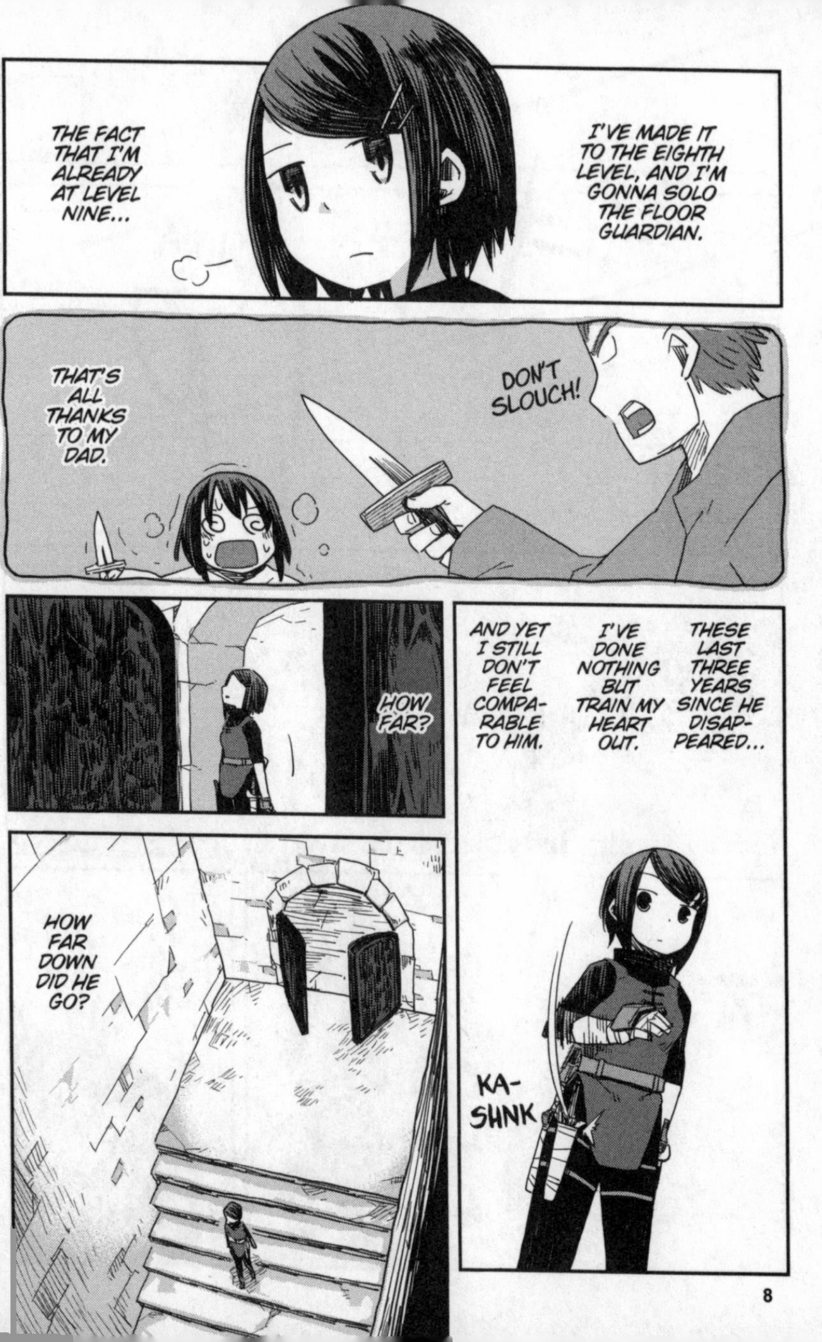

I'VE MADE IT TO THE EIGHTH LEVEL, AND I'M GONNA SOLO THE FLOOR GUARDIAN.
THE FACT THAT I'M ALREADY AT LEVEL NINE...
DON'T SLOUCH!
THAT'S ALL THANKS TO MY DAD.
THESE LAST THREE YEARS SINCE HE DISAP-PEARED...
I'VE DONE NOTHING BUT TRAIN MY HEART OUT.
AND YET I STILL DON'T FEEL COMPA-RABLE TO HIM.
KA-SHNK
HOW FAR?
HOW FAR DOWN DID HE GO?

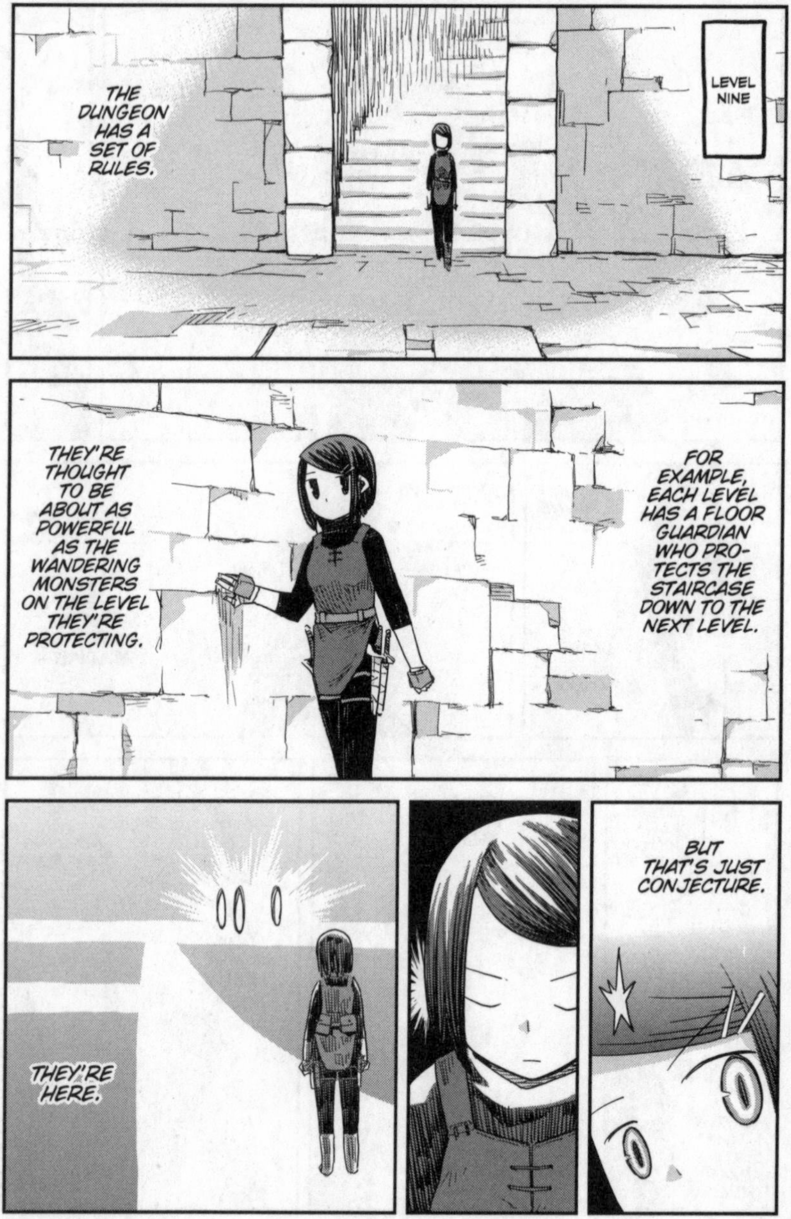
LEVEL NINE
THE DUNGEON HAS A SET OF RULES.
FOR EXAMPLE, EACH LEVEL HAS A FLOOR GUARDIAN WHO PRO-TECTS THE STAIRCASE DOWN TO THE NEXT LEVEL.
THEY'RE THOUGHT TO BE ABOUT AS POWERFUL AS THE WANDERING MONSTERS ON THE LEVEL THEY'RE PROTECTING.
BUT THAT'S JUST CONJECTURE.
THEY'RE HERE.

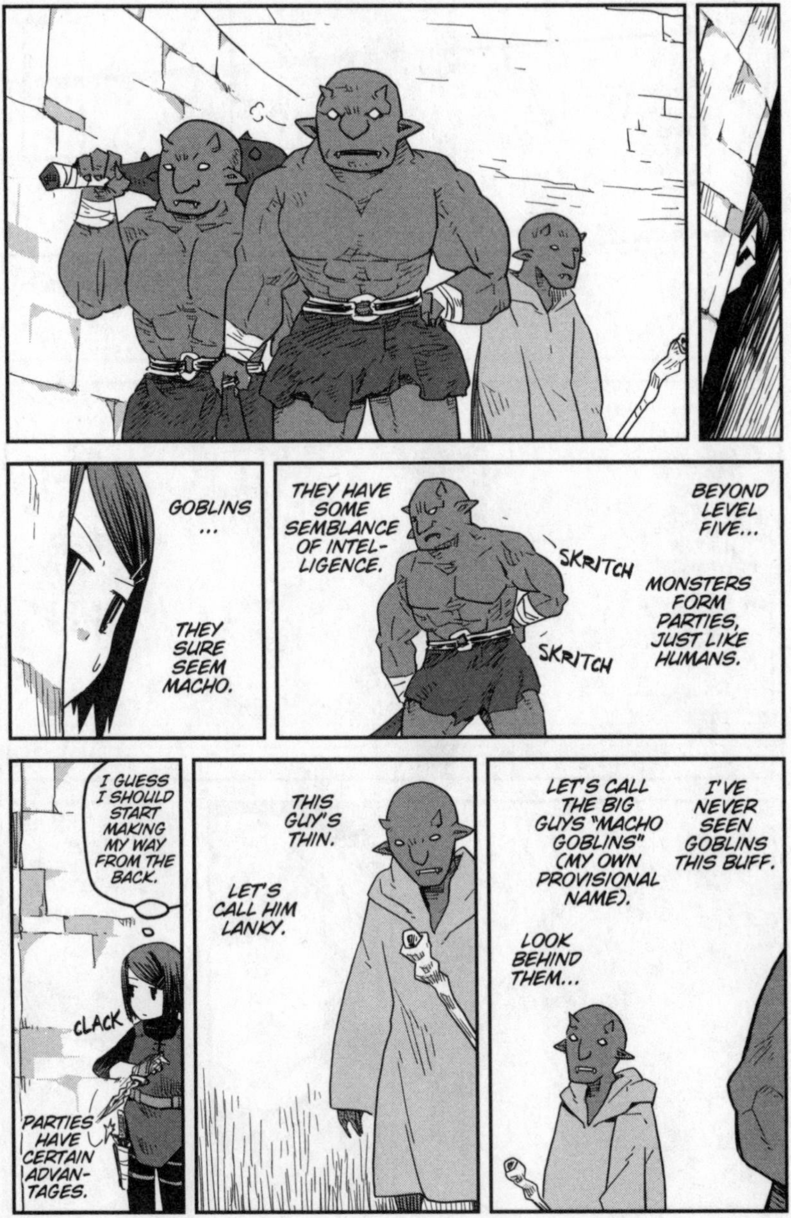
BEYOND LEVEL FIVE...
MONSTERS FORM PARTIES, JUST LIKE HUMANS.
THEY HAVE SOME SEMBLANCE OF INTEL-LIGENCE.
SKRITCH
SKRITCH
GOBLINS ...
THEY SURE SEEM MACHO.
I'VE NEVER SEEN GOBLINS THIS BUFF.
LET'S CALL THE BIG GUYS "MACHO GOBLINS" (MY OWN PROVISIONAL NAME).
LOOK BEHIND THEM...
THIS GUY'S THIN.
LET'S CALL HIM LANKY.
I GUESS I SHOULD START MAKING MY WAY FROM THE BACK.
CLACK
PARTIES HAVE CERTAIN ADVAN-TAGES.

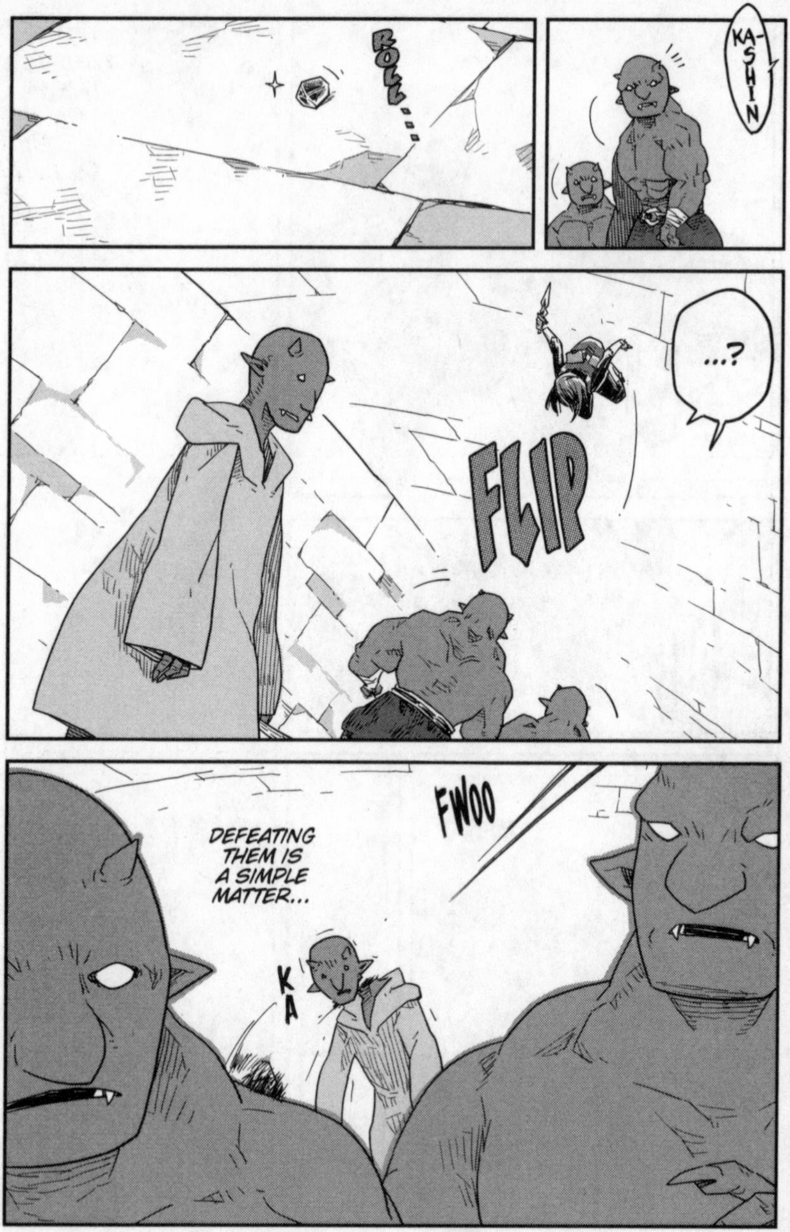
KA-SHIN
ROLL...
...?
FLIP
FWOO
DEFEATING THEM IS A SIMPLE MATTER...
KA

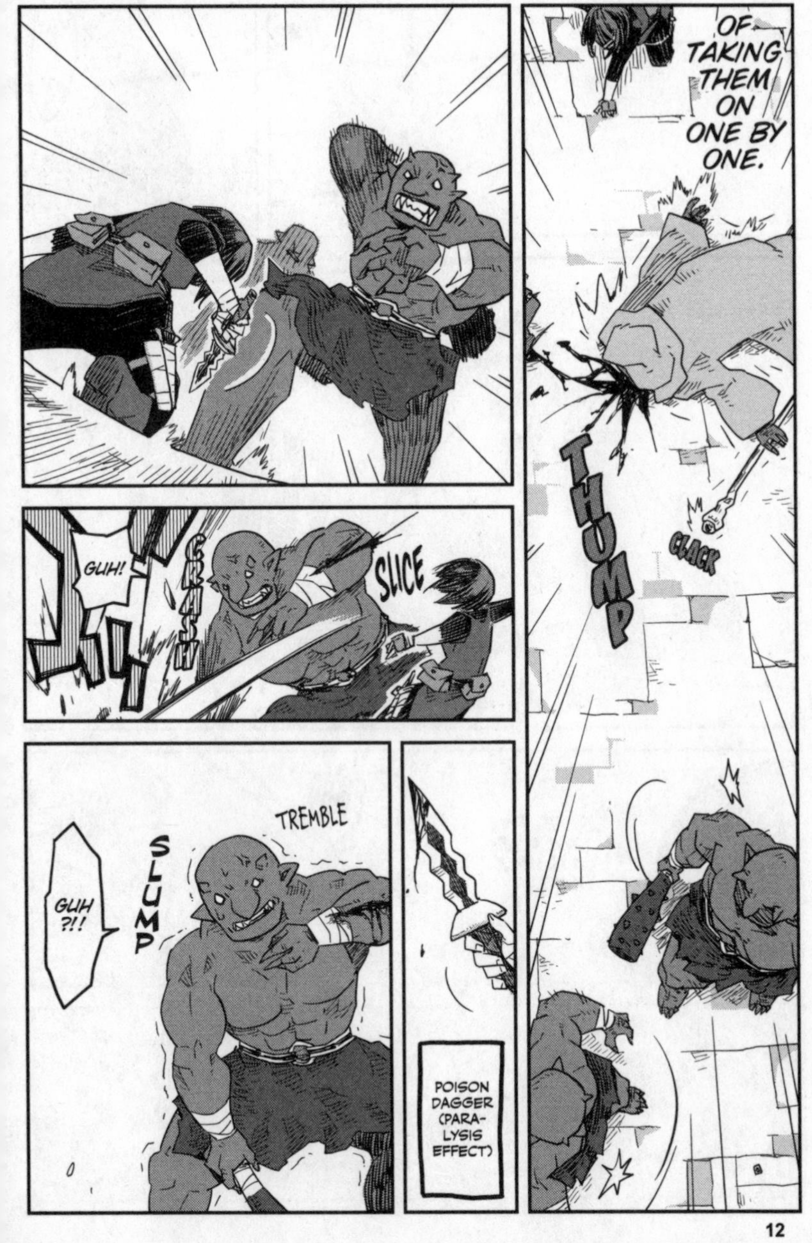
OF TAKING THEM ON ONE BY ONE.
THUMP
CLACK
SLICE
CRASH
GUH!
POISON DAGGER (PARA-LYSIS EFFECT)
TREMBLE
SLUMP
GUH ?!!

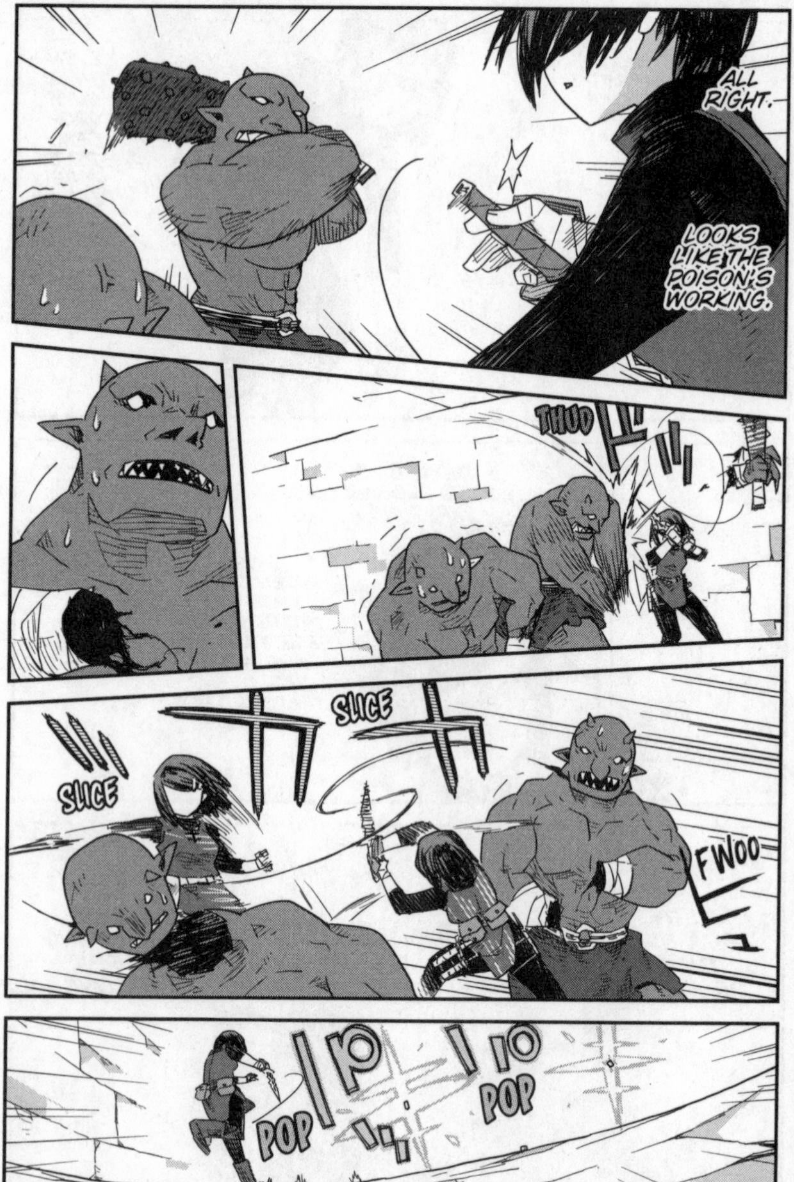
ALL RIGHT.
LOOKS LIKE THE POISON'S WORKING.
THUD
SLICE
FWOO
SLICE
POP
POP

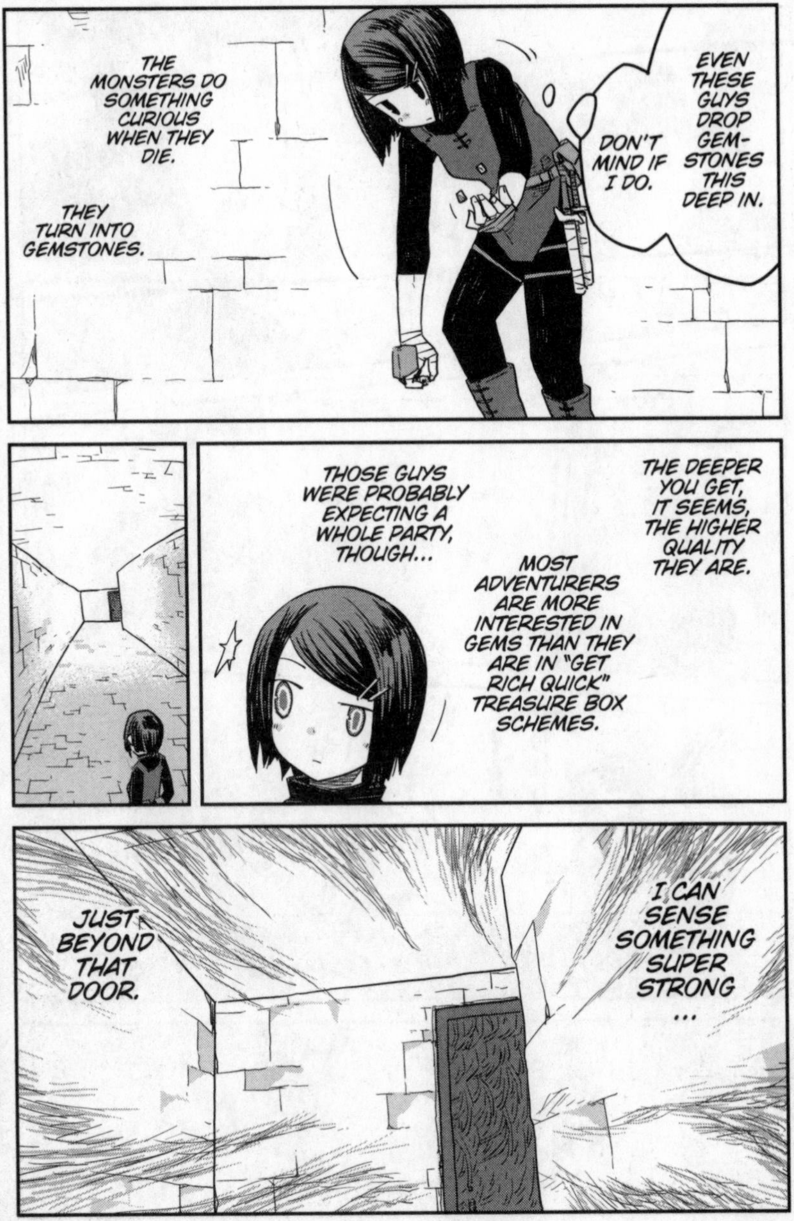
EVEN THESE GUYS DROP GEMSTONES THIS DEEP IN.
DON'T MIND IF I DO.
THE MONSTERS DO SOMETHING CURIOUS WHEN THEY DIE.
THEY TURN INTO GEMSTONES.
THE DEEPER YOU GET, IT SEEMS, THE HIGHER QUALITY THEY ARE.
MOST ADVENTURERS ARE MORE INTERESTED IN GEMS THAN THEY ARE IN "GET RICH QUICK" TREASURE BOX SCHEMES.
THOSE GUYS WERE PROBABLY EXPECTING A WHOLE PARTY, THOUGH...
I CAN SENSE SOMETHING SUPER STRONG...
JUST BEYOND THAT DOOR.

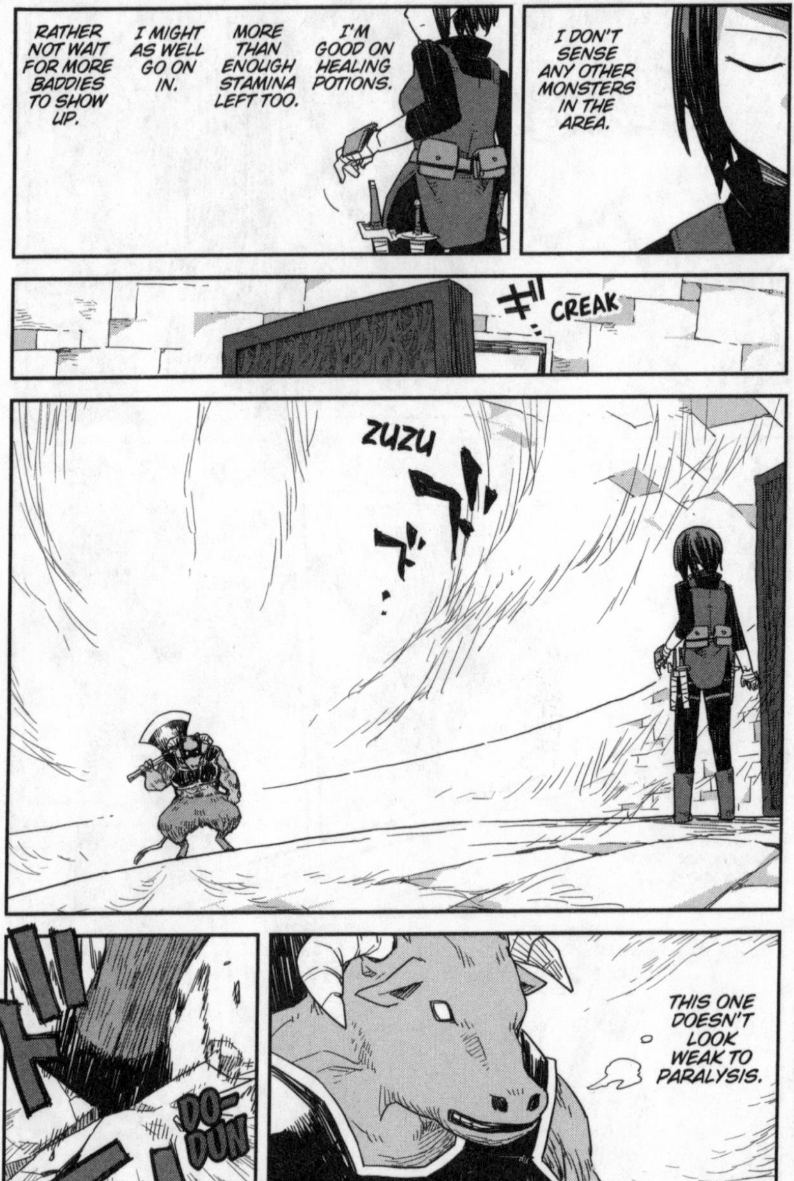
I DON'T SENSE ANY OTHER MONSTERS IN THE AREA.
I'M GOOD ON HEALING POTIONS.
MORE THAN ENOUGH STAMINA LEFT TOO.
I MIGHT AS WELL GO ON IN.
RATHER NOT WAIT FOR MORE BADDIES TO SHOW UP.
CREAK
ZUZU
THIS ONE DOESN'T LOOK WEAK TO PARALYSIS.
DO-DUN

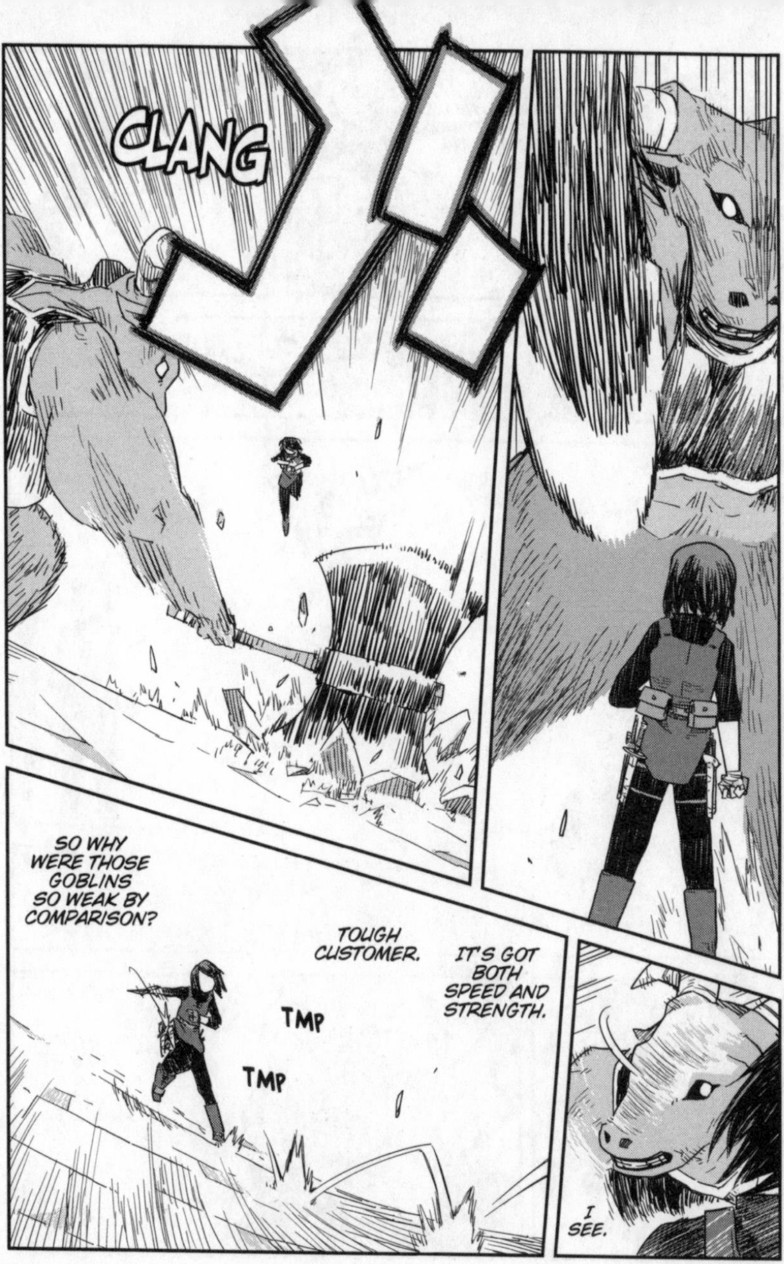
CLANG
I SEE.
TOUGH CUSTOMER.
IT'S GOT BOTH SPEED AND STRENGTH.
SO WHY WERE THOSE GOBLINS SO WEAK BY COMPARISON?
TMP
TMP

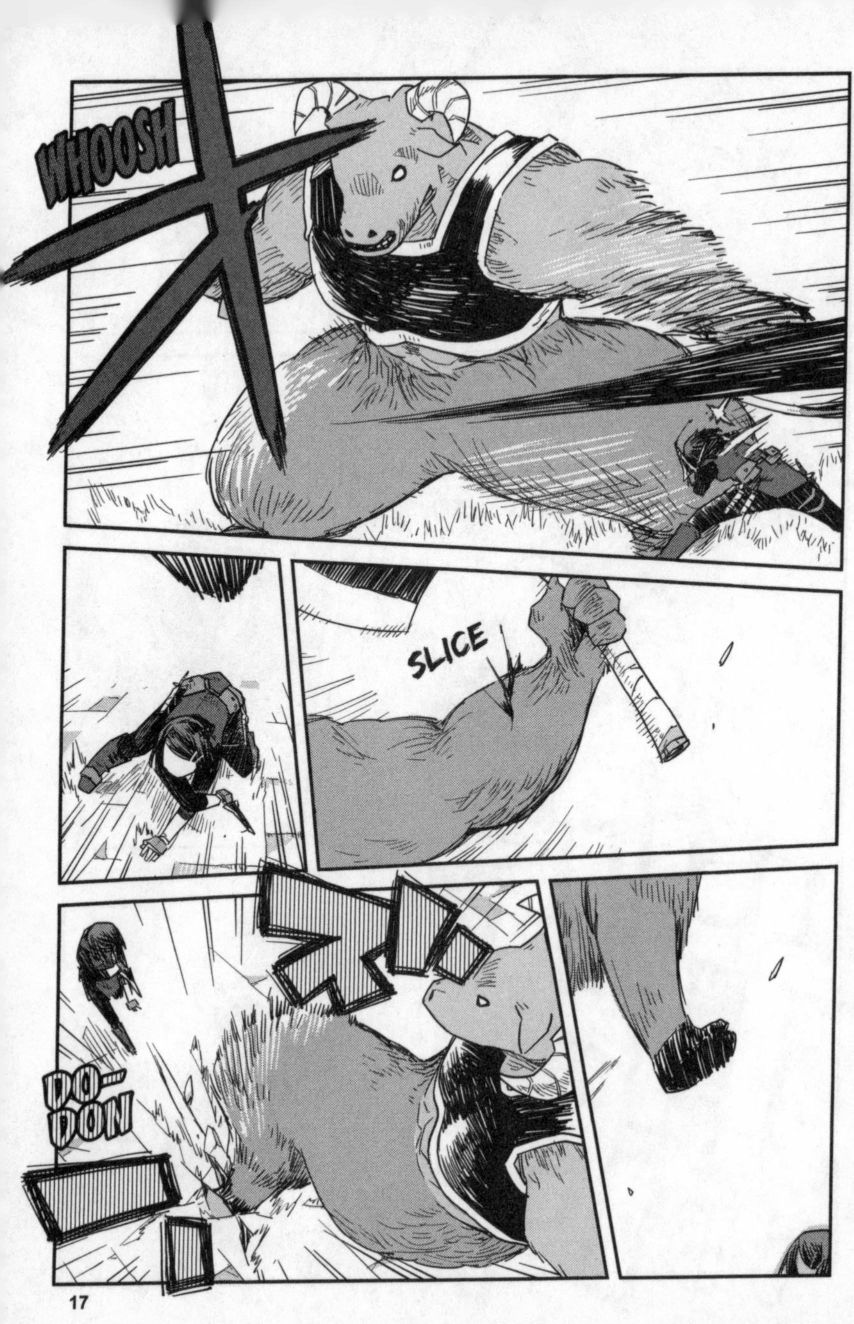
WHOOSH
SLICE
DO-DON

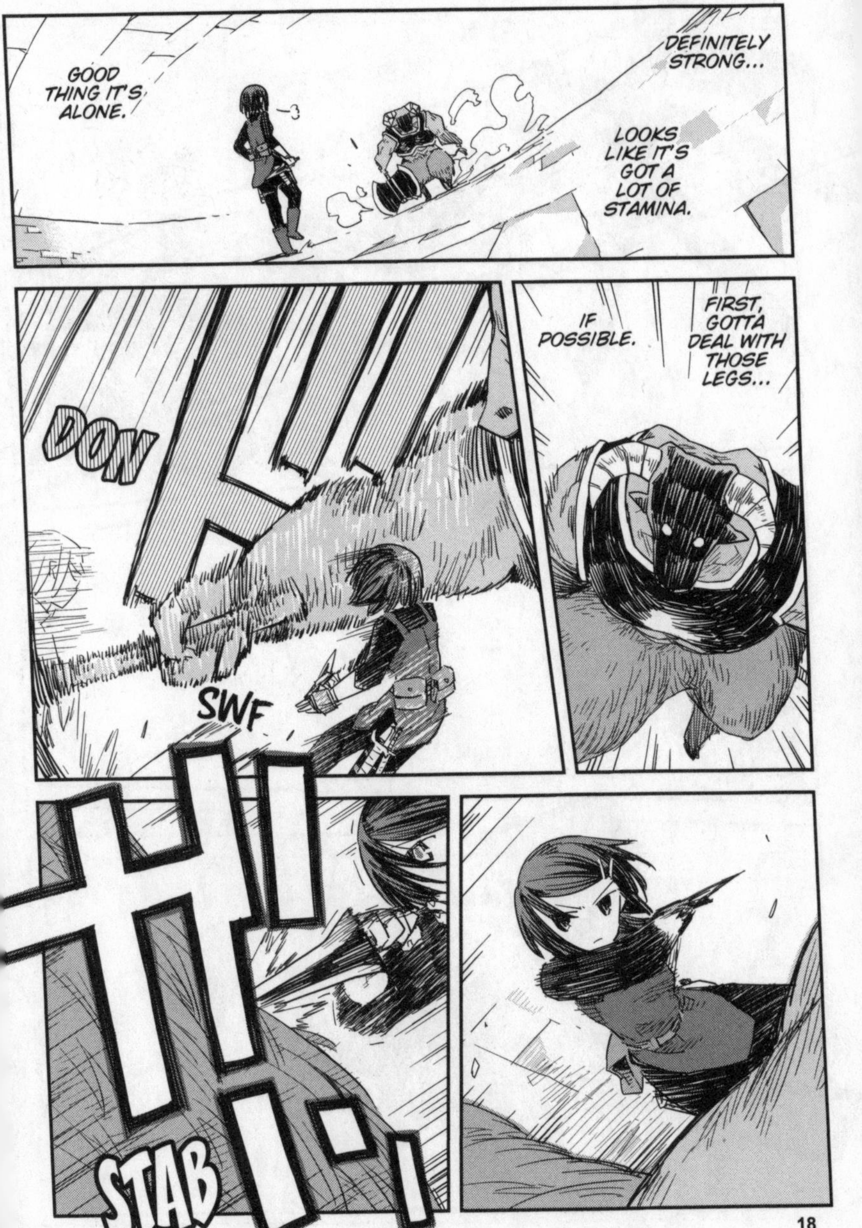
DEFINITELY STRONG...
LOOKS LIKE IT'S GOT A LOT OF STAMINA.
GOOD THING IT'S ALONE.
FIRST, GOTTA DEAL WITH THOSE LEGS...
IF POSSIBLE.
DON
SWF
STAB

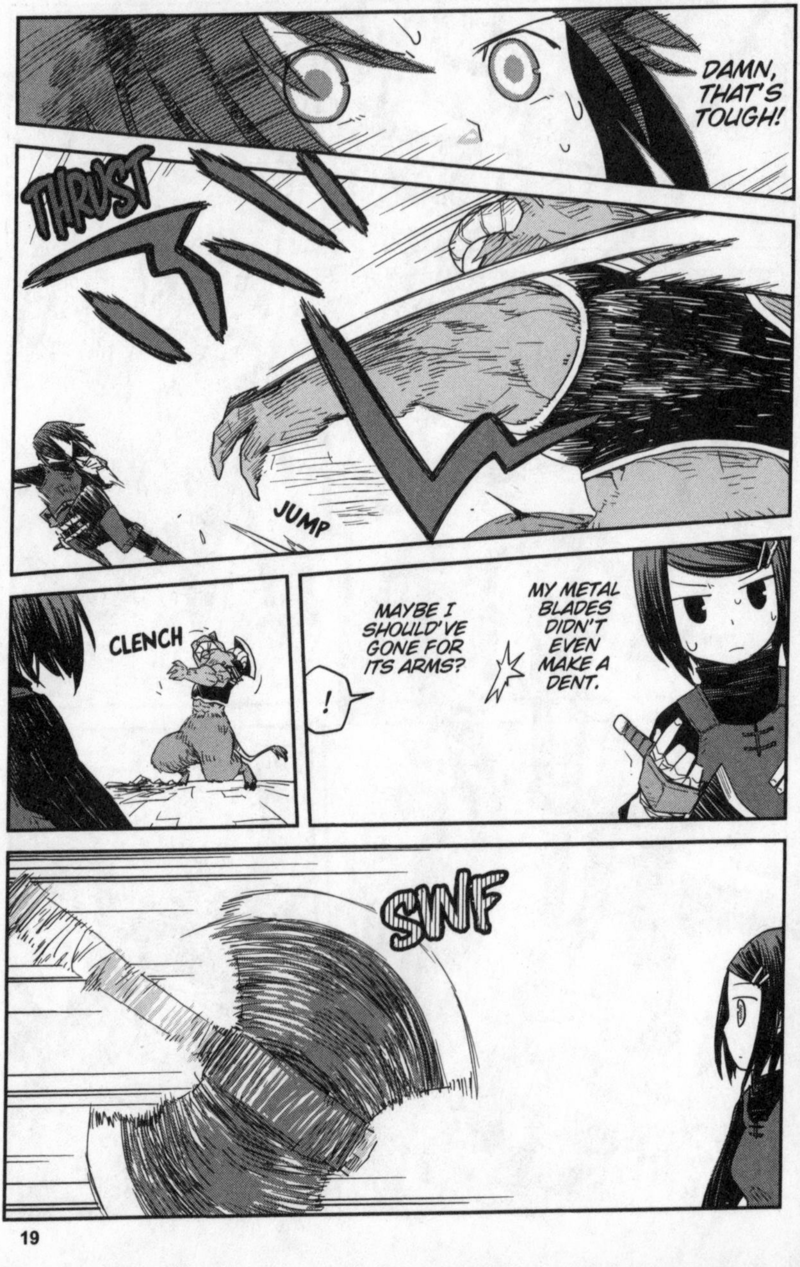
DAMN, THAT'S TOUGH!
THRUST
JUMP
MY METAL BLADES DIDN'T EVEN MAKE A DENT.
MAYBE I SHOULD'VE GONE FOR ITS ARMS?
!
CLENCH
SWF

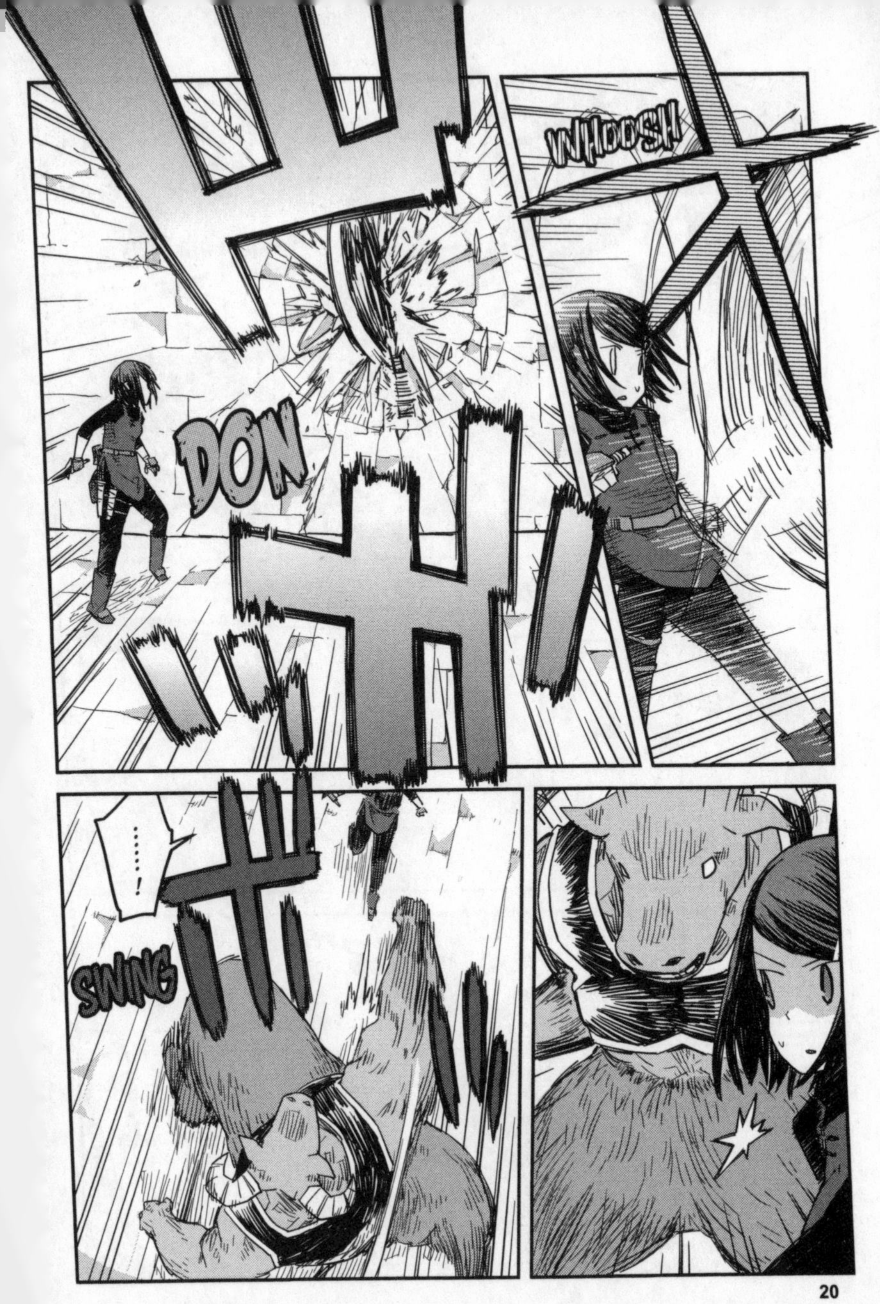
WHOOSH
DON
......!
SWING

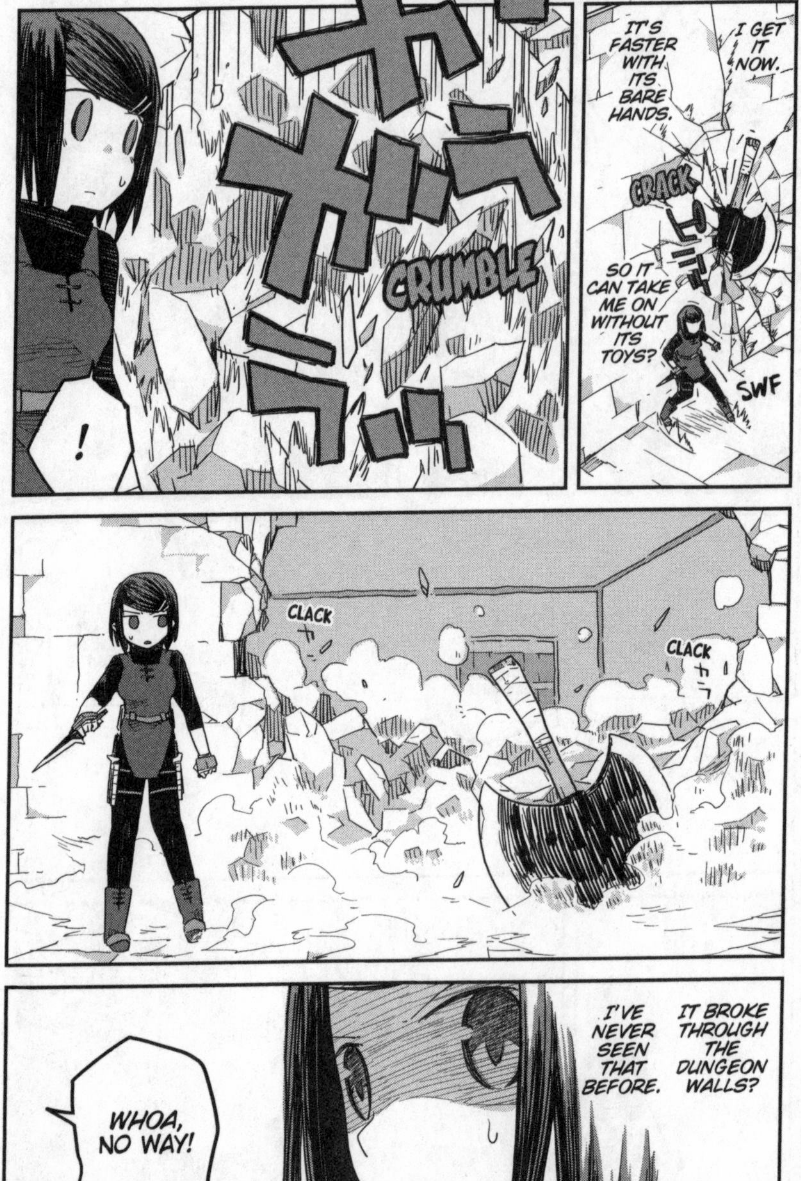
I GET IT NOW.
IT'S FASTER WITH ITS BARE HANDS.
CRACK
SO IT CAN TAKE ME ON WITHOUT ITS TOYS?
SWF
CRUMBLE
!
CLACK
CLACK
IT BROKE THROUGH THE DUNGEON WALLS?
I'VE NEVER SEEN THAT BEFORE.
WHOA, NO WAY!

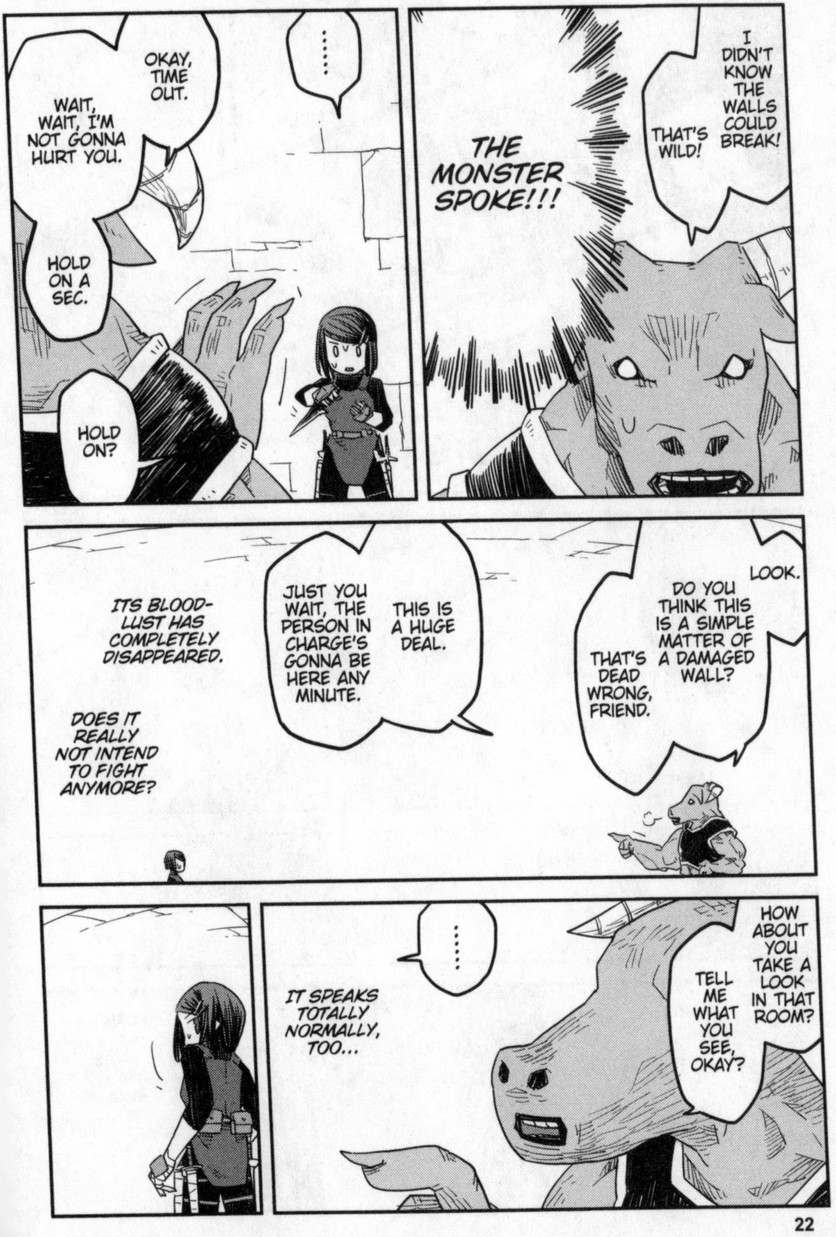
I DIDN'T KNOW THE WALLS COULD BREAK!
THAT'S WILD!
THE MONSTER SPOKE!!!
......
OKAY, TIME OUT.
WAIT, WAIT, I'M NOT GONNA HURT YOU.
HOLD ON A SEC.
HOLD ON?
LOOK.
DO YOU THINK THIS IS A SIMPLE MATTER OF A DAMAGED WALL?
THAT'S DEAD WRONG, FRIEND.
THIS IS A HUGE DEAL.
JUST YOU WAIT, THE PERSON IN CHARGE'S GONNA BE HERE ANY MINUTE.
ITS BLOOD-LUST HAS COMPLETELY DISAPPEARED.
DOES IT REALLY NOT INTEND TO FIGHT ANYMORE?
HOW ABOUT YOU TAKE A LOOK IN THAT ROOM?
TELL ME WHAT YOU SEE, OKAY?
......
IT SPEAKS TOTALLY NORMALLY, TOO...

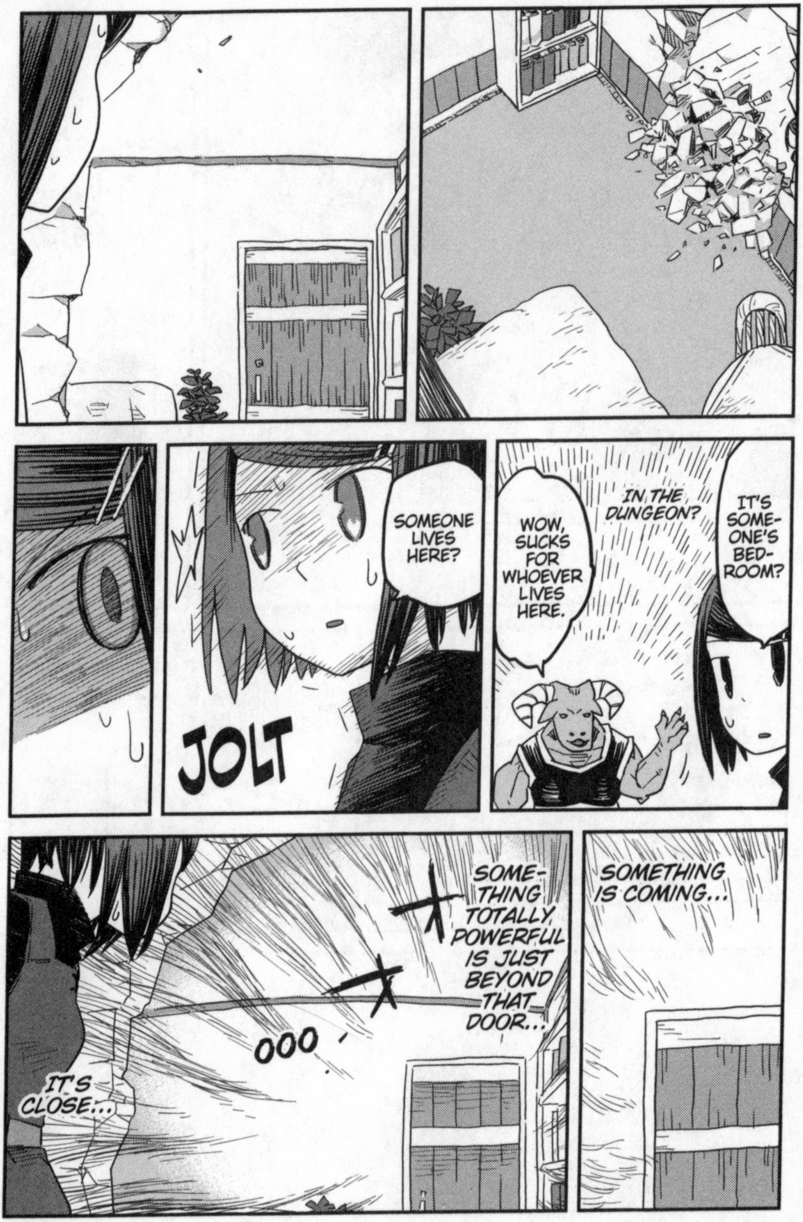
IT'S SOME-ONE'S BED-ROOM?
IN THE DUNGEON?
WOW, SUCKS FOR WHOEVER LIVES HERE.
SOMEONE LIVES HERE?
JOLT
SOMETHING IS COMING...
SOME-THING TOTALLY POWERFUL IS JUST BEYOND THAT DOOR...
OOO
IT'S CLOSE...

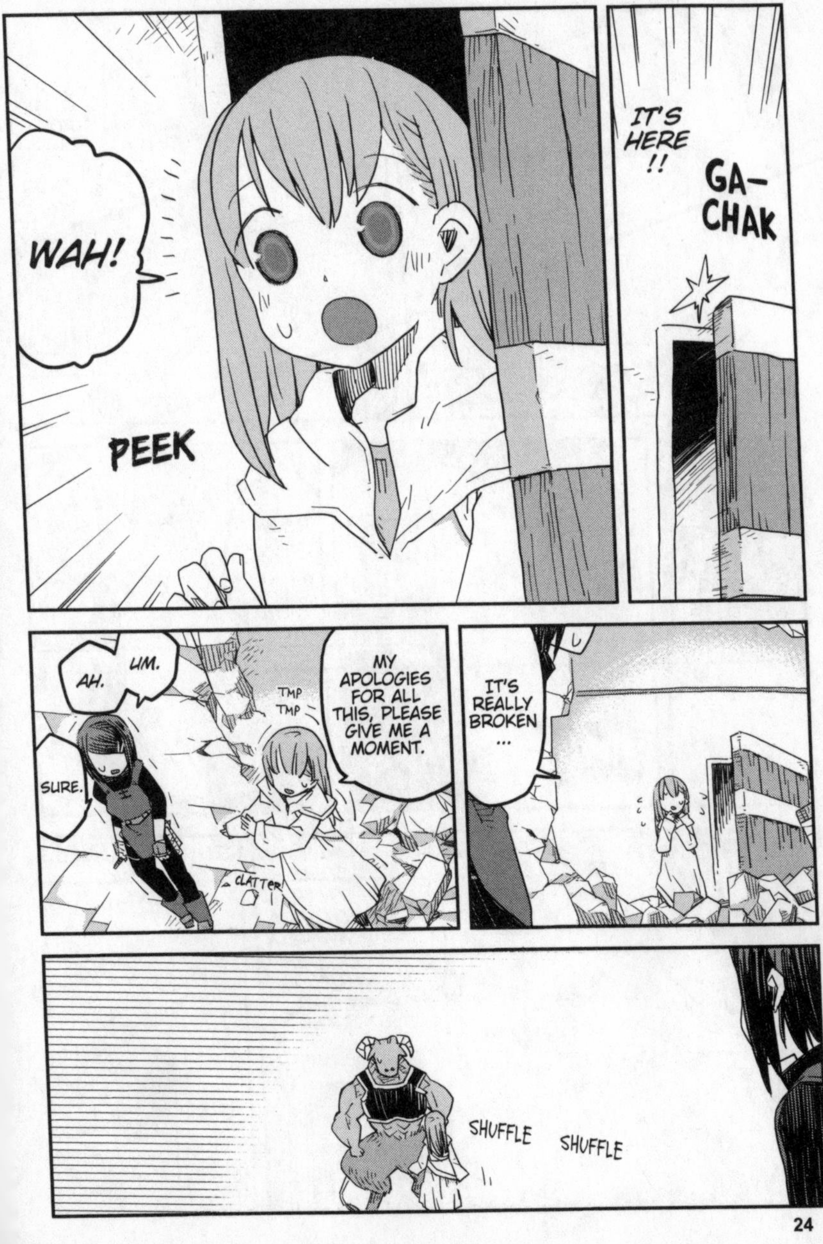
IT'S HERE !!
GA-CHAK
WAH!
PEEK
IT'S REALLY BROKEN ...
MY APOLOGIES FOR ALL THIS, PLEASE GIVE ME A MOMENT.
TMP TMP
UM.
AH.
SURE.
CLATTER
SHUFFLE
SHUFFLE

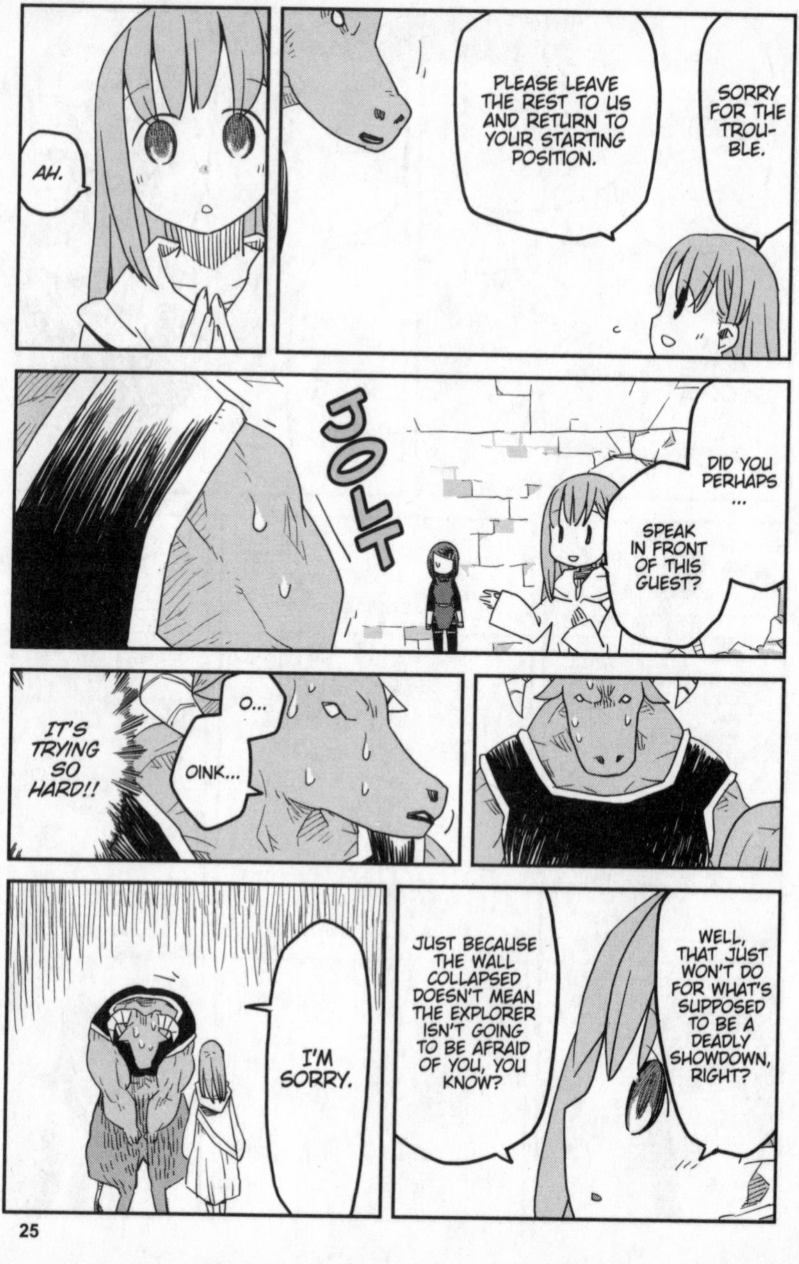
SORRY FOR THE TROU-BLE.
PLEASE LEAVE THE REST TO US AND RETURN TO YOUR STARTING POSITION.
AH.
DID YOU PERHAPS ...
SPEAK IN FRONT OF THIS GUEST?
JOLT
O...
OINK...
IT'S TRYING SO HARD!!
WELL, THAT JUST WON'T DO FOR WHAT'S SUPPOSED TO BE A DEADLY SHOWDOWN, RIGHT?
JUST BECAUSE THE WALL COLLAPSED DOESN'T MEAN THE EXPLORER ISN'T GOING TO BE AFRAID OF YOU, YOU KNOW?
I'M SORRY.

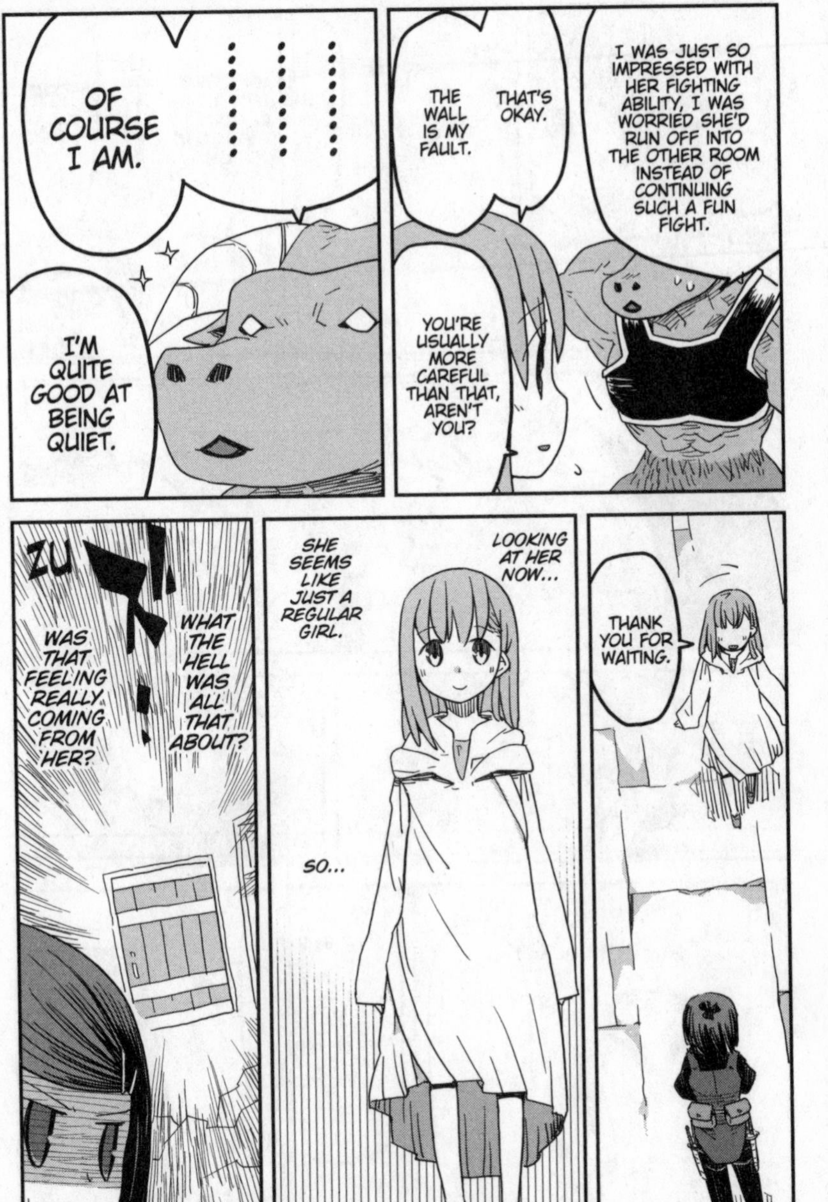
I WAS JUST SO IMPRESSED WITH HER FIGHTING ABILITY, I WAS WORRIED SHE'D RUN OFF INTO THE OTHER ROOM INSTEAD OF CONTINUING SUCH A FUN FIGHT.
THAT'S OKAY.
THE WALL IS MY FAULT.
YOU'RE USUALLY MORE CAREFUL THAN THAT, AREN'T YOU?
......
OF COURSE I AM.
I'M QUITE GOOD AT BEING QUIET.
THANK YOU FOR WAITING.
LOOKING AT HER NOW...
SHE SEEMS LIKE JUST A REGULAR GIRL.
SO...
ZU
WHAT THE HELL WAS ALL THAT ABOUT?
WAS THAT FEELING REALLY COMING FROM HER?

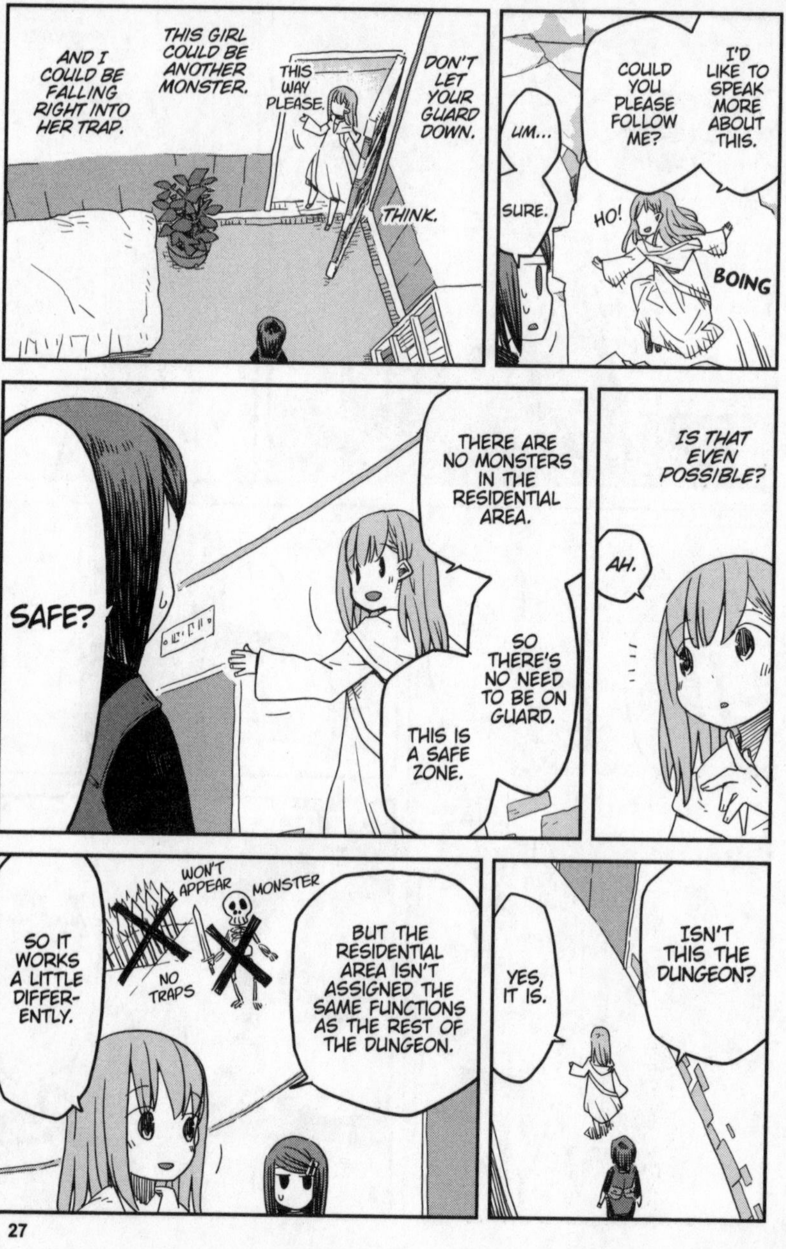
I'D LIKE TO SPEAK MORE ABOUT THIS.
COULD YOU PLEASE FOLLOW ME?
UM...
HO!
SURE.
BOING
DON'T LET YOUR GUARD DOWN.
THIS WAY PLEASE.
THIS GIRL COULD BE ANOTHER MONSTER.
AND I COULD BE FALLING RIGHT INTO HER TRAP.
THINK.
IS THAT EVEN POSSIBLE?
AH.
THERE ARE NO MONSTERS IN THE RESIDENTIAL AREA.
SO THERE'S NO NEED TO BE ON GUARD.
THIS IS A SAFE ZONE.
SAFE?
ISN'T THIS THE DUNGEON?
YES, IT IS.
BUT THE RESIDENTIAL AREA ISN'T ASSIGNED THE SAME FUNCTIONS AS THE REST OF THE DUNGEON.
MONSTER
WON'T APPEAR
NO TRAPS
SO IT WORKS A LITTLE DIFFER-ENTLY.

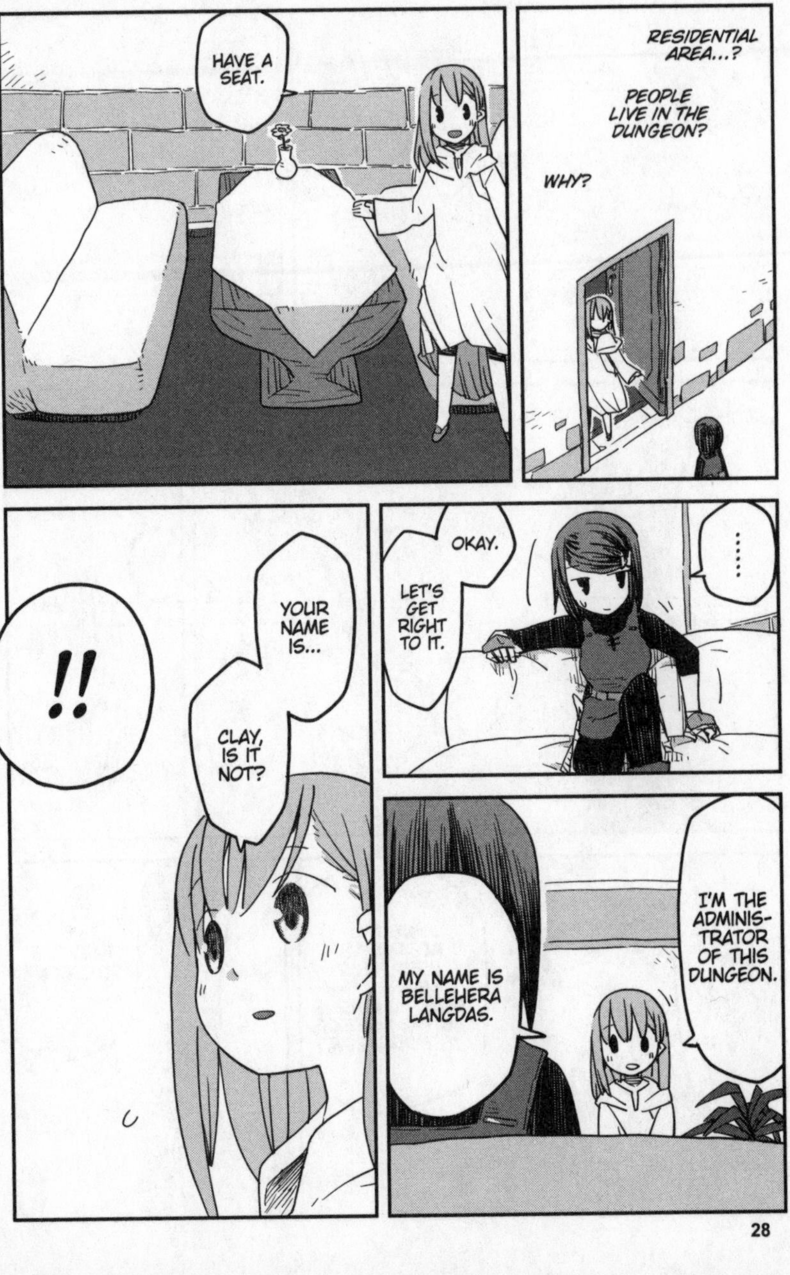
RESIDENTIAL AREA...?
PEOPLE LIVE IN THE DUNGEON?
WHY?
HAVE A SEAT.
......
OKAY.
LET'S GET RIGHT TO IT.
I'M THE ADMINISTRATOR OF THIS DUNGEON.
MY NAME IS BELLEHERA LANGDAS.
YOUR NAME IS...
CLAY, IS IT NOT?
!!

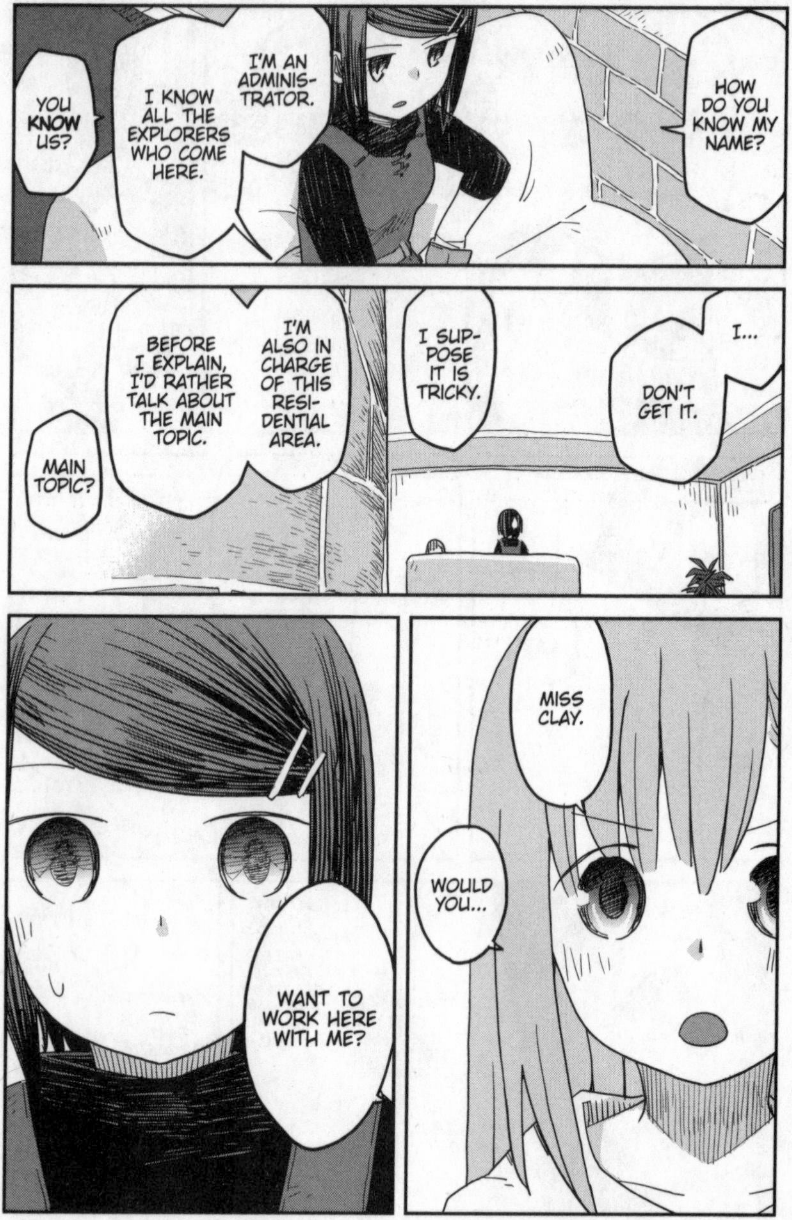
HOW DO YOU KNOW MY NAME?
I'M AN ADMINIS-TRATOR.
I KNOW ALL THE EXPLORERS WHO COME HERE.
YOU KNOW US?
I...
DON'T GET IT.
I SUP-POSE IT IS TRICKY.
I'M ALSO IN CHARGE OF THIS RESI-DENTIAL AREA.
BEFORE I EXPLAIN, I'D RATHER TALK ABOUT THE MAIN TOPIC.
MAIN TOPIC?
MISS CLAY.
WOULD YOU...
WANT TO WORK HERE WITH ME?

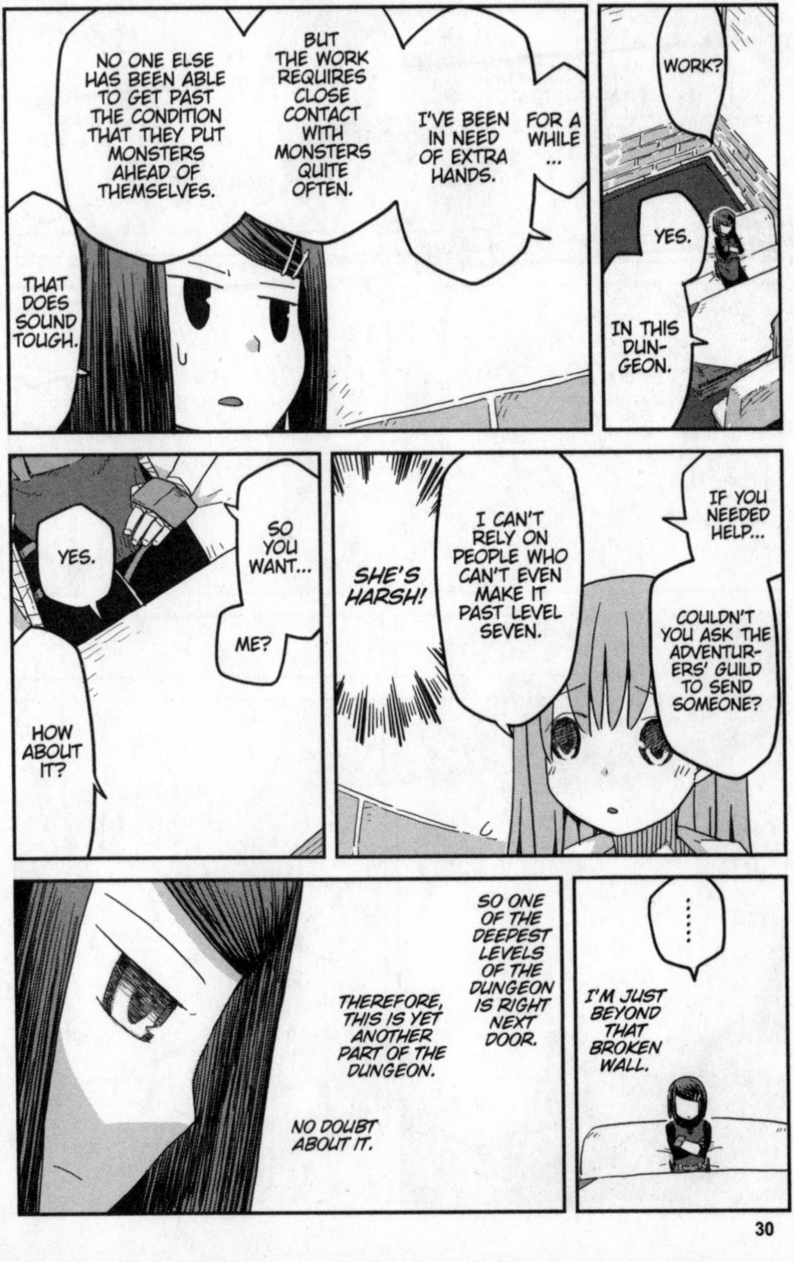
WORK?
YES.
IN THIS DUNGEON.
FOR A WHILE ...
I'VE BEEN IN NEED OF EXTRA HANDS.
BUT THE WORK REQUIRES CLOSE CONTACT WITH MONSTERS QUITE OFTEN.
NO ONE ELSE HAS BEEN ABLE TO GET PAST THE CONDITION THAT THEY PUT MONSTERS AHEAD OF THEMSELVES.
THAT DOES SOUND TOUGH.
IF YOU NEEDED HELP...
COULDN'T YOU ASK THE ADVENTURERS' GUILD TO SEND SOMEONE?
I CAN'T RELY ON PEOPLE WHO CAN'T EVEN MAKE IT PAST LEVEL SEVEN.
SHE'S HARSH!
SO YOU WANT...
ME?
YES.
HOW ABOUT IT?
......
I'M JUST BEYOND THAT BROKEN WALL.
SO ONE OF THE DEEPEST LEVELS OF THE DUNGEON IS RIGHT NEXT DOOR.
THEREFORE, THIS IS YET ANOTHER PART OF THE DUNGEON.
NO DOUBT ABOUT IT.

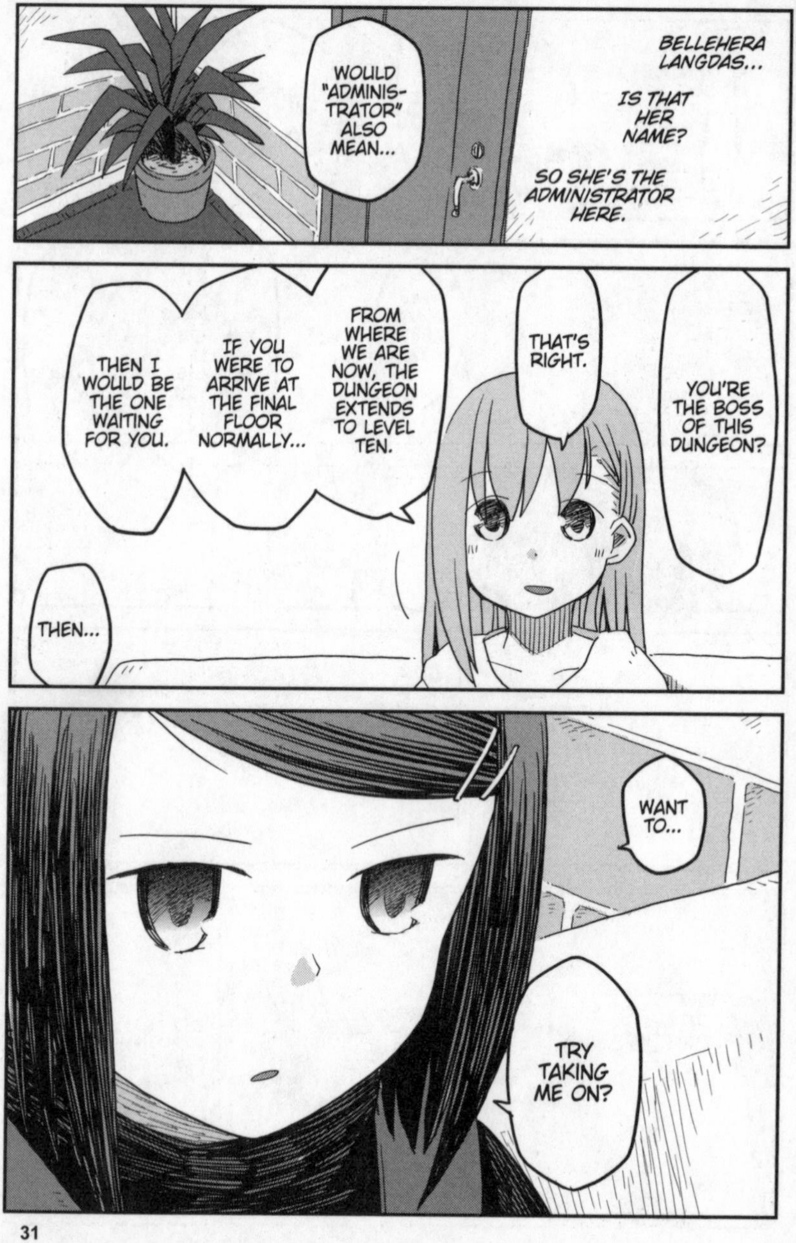
BELLEHERA LANGDAS...
IS THAT HER NAME?
SO SHE'S THE ADMINISTRATOR HERE.
WOULD "ADMINISTRATOR" ALSO MEAN...
YOU'RE THE BOSS OF THIS DUNGEON?
THAT'S RIGHT.
FROM WHERE WE ARE NOW, THE DUNGEON EXTENDS TO LEVEL TEN.
IF YOU WERE TO ARRIVE AT THE FINAL FLOOR NORMALLY...
THEN I WOULD BE THE ONE WAITING FOR YOU.
THEN...
WANT TO...
TRY TAKING ME ON?

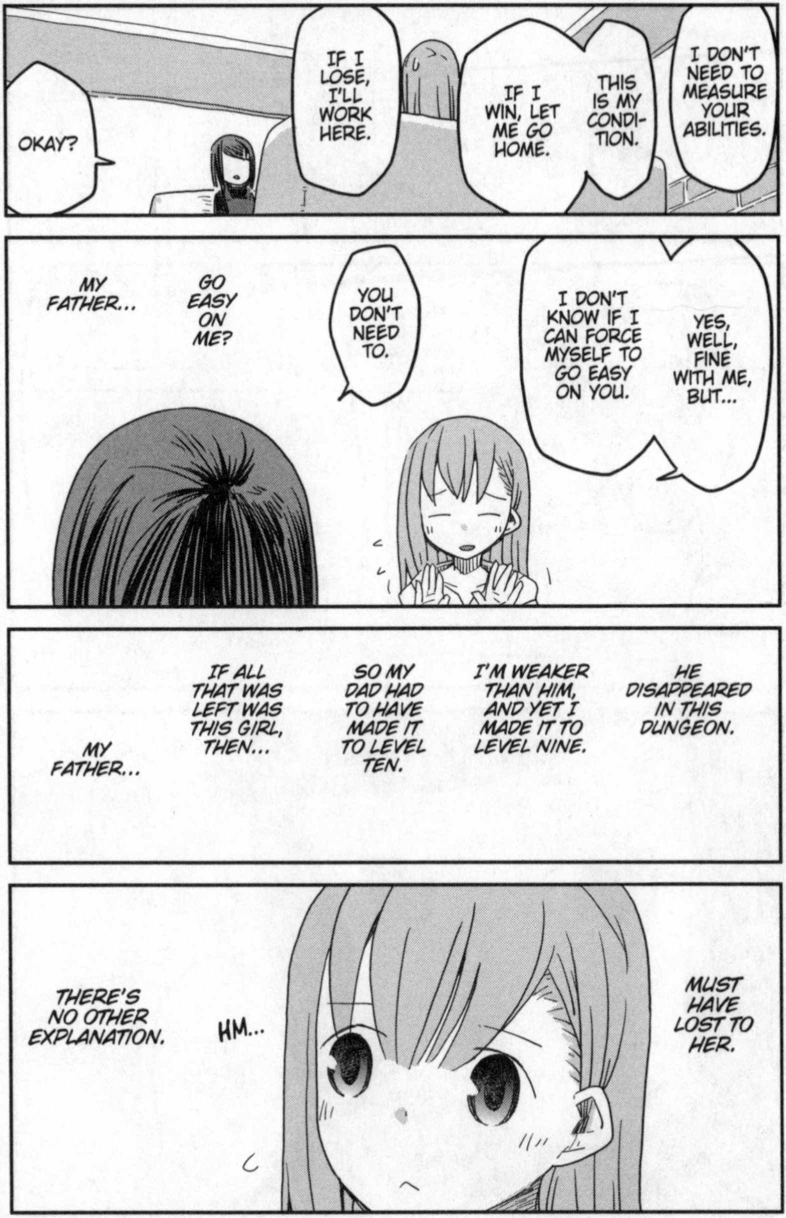
I DON'T NEED TO MEASURE YOUR ABILITIES.
THIS IS MY CONDITION.
IF I WIN, LET ME GO HOME.
IF I LOSE, I'LL WORK HERE.
OKAY?
YES, WELL, FINE WITH ME, BUT...
I DON'T KNOW IF I CAN FORCE MYSELF TO GO EASY ON YOU.
YOU DON'T NEED TO.
GO EASY ON ME?
MY FATHER...
HE DISAPPEARED IN THIS DUNGEON.
I'M WEAKER THAN HIM, AND YET I MADE IT TO LEVEL NINE.
SO MY DAD HAD TO HAVE MADE IT TO LEVEL TEN.
IF ALL THAT WAS LEFT WAS THIS GIRL, THEN...
MY FATHER...
MUST HAVE LOST TO HER.
HM...
THERE'S NO OTHER EXPLANATION.

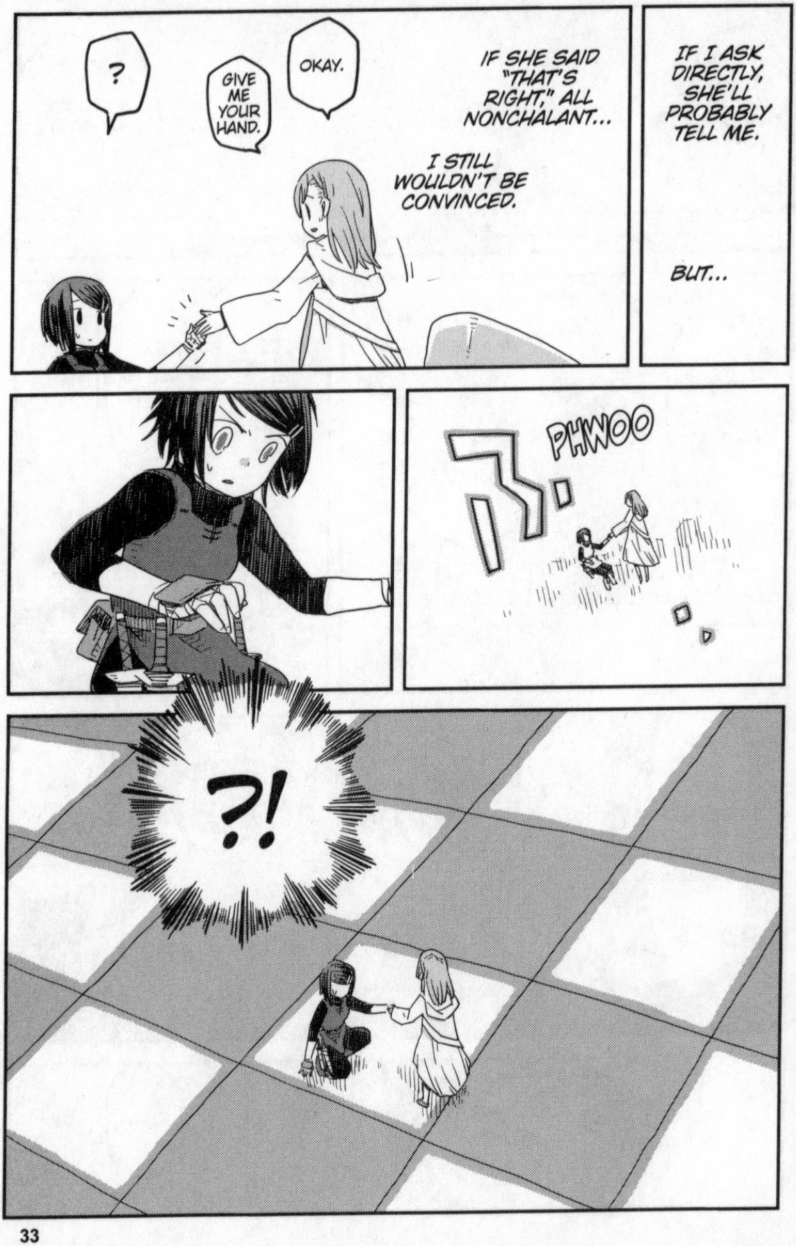
IF I ASK DIRECTLY, SHE'LL PROBABLY TELL ME.
BUT...
IF SHE SAID "THAT'S RIGHT," ALL NONCHALANT...
I STILL WOULDN'T BE CONVINCED.
OKAY.
GIVE ME YOUR HAND.
?
PHWOO
?!

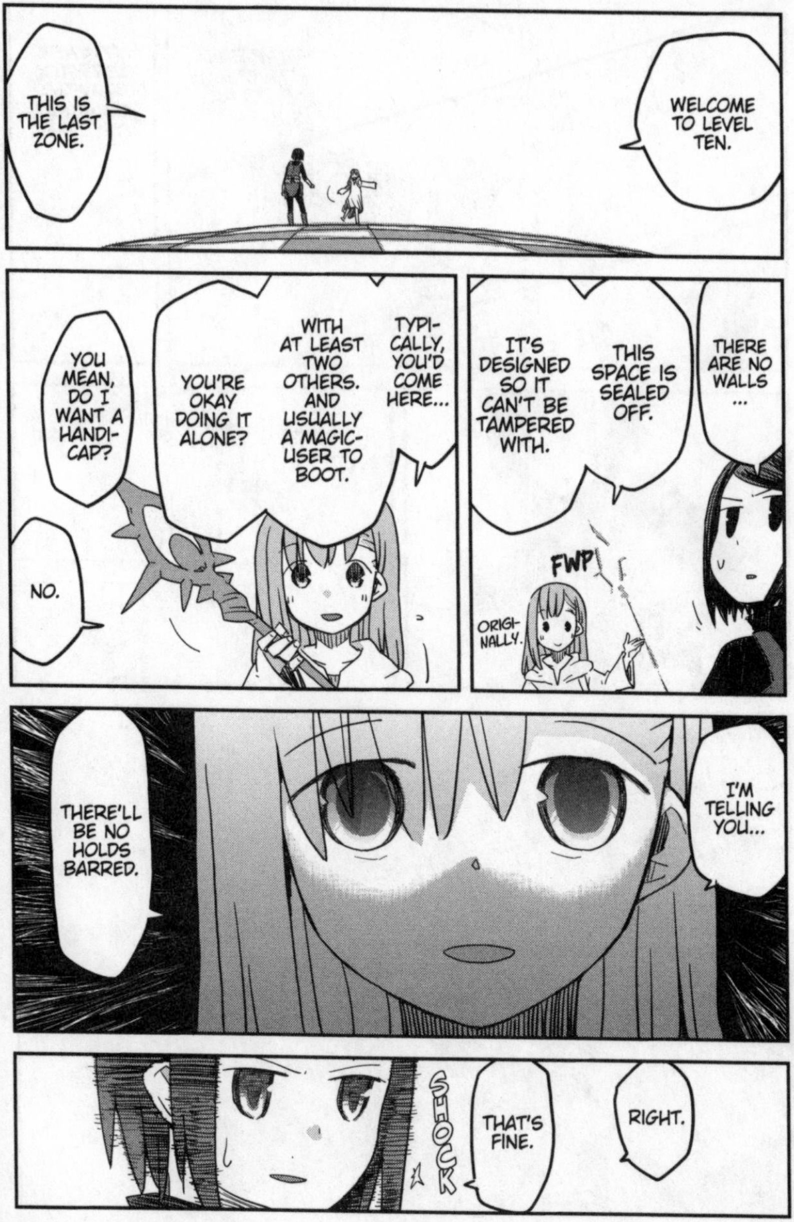
WELCOME TO LEVEL TEN.
THIS IS THE LAST ZONE.
THERE ARE NO WALLS ...
THIS SPACE IS SEALED OFF.
IT'S DESIGNED SO IT CAN'T BE TAMPERED WITH.
FWP
ORIGINALLY.
TYPICALLY, YOU'D COME HERE...
WITH AT LEAST TWO OTHERS. AND USUALLY A MAGIC-USER TO BOOT.
YOU'RE OKAY DOING IT ALONE?
YOU MEAN, DO I WANT A HANDICAP?
NO.
I'M TELLING YOU...
THERE'LL BE NO HOLDS BARRED.
RIGHT.
THAT'S FINE.
SHOCK

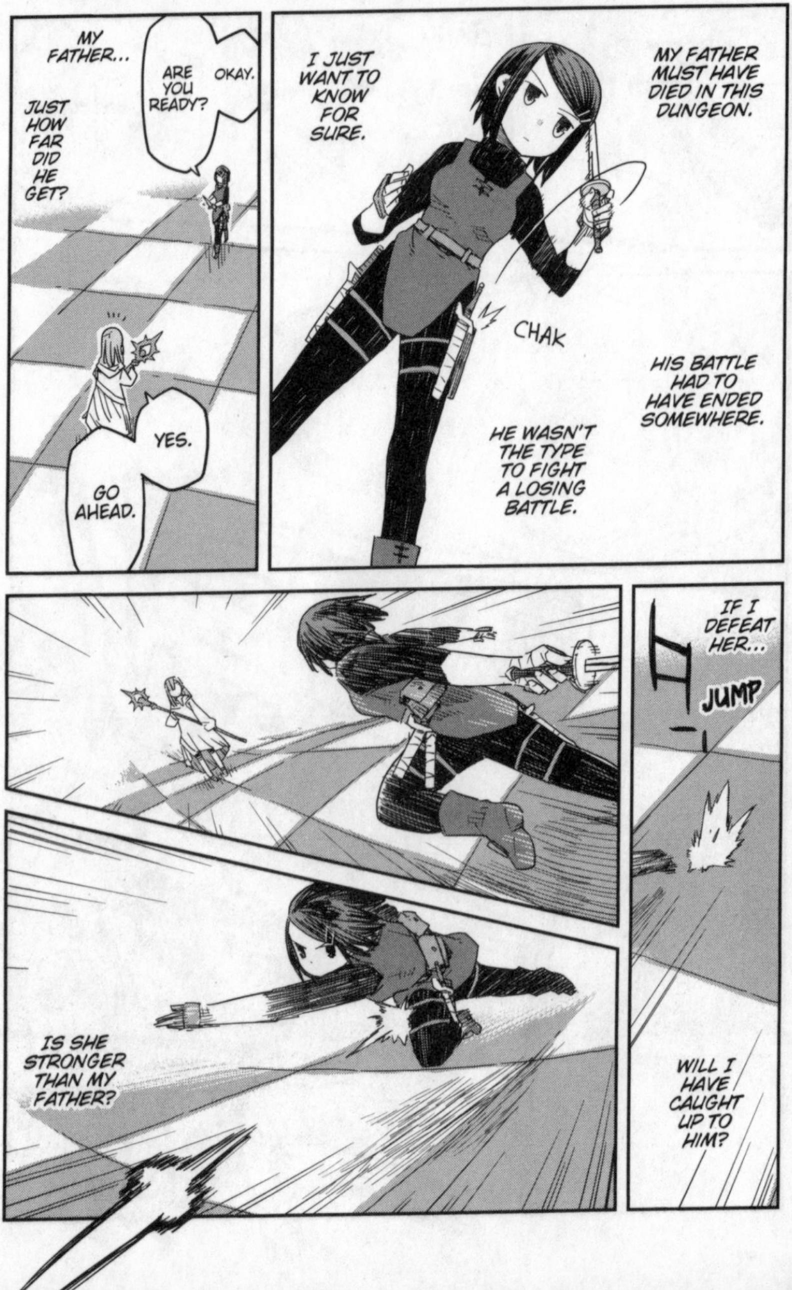
MY FATHER MUST HAVE DIED IN THIS DUNGEON.
I JUST WANT TO KNOW FOR SURE.
CHAK
HIS BATTLE HAD TO HAVE ENDED SOMEWHERE.
HE WASN'T THE TYPE TO FIGHT A LOSING BATTLE.
OKAY.
ARE YOU READY?
MY FATHER...
JUST HOW FAR DID HE GET?
YES.
GO AHEAD.
IF I DEFEAT HER...
JUMP
WILL I HAVE CAUGHT UP TO HIM?
IS SHE STRONGER THAN MY FATHER?

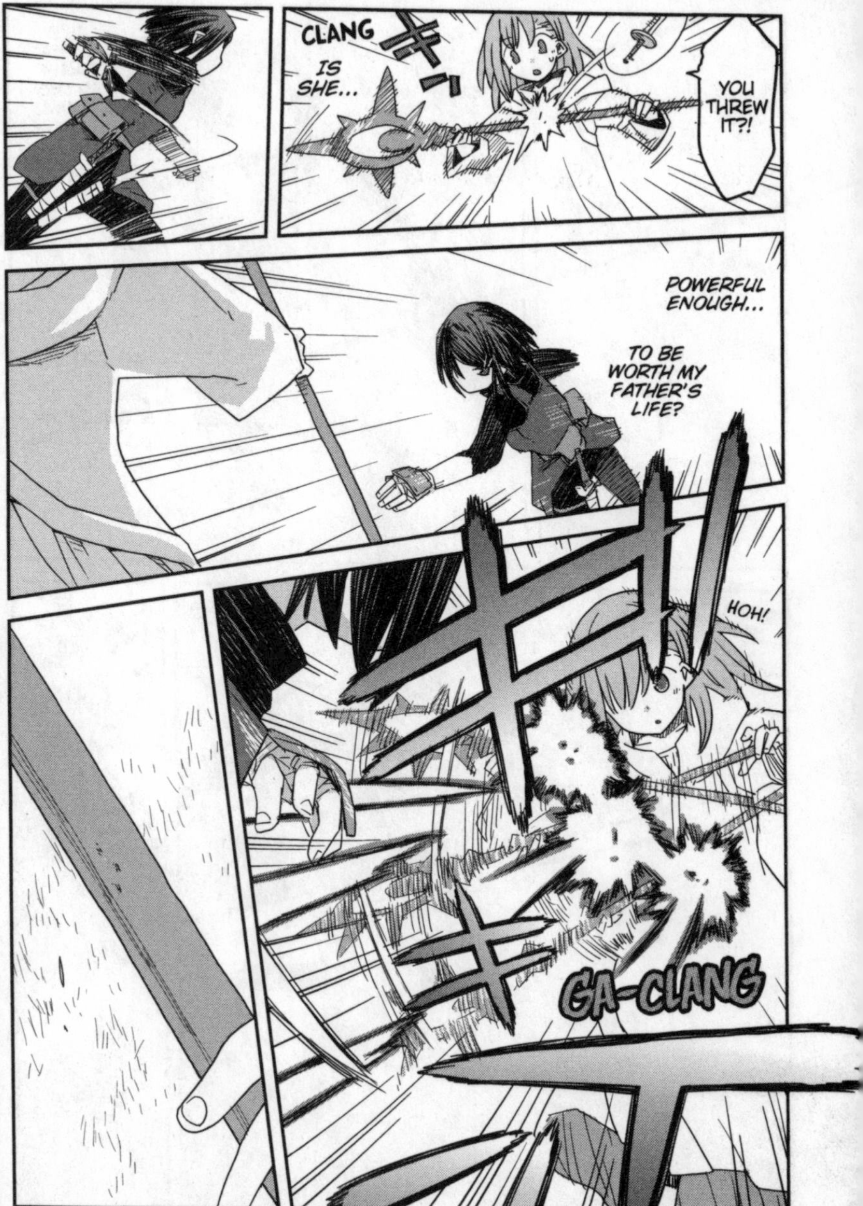
YOU THREW IT?!
CLANG
IS SHE...
POWERFUL ENOUGH...
TO BE WORTH MY FATHER'S LIFE?
HOH!
GA-CLANG

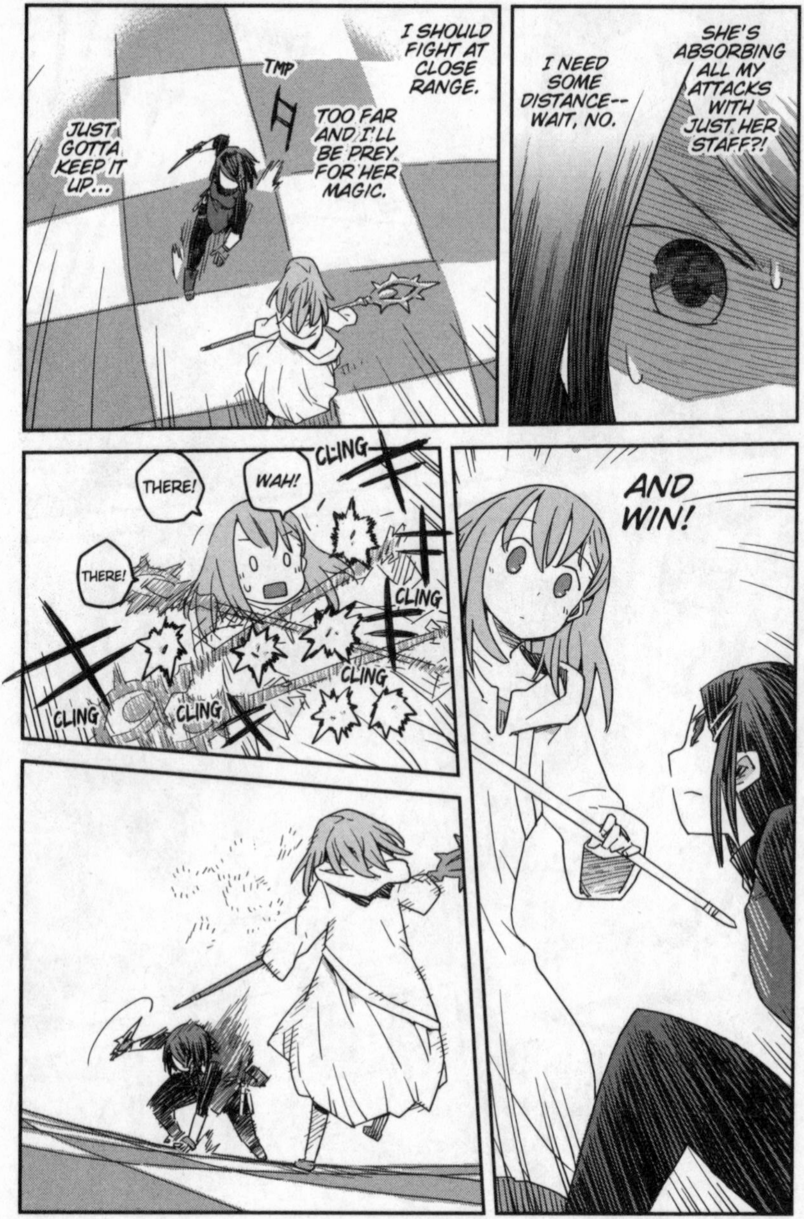
SHE'S ABSORBING ALL MY ATTACKS WITH JUST HER STAFF?!
I NEED SOME DISTANCE-- WAIT, NO.
I SHOULD FIGHT AT CLOSE RANGE.
TOO FAR AND I'LL BE PREY FOR HER MAGIC.
TMP
JUST GOTTA KEEP IT UP...
AND WIN!
CLING
WAH!
THERE!
THERE!
CLING
CLING
CLING
CLING

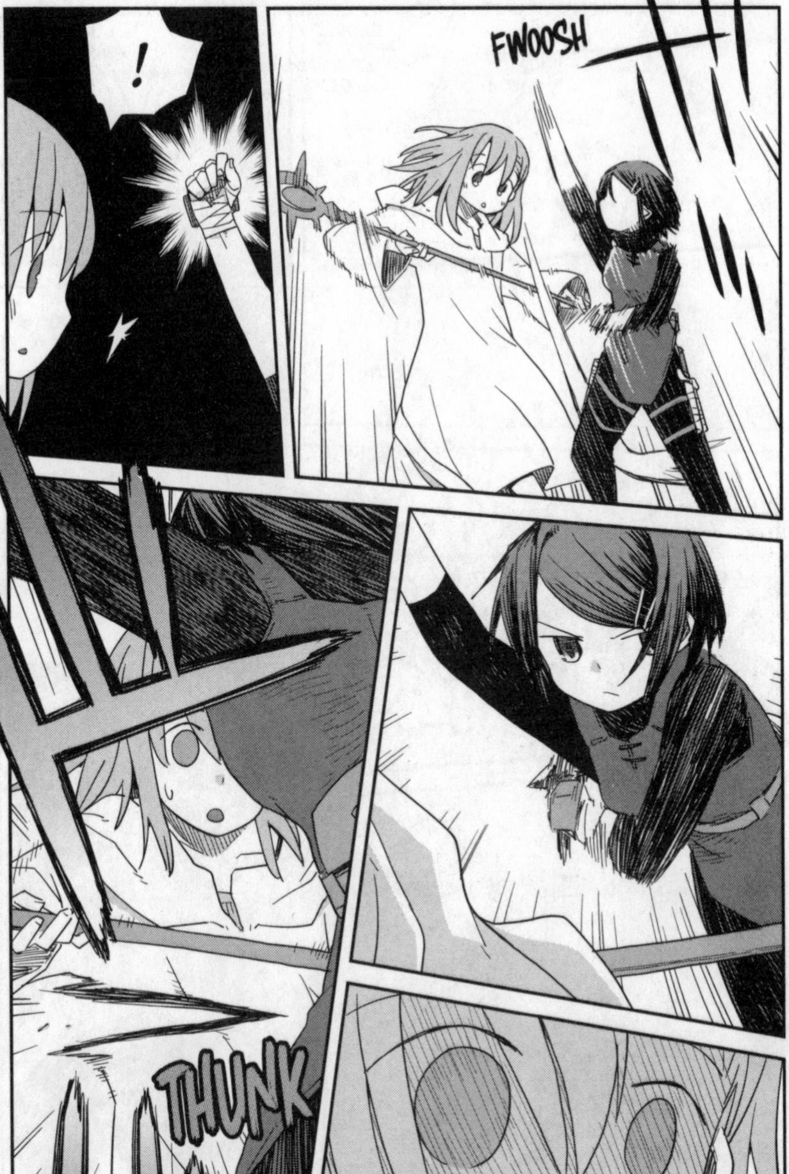
FWOOSH
!
THUNK

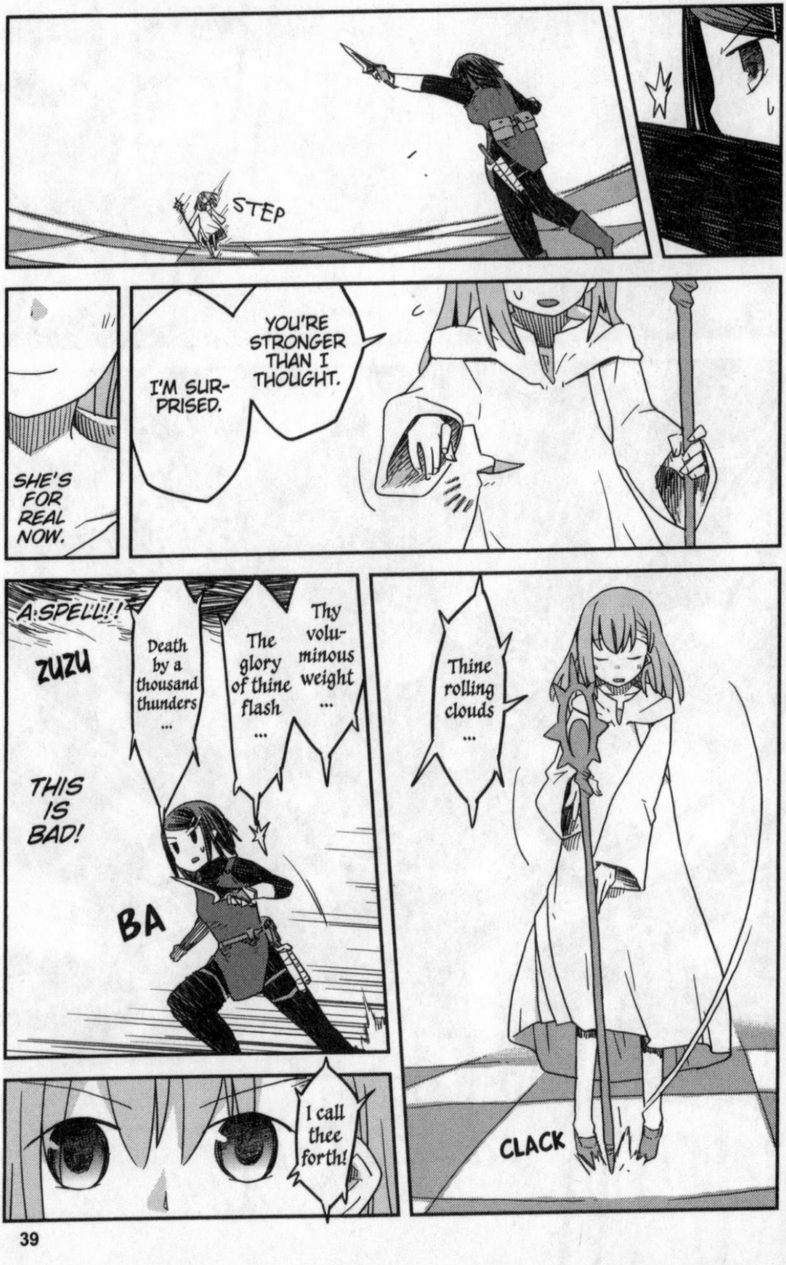
STEP
YOU'RE STRONGER THAN I THOUGHT.
I'M SUR-PRISED.
SHE'S FOR REAL NOW.
Thine rolling clouds ...
CLACK
Thy voluminous weight ...
The glory of thine flash ...
Death by a thousand thunders ...
A SPELL!!
ZUZU
THIS IS BAD!
BA
I call thee forth!

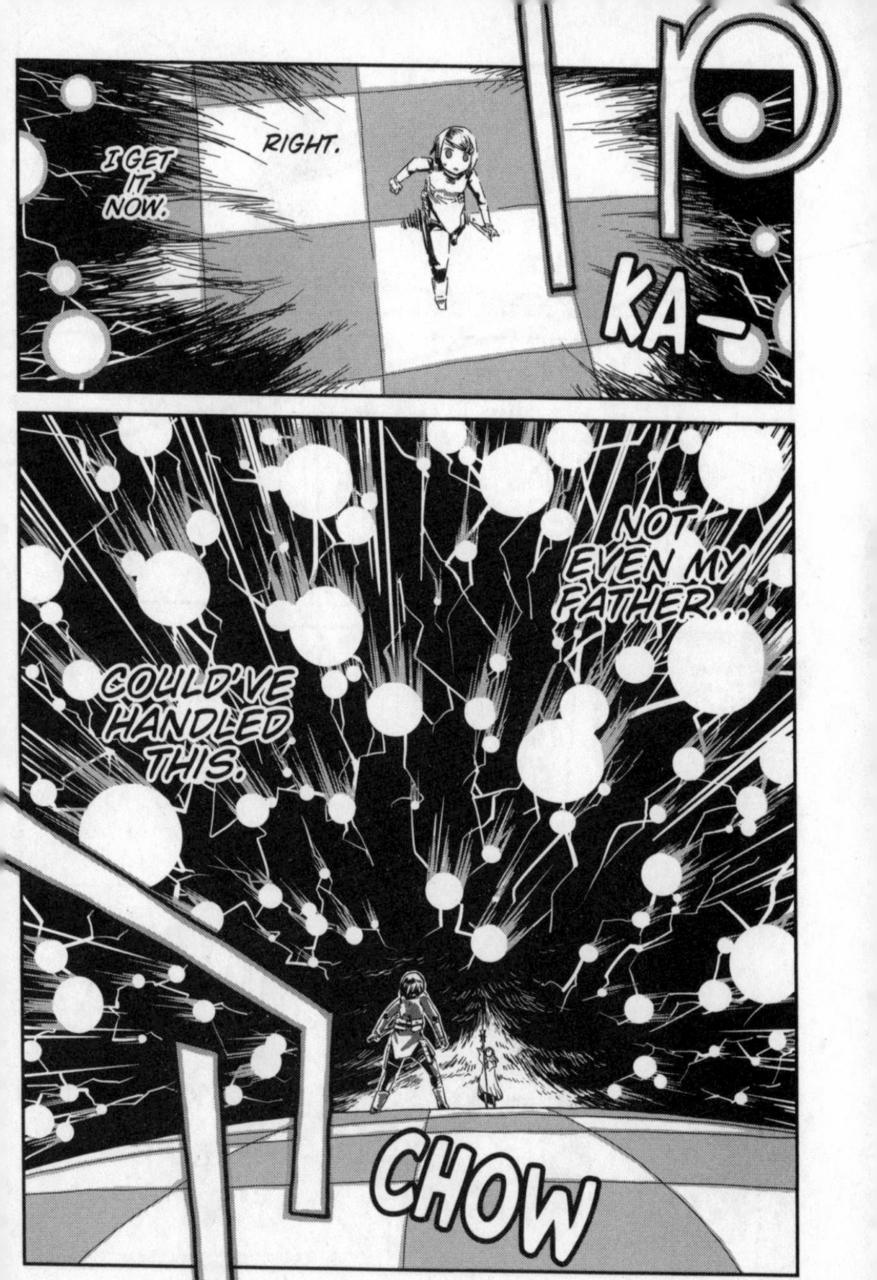
RIGHT.
I GET IT NOW.
KA–
NOT EVEN MY FATHER...
COULD'VE HANDLED THIS.
CHOW

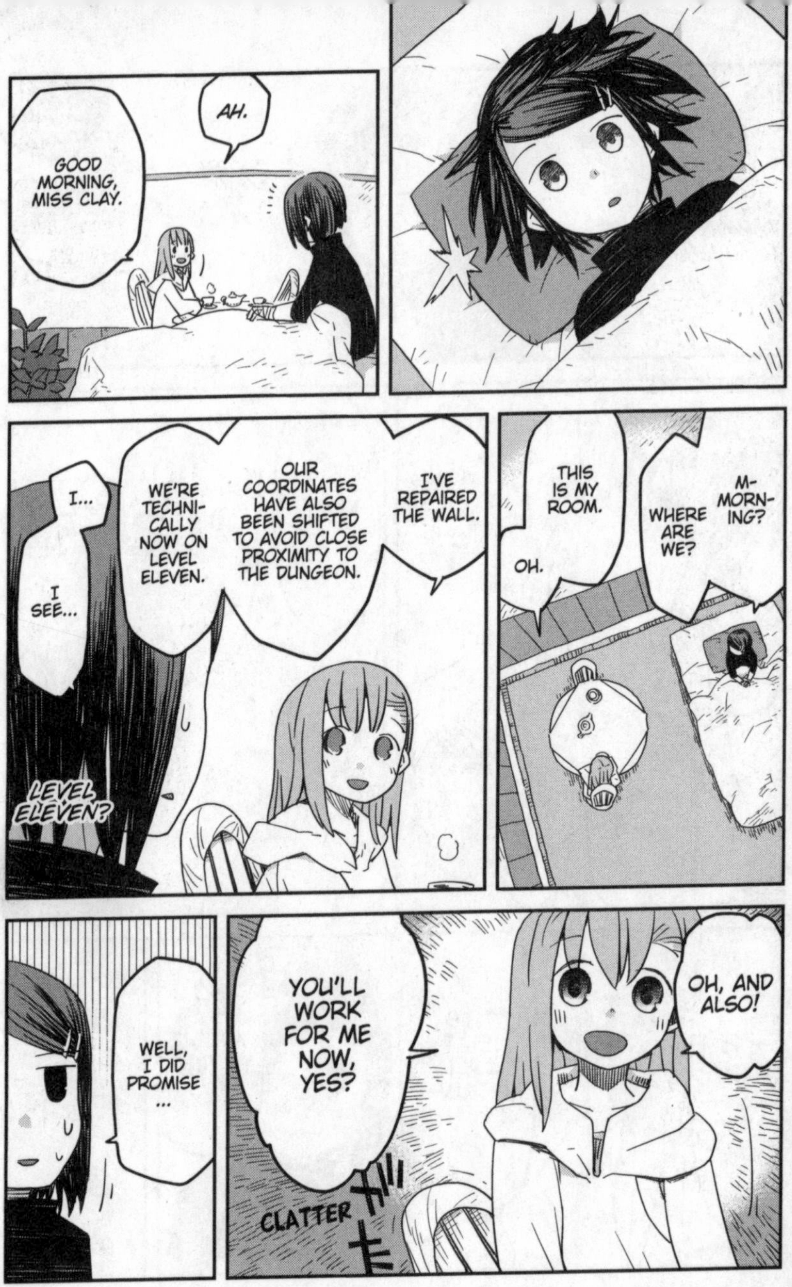
AH.
GOOD MORNING, MISS CLAY.
M-MORNING?
WHERE ARE WE?
THIS IS MY ROOM.
OH.
I'VE REPAIRED THE WALL.
OUR COORDINATES HAVE ALSO BEEN SHIFTED TO AVOID CLOSE PROXIMITY TO THE DUNGEON.
WE'RE TECHNICALLY NOW ON LEVEL ELEVEN.
I...
I SEE...
LEVEL ELEVEN?
OH, AND ALSO!
YOU'LL WORK FOR ME NOW, YES?
CLATTER
WELL, I DID PROMISE ...

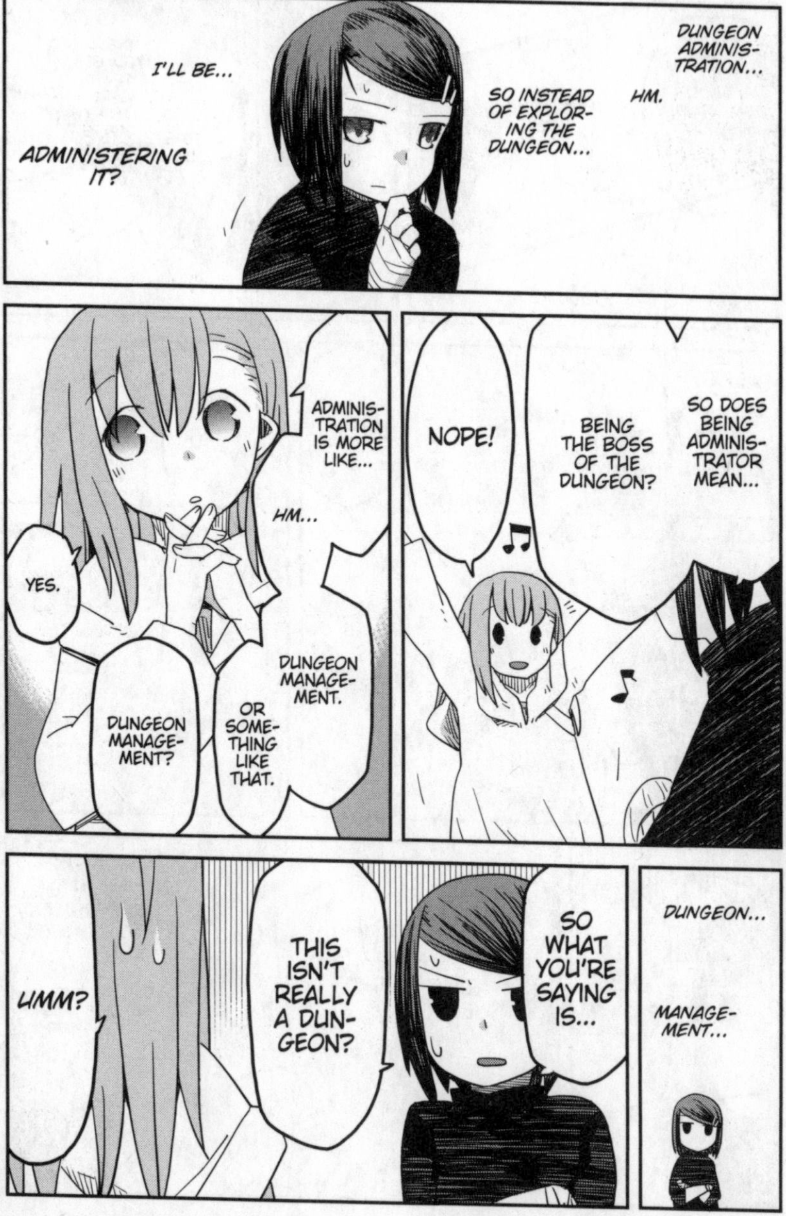
DUNGEON ADMINIS-TRATION...
HM.
SO INSTEAD OF EXPLOR-ING THE DUNGEON...
I'LL BE...
ADMINISTERING IT?
SO DOES BEING ADMINIS-TRATOR MEAN...
BEING THE BOSS OF THE DUNGEON?
NOPE!
ADMINIS-TRATION IS MORE LIKE...
HM...
DUNGEON MANAGE-MENT.
OR SOME-THING LIKE THAT.
DUNGEON MANAGE-MENT?
YES.
DUNGEON...
MANAGE-MENT...
SO WHAT YOU'RE SAYING IS...
THIS ISN'T REALLY A DUN-GEON?
UMM?

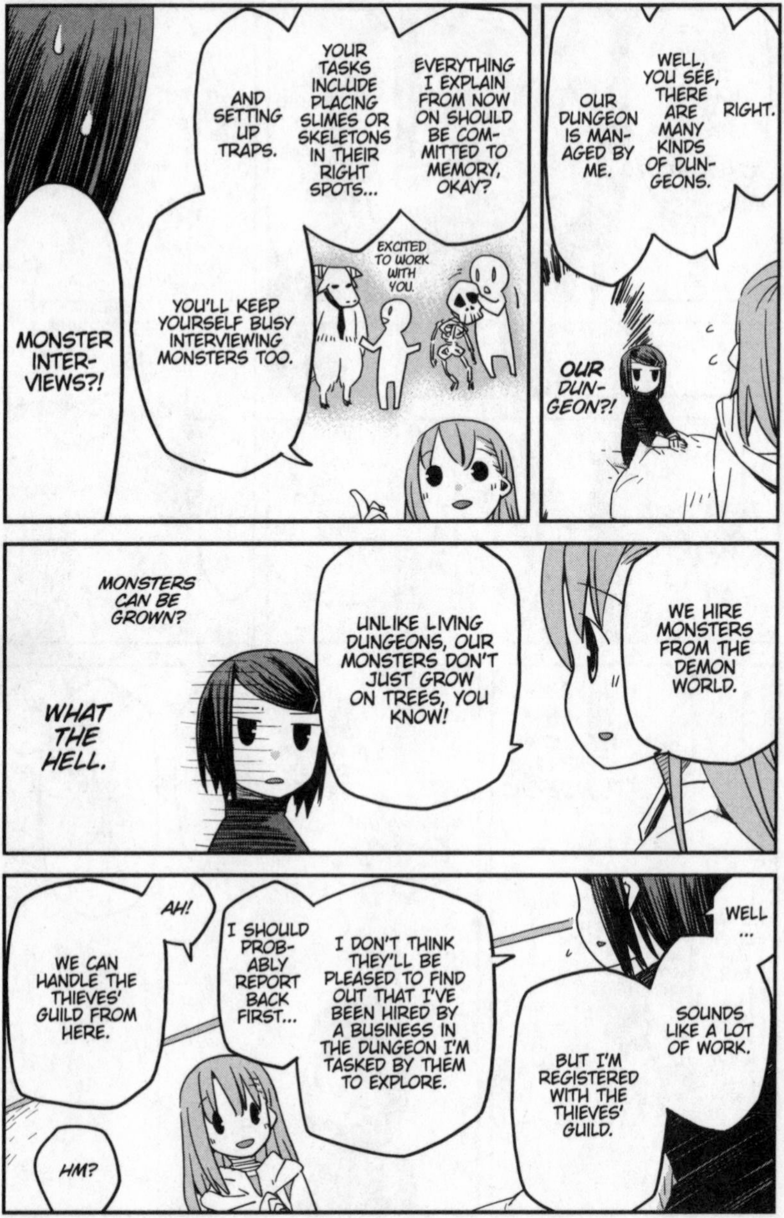
RIGHT.
WELL, YOU SEE, THERE ARE MANY KINDS OF DUN-GEONS.
OUR DUNGEON IS MAN-AGED BY ME.
OUR DUN-GEON?!
EVERYTHING I EXPLAIN FROM NOW ON SHOULD BE COM-MITTED TO MEMORY, OKAY?
YOUR TASKS INCLUDE PLACING SLIMES OR SKELETONS IN THEIR RIGHT SPOTS...
AND SETTING UP TRAPS.
EXCITED TO WORK WITH YOU.
YOU'LL KEEP YOURSELF BUSY INTERVIEWING MONSTERS TOO.
MONSTER INTER-VIEWS?!
WE HIRE MONSTERS FROM THE DEMON WORLD.
UNLIKE LIVING DUNGEONS, OUR MONSTERS DON'T JUST GROW ON TREES, YOU KNOW!
MONSTERS CAN BE GROWN?
WHAT THE HELL.
WELL ...
SOUNDS LIKE A LOT OF WORK.
BUT I'M REGISTERED WITH THE THIEVES' GUILD.
I DON'T THINK THEY'LL BE PLEASED TO FIND OUT THAT I'VE BEEN HIRED BY A BUSINESS IN THE DUNGEON I'M TASKED BY THEM TO EXPLORE.
I SHOULD PROB-ABLY REPORT BACK FIRST...
AH!
WE CAN HANDLE THE THIEVES' GUILD FROM HERE.
HM?

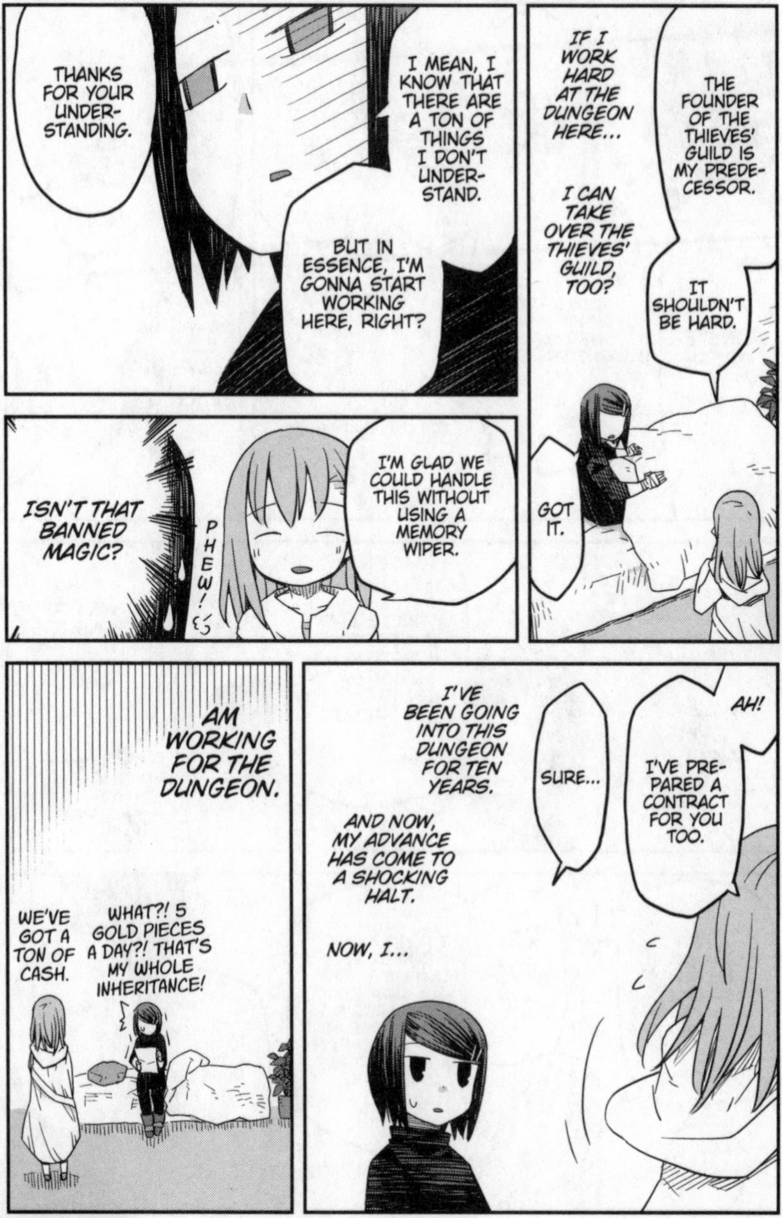
THE FOUNDER OF THE THIEVES' GUILD IS MY PREDE-CESSOR.
IF I WORK HARD AT THE DUNGEON HERE...
I CAN TAKE OVER THE THIEVES' GUILD, TOO?
IT SHOULDN'T BE HARD.
GOT IT.
I MEAN, I KNOW THAT THERE ARE A TON OF THINGS I DON'T UNDER-STAND.
BUT IN ESSENCE, I'M GONNA START WORKING HERE, RIGHT?
THANKS FOR YOUR UNDER-STANDING.
I'M GLAD WE COULD HANDLE THIS WITHOUT USING A MEMORY WIPER.
PHEW!
ISN'T THAT BANNED MAGIC?
AH!
I'VE PRE-PARED A CONTRACT FOR YOU TOO.
SURE...
I'VE BEEN GOING INTO THIS DUNGEON FOR TEN YEARS.
AND NOW, MY ADVANCE HAS COME TO A SHOCKING HALT.
NOW, I...
AM WORKING FOR THE DUNGEON.
WHAT?! 5 GOLD PIECES A DAY?! THAT'S MY WHOLE INHERITANCE!
WE'VE GOT A TON OF CASH.

CHAPTER 1 - END

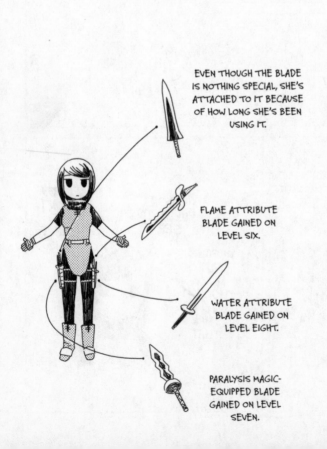

EVEN THOUGH THE BLADE IS NOTHING SPECIAL, SHE'S ATTACHED TO IT BECAUSE OF HOW LONG SHE'S BEEN USING IT.

FLAME ATTRIBUTE BLADE GAINED ON LEVEL SIX.

WATER ATTRIBUTE BLADE GAINED ON LEVEL EIGHT.

PARALYSIS MAGIC-EQUIPPED BLADE GAINED ON LEVEL SEVEN.

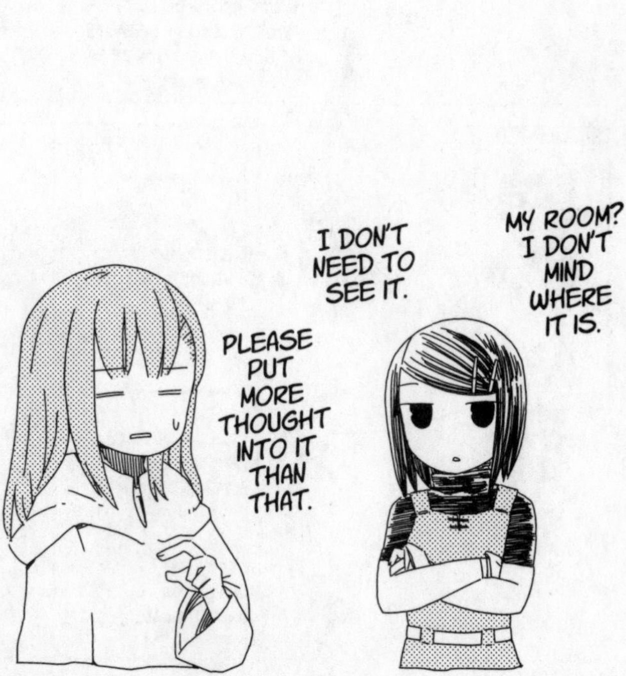
MY ROOM? I DON'T MIND WHERE IT IS.
I DON'T NEED TO SEE IT.
PLEASE PUT MORE THOUGHT INTO IT THAN THAT.

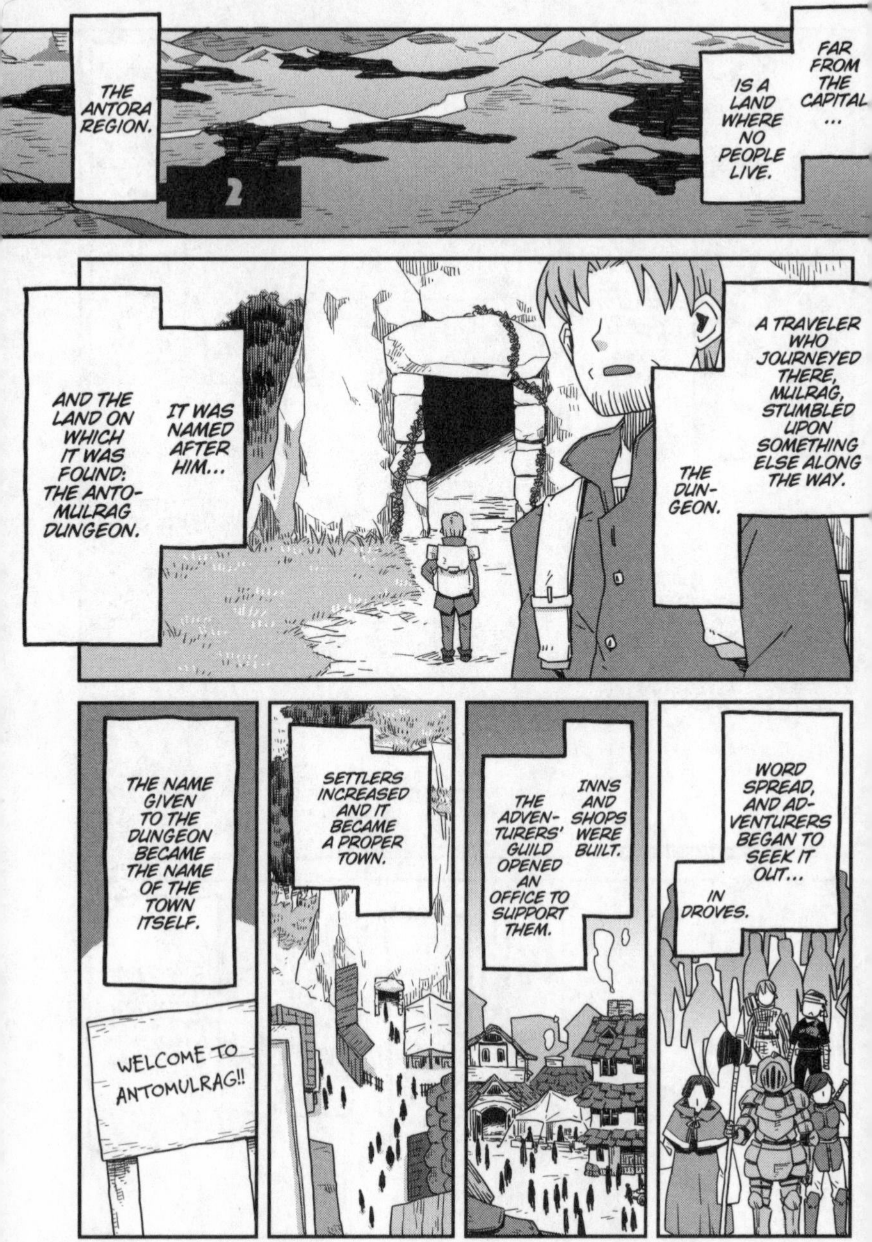
FAR FROM THE CAPITAL...
IS A LAND WHERE NO PEOPLE LIVE.
THE ANTORA REGION.
2
A TRAVELER WHO JOURNEYED THERE, MULRAG, STUMBLED UPON SOMETHING ELSE ALONG THE WAY.
THE DUNGEON.
IT WAS NAMED AFTER HIM...
AND THE LAND ON WHICH IT WAS FOUND: THE ANTO-MULRAG DUNGEON.
WORD SPREAD, AND AD-VENTURERS BEGAN TO SEEK IT OUT...
IN DROVES.
INNS AND SHOPS WERE BUILT.
THE ADVEN-TURERS' GUILD OPENED AN OFFICE TO SUPPORT THEM.
SETTLERS INCREASED AND IT BECAME A PROPER TOWN.
THE NAME GIVEN TO THE DUNGEON BECAME THE NAME OF THE TOWN ITSELF.
WELCOME TO ANTOMULRAG!!

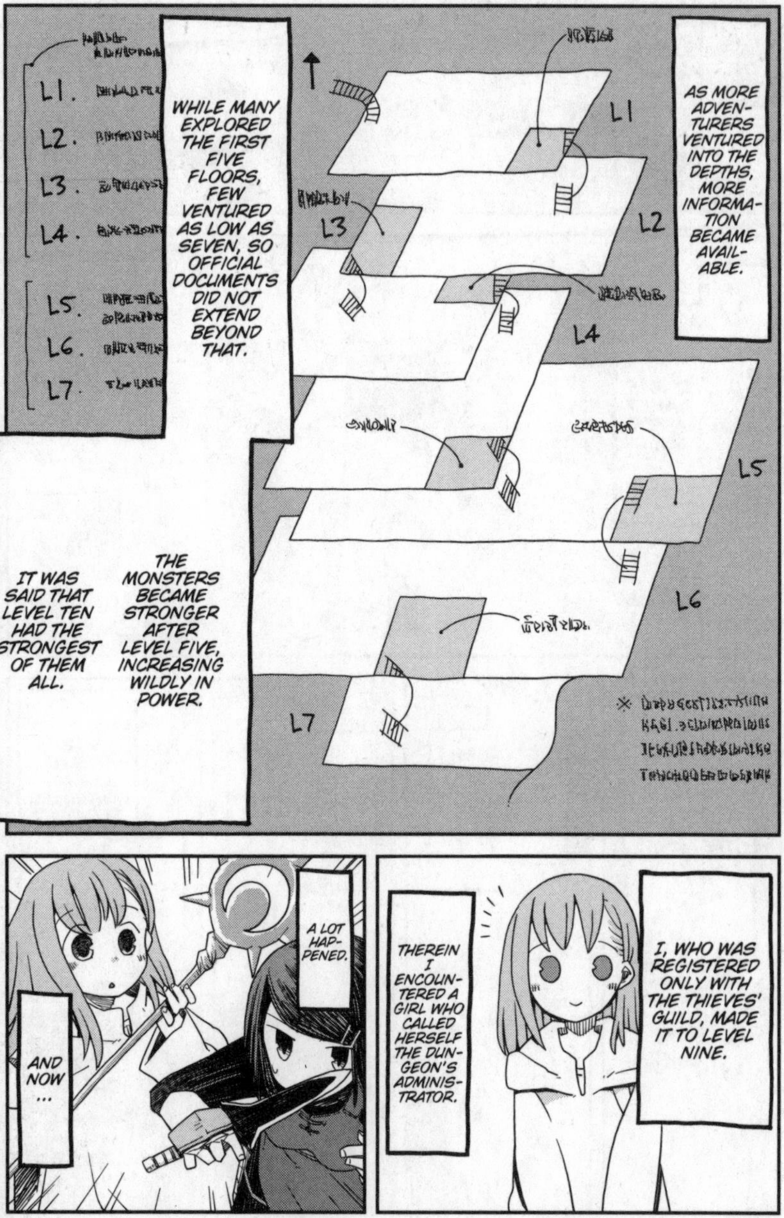
AS MORE ADVENTURERS VENTURED INTO THE DEPTHS, MORE INFORMATION BECAME AVAILABLE.
L1
L2
L3
L4
L5
L6
L7
WHILE MANY EXPLORED THE FIRST FIVE FLOORS, FEW VENTURED AS LOW AS SEVEN, SO OFFICIAL DOCUMENTS DID NOT EXTEND BEYOND THAT.
L1.
L2.
L3.
L4.
L5.
L6.
L7.
THE MONSTERS BECAME STRONGER AFTER LEVEL FIVE, INCREASING WILDLY IN POWER.
IT WAS SAID THAT LEVEL TEN HAD THE STRONGEST OF THEM ALL.
I, WHO WAS REGISTERED ONLY WITH THE THIEVES' GUILD, MADE IT TO LEVEL NINE.
THEREIN I ENCOUNTERED A GIRL WHO CALLED HERSELF THE DUNGEON'S ADMINISTRATOR.
A LOT HAPPENED.
AND NOW ...

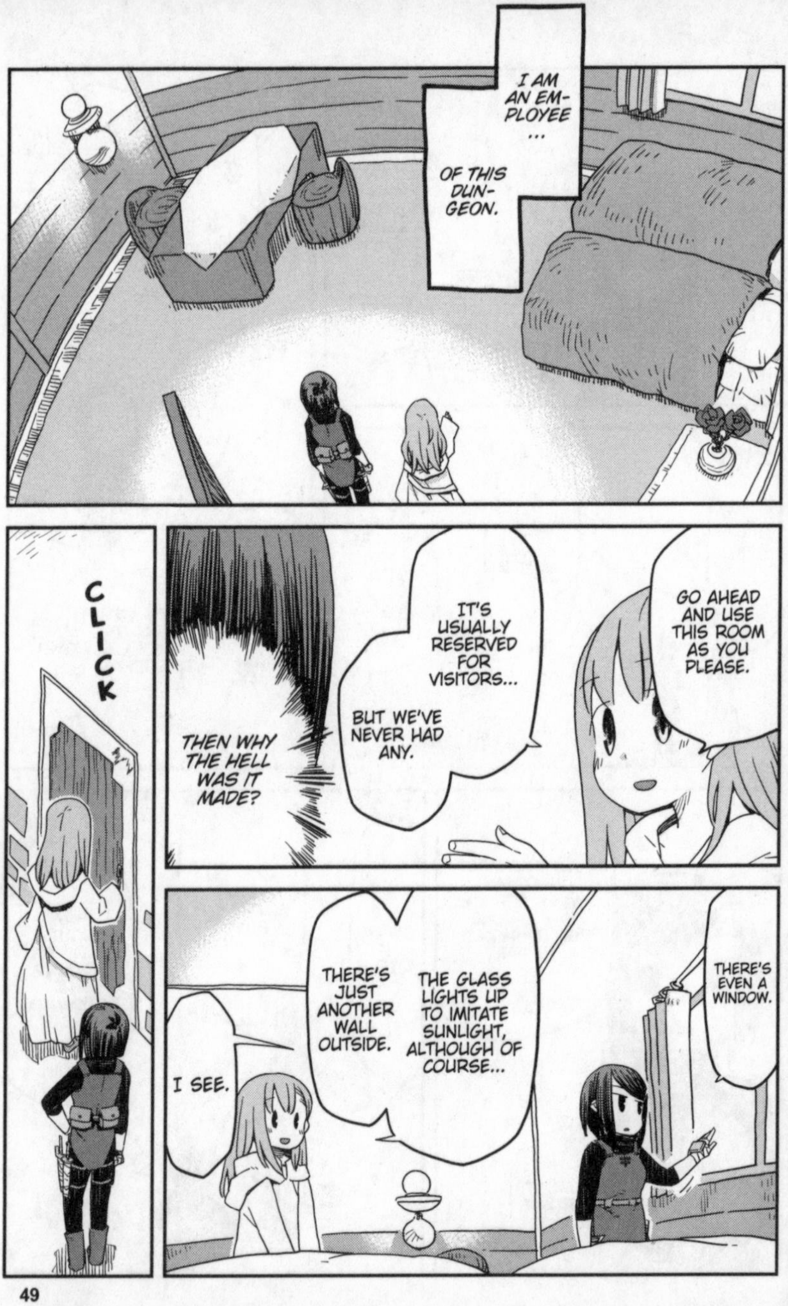
I AM AN EMPLOYEE...
OF THIS DUNGEON.
GO AHEAD AND USE THIS ROOM AS YOU PLEASE.
IT'S USUALLY RESERVED FOR VISITORS...
BUT WE'VE NEVER HAD ANY.
THEN WHY THE HELL WAS IT MADE?
THERE'S EVEN A WINDOW.
THE GLASS LIGHTS UP TO IMITATE SUNLIGHT, ALTHOUGH OF COURSE...
THERE'S JUST ANOTHER WALL OUTSIDE.
I SEE.
CLICK

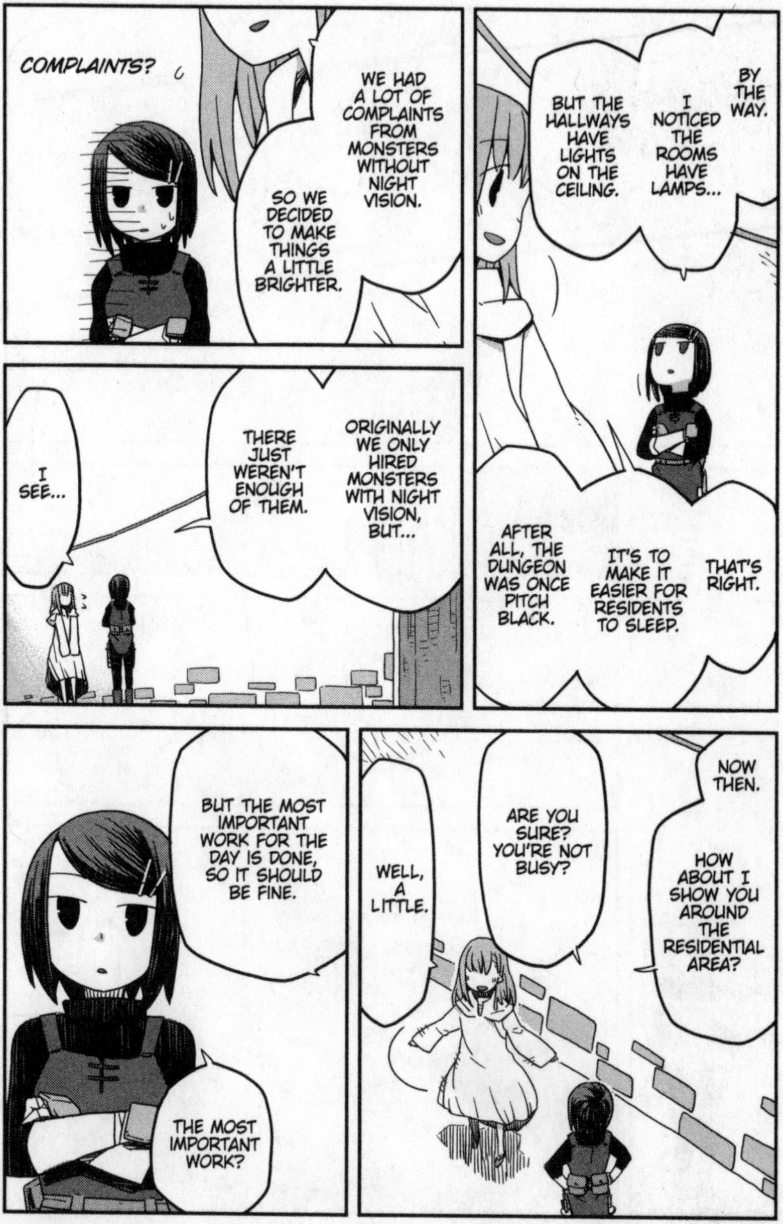
BY THE WAY.
I NOTICED THE ROOMS HAVE LAMPS...
BUT THE HALLWAYS HAVE LIGHTS ON THE CEILING.
THAT'S RIGHT.
IT'S TO MAKE IT EASIER FOR RESIDENTS TO SLEEP.
AFTER ALL, THE DUNGEON WAS ONCE PITCH BLACK.
WE HAD A LOT OF COMPLAINTS FROM MONSTERS WITHOUT NIGHT VISION.
SO WE DECIDED TO MAKE THINGS A LITTLE BRIGHTER.
COMPLAINTS?
ORIGINALLY WE ONLY HIRED MONSTERS WITH NIGHT VISION, BUT...
THERE JUST WEREN'T ENOUGH OF THEM.
I SEE...
NOW THEN.
HOW ABOUT I SHOW YOU AROUND THE RESIDENTIAL AREA?
ARE YOU SURE? YOU'RE NOT BUSY?
WELL, A LITTLE.
BUT THE MOST IMPORTANT WORK FOR THE DAY IS DONE, SO IT SHOULD BE FINE.
THE MOST IMPORTANT WORK?

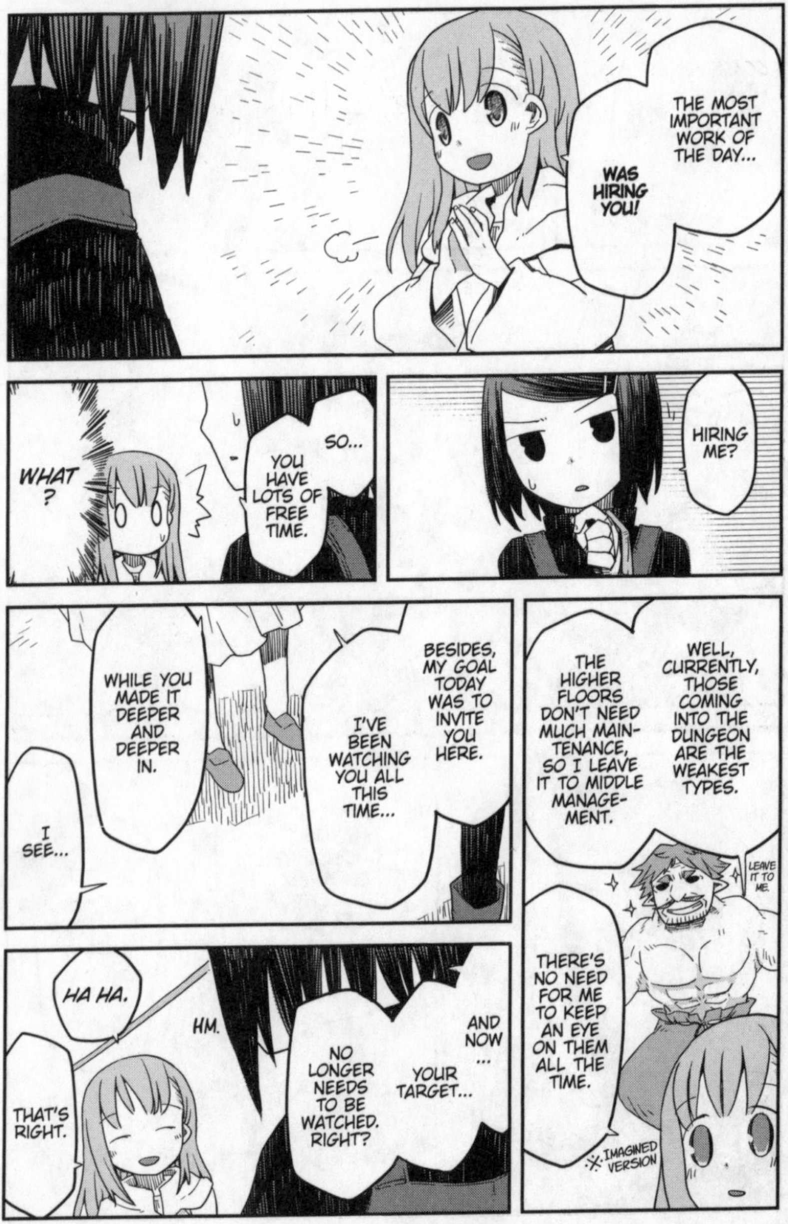
THE MOST IMPORTANT WORK OF THE DAY...
WAS HIRING YOU!
HIRING ME?
SO...
YOU HAVE LOTS OF FREE TIME.
WHAT?
WELL, CURRENTLY, THOSE COMING INTO THE DUNGEON ARE THE WEAKEST TYPES.
THE HIGHER FLOORS DON'T NEED MUCH MAINTENANCE, SO I LEAVE IT TO MIDDLE MANAGEMENT.
LEAVE IT TO ME.
THERE'S NO NEED FOR ME TO KEEP AN EYE ON THEM ALL THE TIME.
※IMAGINED VERSION
BESIDES, MY GOAL TODAY WAS TO INVITE YOU HERE.
I'VE BEEN WATCHING YOU ALL THIS TIME...
WHILE YOU MADE IT DEEPER AND DEEPER IN.
I SEE...
AND NOW...
YOUR TARGET...
NO LONGER NEEDS TO BE WATCHED. RIGHT?
HM.
HA HA.
THAT'S RIGHT.

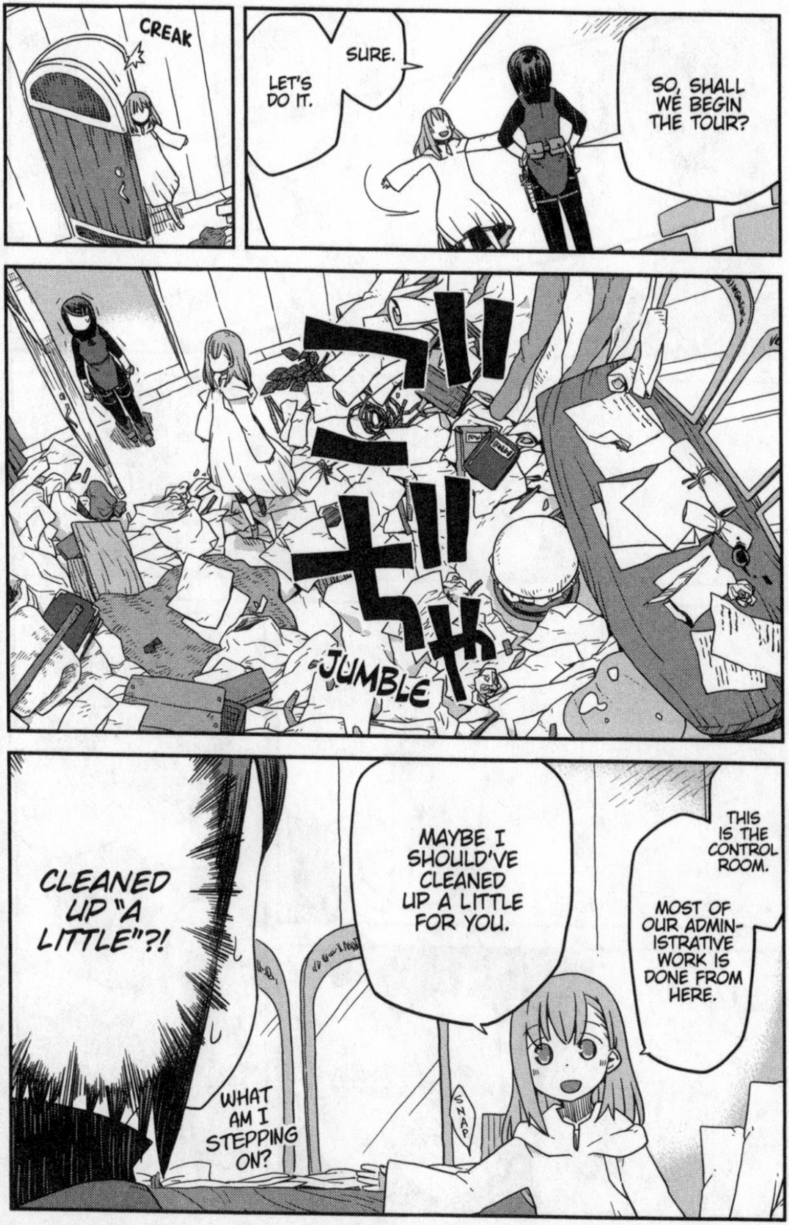
SO, SHALL WE BEGIN THE TOUR?
SURE.
LET'S DO IT.
CREAK
JUMBLE
THIS IS THE CONTROL ROOM.
MOST OF OUR ADMIN-ISTRATIVE WORK IS DONE FROM HERE.
MAYBE I SHOULD'VE CLEANED UP A LITTLE FOR YOU.
SNAP
WHAT AM I STEPPING ON?
CLEANED UP "A LITTLE"?!

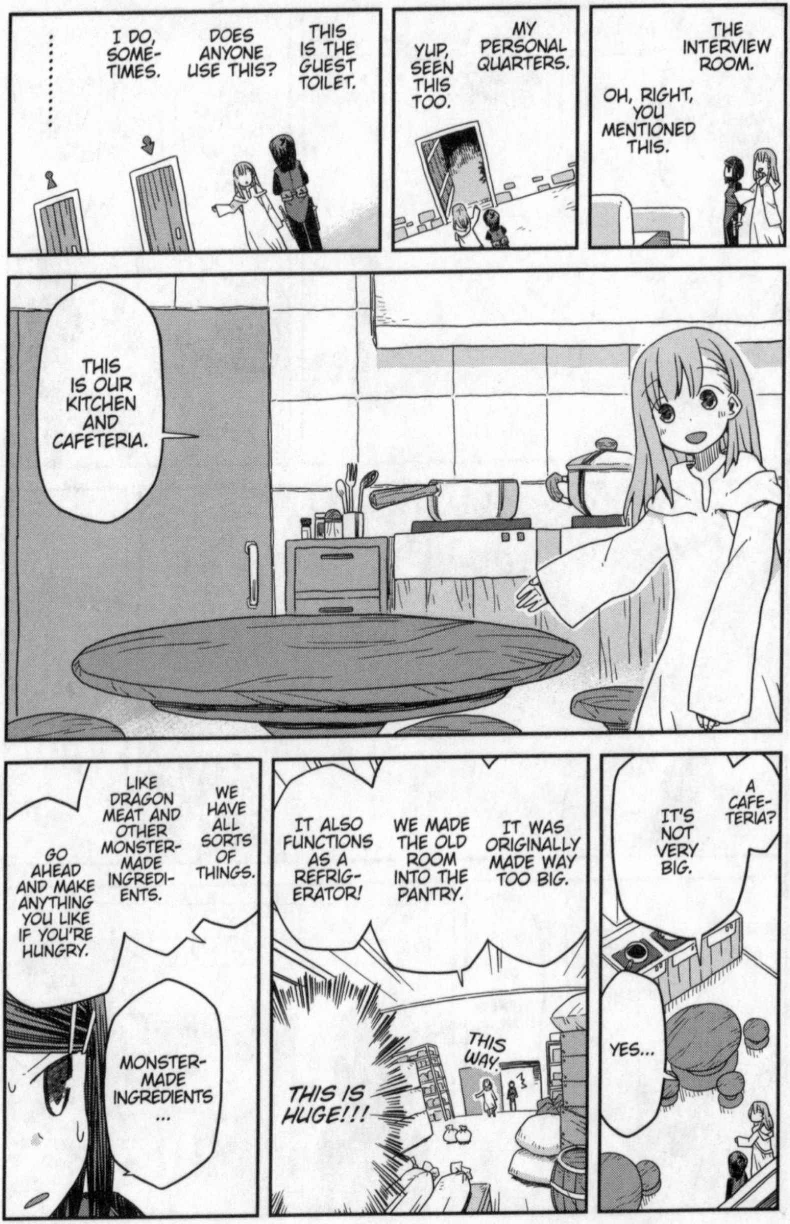
THE INTERVIEW ROOM.
OH, RIGHT, YOU MENTIONED THIS.
MY PERSONAL QUARTERS.
YUP, SEEN THIS TOO.
THIS IS THE GUEST TOILET.
DOES ANYONE USE THIS?
I DO, SOMETIMES.
......
THIS IS OUR KITCHEN AND CAFETERIA.
A CAFETERIA?
IT'S NOT VERY BIG.
YES...
IT WAS ORIGINALLY MADE WAY TOO BIG.
WE MADE THE OLD ROOM INTO THE PANTRY.
IT ALSO FUNCTIONS AS A REFRIGERATOR!
THIS WAY.
THIS IS HUGE!!!
WE HAVE ALL SORTS OF THINGS.
LIKE DRAGON MEAT AND OTHER MONSTER-MADE INGREDIENTS.
GO AHEAD AND MAKE ANYTHING YOU LIKE IF YOU'RE HUNGRY.
MONSTER-MADE INGREDIENTS...

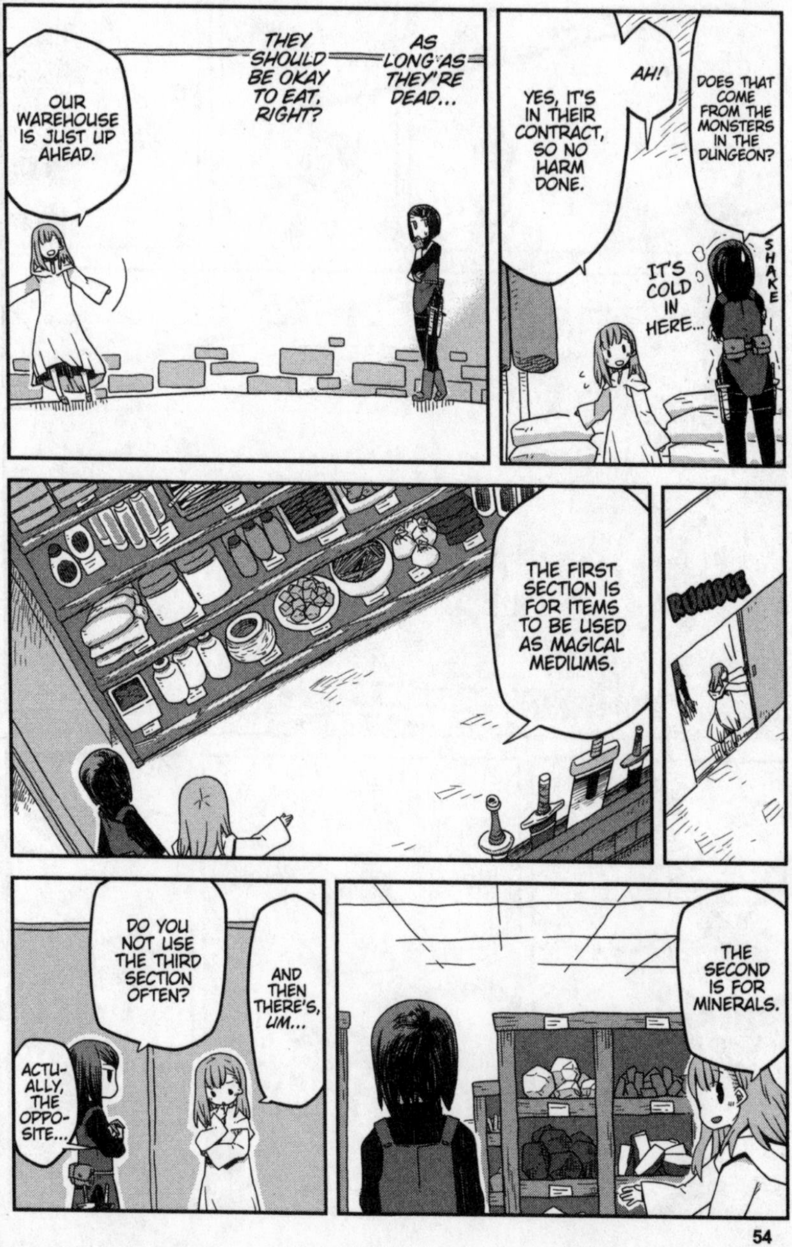
DOES THAT COME FROM THE MONSTERS IN THE DUNGEON?
AH!
YES, IT'S IN THEIR CONTRACT, SO NO HARM DONE.
SHAKE
IT'S COLD IN HERE...
AS LONG AS THEY'RE DEAD...
THEY SHOULD BE OKAY TO EAT, RIGHT?
OUR WAREHOUSE IS JUST UP AHEAD.
RUMBLE
THE FIRST SECTION IS FOR ITEMS TO BE USED AS MAGICAL MEDIUMS.
THE SECOND IS FOR MINERALS.
AND THEN THERE'S, UM...
DO YOU NOT USE THE THIRD SECTION OFTEN?
ACTUALLY, THE OPPOSITE...

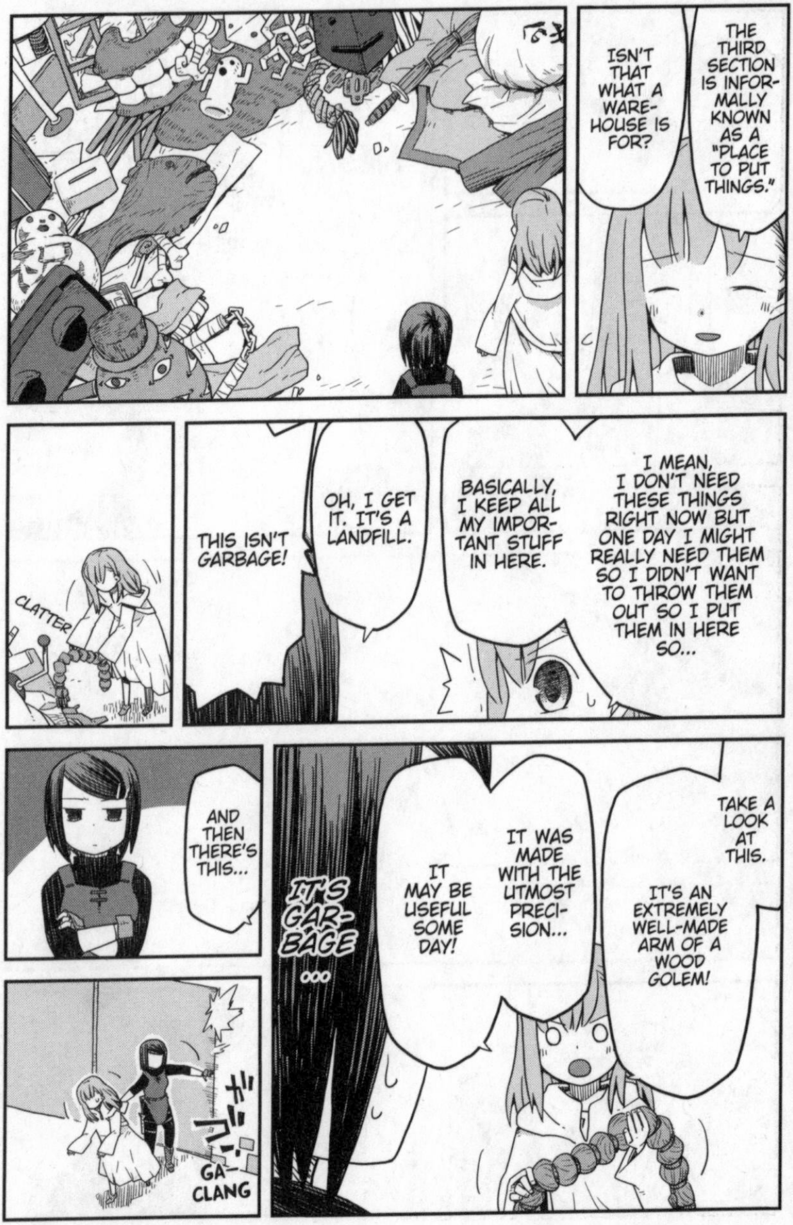
THE THIRD SECTION IS INFORMALLY KNOWN AS A "PLACE TO PUT THINGS."
ISN'T THAT WHAT A WAREHOUSE IS FOR?
I MEAN, I DON'T NEED THESE THINGS RIGHT NOW BUT ONE DAY I MIGHT REALLY NEED THEM SO I DIDN'T WANT TO THROW THEM OUT SO I PUT THEM IN HERE SO...
BASICALLY, I KEEP ALL MY IMPORTANT STUFF IN HERE.
OH, I GET IT. IT'S A LANDFILL.
THIS ISN'T GARBAGE!
CLATTER
TAKE A LOOK AT THIS.
IT'S AN EXTREMELY WELL-MADE ARM OF A WOOD GOLEM!
IT WAS MADE WITH THE UTMOST PRECISION...
IT MAY BE USEFUL SOME DAY!
IT'S GARBAGE...
AND THEN THERE'S THIS...
GA-CLANG

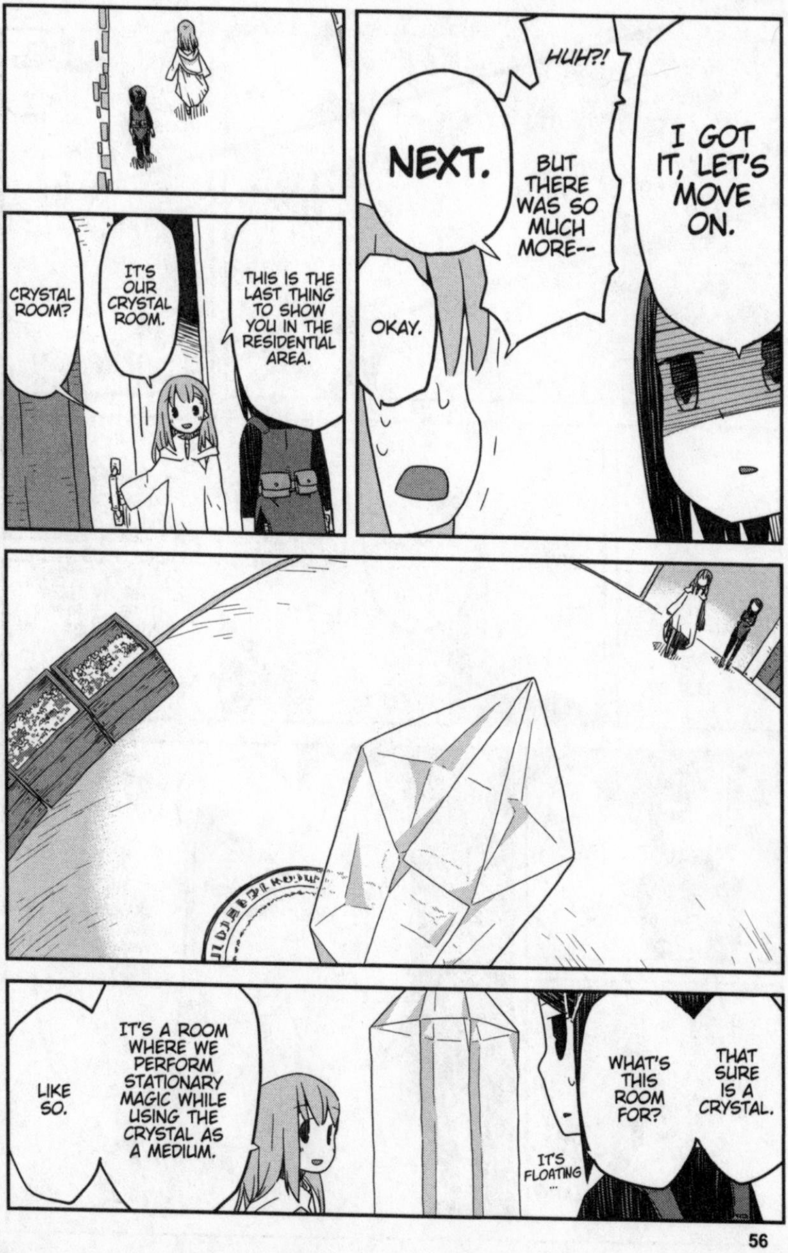
I GOT IT, LET'S MOVE ON.
HUH?!
BUT THERE WAS SO MUCH MORE--
NEXT.
OKAY.
THIS IS THE LAST THING TO SHOW YOU IN THE RESIDENTIAL AREA.
IT'S OUR CRYSTAL ROOM.
CRYSTAL ROOM?
THAT SURE IS A CRYSTAL.
WHAT'S THIS ROOM FOR?
IT'S FLOATING ...
IT'S A ROOM WHERE WE PERFORM STATIONARY MAGIC WHILE USING THE CRYSTAL AS A MEDIUM.
LIKE SO.

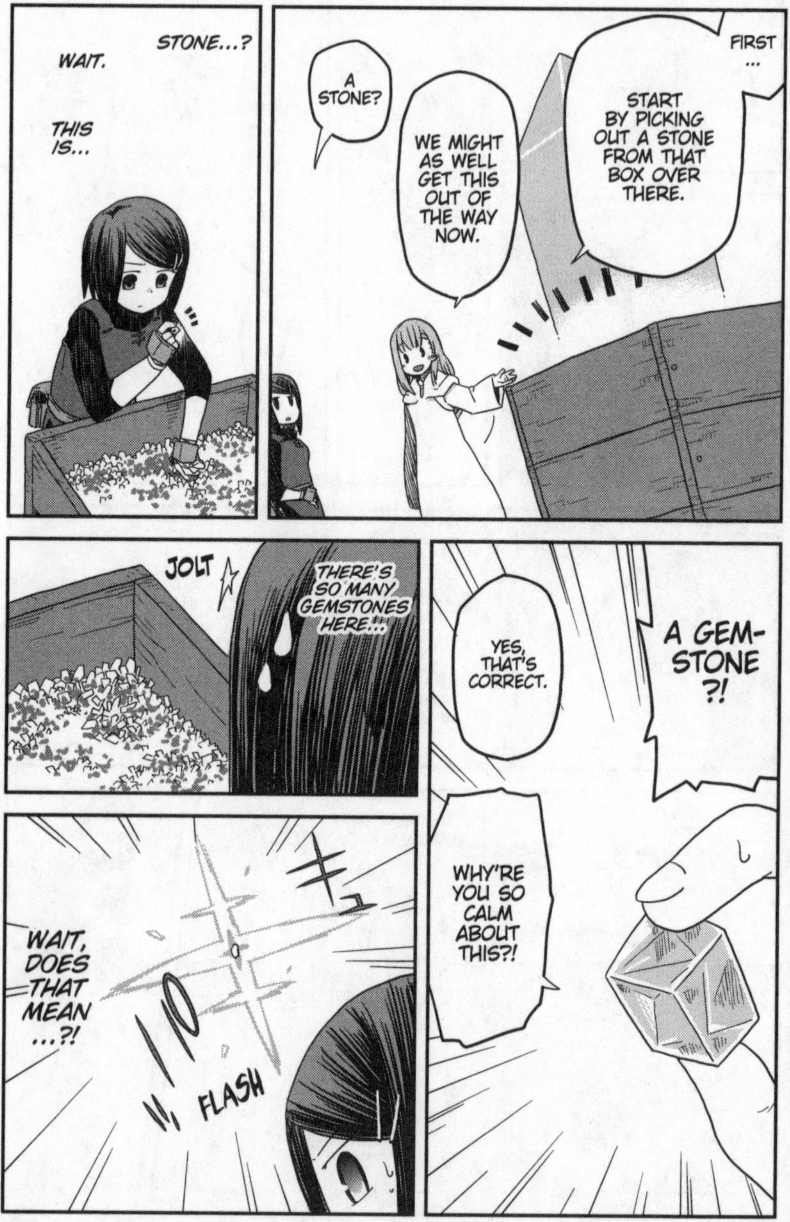
FIRST...
START BY PICKING OUT A STONE FROM THAT BOX OVER THERE.
WE MIGHT AS WELL GET THIS OUT OF THE WAY NOW.
A STONE?
STONE...?
WAIT.
THIS IS...
A GEM-STONE?!
YES, THAT'S CORRECT.
WHY'RE YOU SO CALM ABOUT THIS?!
JOLT
THERE'S SO MANY GEMSTONES HERE...!
WAIT, DOES THAT MEAN...?!
FLASH

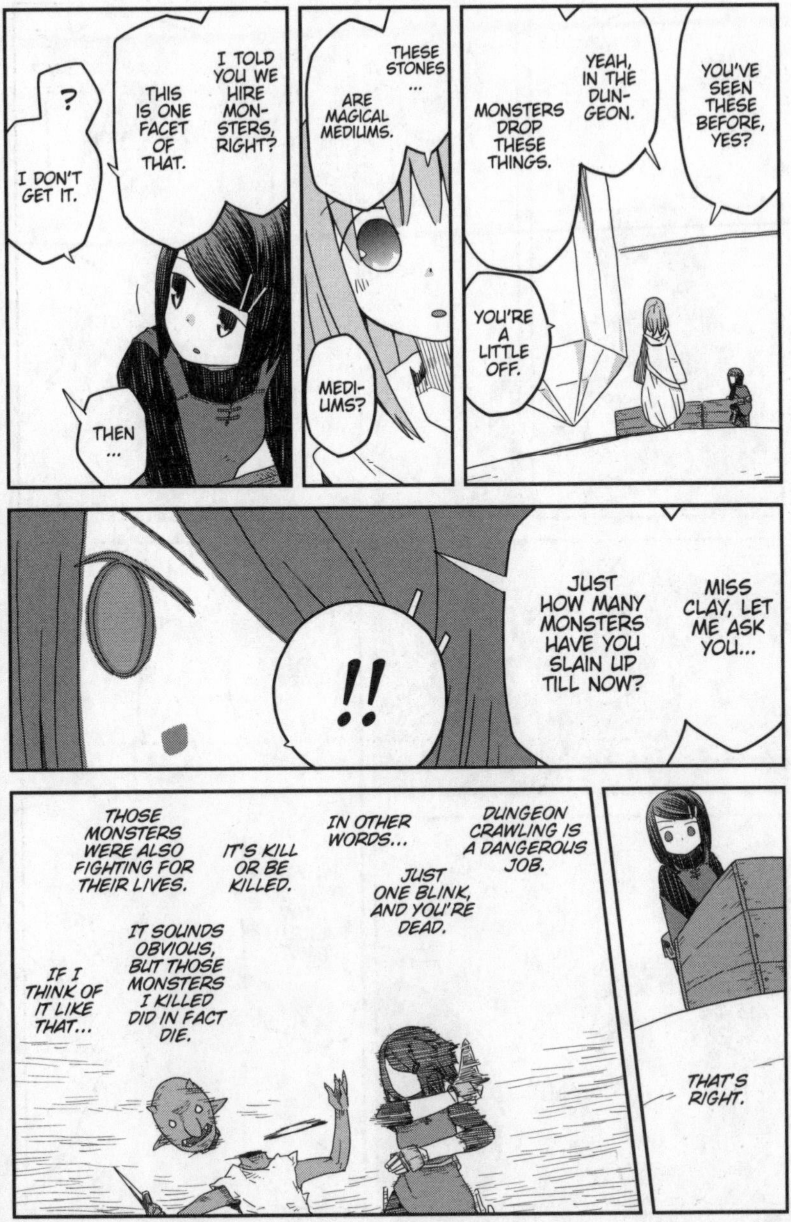
YOU'VE SEEN THESE BEFORE, YES?
YEAH, IN THE DUN-GEON.
MONSTERS DROP THESE THINGS.
YOU'RE A LITTLE OFF.
THESE STONES ...
ARE MAGICAL MEDIUMS.
MEDI-UMS?
I TOLD YOU WE HIRE MON-STERS, RIGHT?
THIS IS ONE FACET OF THAT.
?
I DON'T GET IT.
THEN ...
MISS CLAY, LET ME ASK YOU...
JUST HOW MANY MONSTERS HAVE YOU SLAIN UP TILL NOW?
!!
THAT'S RIGHT.
DUNGEON CRAWLING IS A DANGEROUS JOB.
JUST ONE BLINK, AND YOU'RE DEAD.
IN OTHER WORDS...
IT'S KILL OR BE KILLED.
THOSE MONSTERS WERE ALSO FIGHTING FOR THEIR LIVES.
IT SOUNDS OBVIOUS, BUT THOSE MONSTERS I KILLED DID IN FACT DIE.
IF I THINK OF IT LIKE THAT...

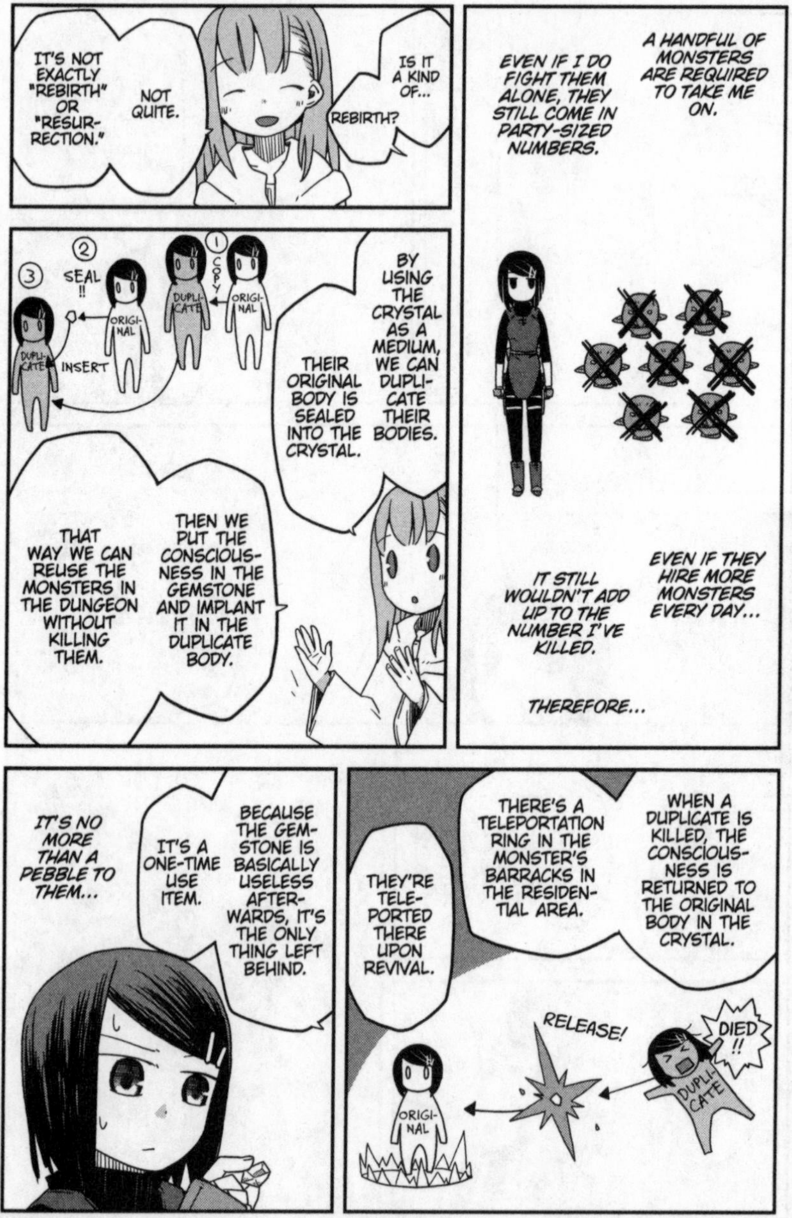
A HANDFUL OF MONSTERS ARE REQUIRED TO TAKE ME ON.
EVEN IF I DO FIGHT THEM ALONE, THEY STILL COME IN PARTY-SIZED NUMBERS.
EVEN IF THEY HIRE MORE MONSTERS EVERY DAY…
IT STILL WOULDN'T ADD UP TO THE NUMBER I'VE KILLED.
THEREFORE…
IS IT A KIND OF…
REBIRTH?
NOT QUITE.
IT'S NOT EXACTLY "REBIRTH" OR "RESURRECTION."
BY USING THE CRYSTAL AS A MEDIUM, WE CAN DUPLICATE THEIR BODIES.
THEIR ORIGINAL BODY IS SEALED INTO THE CRYSTAL.
① COPY
ORIGINAL
DUPLICATE
② SEAL!!
ORIGINAL
③
DUPLICATE
INSERT
THEN WE PUT THE CONSCIOUSNESS IN THE GEMSTONE AND IMPLANT IT IN THE DUPLICATE BODY.
THAT WAY WE CAN REUSE THE MONSTERS IN THE DUNGEON WITHOUT KILLING THEM.
WHEN A DUPLICATE IS KILLED, THE CONSCIOUSNESS IS RETURNED TO THE ORIGINAL BODY IN THE CRYSTAL.
THERE'S A TELEPORTATION RING IN THE MONSTER'S BARRACKS IN THE RESIDENTIAL AREA.
THEY'RE TELEPORTED THERE UPON REVIVAL.
DIED!!
DUPLICATE
RELEASE!
ORIGINAL
BECAUSE THE GEMSTONE IS BASICALLY USELESS AFTERWARDS, IT'S THE ONLY THING LEFT BEHIND.
IT'S A ONE-TIME USE ITEM.
IT'S NO MORE THAN A PEBBLE TO THEM…

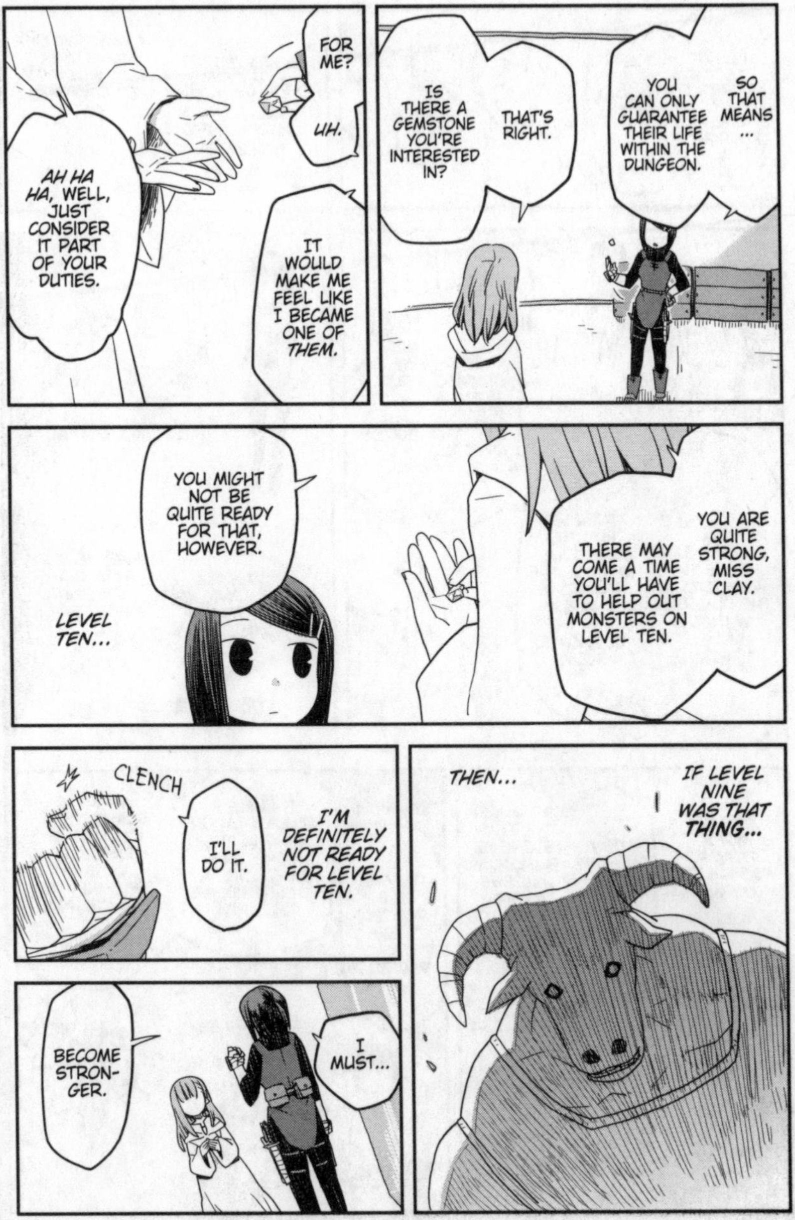
SO THAT MEANS ...
YOU CAN ONLY GUARANTEE THEIR LIFE WITHIN THE DUNGEON.
THAT'S RIGHT.
IS THERE A GEMSTONE YOU'RE INTERESTED IN?
FOR ME?
UH.
IT WOULD MAKE ME FEEL LIKE I BECAME ONE OF *THEM*.
AH HA HA, WELL, JUST CONSIDER IT PART OF YOUR DUTIES.
YOU ARE QUITE STRONG, MISS CLAY.
THERE MAY COME A TIME YOU'LL HAVE TO HELP OUT MONSTERS ON LEVEL TEN.
YOU MIGHT NOT BE QUITE READY FOR THAT, HOWEVER.
LEVEL TEN...
IF LEVEL NINE WAS THAT THING...
THEN...
I'M DEFINITELY NOT READY FOR LEVEL TEN.
I'LL DO IT.
CLENCH
I MUST...
BECOME STRONGER.

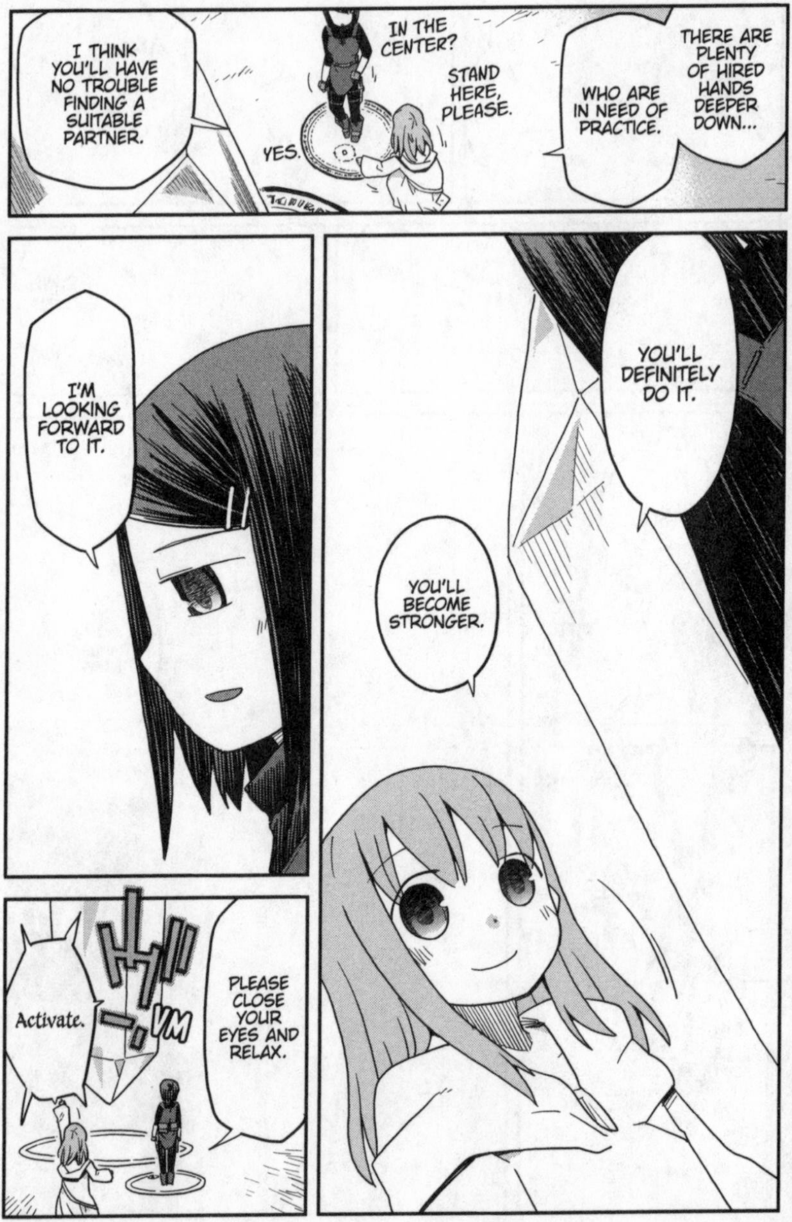
THERE ARE PLENTY OF HIRED HANDS DEEPER DOWN...
WHO ARE IN NEED OF PRACTICE.
STAND HERE, PLEASE.
IN THE CENTER?
YES.
I THINK YOU'LL HAVE NO TROUBLE FINDING A SUITABLE PARTNER.
YOU'LL DEFINITELY DO IT.
YOU'LL BECOME STRONGER.
I'M LOOKING FORWARD TO IT.
PLEASE CLOSE YOUR EYES AND RELAX.
VM
Activate.

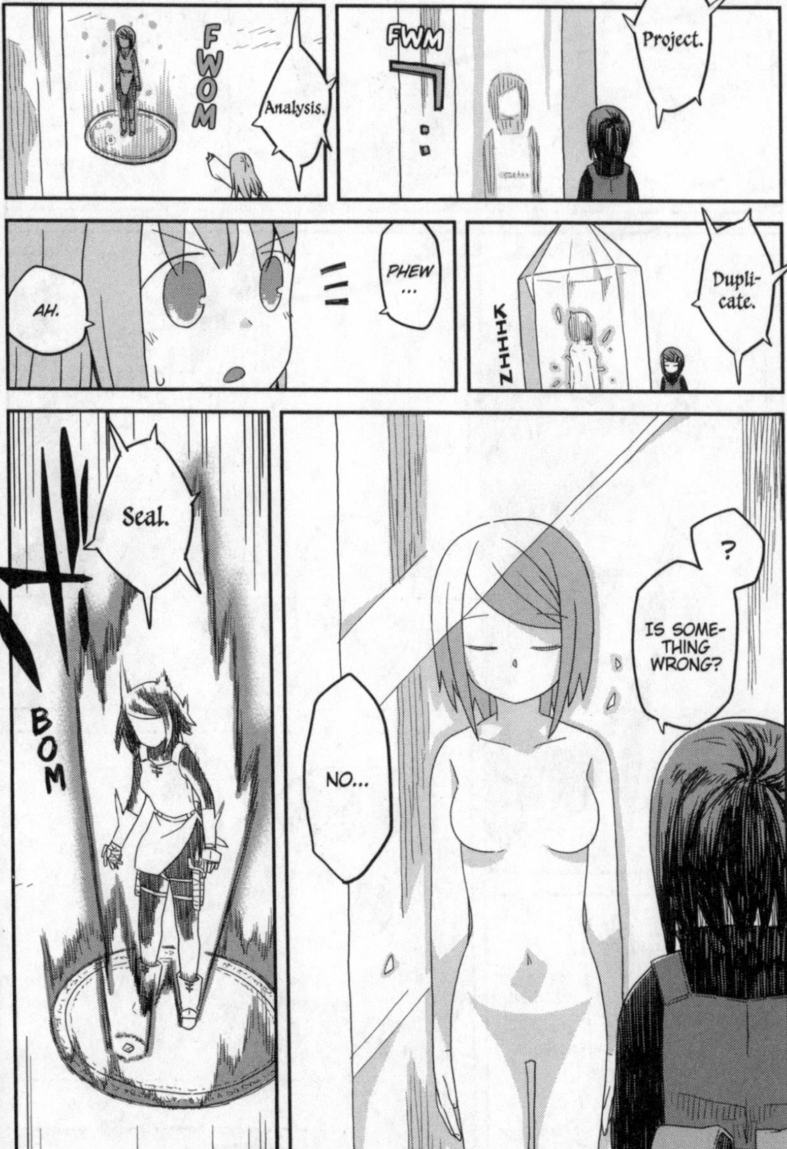
Project.
FWM
Analysis.
FWOM
Dupli-cate.
ZHHHK
PHEW...
AH.
?
IS SOME-THING WRONG?
NO...
Seal.
BOM

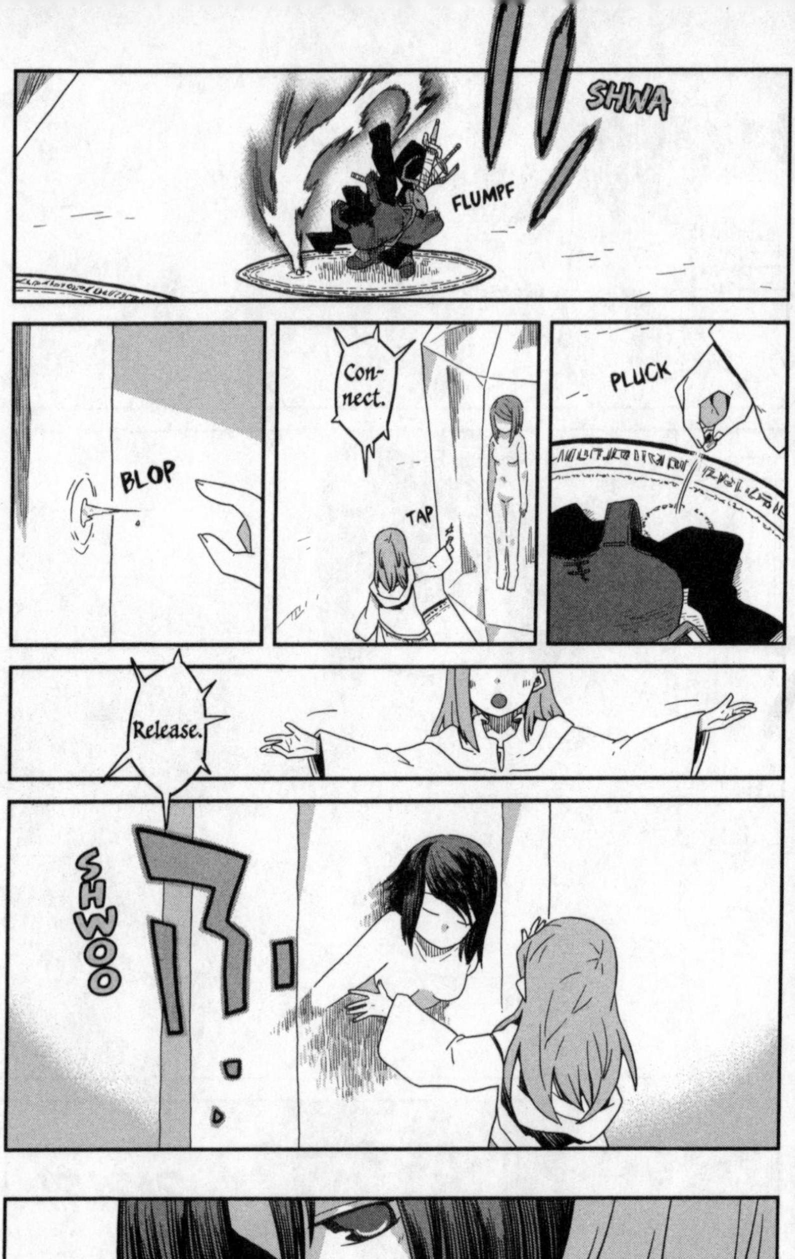
SHWA
FLUMPF
PLUCK
Con-
nect.
TAP
BLOP
Release.
SHWOO

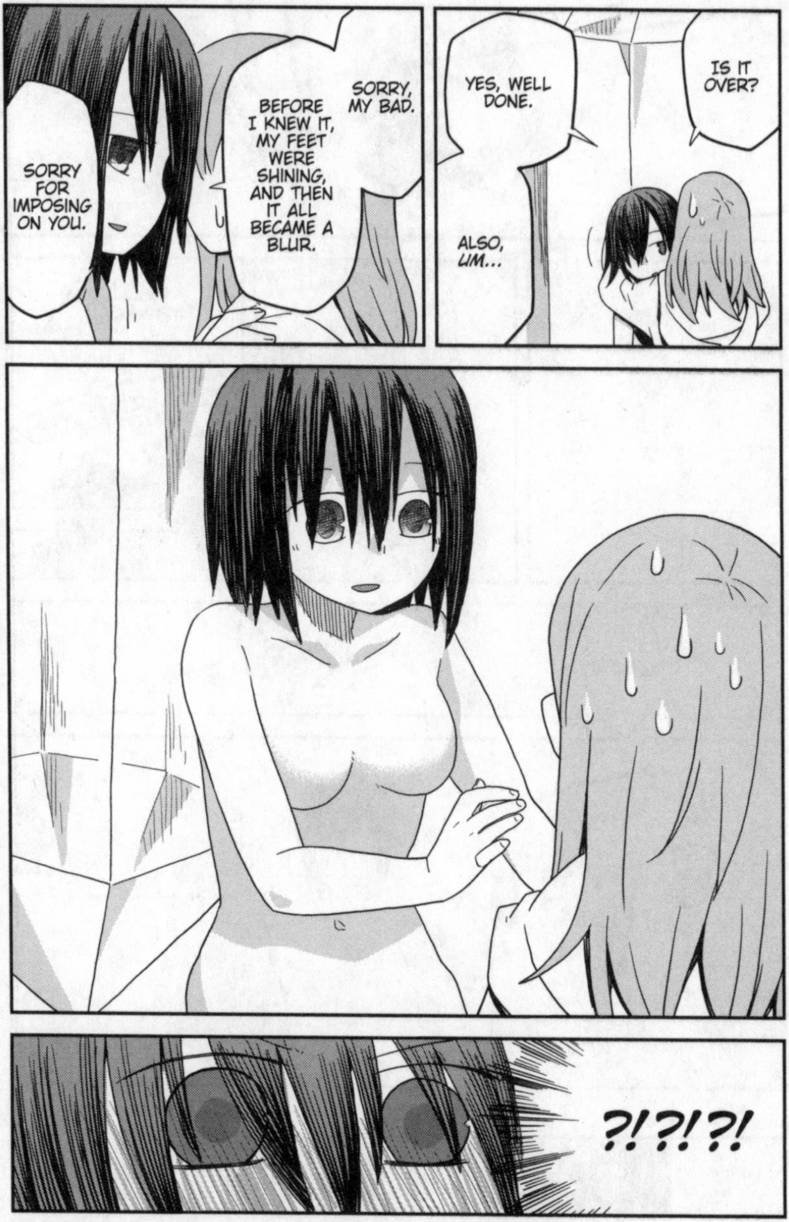
IS IT OVER?
YES, WELL DONE.
ALSO, UM...
SORRY, MY BAD.
BEFORE I KNEW IT, MY FEET WERE SHINING, AND THEN IT ALL BECAME A BLUR.
SORRY FOR IMPOSING ON YOU.
?!?!?!

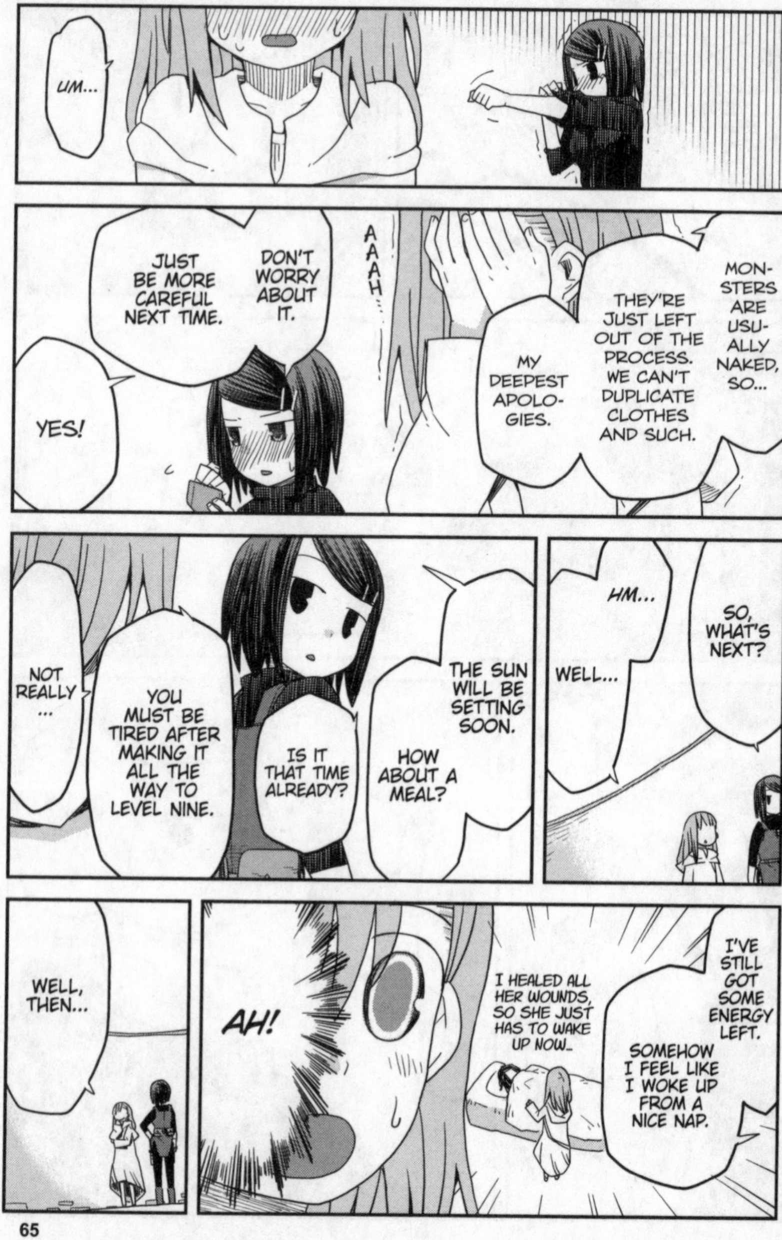
UM...
MON-STERS ARE USU-ALLY NAKED, SO...
THEY'RE JUST LEFT OUT OF THE PROCESS. WE CAN'T DUPLICATE CLOTHES AND SUCH.
MY DEEPEST APOLO-GIES.
AAAAH...
DON'T WORRY ABOUT IT.
JUST BE MORE CAREFUL NEXT TIME.
YES!
SO, WHAT'S NEXT?
HM...
WELL...
THE SUN WILL BE SETTING SOON.
HOW ABOUT A MEAL?
IS IT THAT TIME ALREADY?
YOU MUST BE TIRED AFTER MAKING IT ALL THE WAY TO LEVEL NINE.
NOT REALLY ...
I'VE STILL GOT SOME ENERGY LEFT.
SOMEHOW I FEEL LIKE I WOKE UP FROM A NICE NAP.
I HEALED ALL HER WOUNDS, SO SHE JUST HAS TO WAKE UP NOW..
AH!
WELL, THEN...

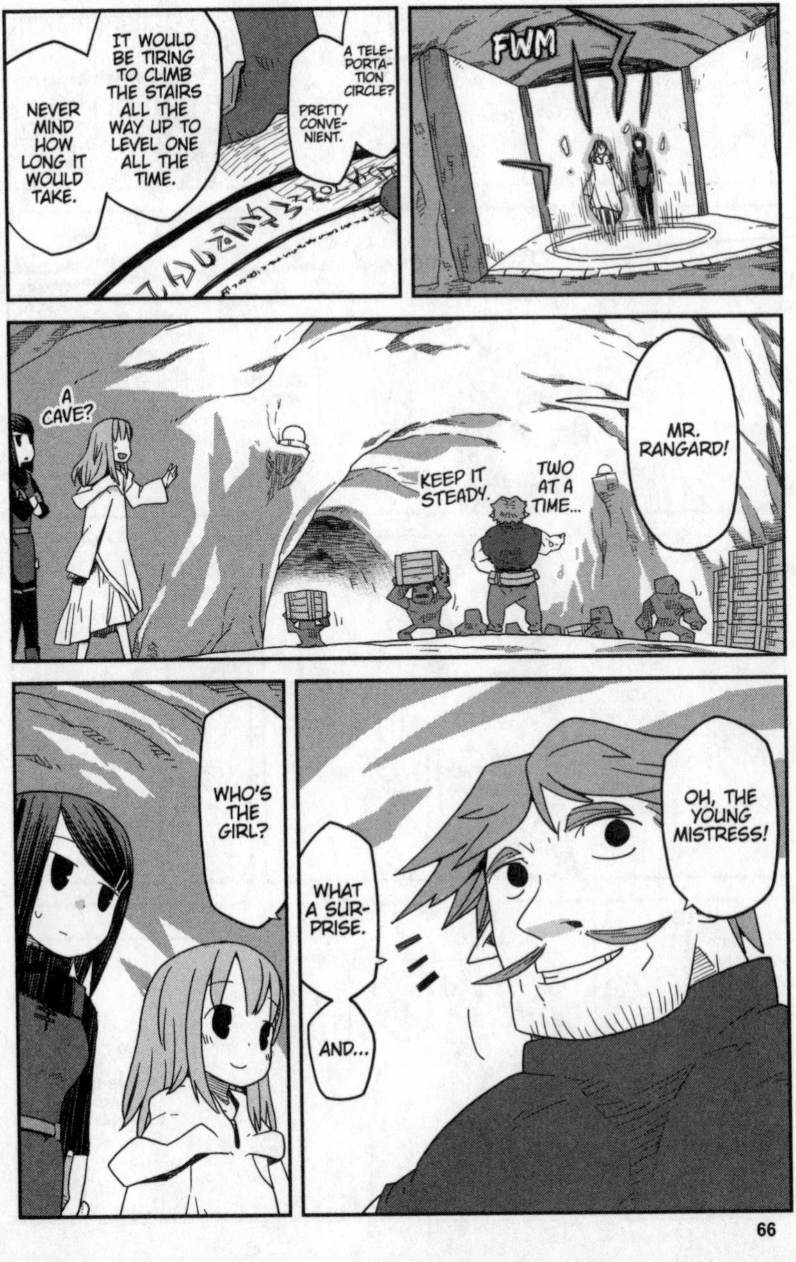
FWM
A TELEPORTATION CIRCLE?
PRETTY CONVENIENT.
IT WOULD BE TIRING TO CLIMB THE STAIRS ALL THE WAY UP TO LEVEL ONE ALL THE TIME.
NEVER MIND HOW LONG IT WOULD TAKE.
MR. RANGARD!
TWO AT A TIME...
KEEP IT STEADY.
A CAVE?
OH, THE YOUNG MISTRESS!
WHAT A SURPRISE.
AND...
WHO'S THE GIRL?

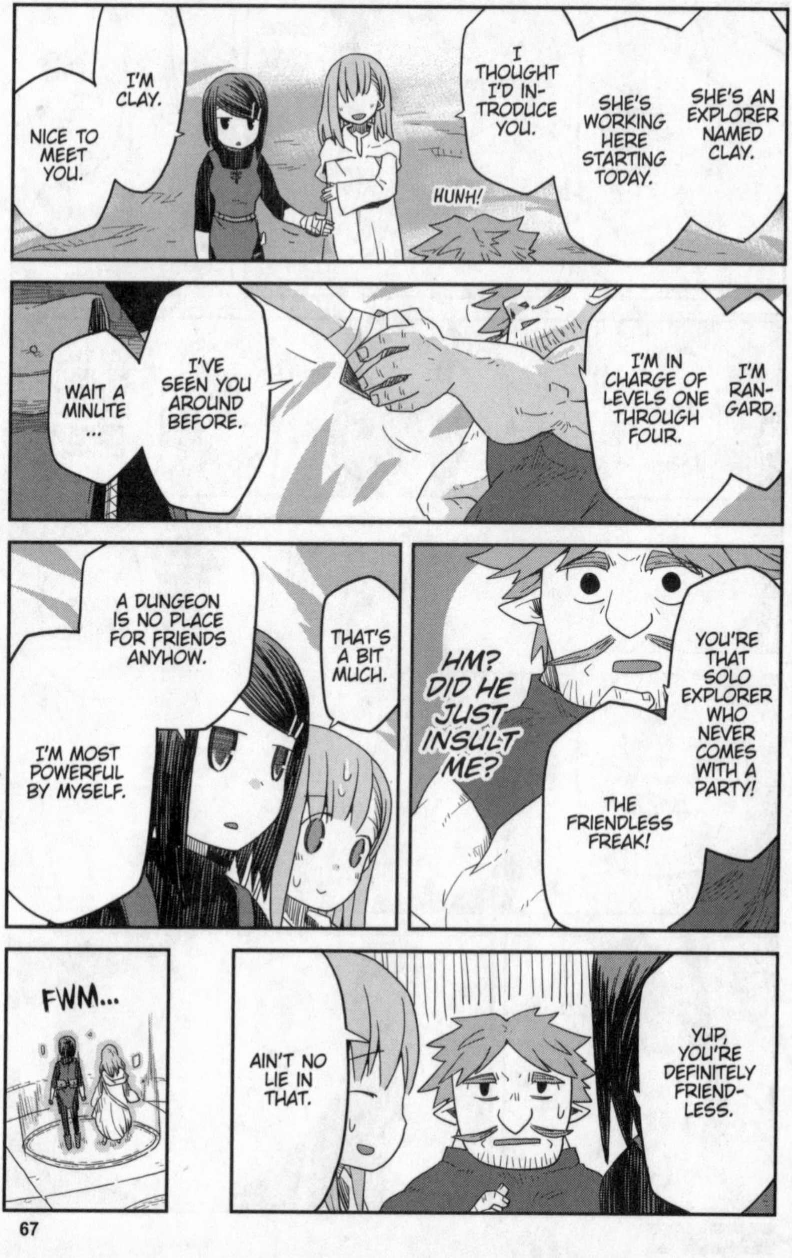
SHE'S AN EXPLORER NAMED CLAY.
SHE'S WORKING HERE STARTING TODAY.
I THOUGHT I'D IN-TRODUCE YOU.
HUNH!
I'M CLAY.
NICE TO MEET YOU.
I'M RAN-GARD.
I'M IN CHARGE OF LEVELS ONE THROUGH FOUR.
I'VE SEEN YOU AROUND BEFORE.
WAIT A MINUTE ...
YOU'RE THAT SOLO EXPLORER WHO NEVER COMES WITH A PARTY!
THE FRIENDLESS FREAK!
HM? DID HE JUST INSULT ME?
THAT'S A BIT MUCH.
A DUNGEON IS NO PLACE FOR FRIENDS ANYHOW.
I'M MOST POWERFUL BY MYSELF.
YUP, YOU'RE DEFINITELY FRIEND-LESS.
AIN'T NO LIE IN THAT.
FWM...

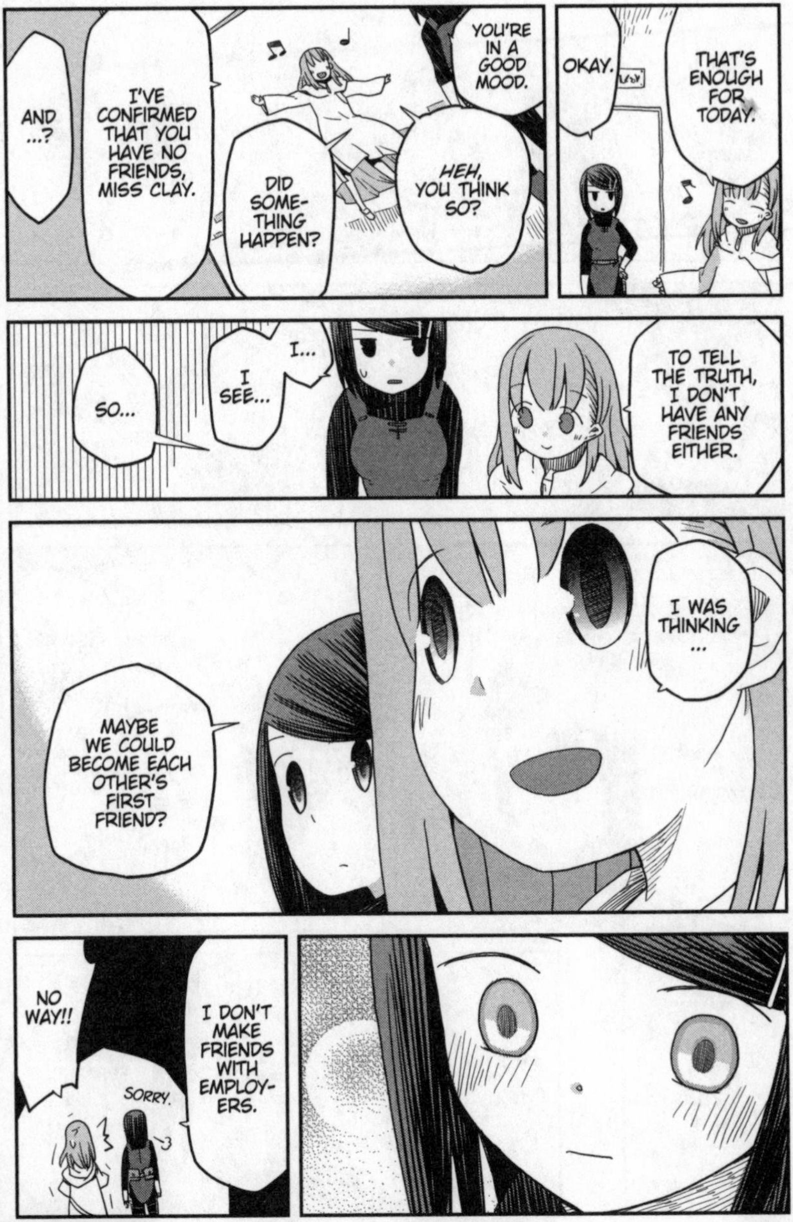
THAT'S ENOUGH FOR TODAY.
OKAY.
YOU'RE IN A GOOD MOOD.
HEH, YOU THINK SO?
DID SOME-THING HAPPEN?
I'VE CONFIRMED THAT YOU HAVE NO FRIENDS, MISS CLAY.
AND ...?
TO TELL THE TRUTH, I DON'T HAVE ANY FRIENDS EITHER.
I...
I SEE...
SO...
I WAS THINKING ...
MAYBE WE COULD BECOME EACH OTHER'S FIRST FRIEND?
I DON'T MAKE FRIENDS WITH EMPLOY-ERS.
NO WAY!!
SORRY.

CHAPTER 2 - END

I SHOULD'VE JUST GIVEN YOU THE SAME JOB TITLE AS ME!
THIS IS ONLY OCCURRING TO YOU NOW?

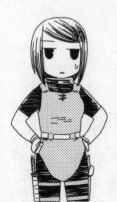

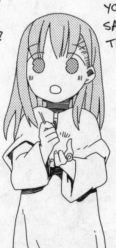

HELP?
SURE,
BUT...

CLEANING
UP A
ROOM?

SEEMS A
BIT OUT
OF MY PAY
GRADE...

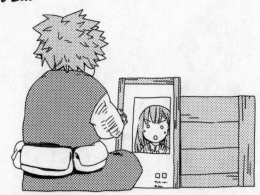

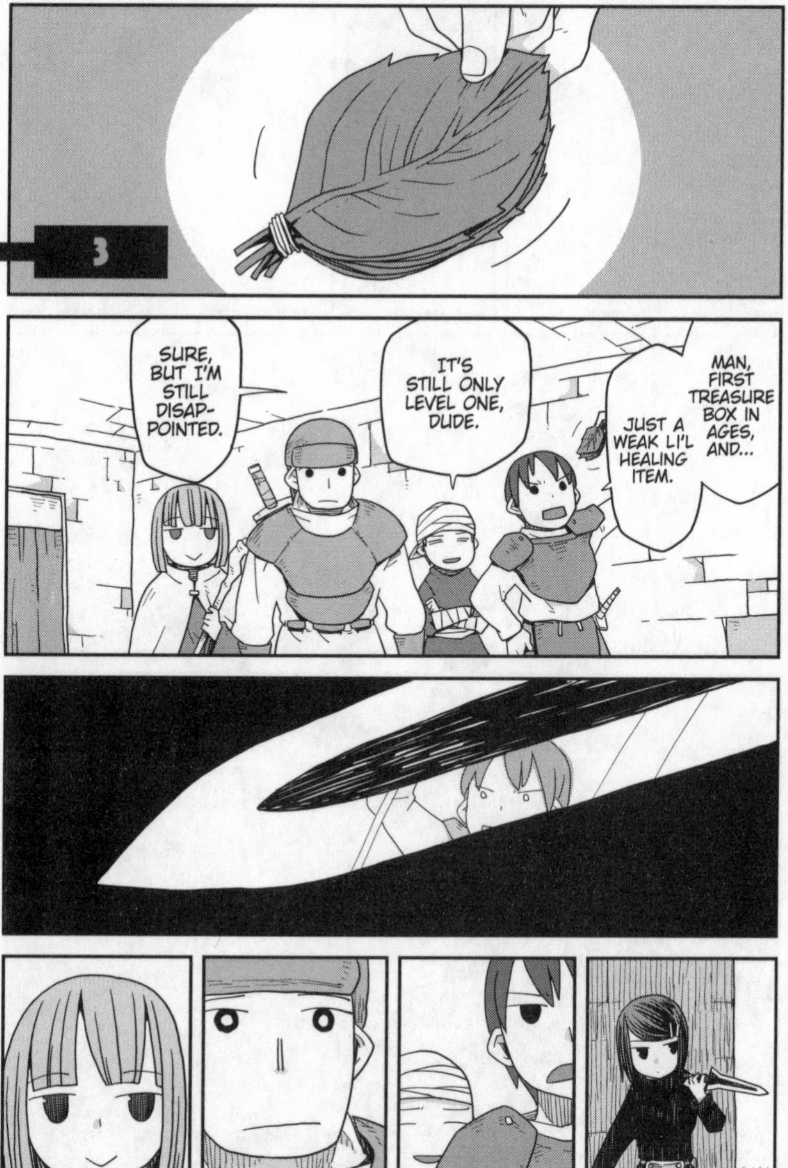
3
MAN, FIRST TREASURE BOX IN AGES, AND...
JUST A WEAK LI'L HEALING ITEM.
IT'S STILL ONLY LEVEL ONE, DUDE.
SURE, BUT I'M STILL DISAP-POINTED.

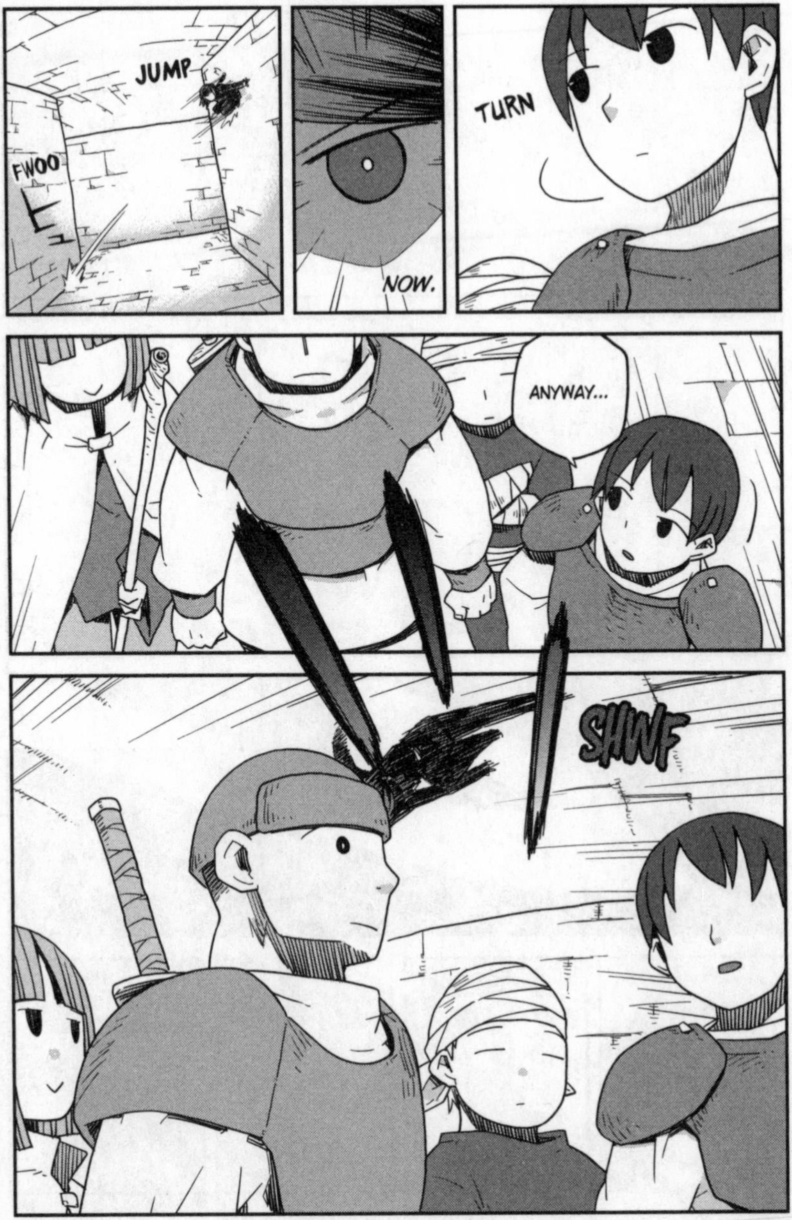
TURN
NOW.
JUMP
FWOO
ANYWAY...
SHWF

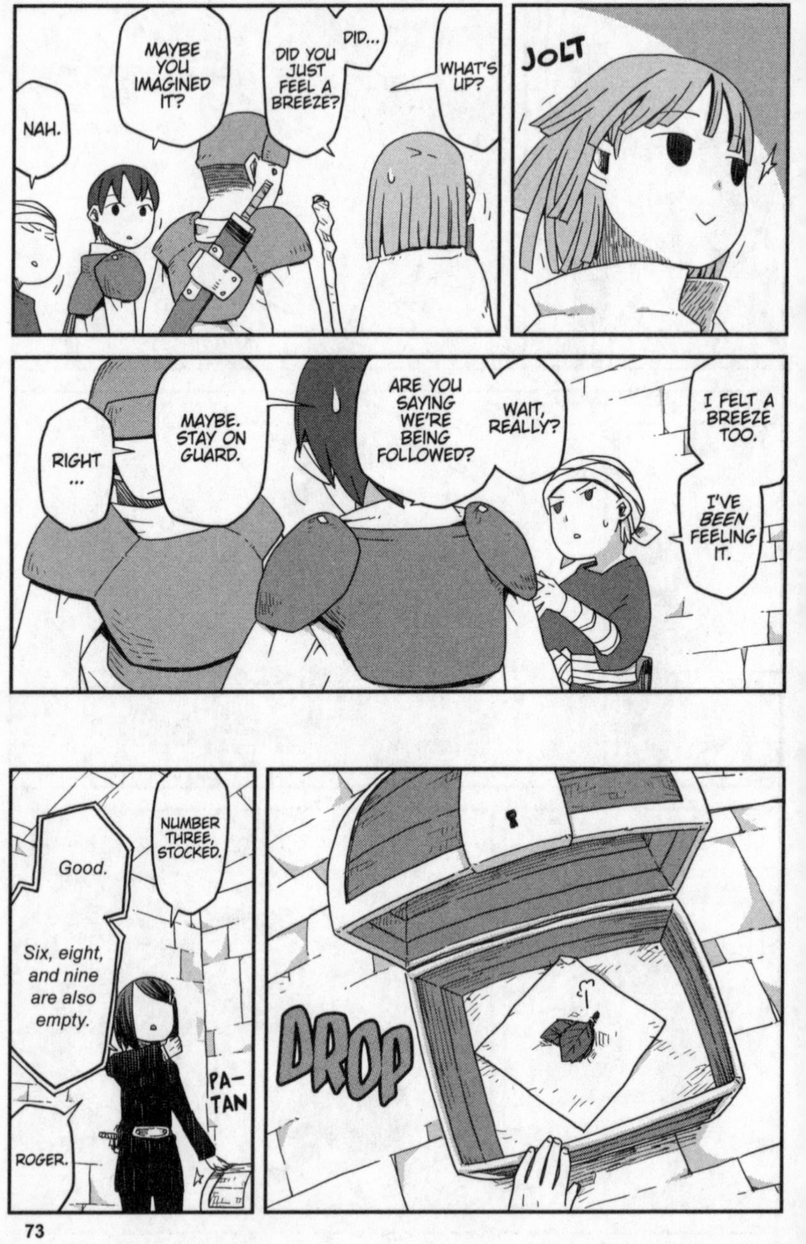

JOLT
WHAT'S UP?
DID...
DID YOU JUST FEEL A BREEZE?
MAYBE YOU IMAGINED IT?
NAH.
I FELT A BREEZE TOO.
I'VE *BEEN* FEELING IT.
WAIT, REALLY?
ARE YOU SAYING WE'RE BEING FOLLOWED?
MAYBE. STAY ON GUARD.
RIGHT ...
DROP
NUMBER THREE, STOCKED.
Good.
Six, eight, and nine are also empty.
PA-TAN
ROGER.

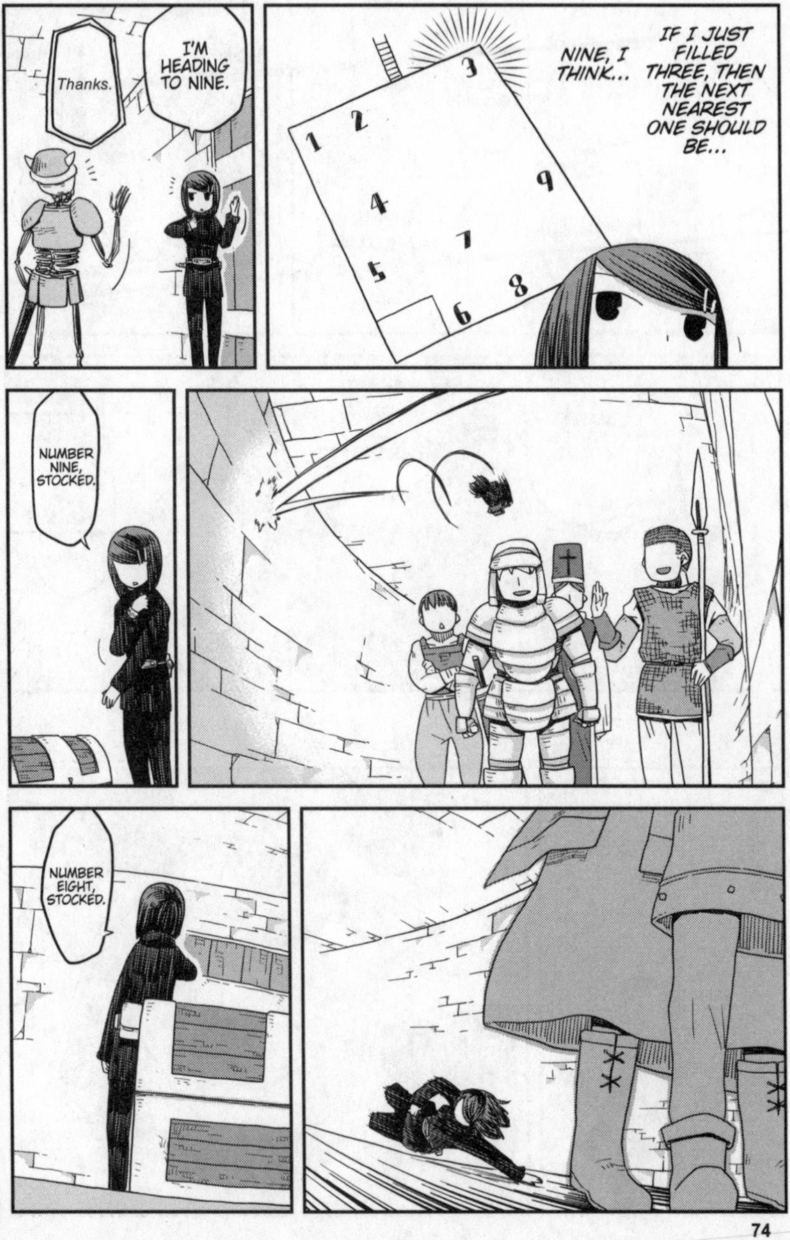
IF I JUST FILLED THREE, THEN THE NEXT NEAREST ONE SHOULD BE...
NINE, I THINK...
I'M HEADING TO NINE.
Thanks.
NUMBER NINE, STOCKED.
NUMBER EIGHT, STOCKED.

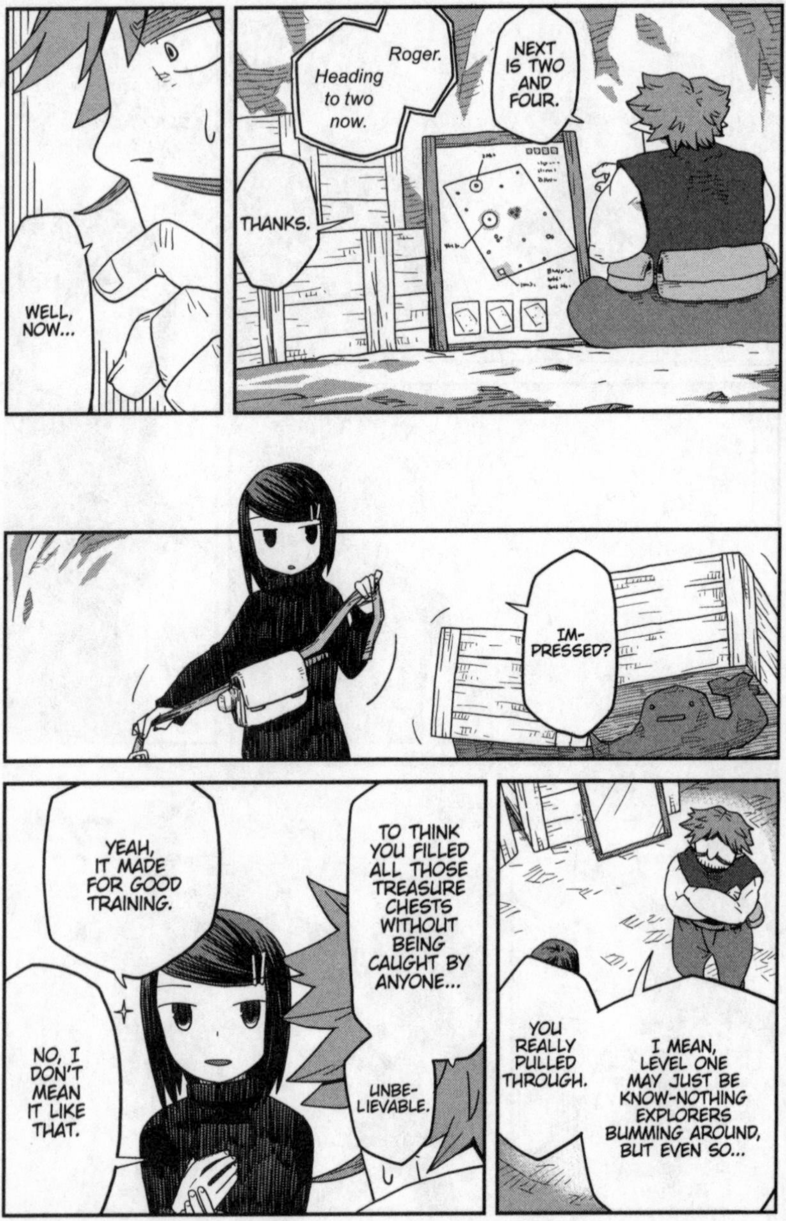
NEXT IS TWO AND FOUR.
Roger. Heading to two now.
THANKS.
WELL, NOW...
IM-PRESSED?
YOU REALLY PULLED THROUGH.
I MEAN, LEVEL ONE MAY JUST BE KNOW-NOTHING EXPLORERS BUMMING AROUND, BUT EVEN SO...
TO THINK YOU FILLED ALL THOSE TREASURE CHESTS WITHOUT BEING CAUGHT BY ANYONE...
UNBE-LIEVABLE.
YEAH, IT MADE FOR GOOD TRAINING.
NO, I DON'T MEAN IT LIKE THAT.

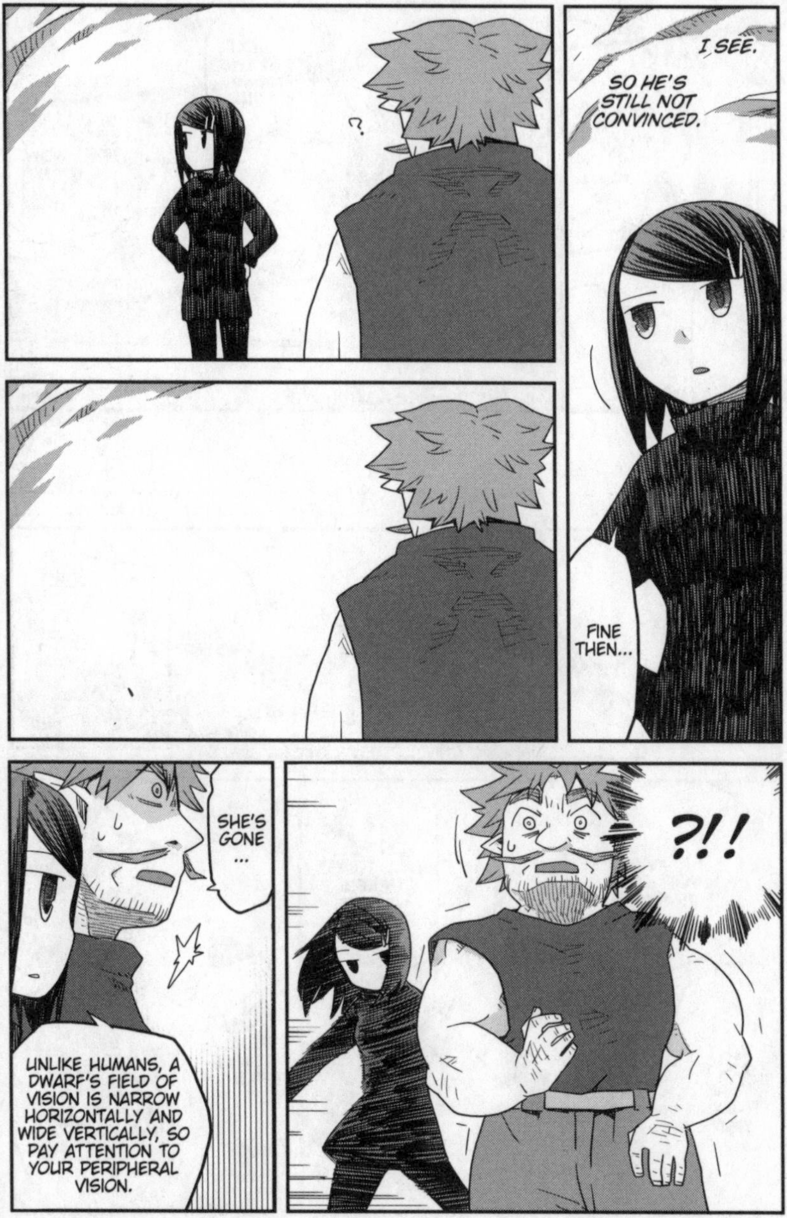

I SEE.
SO HE'S STILL NOT CONVINCED.
FINE THEN...
?
?!!
SHE'S GONE ...
UNLIKE HUMANS, A DWARF'S FIELD OF VISION IS NARROW HORIZONTALLY AND WIDE VERTICALLY, SO PAY ATTENTION TO YOUR PERIPHERAL VISION.

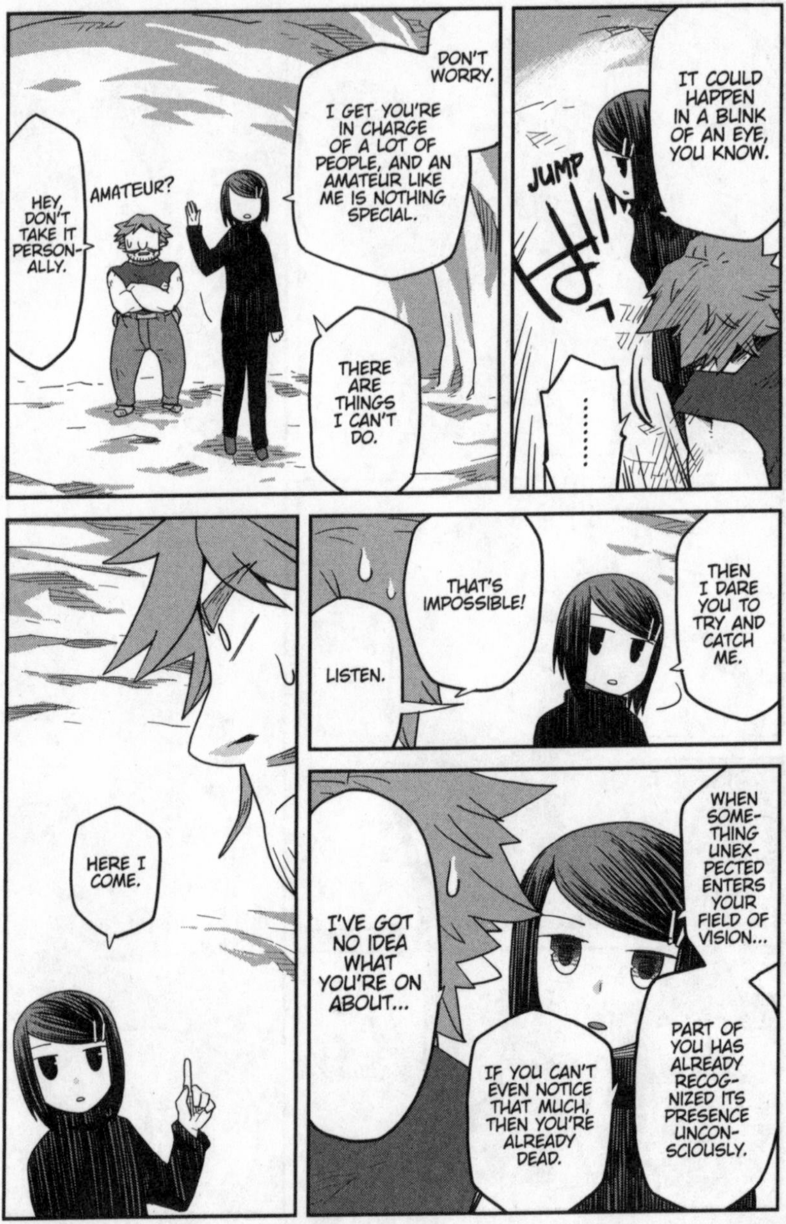
IT COULD HAPPEN IN A BLINK OF AN EYE, YOU KNOW.
JUMP
DON'T WORRY.
I GET YOU'RE IN CHARGE OF A LOT OF PEOPLE, AND AN AMATEUR LIKE ME IS NOTHING SPECIAL.
AMATEUR?
HEY, DON'T TAKE IT PERSON-ALLY.
THERE ARE THINGS I CAN'T DO.
THEN I DARE YOU TO TRY AND CATCH ME.
THAT'S IMPOSSIBLE!
LISTEN.
WHEN SOME-THING UNEX-PECTED ENTERS YOUR FIELD OF VISION...
PART OF YOU HAS ALREADY RECOG-NIZED ITS PRESENCE UNCON-SCIOUSLY.
IF YOU CAN'T EVEN NOTICE THAT MUCH, THEN YOU'RE ALREADY DEAD.
I'VE GOT NO IDEA WHAT YOU'RE ON ABOUT...
HERE I COME.

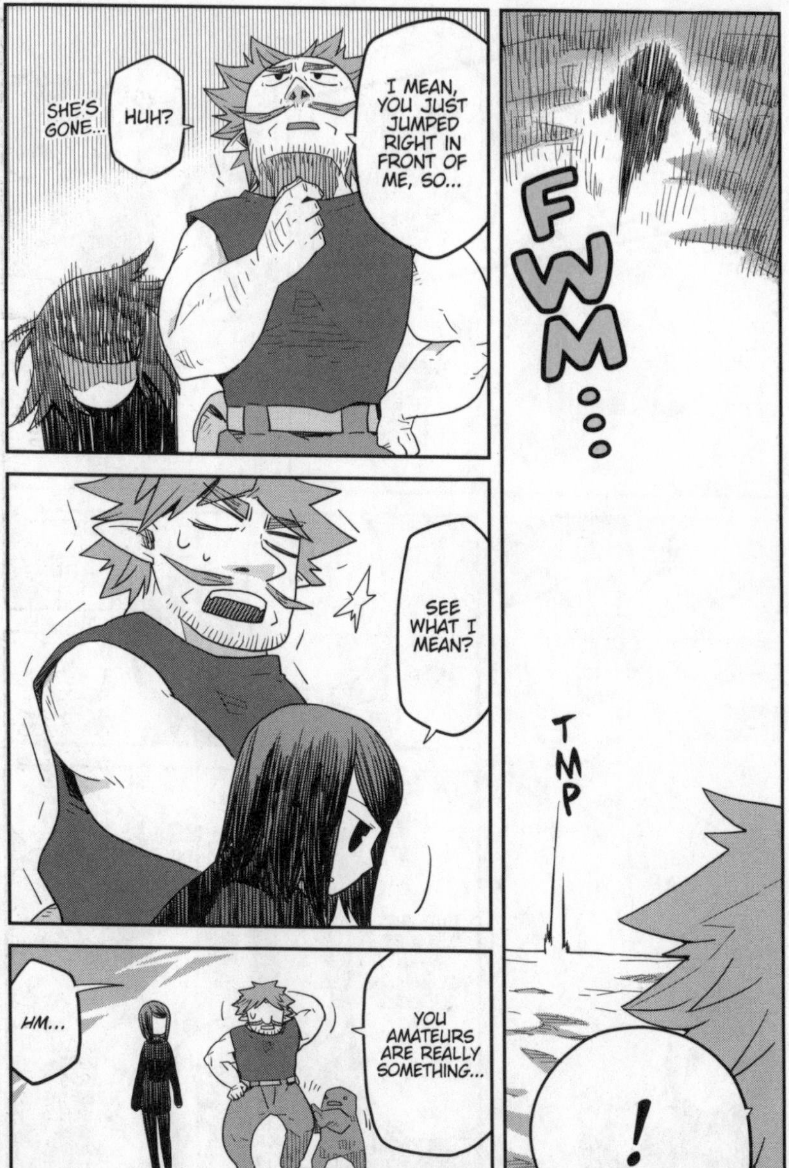

FWM...
TMP
!
I MEAN, YOU JUST JUMPED RIGHT IN FRONT OF ME, SO...
HUH?
SHE'S GONE...
SEE WHAT I MEAN?
YOU AMATEURS ARE REALLY SOMETHING...
HM...

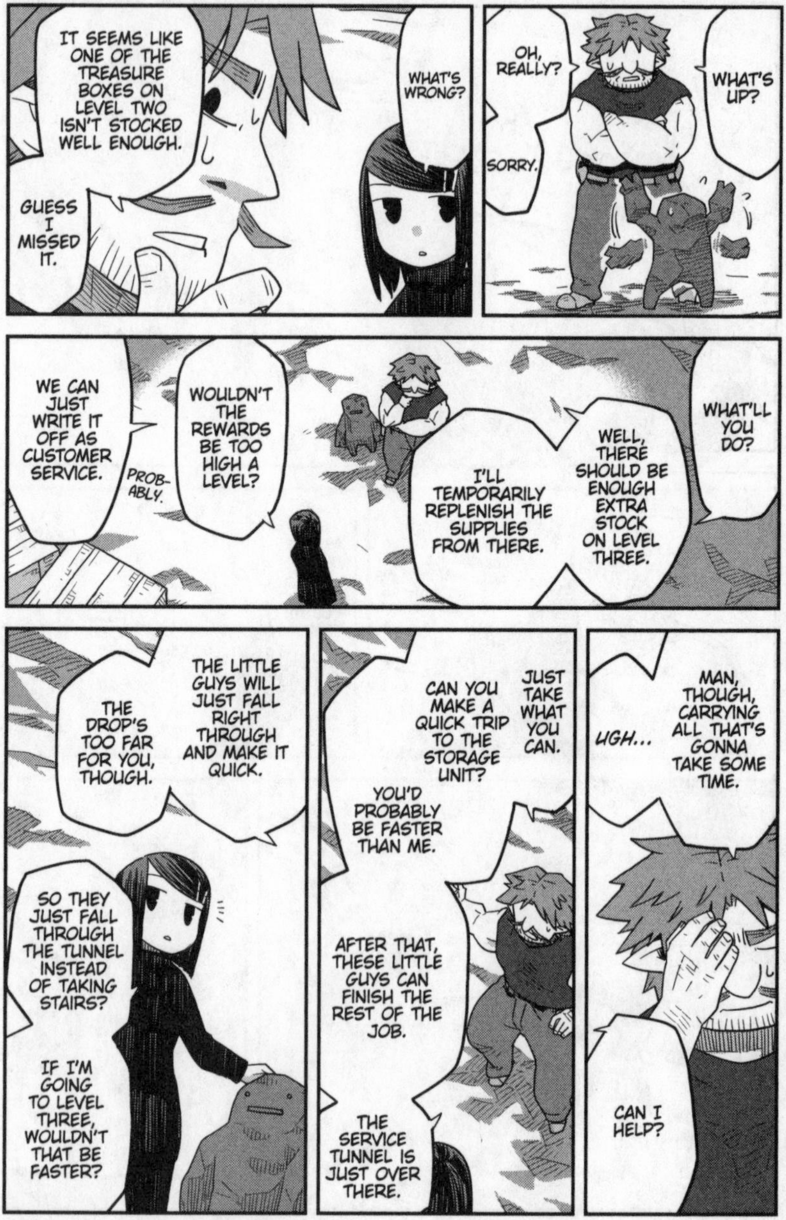
WHAT'S UP?
OH, REALLY?
SORRY.
WHAT'S WRONG?
IT SEEMS LIKE ONE OF THE TREASURE BOXES ON LEVEL TWO ISN'T STOCKED WELL ENOUGH.
GUESS I MISSED IT.
WHAT'LL YOU DO?
WELL, THERE SHOULD BE ENOUGH EXTRA STOCK ON LEVEL THREE.
I'LL TEMPORARILY REPLENISH THE SUPPLIES FROM THERE.
WOULDN'T THE REWARDS BE TOO HIGH A LEVEL?
PROB-ABLY.
WE CAN JUST WRITE IT OFF AS CUSTOMER SERVICE.
MAN, THOUGH, CARRYING ALL THAT'S GONNA TAKE SOME TIME.
UGH...
CAN I HELP?
JUST TAKE WHAT YOU CAN.
CAN YOU MAKE A QUICK TRIP TO THE STORAGE UNIT?
YOU'D PROBABLY BE FASTER THAN ME.
AFTER THAT, THESE LITTLE GUYS CAN FINISH THE REST OF THE JOB.
THE SERVICE TUNNEL IS JUST OVER THERE.
THE LITTLE GUYS WILL JUST FALL RIGHT THROUGH AND MAKE IT QUICK.
THE DROP'S TOO FAR FOR YOU, THOUGH.
SO THEY JUST FALL THROUGH THE TUNNEL INSTEAD OF TAKING STAIRS?
IF I'M GOING TO LEVEL THREE, WOULDN'T THAT BE FASTER?

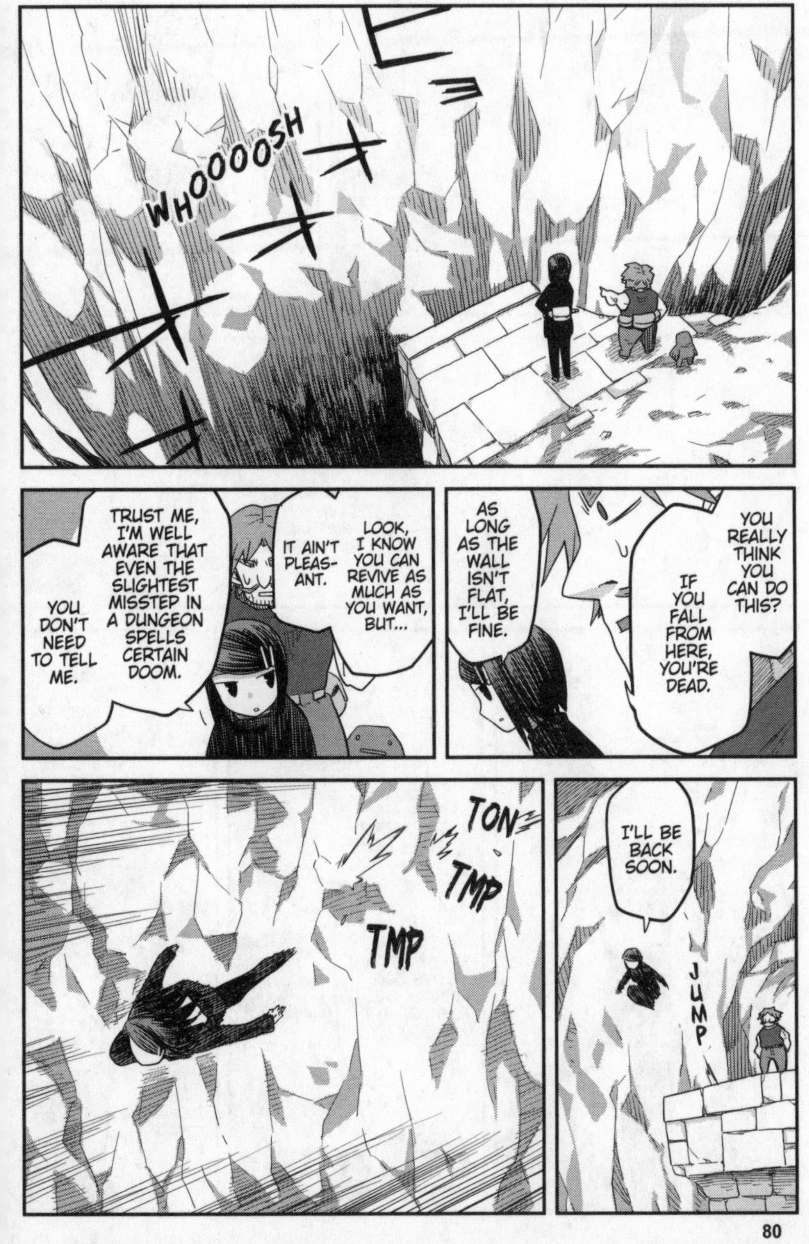
WHOOOOSH
YOU REALLY THINK YOU CAN DO THIS?
IF YOU FALL FROM HERE, YOU'RE DEAD.
AS LONG AS THE WALL ISN'T FLAT, I'LL BE FINE.
LOOK, I KNOW YOU CAN REVIVE AS MUCH AS YOU WANT, BUT...
IT AIN'T PLEAS-ANT.
TRUST ME, I'M WELL AWARE THAT EVEN THE SLIGHTEST MISSTEP IN A DUNGEON SPELLS CERTAIN DOOM.
YOU DON'T NEED TO TELL ME.
I'LL BE BACK SOON.
JUMP
TON
TMP
TMP

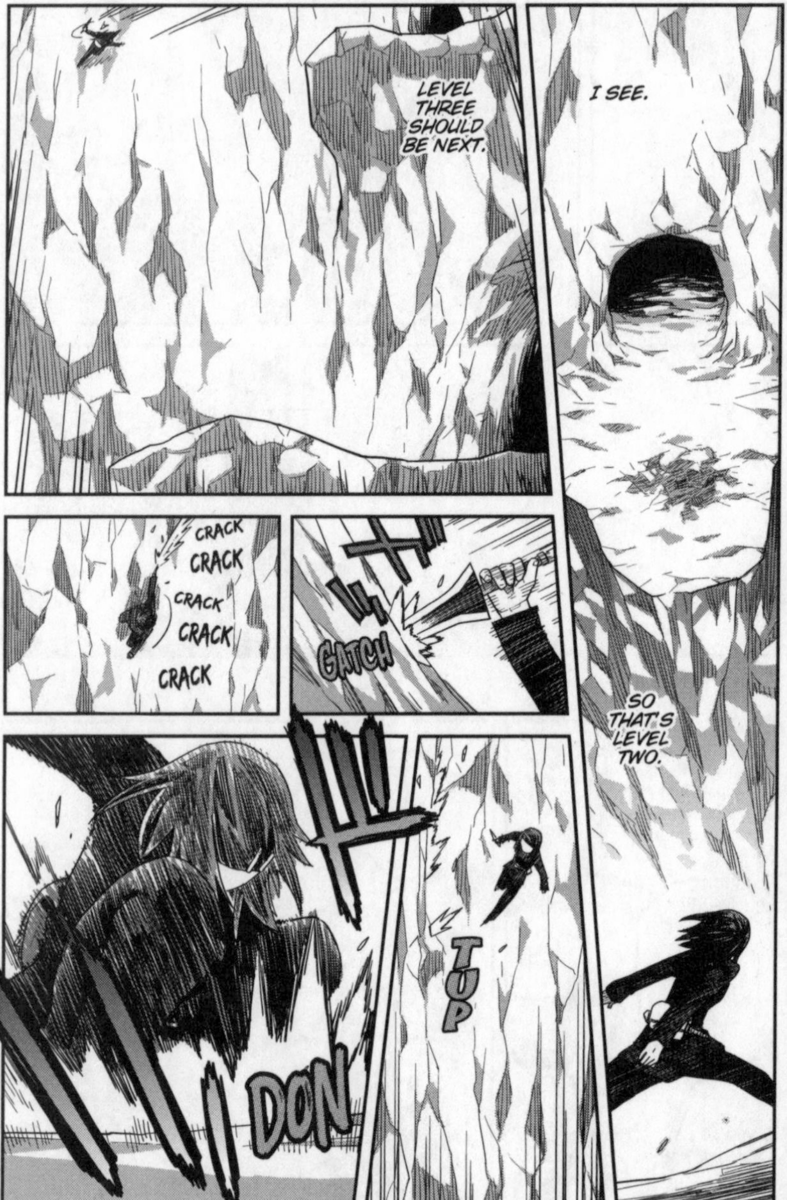
I SEE.
SO THAT'S LEVEL TWO.
LEVEL THREE SHOULD BE NEXT.
GATCH
CRACK
CRACK
CRACK
CRACK
CRACK
TUP
DON

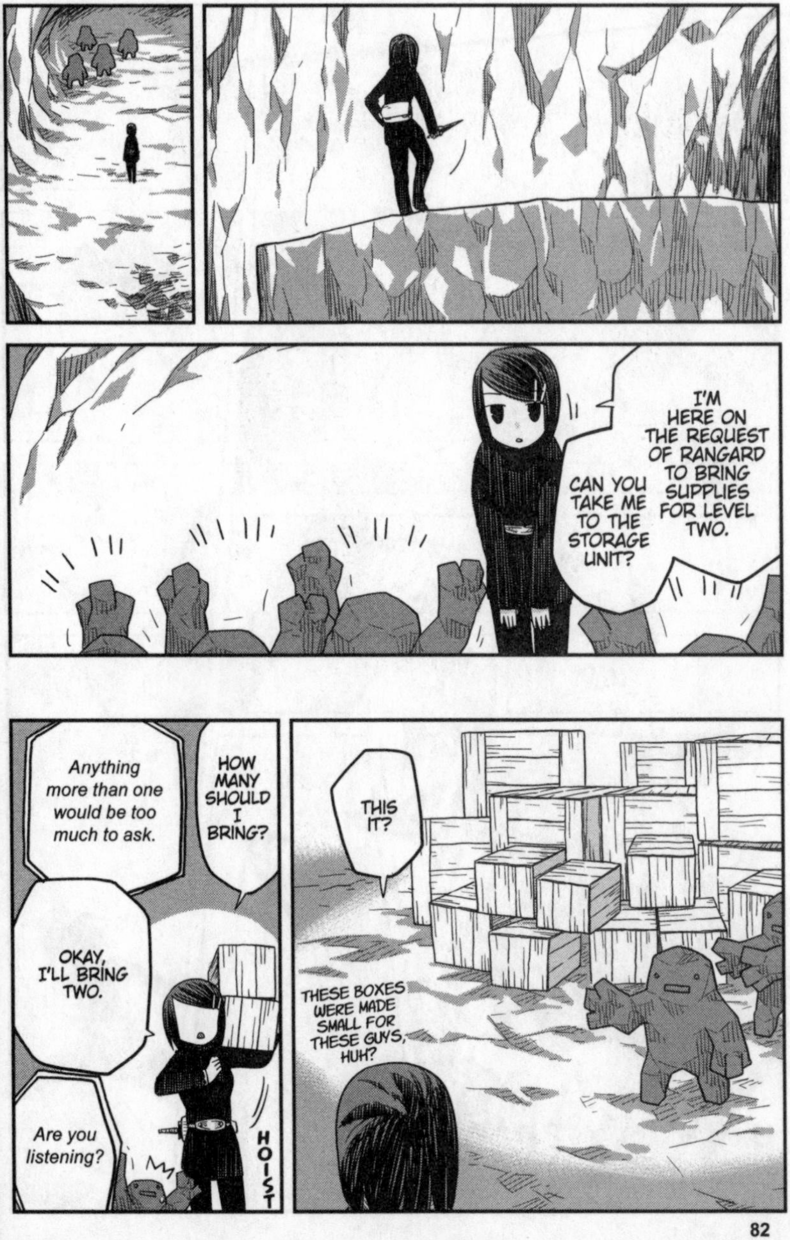
I'M HERE ON THE REQUEST OF RANGARD TO BRING SUPPLIES FOR LEVEL TWO.
CAN YOU TAKE ME TO THE STORAGE UNIT?
THIS IT?
THESE BOXES WERE MADE SMALL FOR THESE GUYS, HUH?
HOW MANY SHOULD I BRING?
Anything more than one would be too much to ask.
OKAY, I'LL BRING TWO.
HOIST
Are you listening?

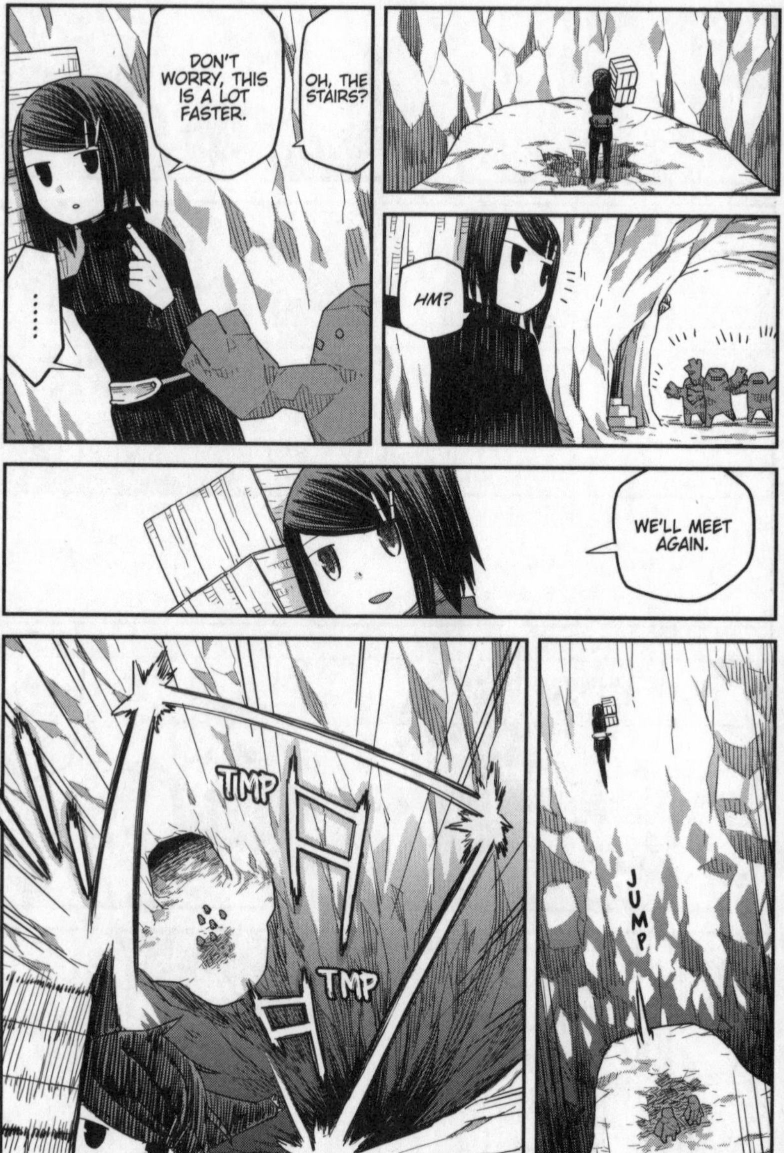
HM?
OH, THE STAIRS?
DON'T WORRY, THIS IS A LOT FASTER.
......
WE'LL MEET AGAIN.
JUMP
TMP
TMP

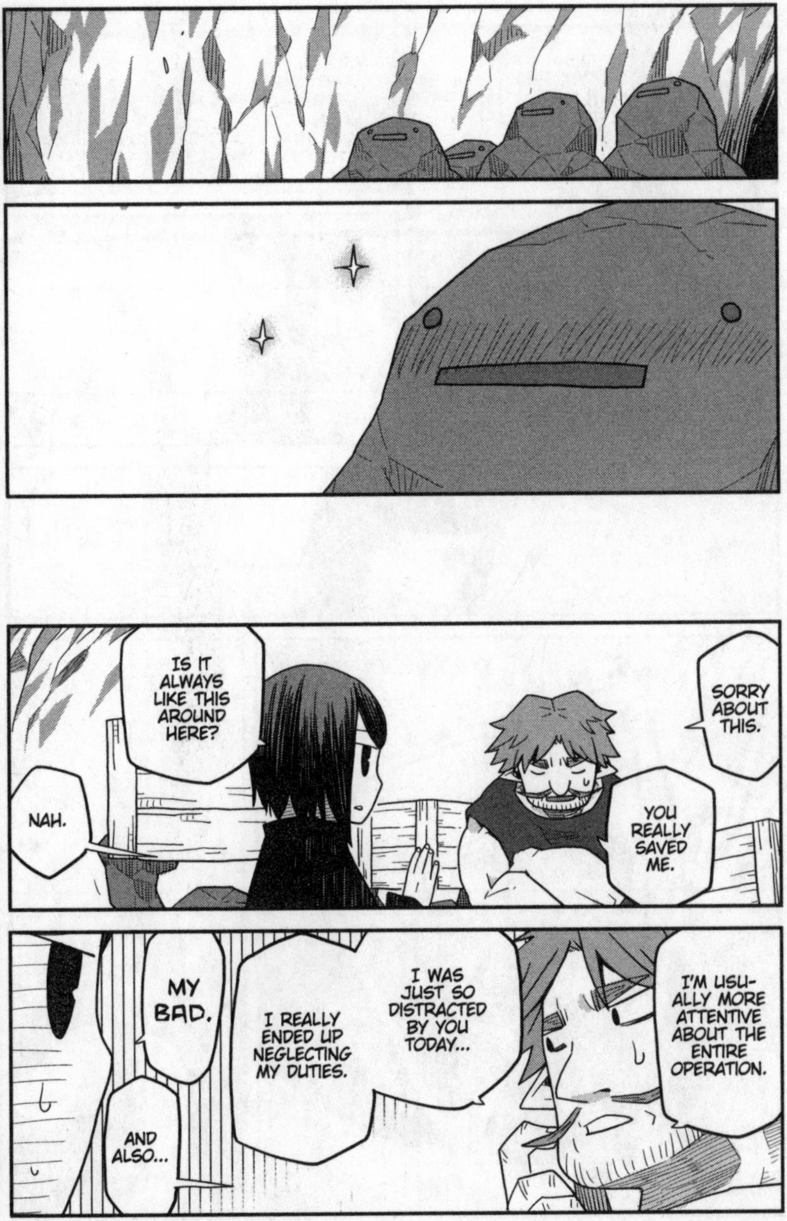
SORRY ABOUT THIS.
YOU REALLY SAVED ME.
IS IT ALWAYS LIKE THIS AROUND HERE?
NAH.
I'M USU-ALLY MORE ATTENTIVE ABOUT THE ENTIRE OPERATION.
I WAS JUST SO DISTRACTED BY YOU TODAY...
I REALLY ENDED UP NEGLECTING MY DUTIES.
MY BAD.
AND ALSO...

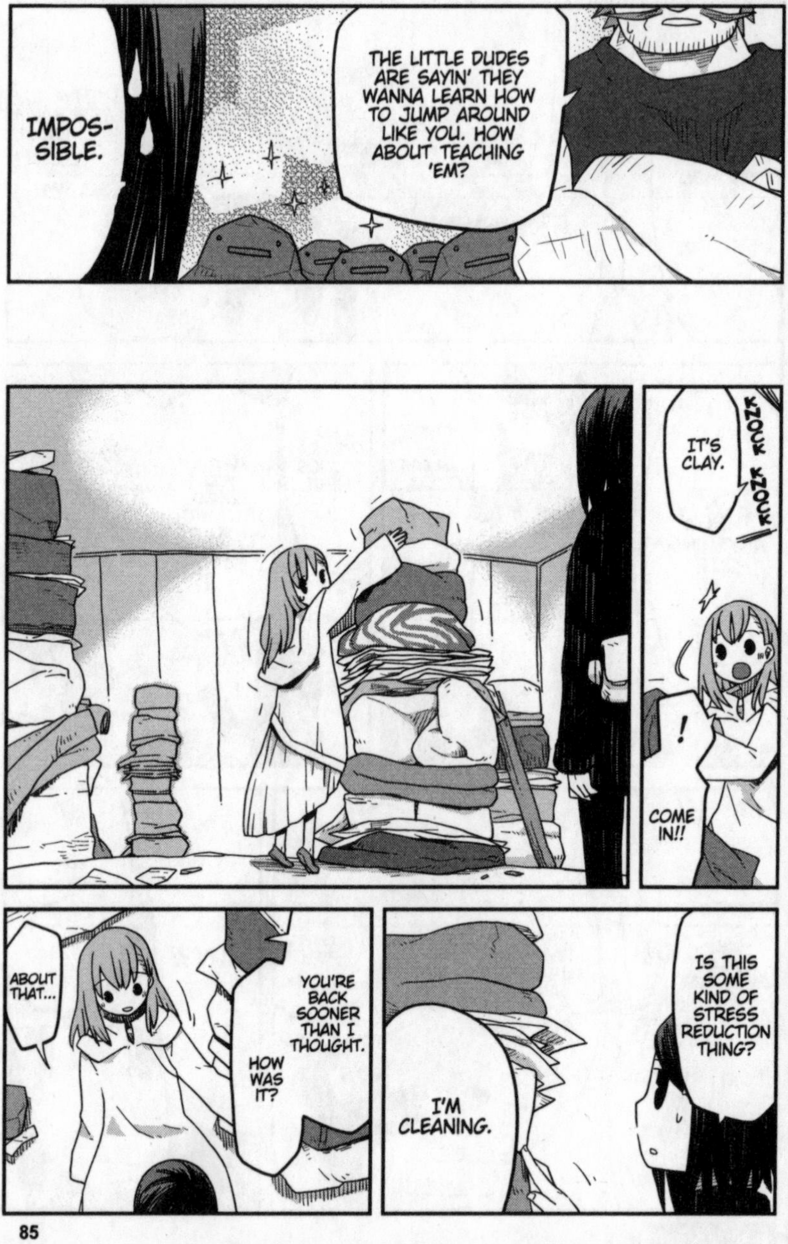
THE LITTLE DUDES ARE SAYIN' THEY WANNA LEARN HOW TO JUMP AROUND LIKE YOU. HOW ABOUT TEACHING 'EM?
IMPOS-SIBLE.
KNOCK KNOCK
IT'S CLAY.
COME IN!!
IS THIS SOME KIND OF STRESS REDUCTION THING?
I'M CLEANING.
YOU'RE BACK SOONER THAN I THOUGHT.
HOW WAS IT?
ABOUT THAT...

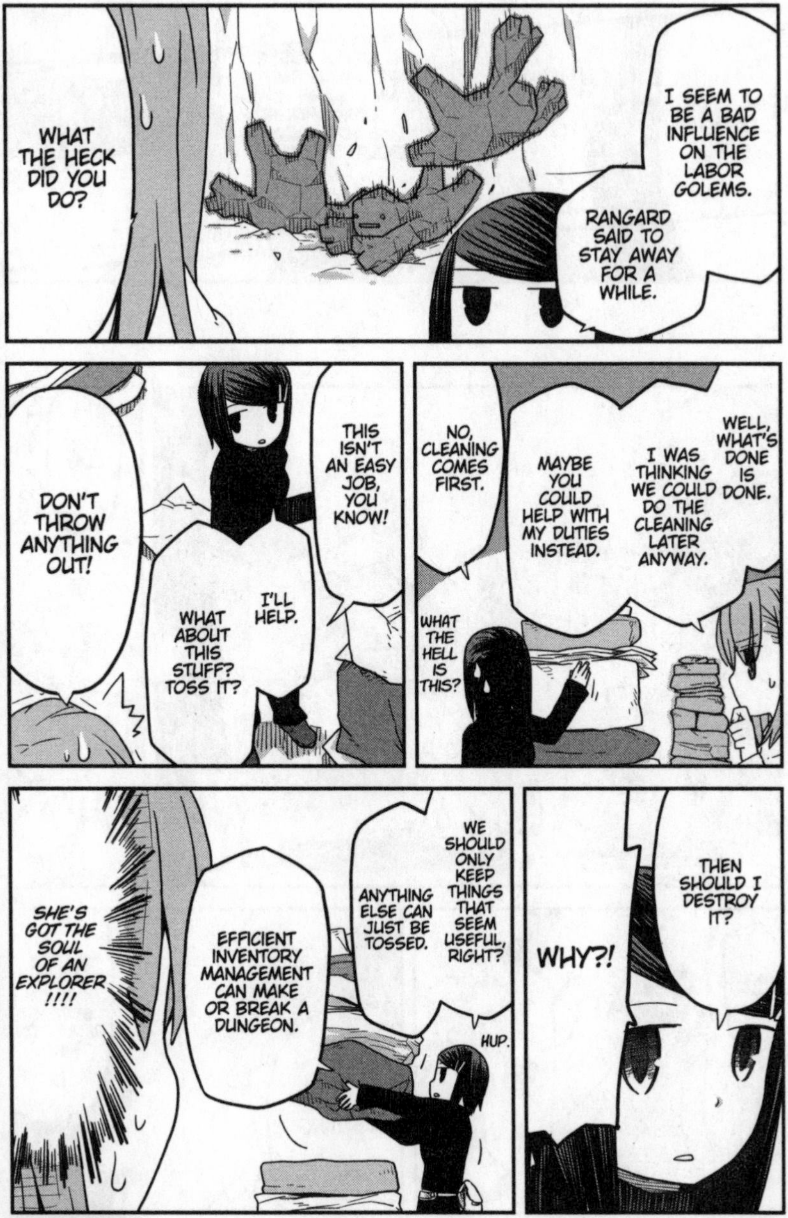
I SEEM TO BE A BAD INFLUENCE ON THE LABOR GOLEMS.
RANGARD SAID TO STAY AWAY FOR A WHILE.
WHAT THE HECK DID YOU DO?
WELL, WHAT'S DONE IS DONE.
I WAS THINKING WE COULD DO THE CLEANING LATER ANYWAY.
MAYBE YOU COULD HELP WITH MY DUTIES INSTEAD.
NO, CLEANING COMES FIRST.
WHAT THE HELL IS THIS?
THIS ISN'T AN EASY JOB, YOU KNOW!
I'LL HELP.
WHAT ABOUT THIS STUFF? TOSS IT?
DON'T THROW ANYTHING OUT!
THEN SHOULD I DESTROY IT?
WHY?!
WE SHOULD ONLY KEEP THINGS THAT SEEM USEFUL, RIGHT?
HUP.
ANYTHING ELSE CAN JUST BE TOSSED.
EFFICIENT INVENTORY MANAGEMENT CAN MAKE OR BREAK A DUNGEON.
SHE'S GOT THE SOUL OF AN EXPLORER!!!!

CHAPTER 3 - END

WHAT KIND OF THINGS DO YOU THROW AWAY THE MOST OFTEN, MISS CLAY?
HM... I DON'T REALLY HAVE AN ANSWER OTHER THAN 'WHATEVER SEEMS USELESS.'

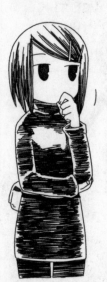

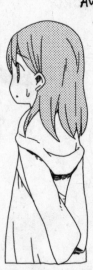

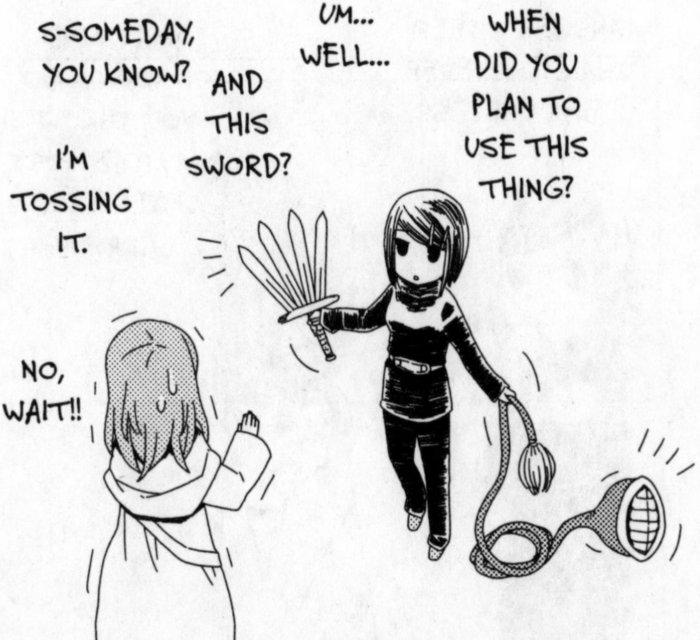
WHEN DID YOU PLAN TO USE THIS THING?
UM... WELL...
AND THIS SWORD?
S-SOMEDAY, YOU KNOW?
I'M TOSSING IT.
NO, WAIT!!

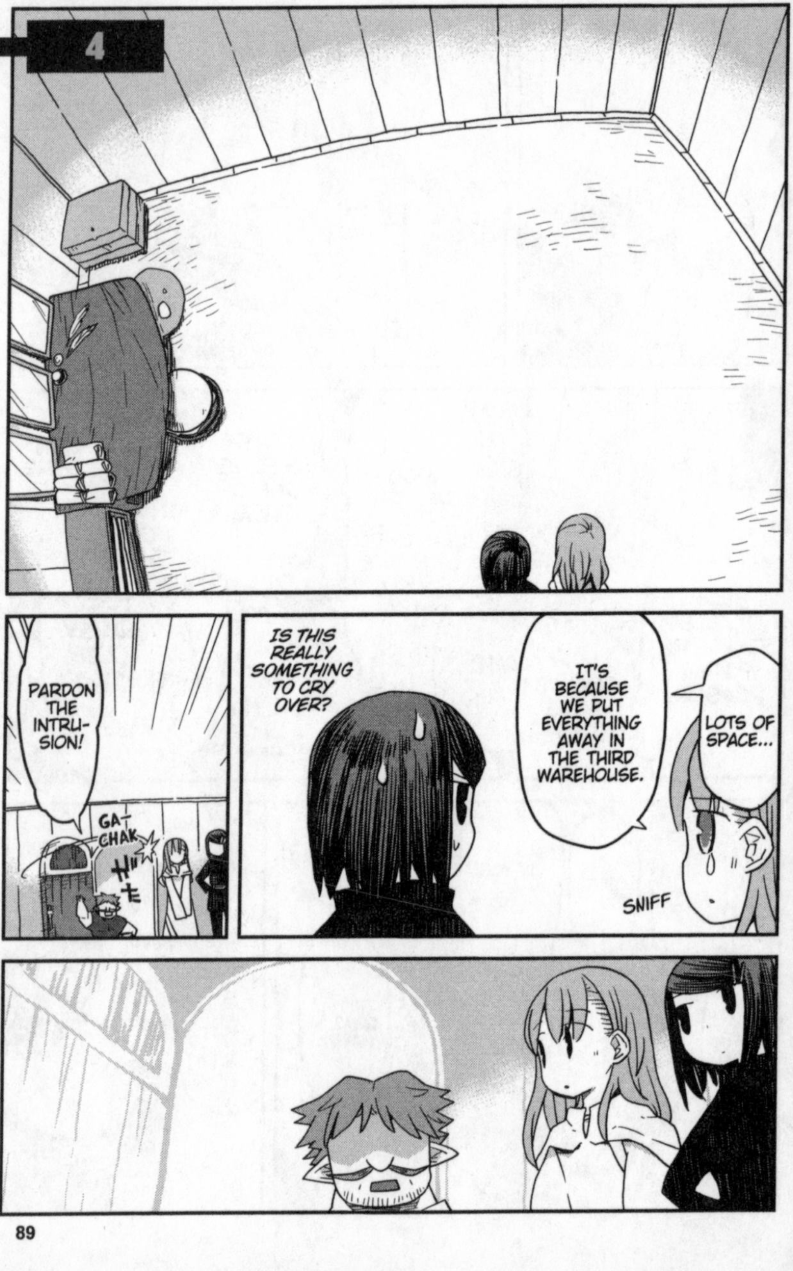
4
LOTS OF SPACE...
SNIFF
IT'S BECAUSE WE PUT EVERYTHING AWAY IN THE THIRD WAREHOUSE.
IS THIS REALLY SOMETHING TO CRY OVER?
PARDON THE INTRU-SION!
GA-CHAK

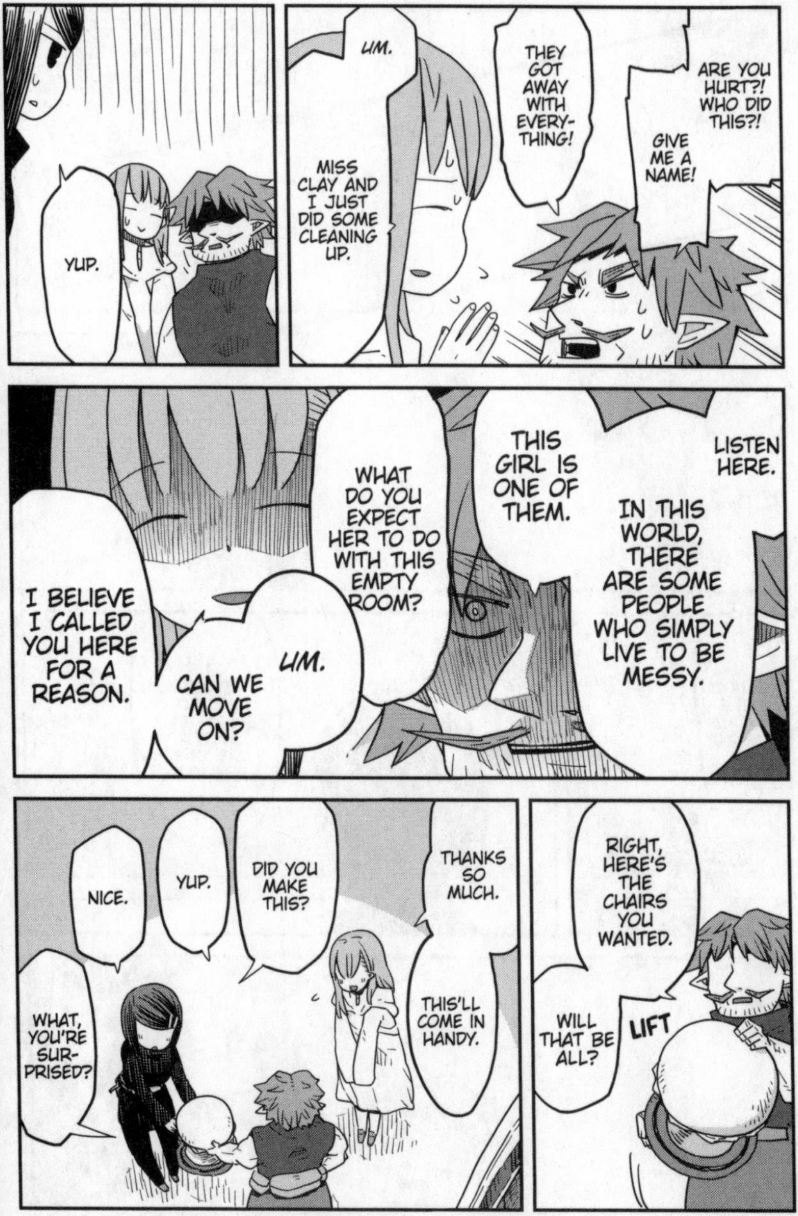
ARE YOU HURT?! WHO DID THIS?!
GIVE ME A NAME!
THEY GOT AWAY WITH EVERY-THING!
UM.
MISS CLAY AND I JUST DID SOME CLEANING UP.
YUP.
LISTEN HERE.
IN THIS WORLD, THERE ARE SOME PEOPLE WHO SIMPLY LIVE TO BE MESSY.
THIS GIRL IS ONE OF THEM.
WHAT DO YOU EXPECT HER TO DO WITH THIS EMPTY ROOM?
UM.
CAN WE MOVE ON?
I BELIEVE I CALLED YOU HERE FOR A REASON.
RIGHT, HERE'S THE CHAIRS YOU WANTED.
LIFT
WILL THAT BE ALL?
THANKS SO MUCH.
THIS'LL COME IN HANDY.
DID YOU MAKE THIS?
YUP.
NICE.
WHAT, YOU'RE SUR-PRISED?

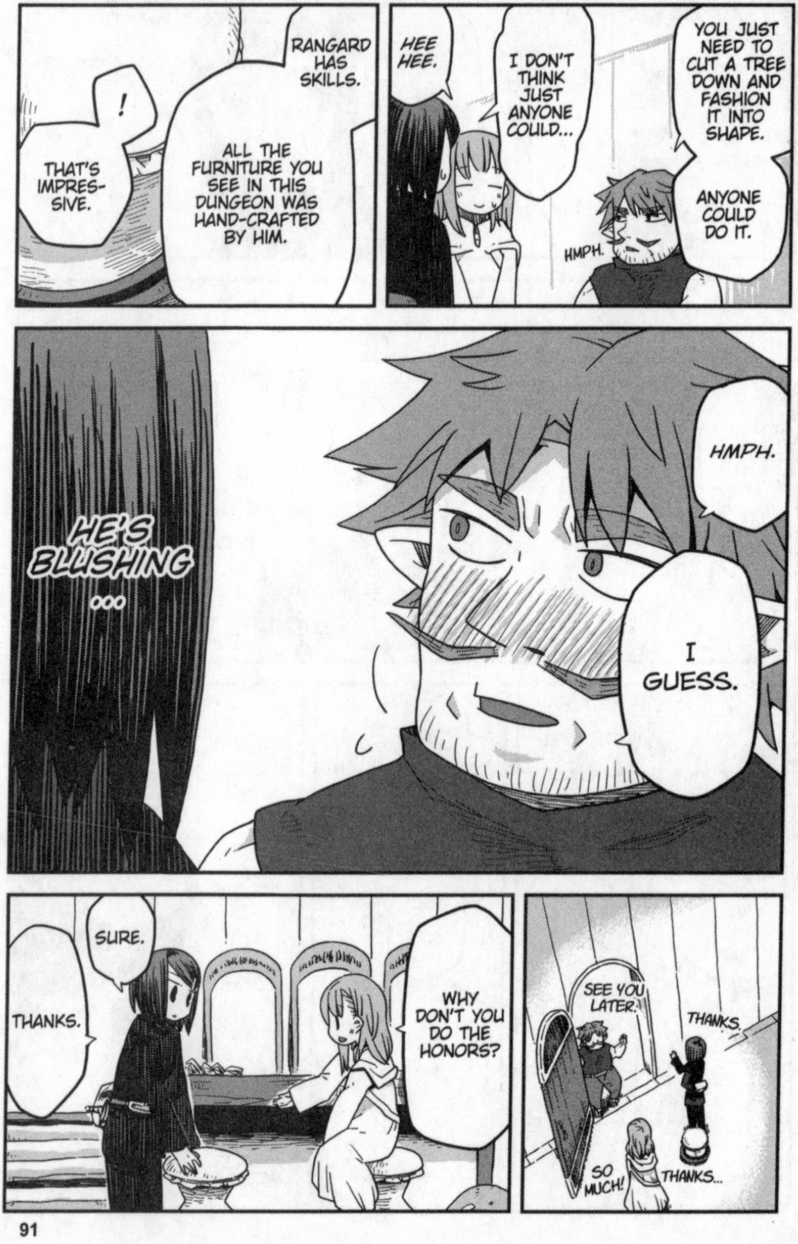
YOU JUST NEED TO CUT A TREE DOWN AND FASHION IT INTO SHAPE.
ANYONE COULD DO IT.
I DON'T THINK JUST ANYONE COULD...
HEE HEE.
HMPH.
RANGARD HAS SKILLS.
ALL THE FURNITURE YOU SEE IN THIS DUNGEON WAS HAND-CRAFTED BY HIM.
!
THAT'S IMPRES-SIVE.
HMPH.
I GUESS.
HE'S BLUSHING...
SEE YOU LATER.
THANKS.
THANKS...
SO MUCH!
WHY DON'T YOU DO THE HONORS?
SURE.
THANKS.

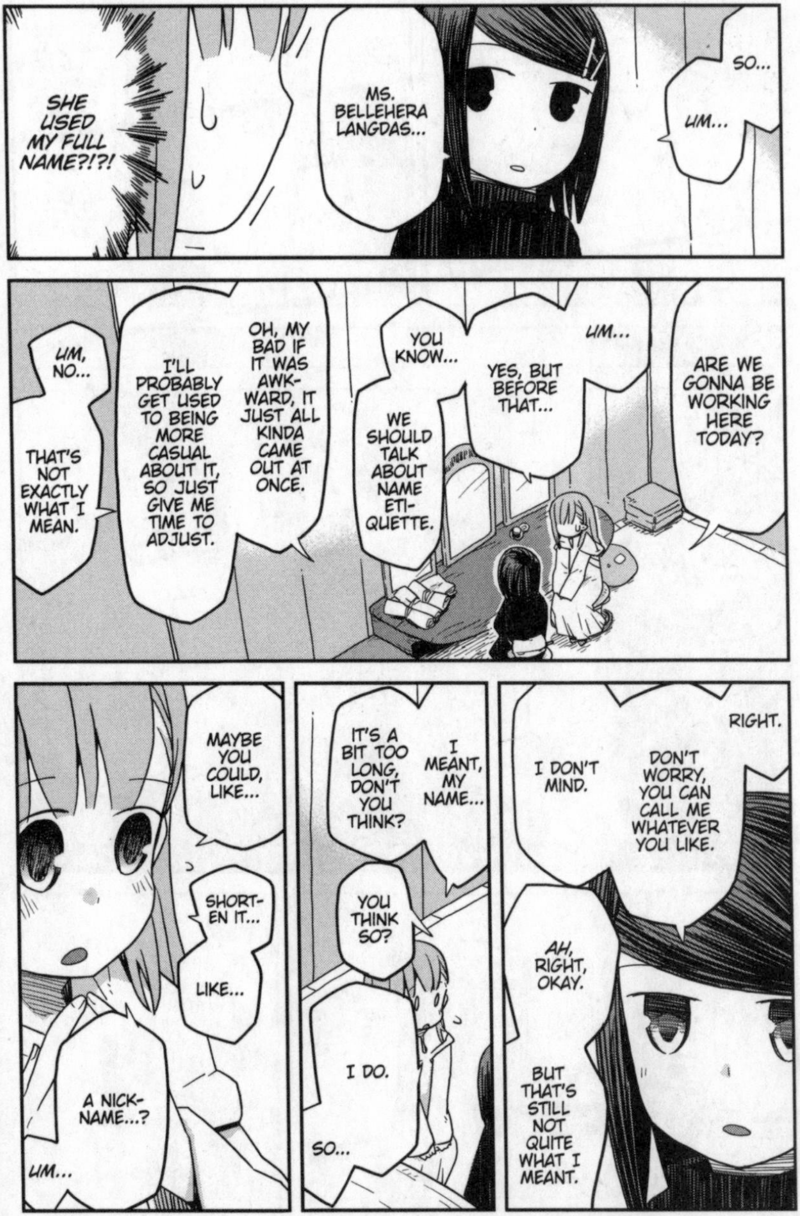
SO...
UM...
MS. BELLEHERA LANGDAS...
SHE USED MY FULL NAME?!?!
ARE WE GONNA BE WORKING HERE TODAY?
UM...
YES, BUT BEFORE THAT...
YOU KNOW...
WE SHOULD TALK ABOUT NAME ETI-QUETTE.
OH, MY BAD IF IT WAS AWK-WARD, IT JUST ALL KINDA CAME OUT AT ONCE.
I'LL PROBABLY GET USED TO BEING MORE CASUAL ABOUT IT, SO JUST GIVE ME TIME TO ADJUST.
UM, NO...
THAT'S NOT EXACTLY WHAT I MEAN.
RIGHT.
DON'T WORRY, YOU CAN CALL ME WHATEVER YOU LIKE.
I DON'T MIND.
AH, RIGHT, OKAY.
BUT THAT'S STILL NOT QUITE WHAT I MEANT.
I MEANT, MY NAME...
IT'S A BIT TOO LONG, DON'T YOU THINK?
YOU THINK SO?
I DO.
SO...
MAYBE YOU COULD, LIKE...
SHORT-EN IT...
LIKE...
A NICK-NAME...?
UM...

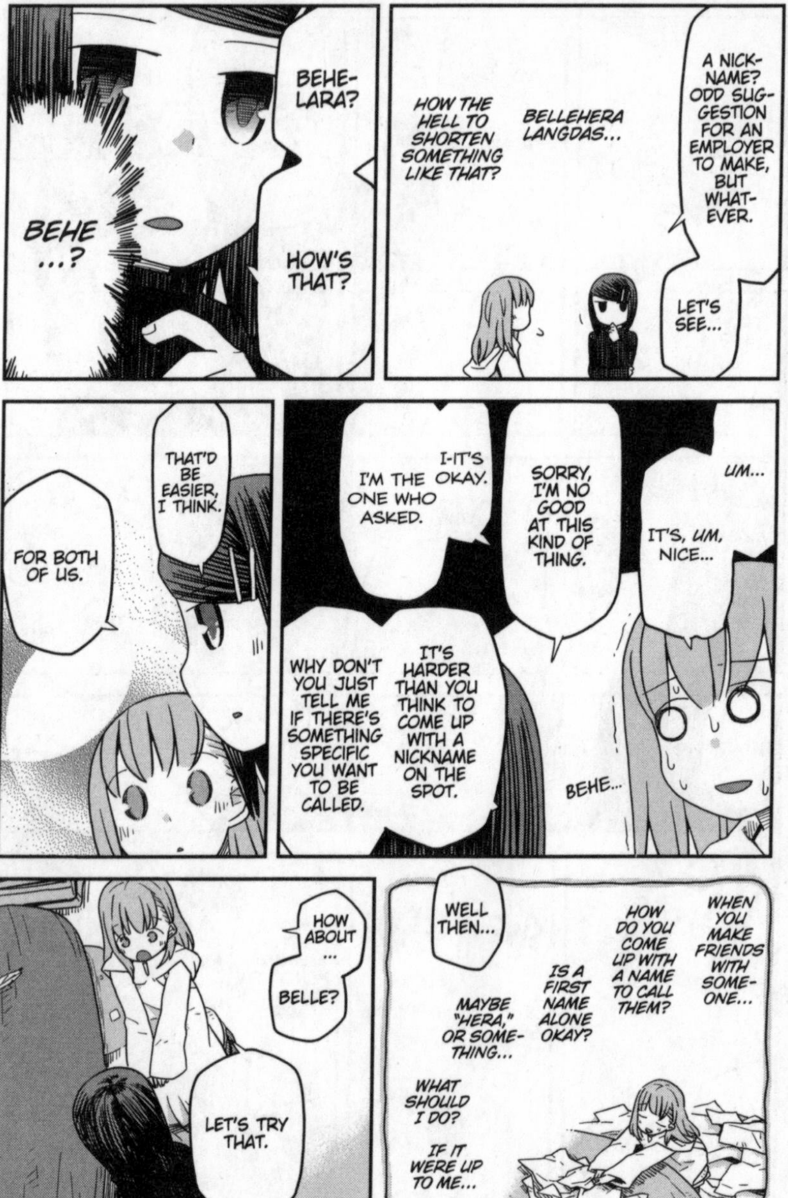
A NICKNAME? ODD SUGGESTION FOR AN EMPLOYER TO MAKE, BUT WHATEVER.
LET'S SEE...
BELLEHERA LANGDAS...
HOW THE HELL TO SHORTEN SOMETHING LIKE THAT?
BEHE-LARA?
HOW'S THAT?
BEHE ...?
UM...
IT'S, UM, NICE...
BEHE...
SORRY, I'M NO GOOD AT THIS KIND OF THING.
I-IT'S OKAY.
I'M THE ONE WHO ASKED.
IT'S HARDER THAN YOU THINK TO COME UP WITH A NICKNAME ON THE SPOT.
WHY DON'T YOU JUST TELL ME IF THERE'S SOMETHING SPECIFIC YOU WANT TO BE CALLED.
THAT'D BE EASIER, I THINK.
FOR BOTH OF US.
WHEN YOU MAKE FRIENDS WITH SOMEONE...
HOW DO YOU COME UP WITH A NAME TO CALL THEM?
IS A FIRST NAME ALONE OKAY?
WELL THEN...
MAYBE "HERA," OR SOMETHING...
WHAT SHOULD I DO?
IF IT WERE UP TO ME...
HOW ABOUT ...
BELLE?
LET'S TRY THAT.

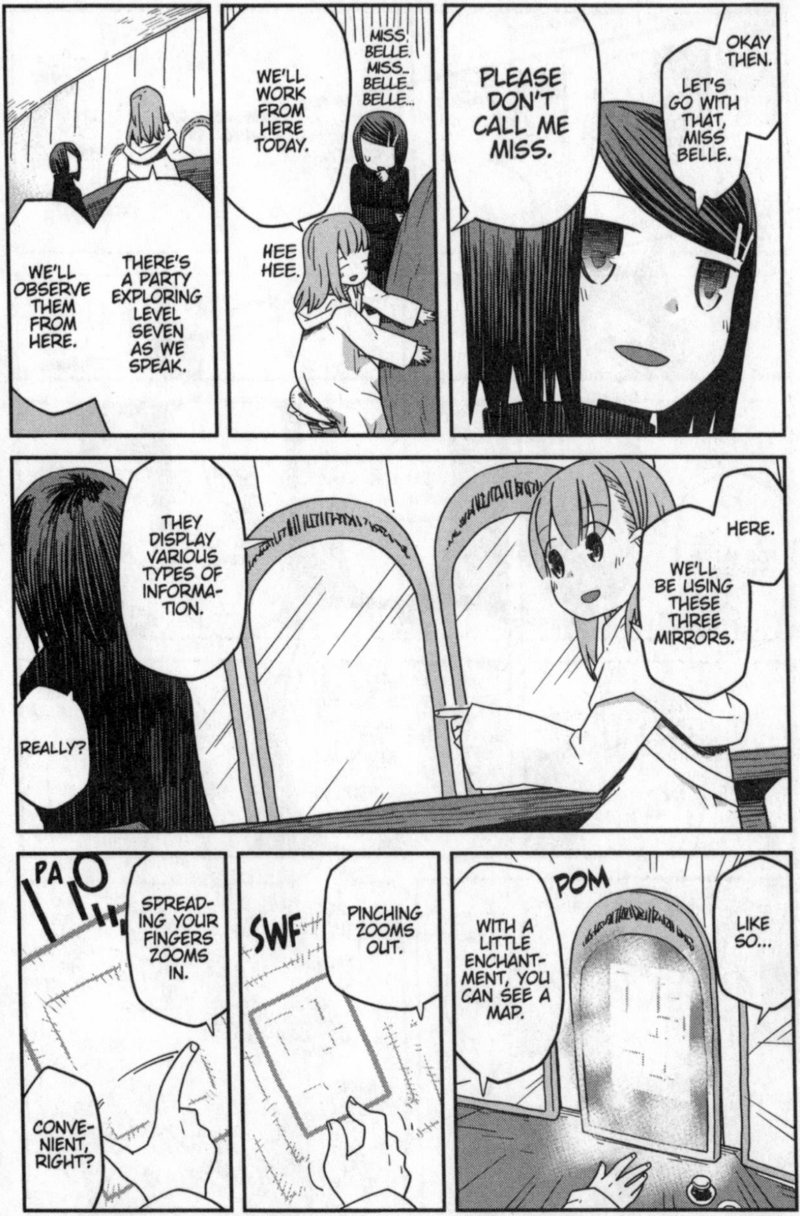
OKAY THEN. LET'S GO WITH THAT, MISS BELLE.
PLEASE DON'T CALL ME MISS.
MISS. BELLE. MISS.. BELLE. BELLE...
WE'LL WORK FROM HERE TODAY.
HEE HEE.
THERE'S A PARTY EXPLORING LEVEL SEVEN AS WE SPEAK.
WE'LL OBSERVE THEM FROM HERE.
HERE. WE'LL BE USING THESE THREE MIRRORS.
THEY DISPLAY VARIOUS TYPES OF INFORMATION.
REALLY?
LIKE SO...
POM
WITH A LITTLE ENCHANTMENT, YOU CAN SEE A MAP.
PINCHING ZOOMS OUT.
SWF
PA
SPREADING YOUR FINGERS ZOOMS IN.
CONVENIENT, RIGHT?

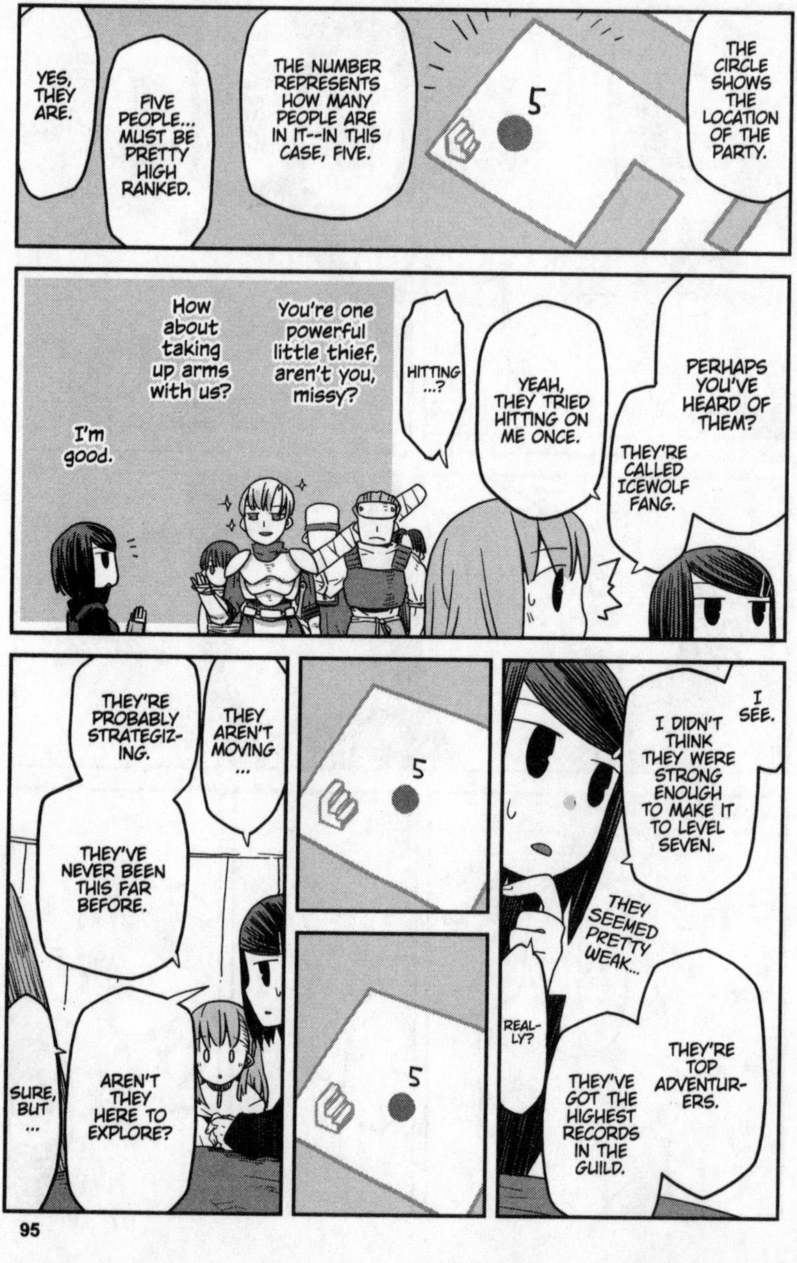
THE CIRCLE SHOWS THE LOCATION OF THE PARTY.
5
THE NUMBER REPRESENTS HOW MANY PEOPLE ARE IN IT--IN THIS CASE, FIVE.
FIVE PEOPLE... MUST BE PRETTY HIGH RANKED.
YES, THEY ARE.
PERHAPS YOU'VE HEARD OF THEM?
THEY'RE CALLED ICEWOLF FANG.
YEAH, THEY TRIED HITTING ON ME ONCE.
HITTING ...?
You're one powerful little thief, aren't you, missy?
How about taking up arms with us?
I'm good.
I SEE.
I DIDN'T THINK THEY WERE STRONG ENOUGH TO MAKE IT TO LEVEL SEVEN.
THEY SEEMED PRETTY WEAK...
REAL-LY?
THEY'RE TOP ADVENTUR-ERS.
THEY'VE GOT THE HIGHEST RECORDS IN THE GUILD.
5
5
THEY AREN'T MOVING ...
THEY'RE PROBABLY STRATEGIZ-ING.
THEY'VE NEVER BEEN THIS FAR BEFORE.
AREN'T THEY HERE TO EXPLORE?
SURE, BUT ...

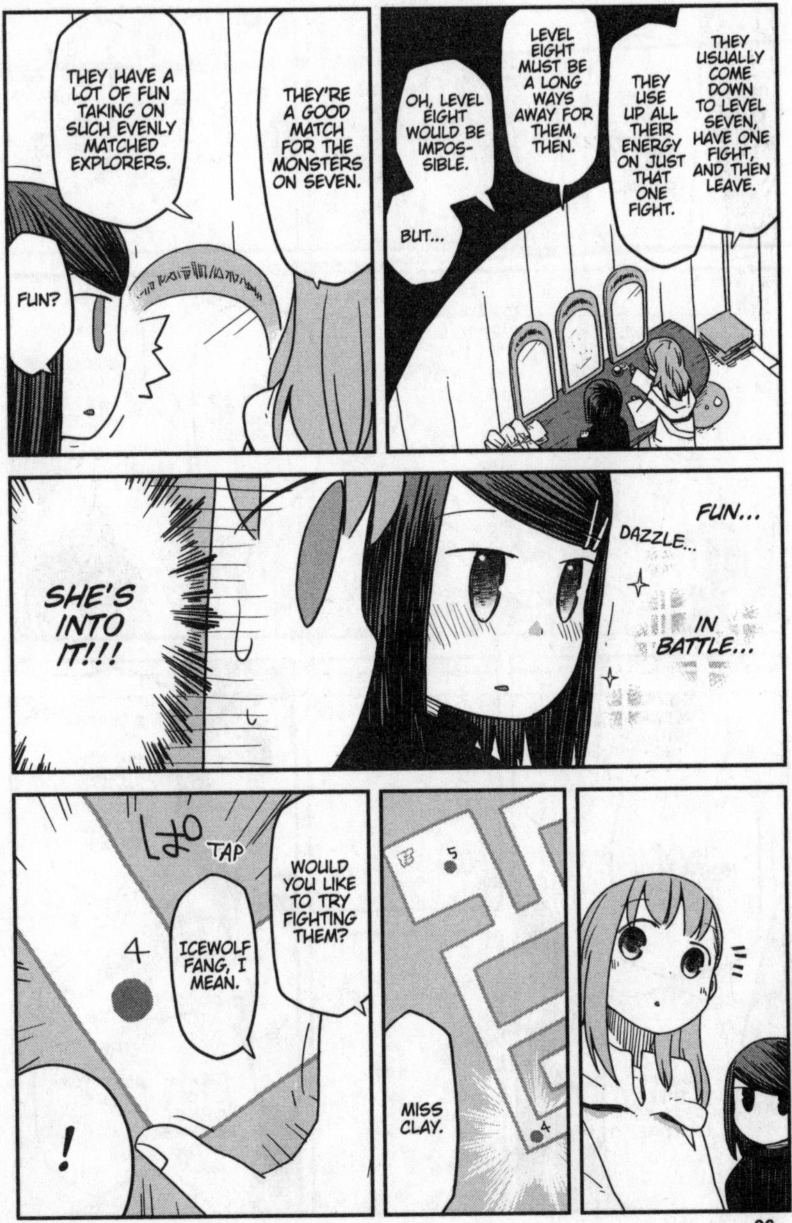
THEY USUALLY COME DOWN TO LEVEL SEVEN, HAVE ONE FIGHT, AND THEN LEAVE.
THEY USE UP ALL THEIR ENERGY ON JUST THAT ONE FIGHT.
LEVEL EIGHT MUST BE A LONG WAYS AWAY FOR THEM, THEN.
OH, LEVEL EIGHT WOULD BE IMPOSSIBLE.
BUT...
THEY'RE A GOOD MATCH FOR THE MONSTERS ON SEVEN.
THEY HAVE A LOT OF FUN TAKING ON SUCH EVENLY MATCHED EXPLORERS.
FUN?
FUN...
DAZZLE...
IN BATTLE...
SHE'S INTO IT!!!
MISS CLAY.
WOULD YOU LIKE TO TRY FIGHTING THEM?
TAP
ICEWOLF FANG, I MEAN.
!

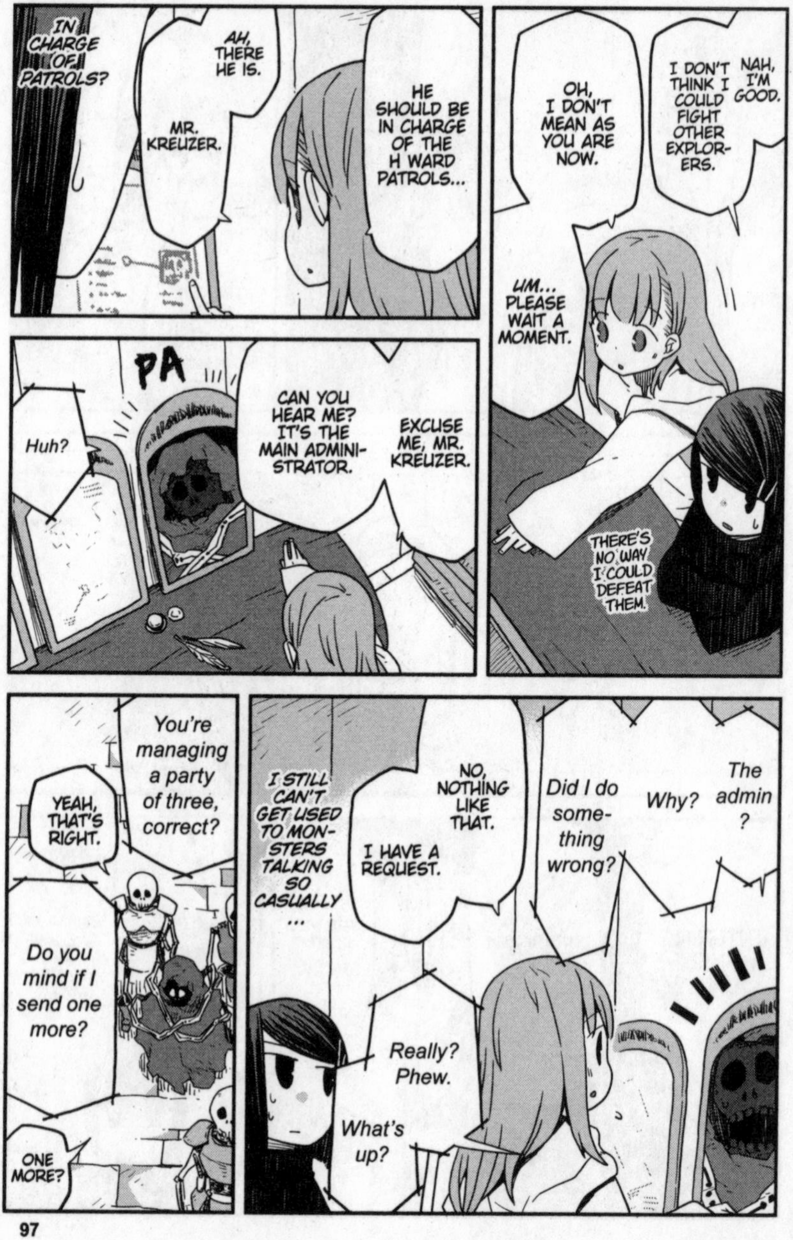
NAH, I'M GOOD.
I DON'T THINK I COULD FIGHT OTHER EXPLORERS.
OH, I DON'T MEAN AS YOU ARE NOW.
UM... PLEASE WAIT A MOMENT.
THERE'S NO WAY I COULD DEFEAT THEM.
HE SHOULD BE IN CHARGE OF THE H WARD PATROLS...
AH, THERE HE IS.
MR. KREUZER.
IN CHARGE OF PATROLS?
EXCUSE ME, MR. KREUZER.
CAN YOU HEAR ME? IT'S THE MAIN ADMINISTRATOR.
PA
Huh?
The admin?
Why?
Did I do something wrong?
NO, NOTHING LIKE THAT.
I HAVE A REQUEST.
I STILL CAN'T GET USED TO MONSTERS TALKING SO CASUALLY...
Really? Phew.
What's up?
You're managing a party of three, correct?
YEAH, THAT'S RIGHT.
Do you mind if I send one more?
ONE MORE?

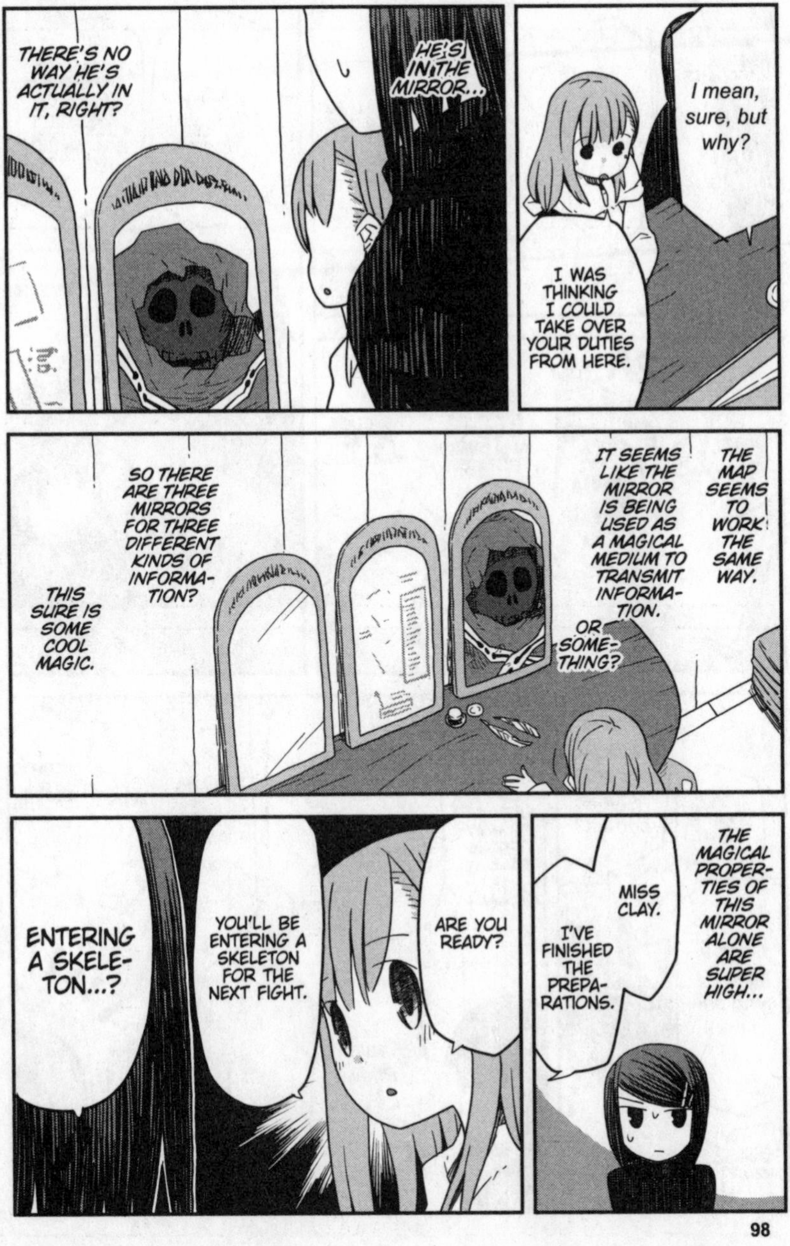
I mean, sure, but why?
I WAS THINKING I COULD TAKE OVER YOUR DUTIES FROM HERE.
HE'S IN THE MIRROR...
THERE'S NO WAY HE'S ACTUALLY IN IT, RIGHT?
THE MAP SEEMS TO WORK THE SAME WAY.
IT SEEMS LIKE THE MIRROR IS BEING USED AS A MAGICAL MEDIUM TO TRANSMIT INFORMATION.
OR SOMETHING?
SO THERE ARE THREE MIRRORS FOR THREE DIFFERENT KINDS OF INFORMATION?
THIS SURE IS SOME COOL MAGIC.
THE MAGICAL PROPERTIES OF THIS MIRROR ALONE ARE SUPER HIGH...
MISS CLAY.
I'VE FINISHED THE PREPARATIONS.
ARE YOU READY?
YOU'LL BE ENTERING A SKELETON FOR THE NEXT FIGHT.
ENTERING A SKELETON...?

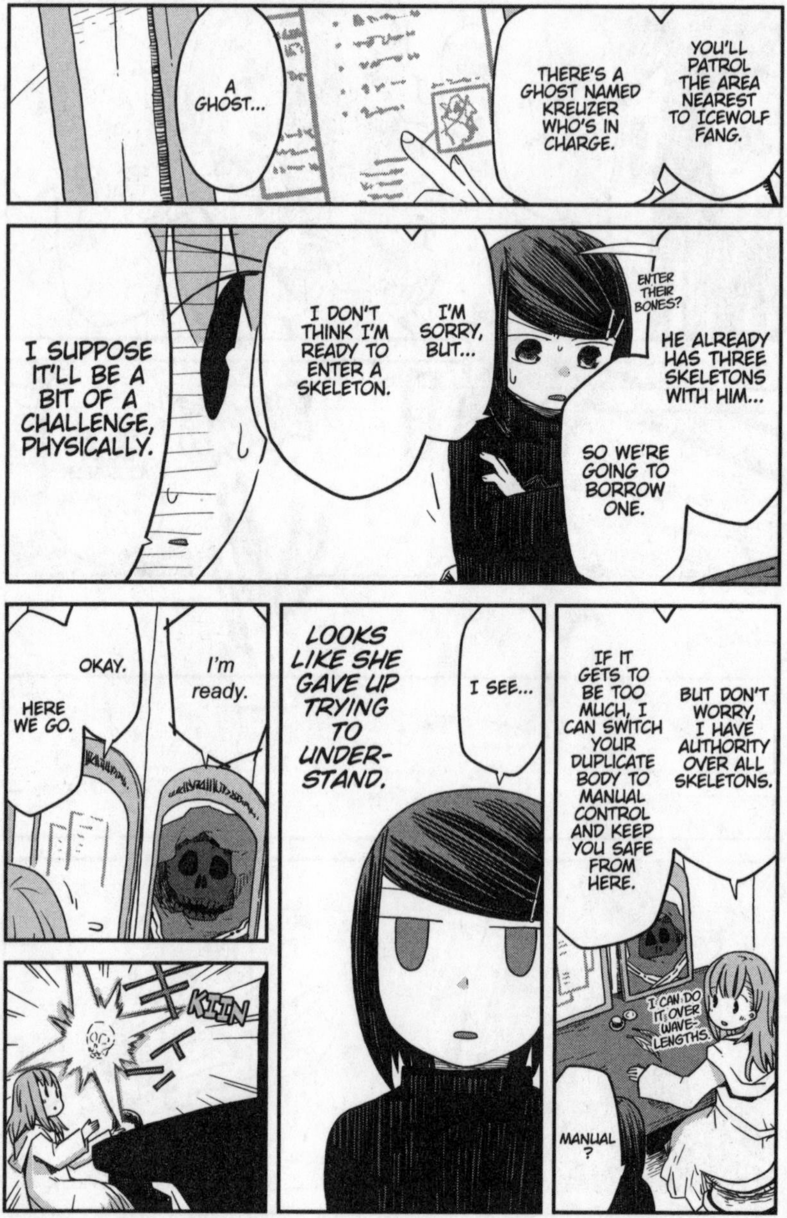
YOU'LL PATROL THE AREA NEAREST TO ICEWOLF FANG.
THERE'S A GHOST NAMED KREUZER WHO'S IN CHARGE.
A GHOST...
ENTER THEIR BONES?
HE ALREADY HAS THREE SKELETONS WITH HIM...
SO WE'RE GOING TO BORROW ONE.
I'M SORRY, BUT...
I DON'T THINK I'M READY TO ENTER A SKELETON.
I SUPPOSE IT'LL BE A BIT OF A CHALLENGE, PHYSICALLY.
BUT DON'T WORRY, I HAVE AUTHORITY OVER ALL SKELETONS.
IF IT GETS TO BE TOO MUCH, I CAN SWITCH YOUR DUPLICATE BODY TO MANUAL CONTROL AND KEEP YOU SAFE FROM HERE.
I CAN DO IT OVER WAVE-LENGTHS.
MANUAL?
I SEE...
LOOKS LIKE SHE GAVE UP TRYING TO UNDER-STAND.
I'm ready.
OKAY.
HERE WE GO.
KIIN

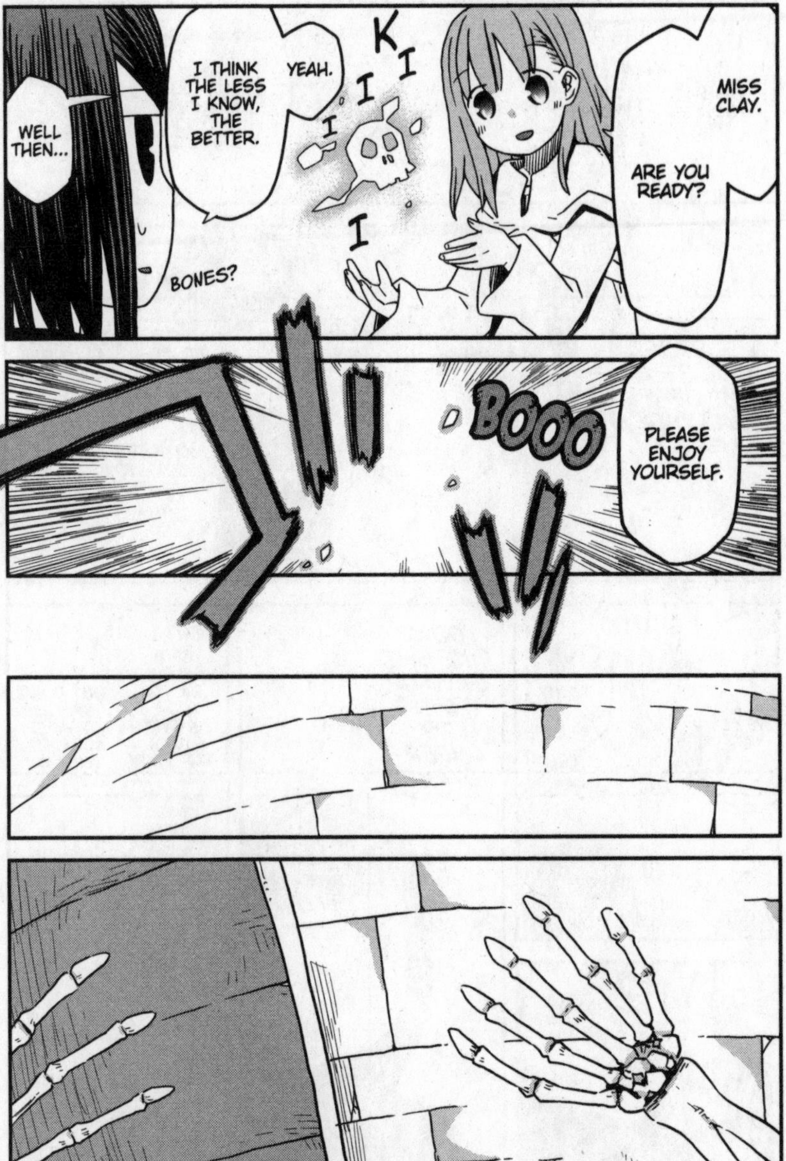
MISS CLAY.
ARE YOU READY?
KIIII
YEAH.
I THINK THE LESS I KNOW, THE BETTER.
BONES?
WELL THEN...
PLEASE ENJOY YOURSELF.
BOOO

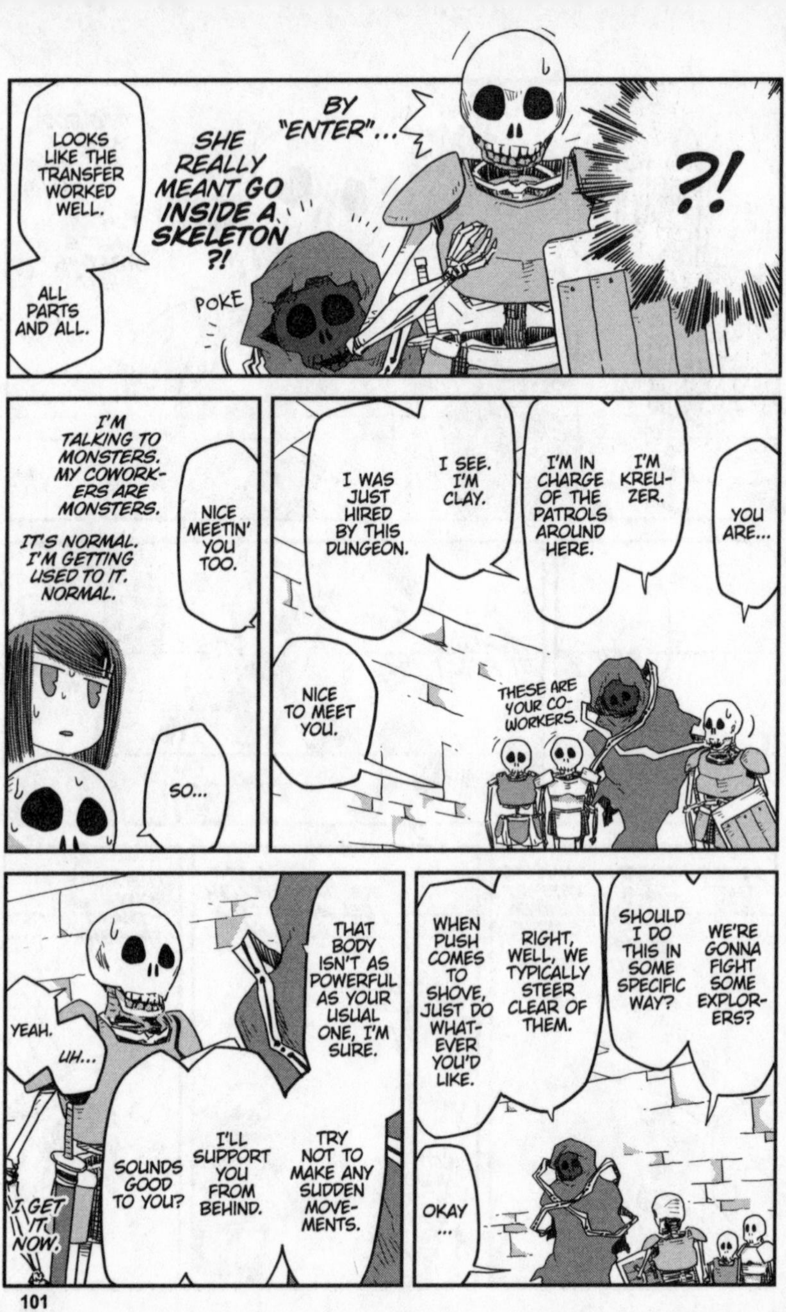
?!
BY "ENTER"...
SHE REALLY MEANT GO INSIDE A SKELETON ?!
LOOKS LIKE THE TRANSFER WORKED WELL.
POKE
ALL PARTS AND ALL.
YOU ARE...
I'M KREUZER.
I'M IN CHARGE OF THE PATROLS AROUND HERE.
I SEE. I'M CLAY.
I WAS JUST HIRED BY THIS DUNGEON.
THESE ARE YOUR CO-WORKERS.
NICE TO MEET YOU.
NICE MEETIN' YOU TOO.
I'M TALKING TO MONSTERS. MY COWORKERS ARE MONSTERS.
IT'S NORMAL. I'M GETTING USED TO IT. NORMAL.
SO...
WE'RE GONNA FIGHT SOME EXPLORERS?
SHOULD I DO THIS IN SOME SPECIFIC WAY?
RIGHT, WELL, WE TYPICALLY STEER CLEAR OF THEM.
WHEN PUSH COMES TO SHOVE, JUST DO WHATEVER YOU'D LIKE.
OKAY ...
THAT BODY ISN'T AS POWERFUL AS YOUR USUAL ONE, I'M SURE.
TRY NOT TO MAKE ANY SUDDEN MOVEMENTS.
I'LL SUPPORT YOU FROM BEHIND.
SOUNDS GOOD TO YOU?
YEAH.
UH...
I GET IT. NOW.

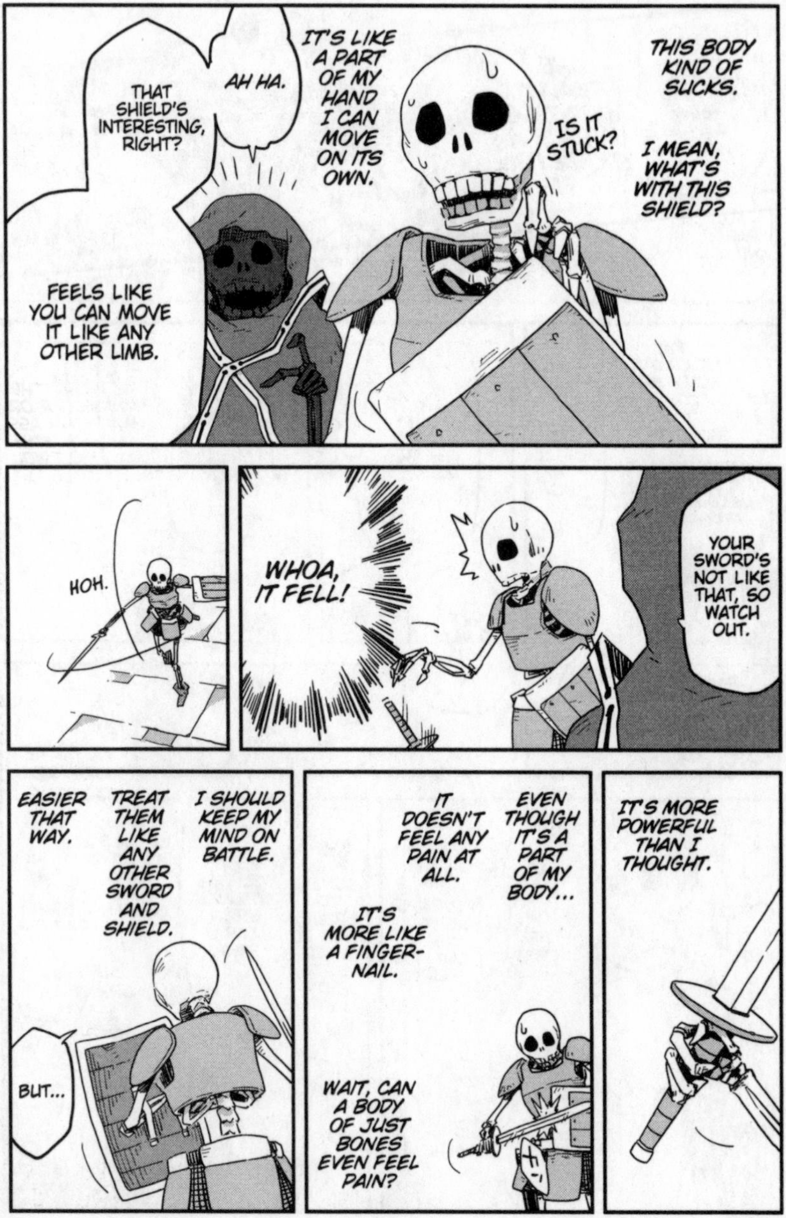
THIS BODY KIND OF SUCKS.
I MEAN, WHAT'S WITH THIS SHIELD?
IS IT STUCK?
IT'S LIKE A PART OF MY HAND I CAN MOVE ON ITS OWN.
AH HA.
THAT SHIELD'S INTERESTING, RIGHT?
FEELS LIKE YOU CAN MOVE IT LIKE ANY OTHER LIMB.
YOUR SWORD'S NOT LIKE THAT, SO WATCH OUT.
WHOA, IT FELL!
HOH.
IT'S MORE POWERFUL THAN I THOUGHT.
EVEN THOUGH IT'S A PART OF MY BODY...
IT DOESN'T FEEL ANY PAIN AT ALL.
IT'S MORE LIKE A FINGER-NAIL.
WAIT, CAN A BODY OF JUST BONES EVEN FEEL PAIN?
I SHOULD KEEP MY MIND ON BATTLE.
TREAT THEM LIKE ANY OTHER SWORD AND SHIELD.
EASIER THAT WAY.
BUT...

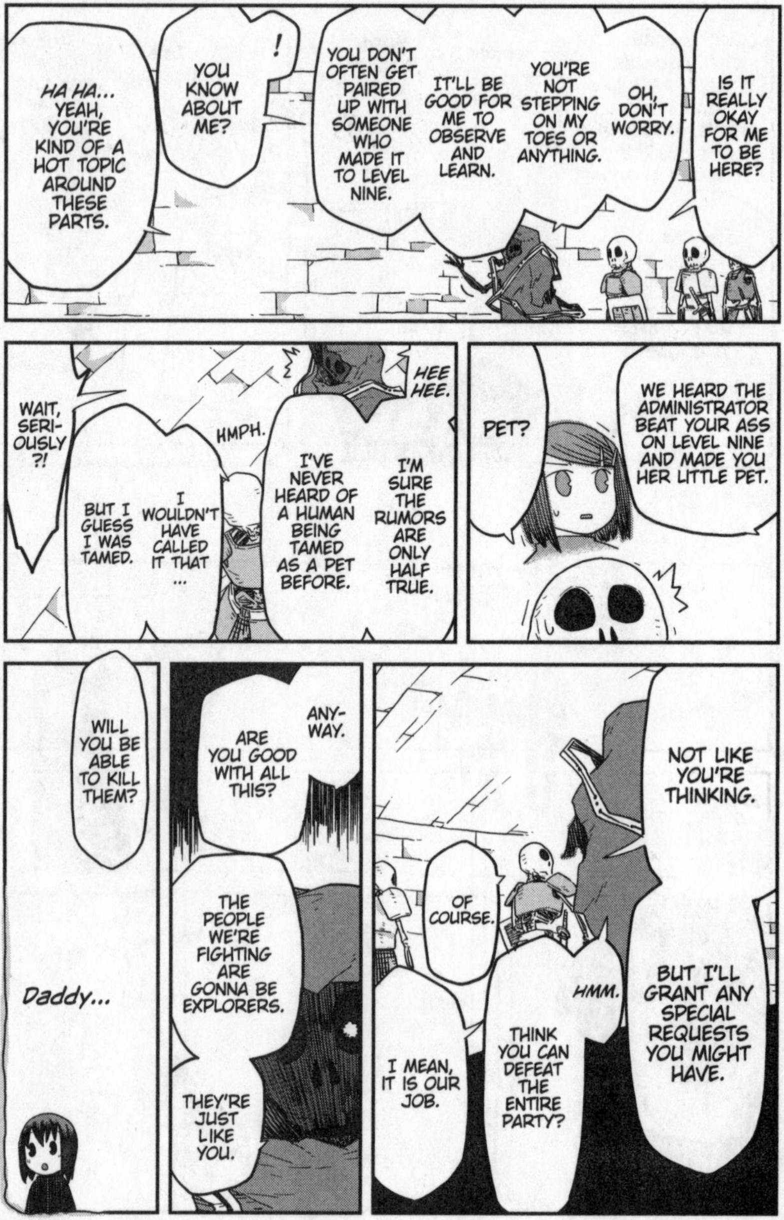

IS IT REALLY OKAY FOR ME TO BE HERE?
OH, DON'T WORRY.
YOU'RE NOT STEPPING ON MY TOES OR ANYTHING.
IT'LL BE GOOD FOR ME TO OBSERVE AND LEARN.
YOU DON'T OFTEN GET PAIRED UP WITH SOMEONE WHO MADE IT TO LEVEL NINE.
!
YOU KNOW ABOUT ME?
HA HA... YEAH, YOU'RE KIND OF A HOT TOPIC AROUND THESE PARTS.
WE HEARD THE ADMINISTRATOR BEAT YOUR ASS ON LEVEL NINE AND MADE YOU HER LITTLE PET.
PET?
HEE HEE.
I'M SURE THE RUMORS ARE ONLY HALF TRUE.
I'VE NEVER HEARD OF A HUMAN BEING TAMED AS A PET BEFORE.
HMPH.
I WOULDN'T HAVE CALLED IT THAT ...
BUT I GUESS I WAS TAMED.
WAIT, SERIOUSLY?!
NOT LIKE YOU'RE THINKING.
OF COURSE.
BUT I'LL GRANT ANY SPECIAL REQUESTS YOU MIGHT HAVE.
HMM.
THINK YOU CAN DEFEAT THE ENTIRE PARTY?
I MEAN, IT IS OUR JOB.
ANYWAY.
ARE YOU GOOD WITH ALL THIS?
THE PEOPLE WE'RE FIGHTING ARE GONNA BE EXPLORERS.
THEY'RE JUST LIKE YOU.
WILL YOU BE ABLE TO KILL THEM?
Daddy...

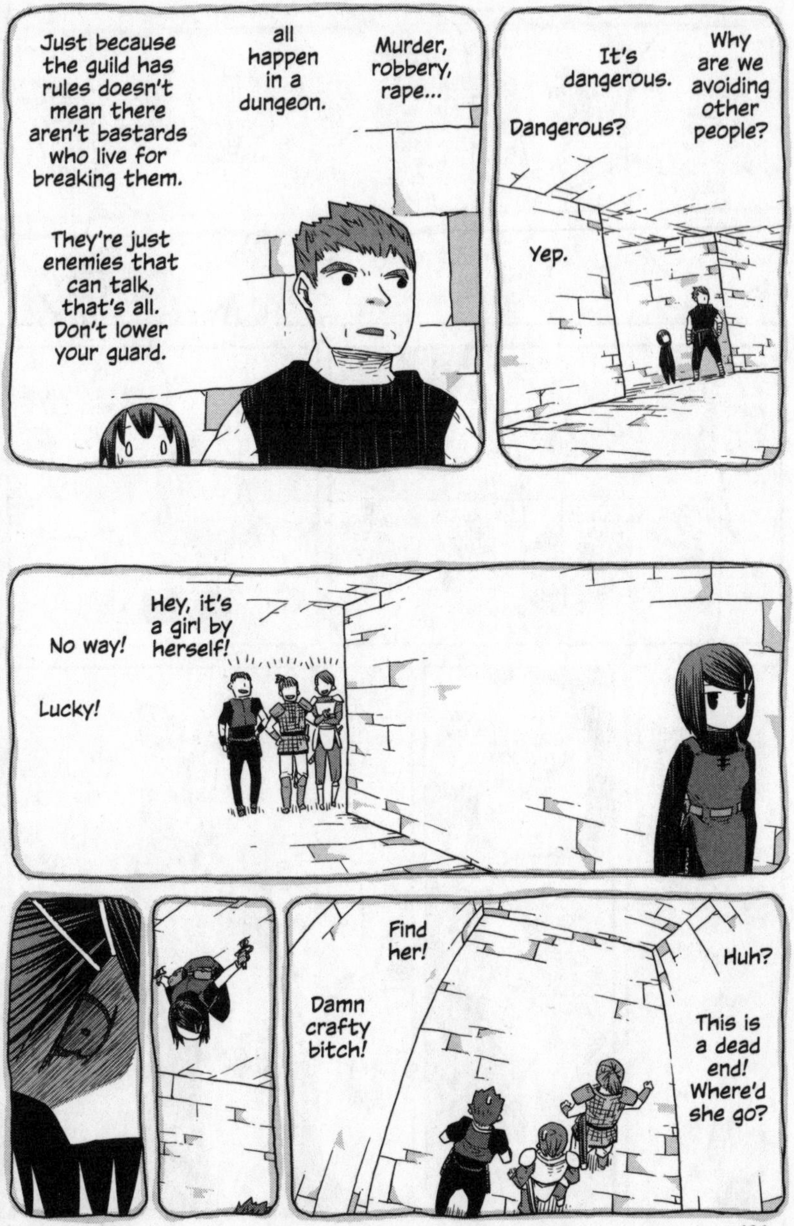
Why are we avoiding other people?
It's dangerous.
Dangerous?
Yep.
Murder, robbery, rape...
all happen in a dungeon.
Just because the guild has rules doesn't mean there aren't bastards who live for breaking them.
They're just enemies that can talk, that's all. Don't lower your guard.
Hey, it's a girl by herself!
No way!
Lucky!
Huh?
This is a dead end! Where'd she go?
Find her!
Damn crafty bitch!

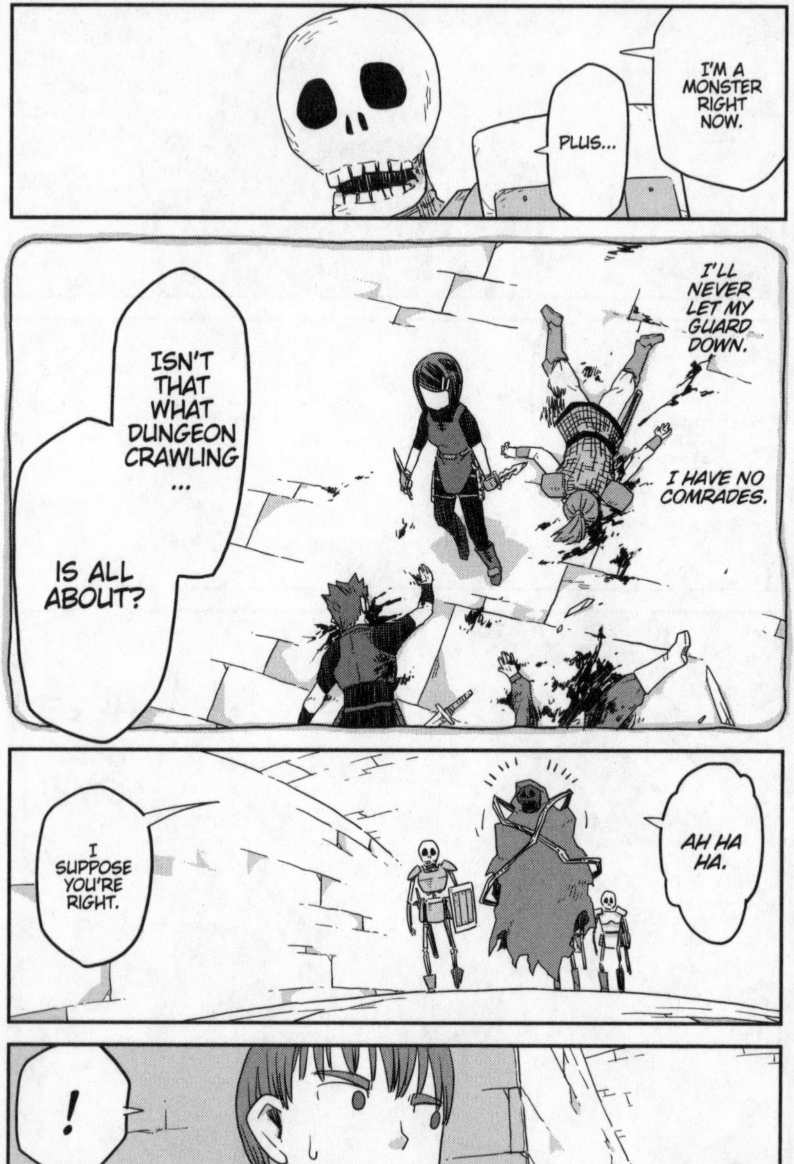
I'M A MONSTER RIGHT NOW.
PLUS...
I'LL NEVER LET MY GUARD DOWN.
I HAVE NO COMRADES.
ISN'T THAT WHAT DUNGEON CRAWLING ...
IS ALL ABOUT?
AH HA HA.
I SUPPOSE YOU'RE RIGHT.
!

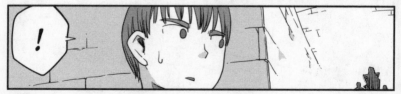

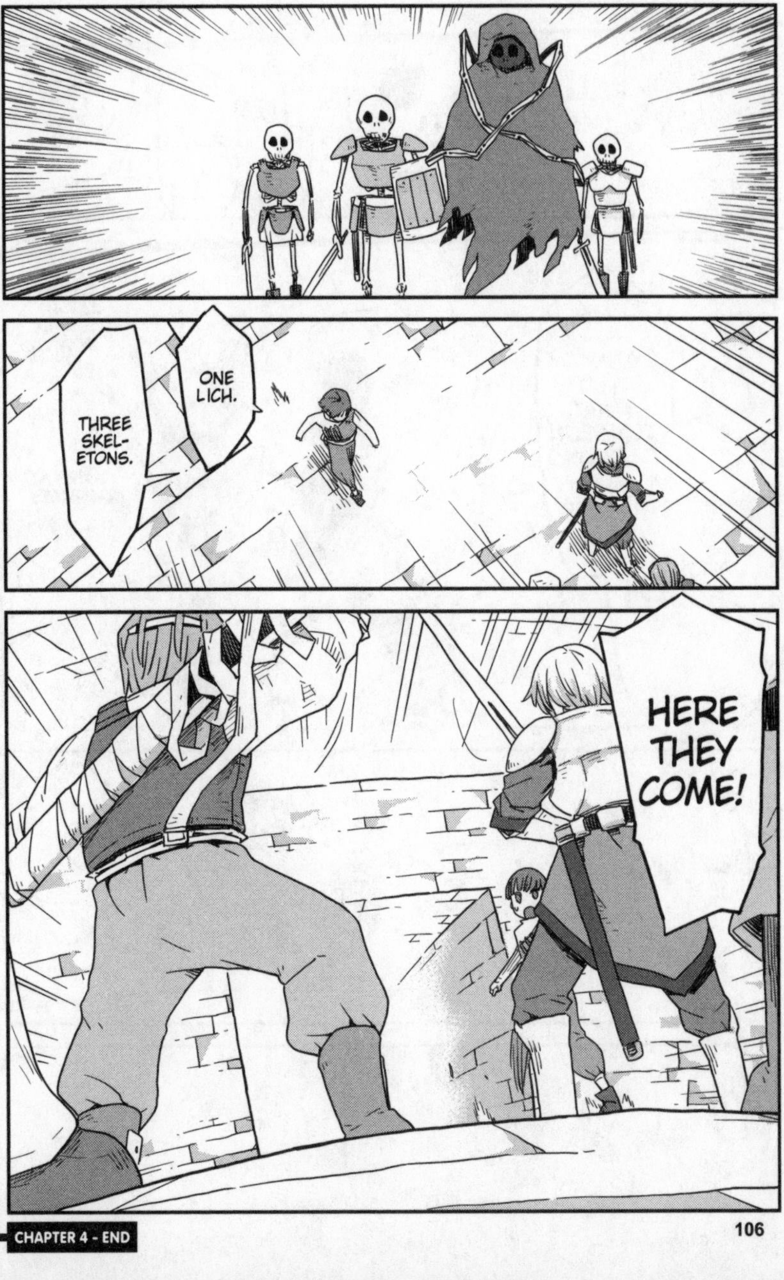
ONE LICH.
THREE SKELETONS.
HERE THEY COME!

CHAPTER 4 - END

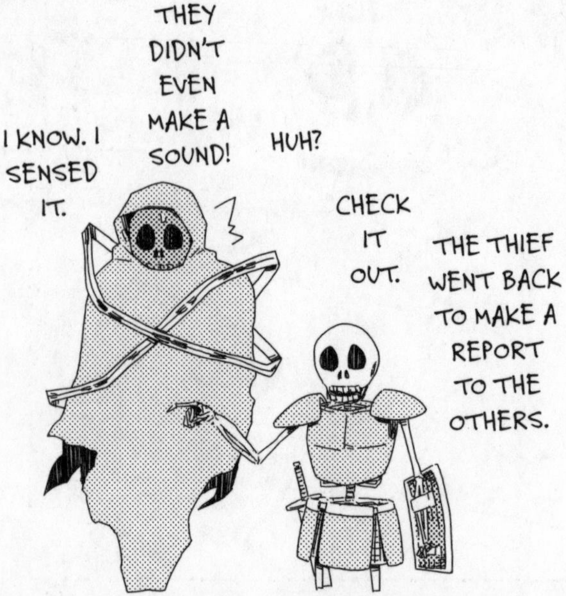
CHECK IT OUT.
THE THIEF WENT BACK TO MAKE A REPORT TO THE OTHERS.
HUH?
THEY DIDN'T EVEN MAKE A SOUND!
I KNOW. I SENSED IT.

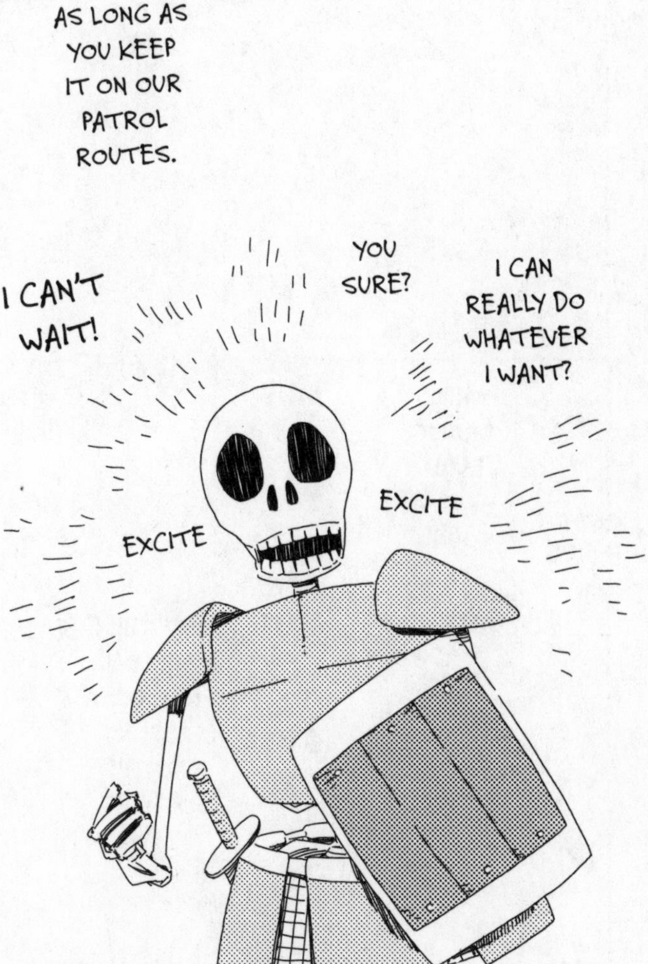
AS LONG AS YOU KEEP IT ON OUR PATROL ROUTES.
I CAN REALLY DO WHATEVER I WANT?
YOU SURE?
I CAN'T WAIT!
EXCITE
EXCITE

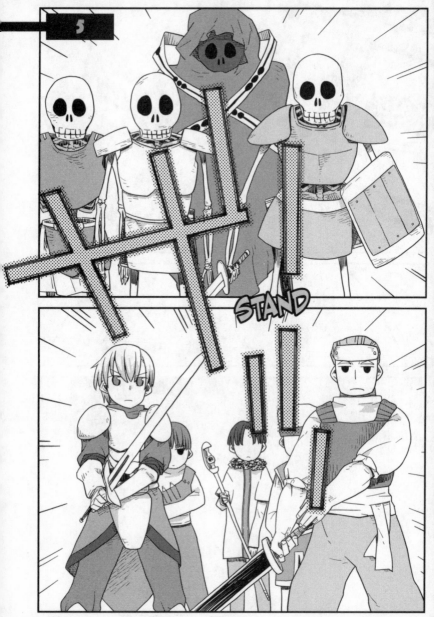

STAND

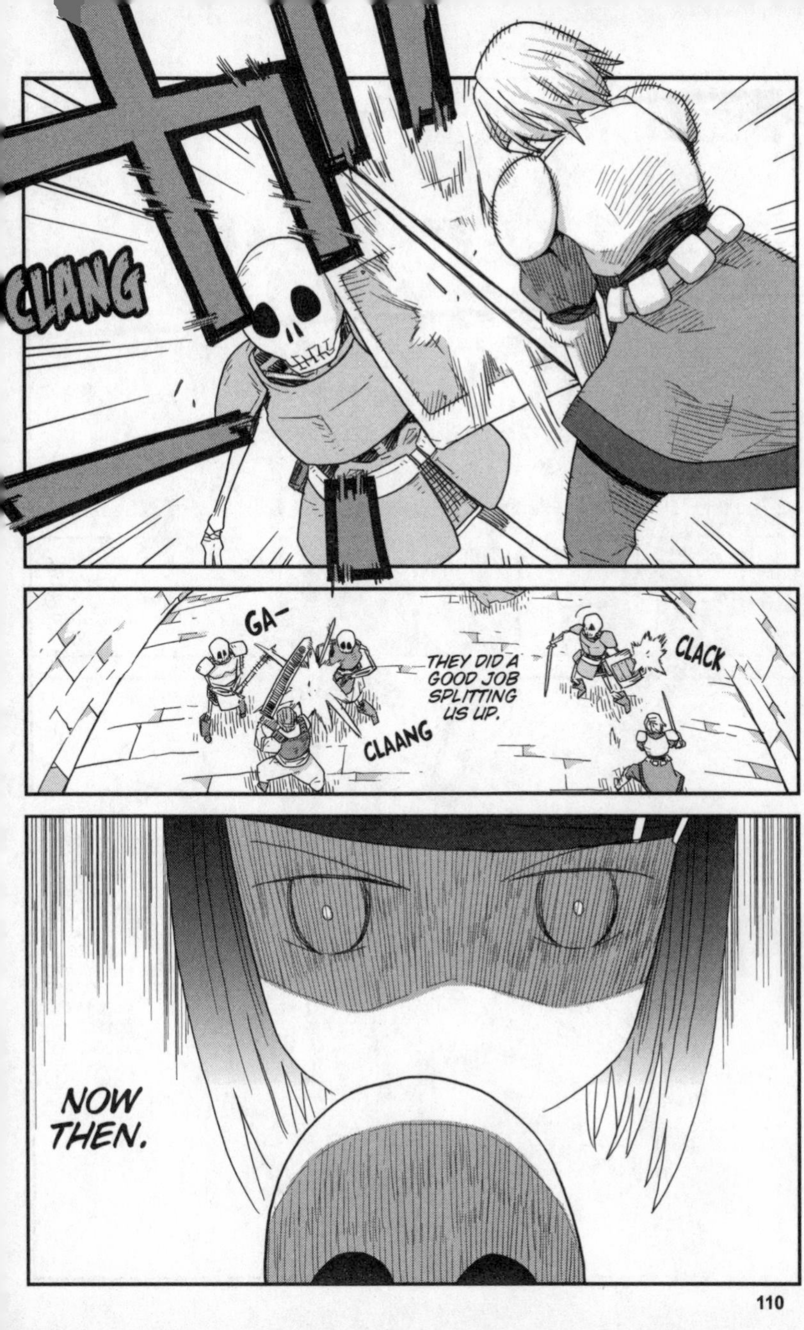
CLANG
CLACK
THEY DID A GOOD JOB SPLITTING US UP.
GA-
CLAANG
NOW THEN.

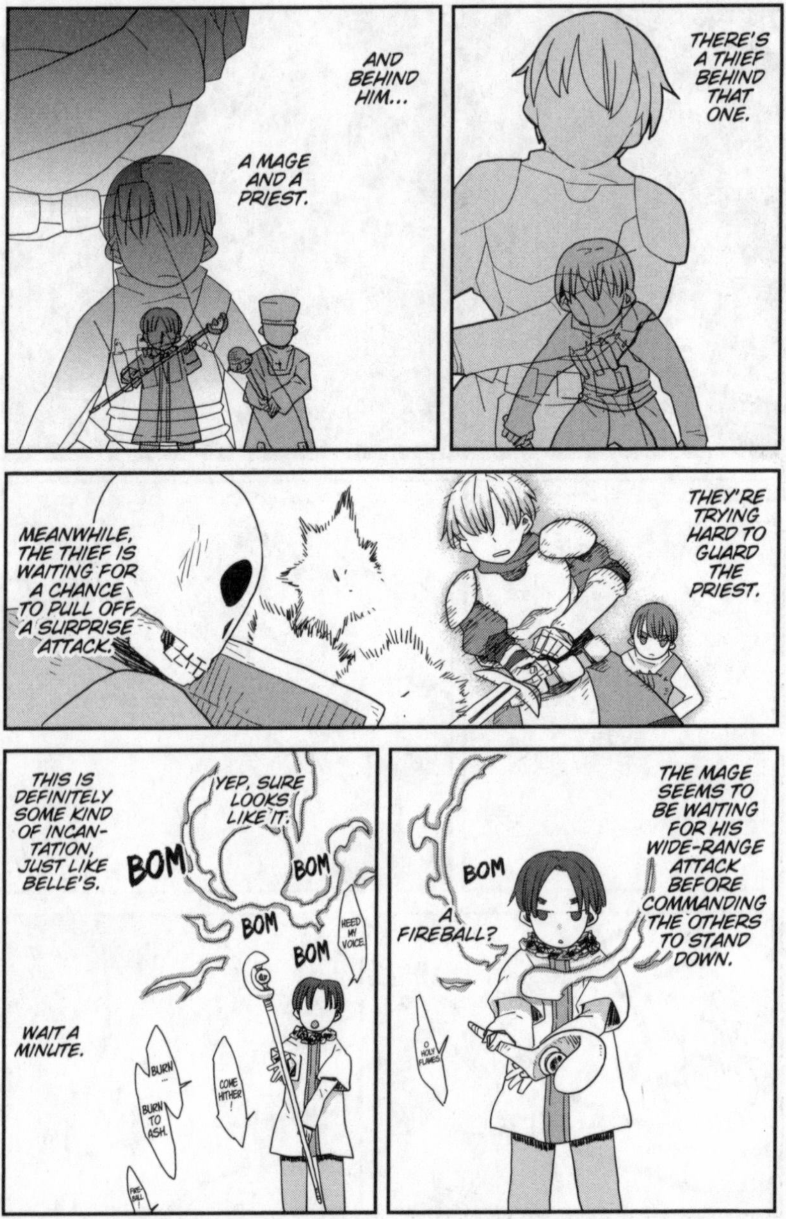
THERE'S A THIEF BEHIND THAT ONE.
AND BEHIND HIM...
A MAGE AND A PRIEST.
THEY'RE TRYING HARD TO GUARD THE PRIEST.
MEANWHILE, THE THIEF IS WAITING FOR A CHANCE TO PULL OFF A SURPRISE ATTACK.
THE MAGE SEEMS TO BE WAITING FOR HIS WIDE-RANGE ATTACK BEFORE COMMANDING THE OTHERS TO STAND DOWN.
BOM
A FIREBALL?
O HOLY FLAMES
YEP, SURE LOOKS LIKE IT.
THIS IS DEFINITELY SOME KIND OF INCAN-TATION, JUST LIKE BELLE'S.
BOM
BOM
BOM
BOM
HEED MY VOICE
COME HITHER!
BURN... BURN TO ASH.
FIRE-BALL!
WAIT A MINUTE.

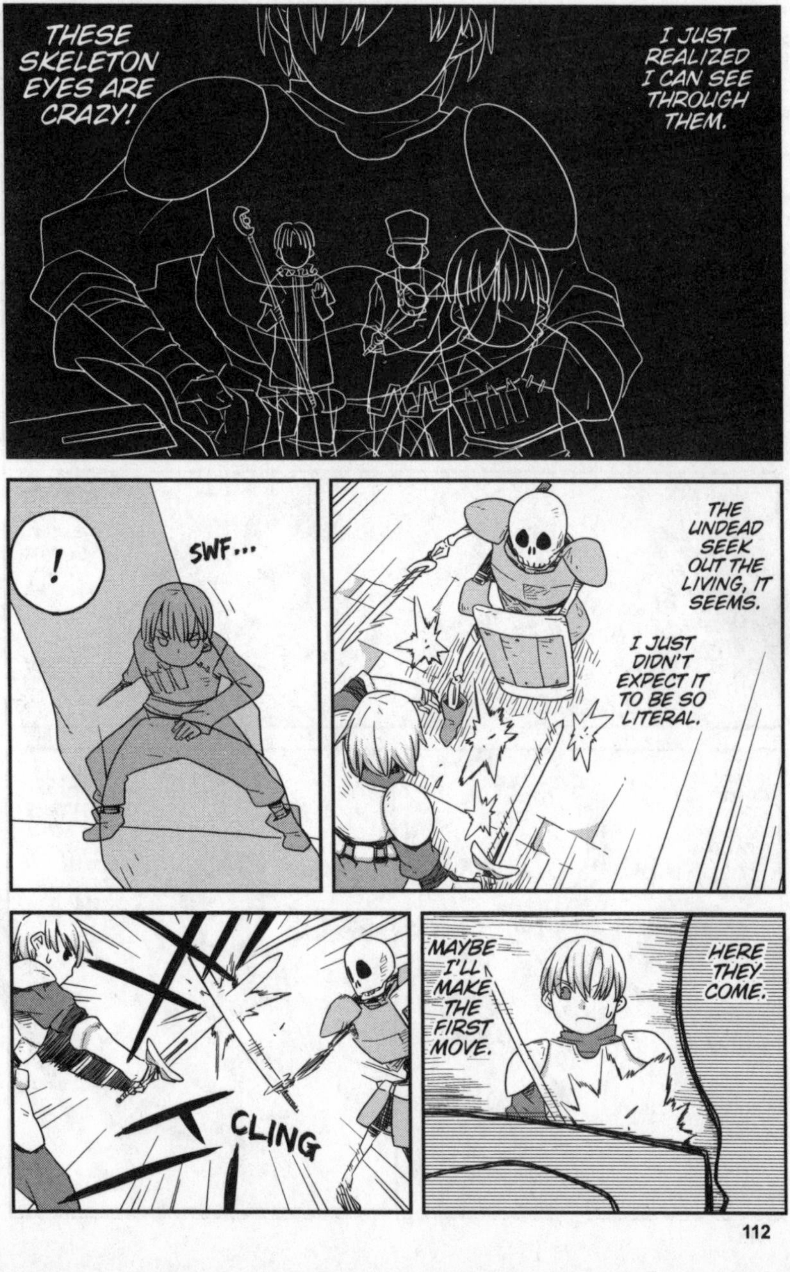
I JUST REALIZED I CAN SEE THROUGH THEM.
THESE SKELETON EYES ARE CRAZY!
THE UNDEAD SEEK OUT THE LIVING, IT SEEMS.
I JUST DIDN'T EXPECT IT TO BE SO LITERAL.
SWF...
!
HERE THEY COME.
MAYBE I'LL MAKE THE FIRST MOVE.
CLING

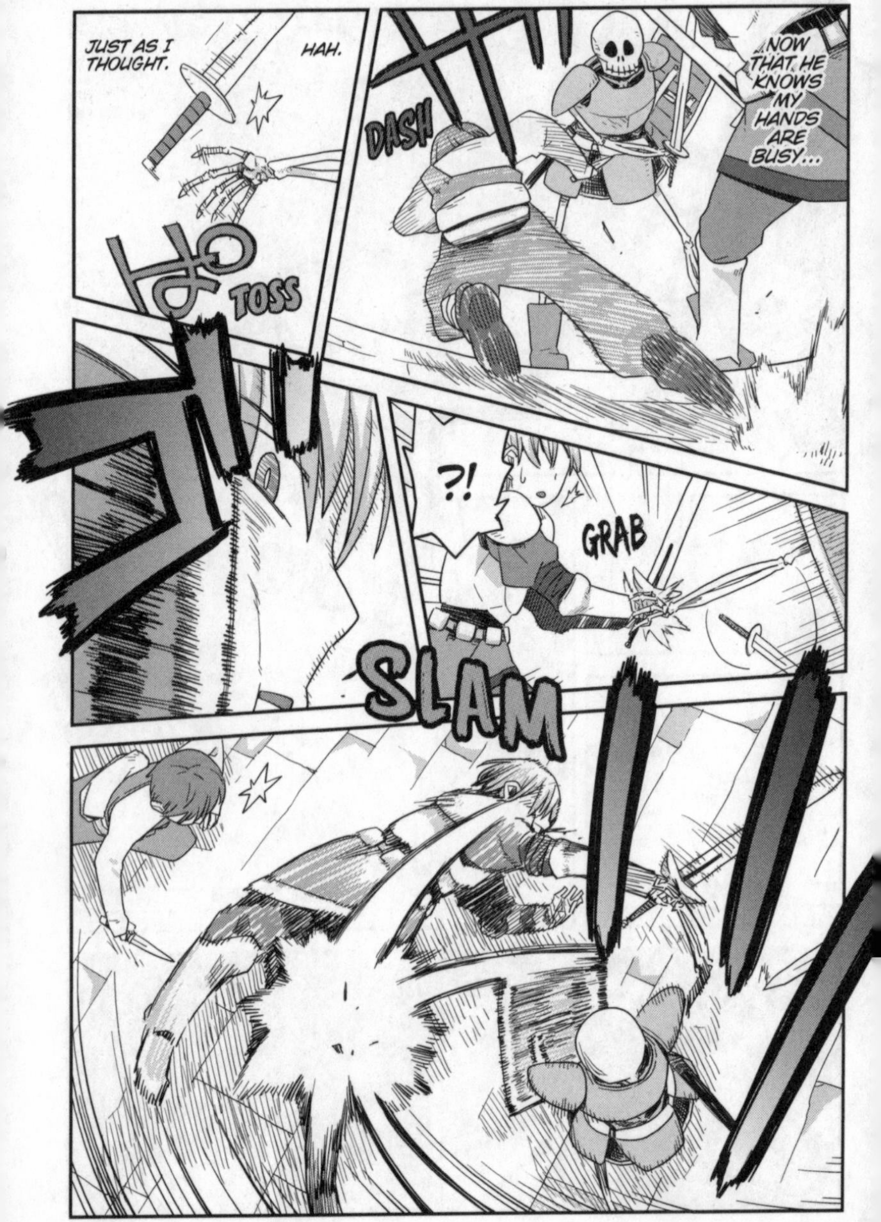
NOW THAT HE KNOWS MY HANDS ARE BUSY...
DASH
HAH.
JUST AS I THOUGHT.
TOSS
?!
GRAB
SLAM

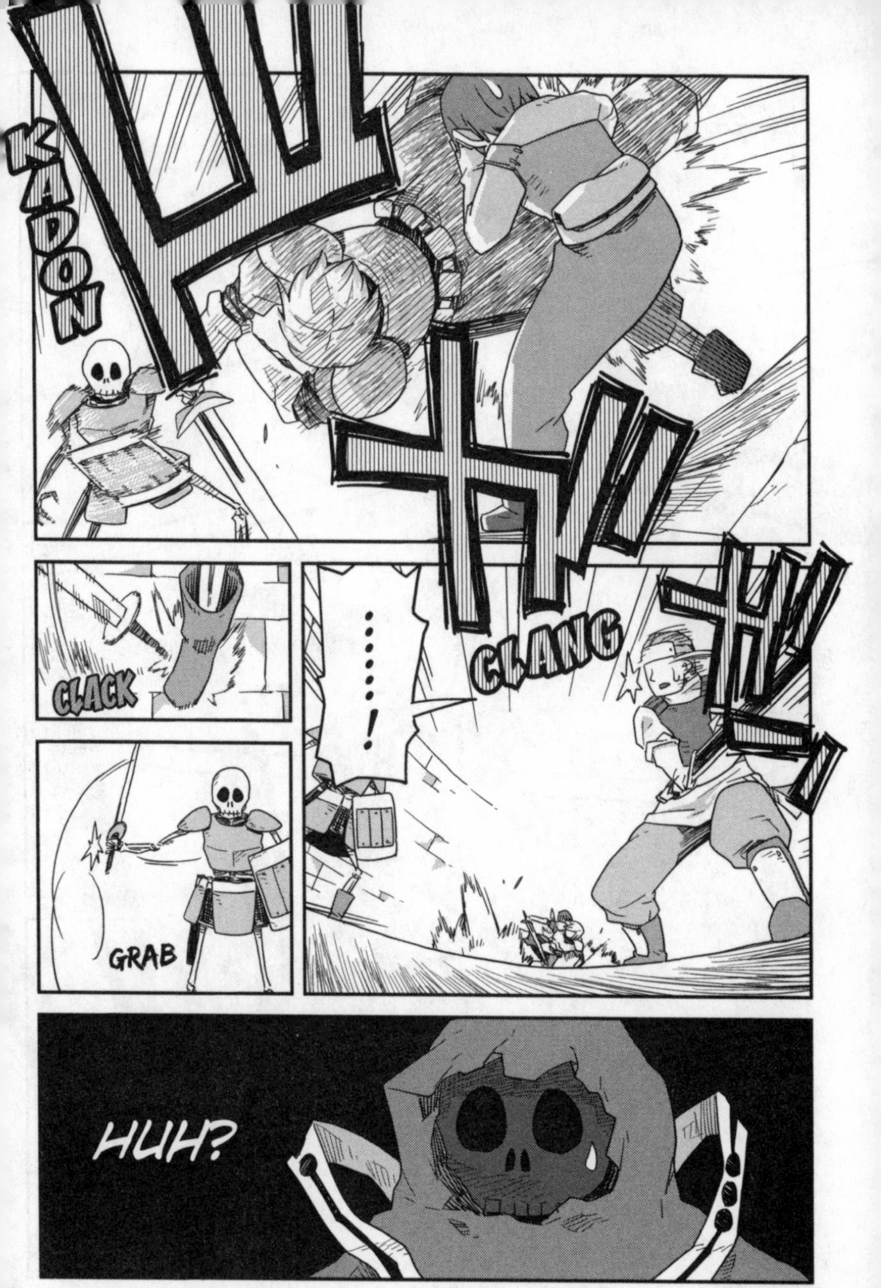
KADON
CLANG
......!
CLACK
GRAB
HUH?

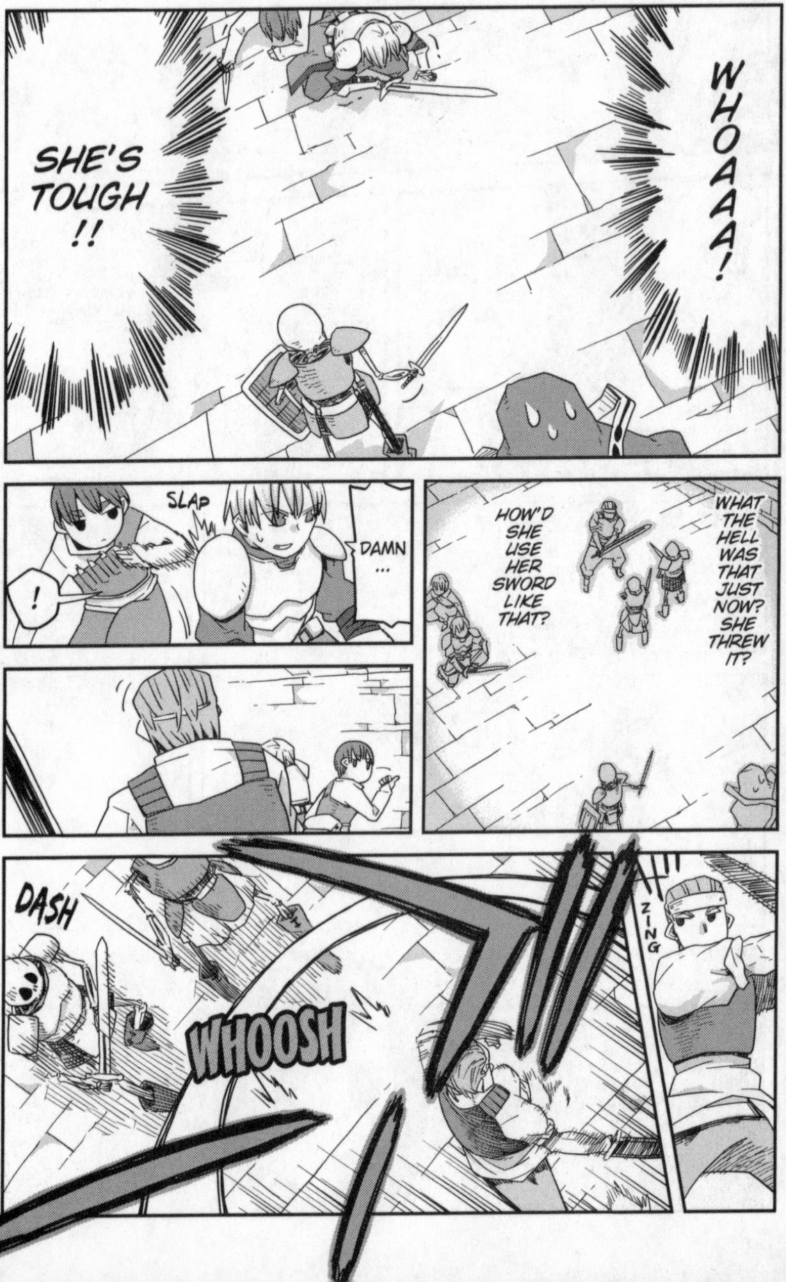
WHOAAAA!
SHE'S TOUGH!!
WHAT THE HELL WAS THAT JUST NOW? SHE THREW IT?
HOW'D SHE USE HER SWORD LIKE THAT?
DAMN ...
SLAP
!
ZING
WHOOSH
DASH

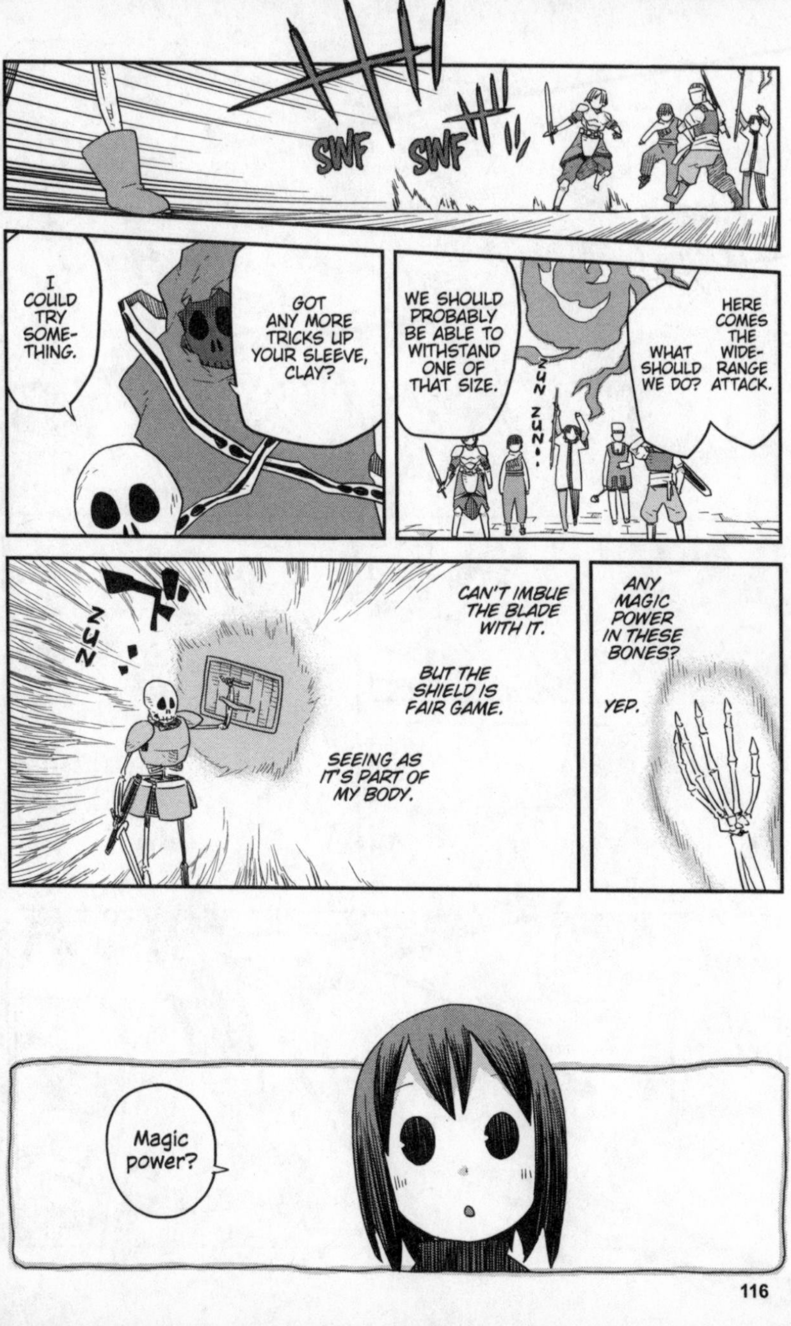
SWF
SWF
HERE COMES THE WIDE-RANGE ATTACK.
WHAT SHOULD WE DO?
ZUN ZUN...
WE SHOULD PROBABLY BE ABLE TO WITHSTAND ONE OF THAT SIZE.
GOT ANY MORE TRICKS UP YOUR SLEEVE, CLAY?
I COULD TRY SOME-THING.
ANY MAGIC POWER IN THESE BONES?
YEP.
CAN'T IMBUE THE BLADE WITH IT.
BUT THE SHIELD IS FAIR GAME.
SEEING AS IT'S PART OF MY BODY.
ZUN
Magic power?

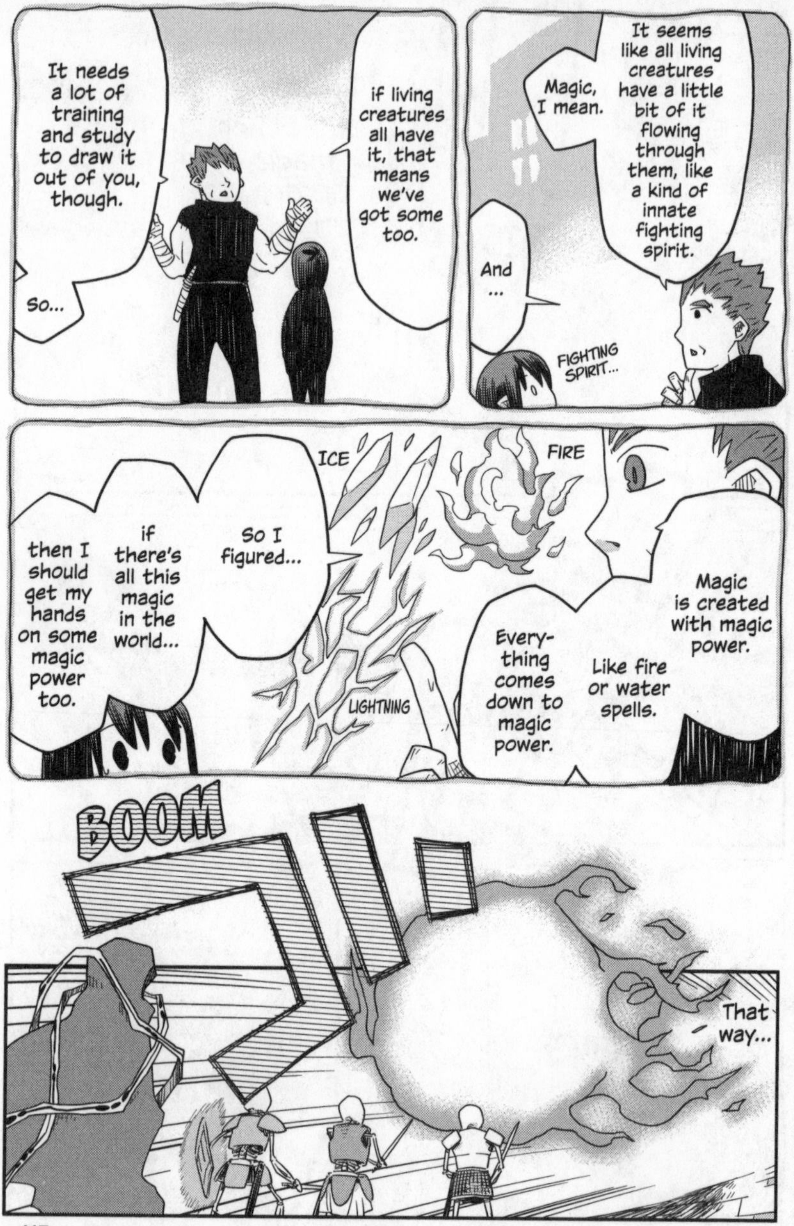
It seems like all living creatures have a little bit of it flowing through them, like a kind of innate fighting spirit.
Magic, I mean.
And ...
FIGHTING SPIRIT...
if living creatures all have it, that means we've got some too.
It needs a lot of training and study to draw it out of you, though.
So...
Magic is created with magic power.
Like fire or water spells.
Every-thing comes down to magic power.
FIRE
ICE
LIGHTNING
So I figured...
if there's all this magic in the world...
then I should get my hands on some magic power too.
BOOM
That way...

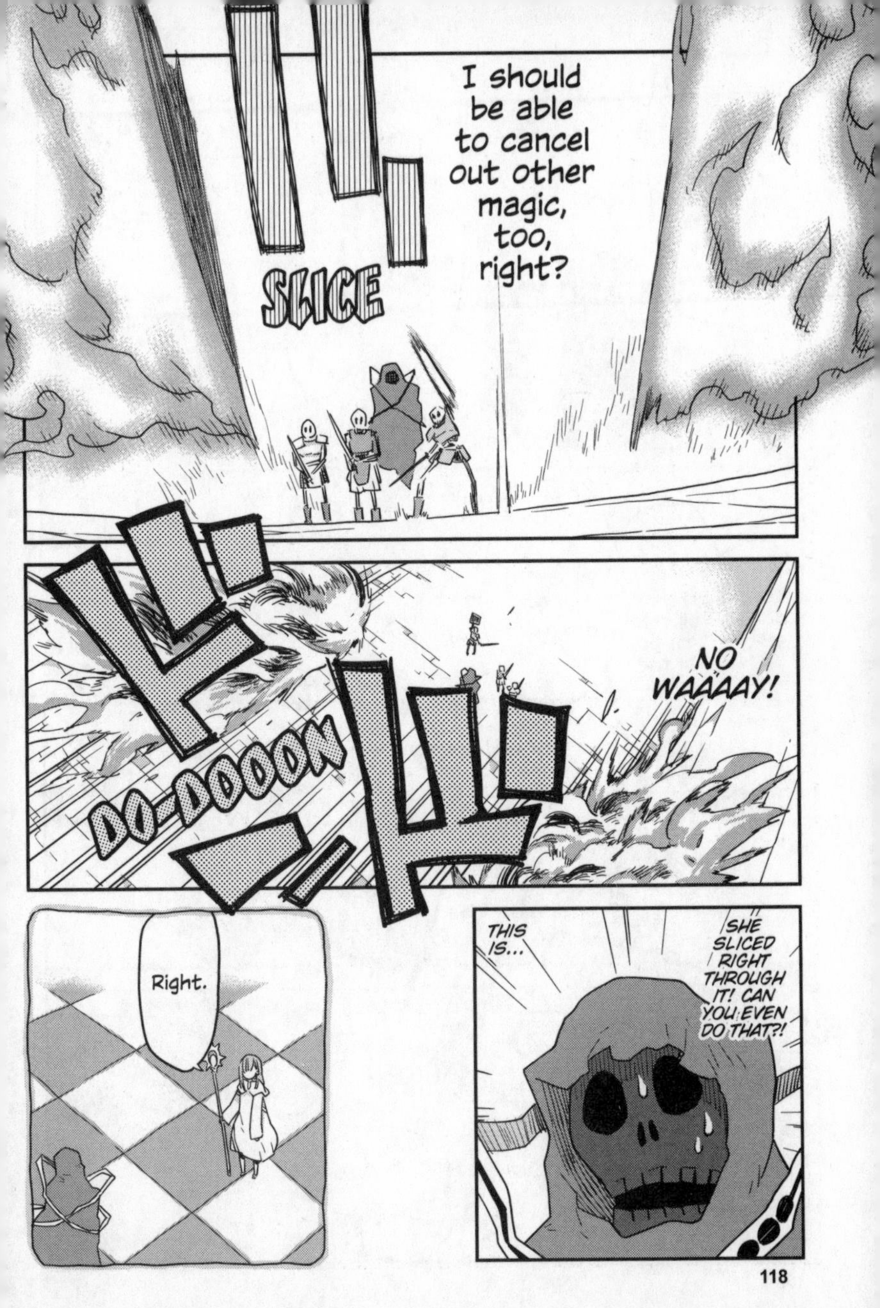
I should be able to cancel out other magic, too, right?
SLICE
NO WAAAAY!
DO-DOOON
SHE SLICED RIGHT THROUGH IT! CAN YOU EVEN DO THAT?!
THIS IS...
Right.

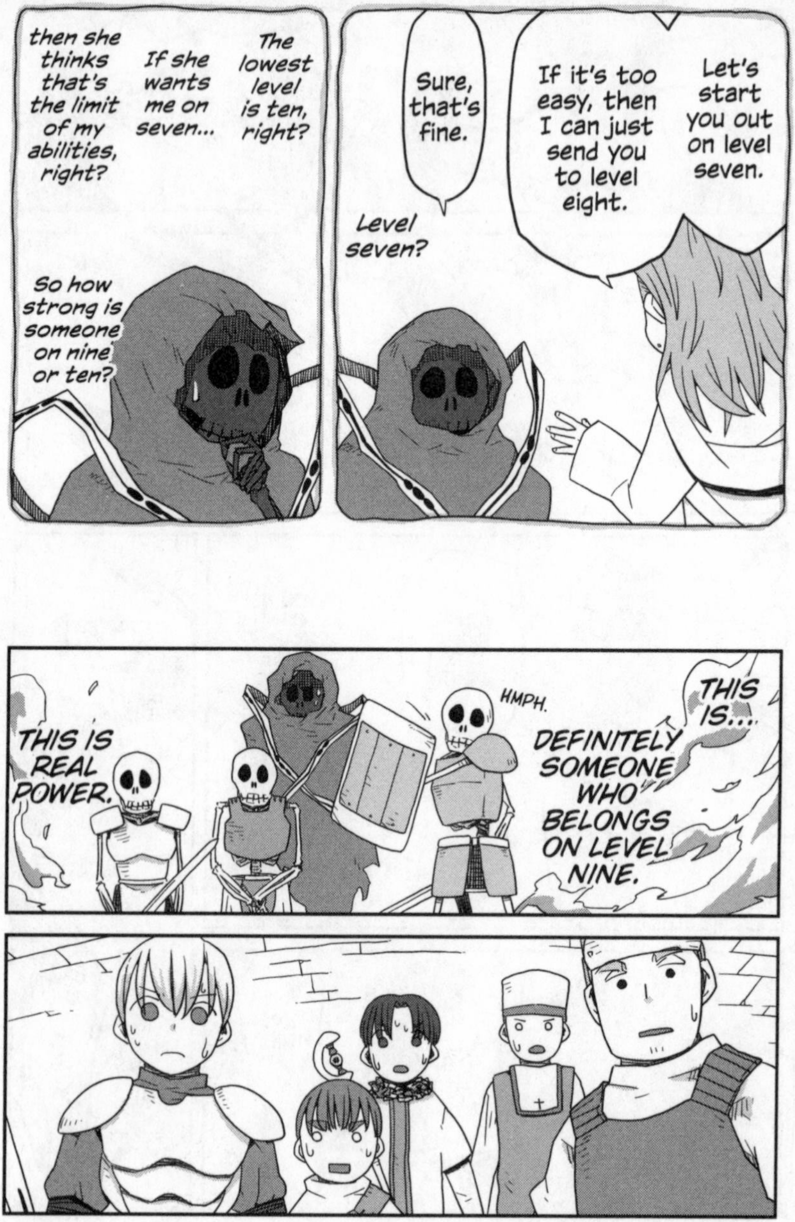
Let's start you out on level seven.
If it's too easy, then I can just send you to level eight.
Sure, that's fine.
Level seven?
The lowest level is ten, right?
If she wants me on seven...
then she thinks that's the limit of my abilities, right?
So how strong is someone on nine or ten?
THIS IS... DEFINITELY SOMEONE WHO BELONGS ON LEVEL NINE.
HMPH.
THIS IS REAL POWER.

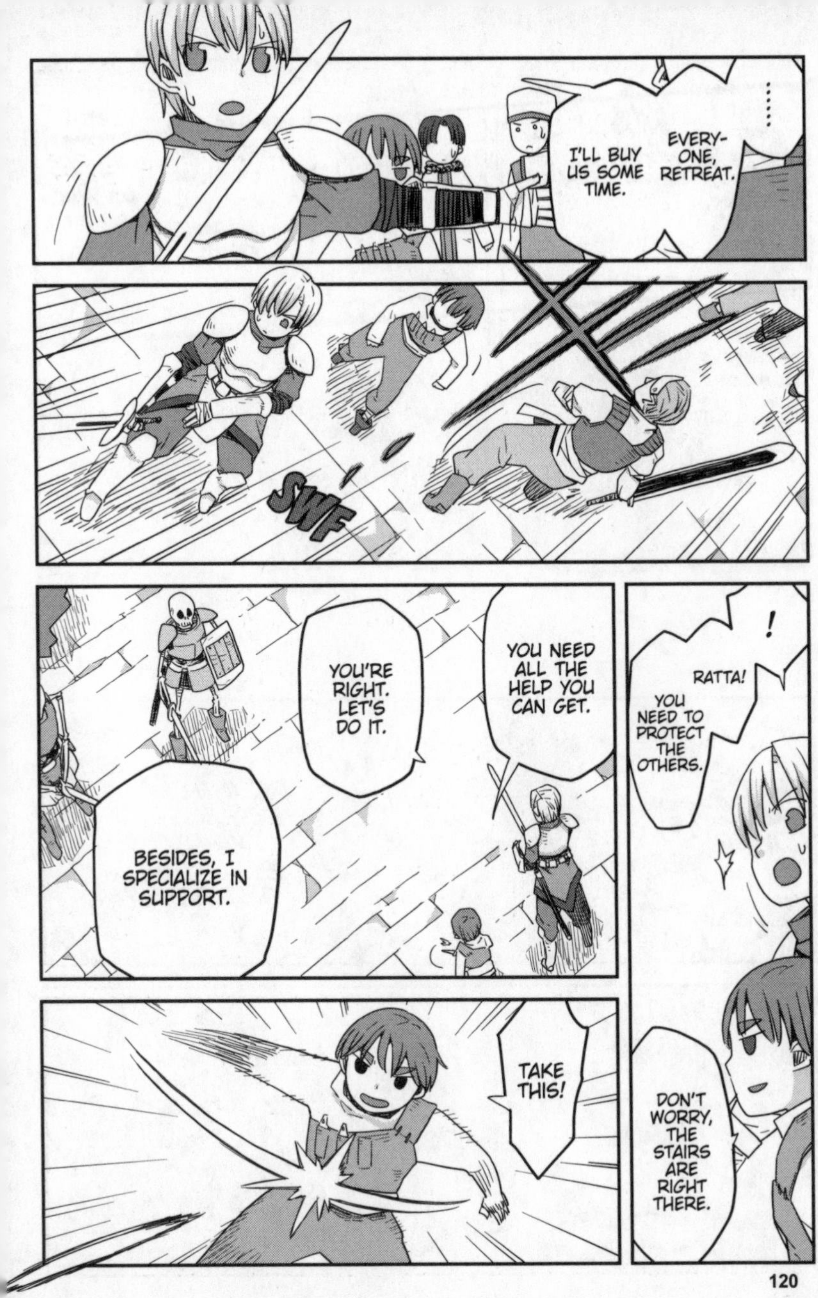
……
EVERY-ONE, RETREAT.
I'LL BUY US SOME TIME.
SWF
!
RATTA! YOU NEED TO PROTECT THE OTHERS.
DON'T WORRY, THE STAIRS ARE RIGHT THERE.
YOU NEED ALL THE HELP YOU CAN GET.
YOU'RE RIGHT. LET'S DO IT.
BESIDES, I SPECIALIZE IN SUPPORT.
TAKE THIS!

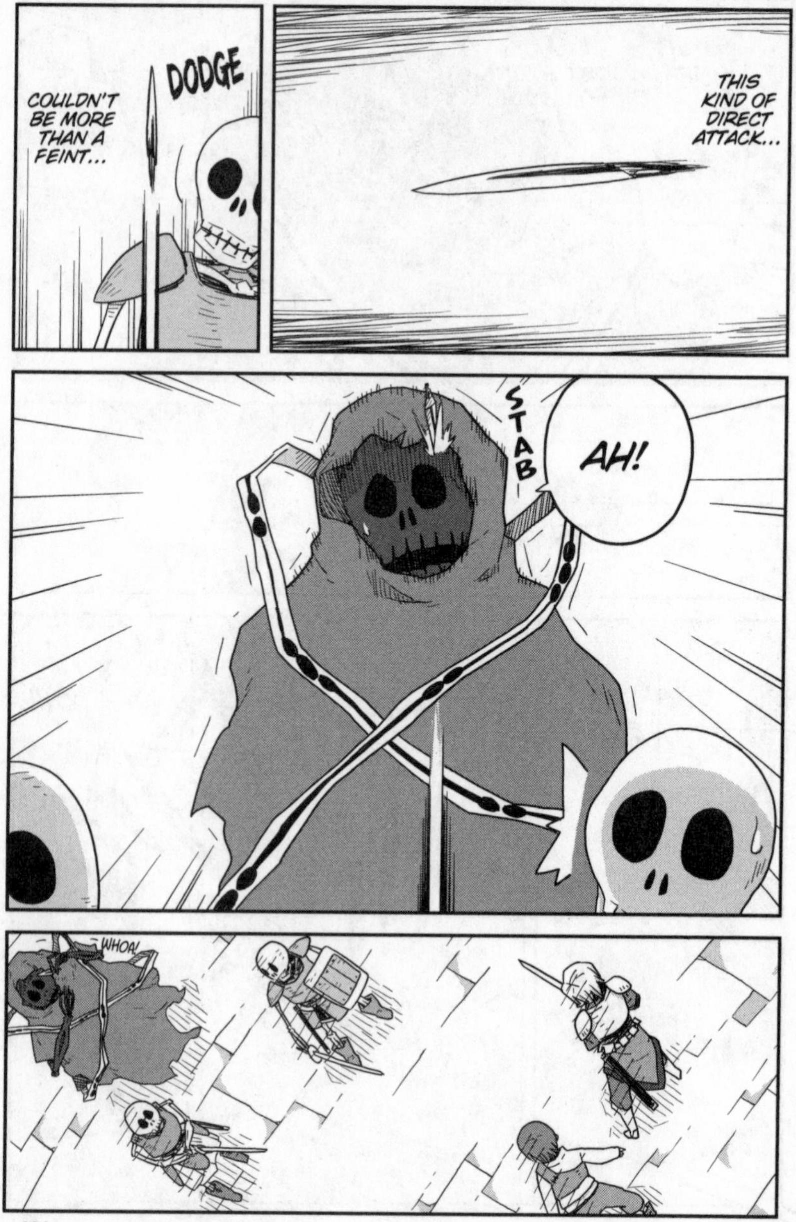
THIS KIND OF DIRECT ATTACK...
DODGE
COULDN'T BE MORE THAN A FEINT...
AH!
STAB
WHOA!

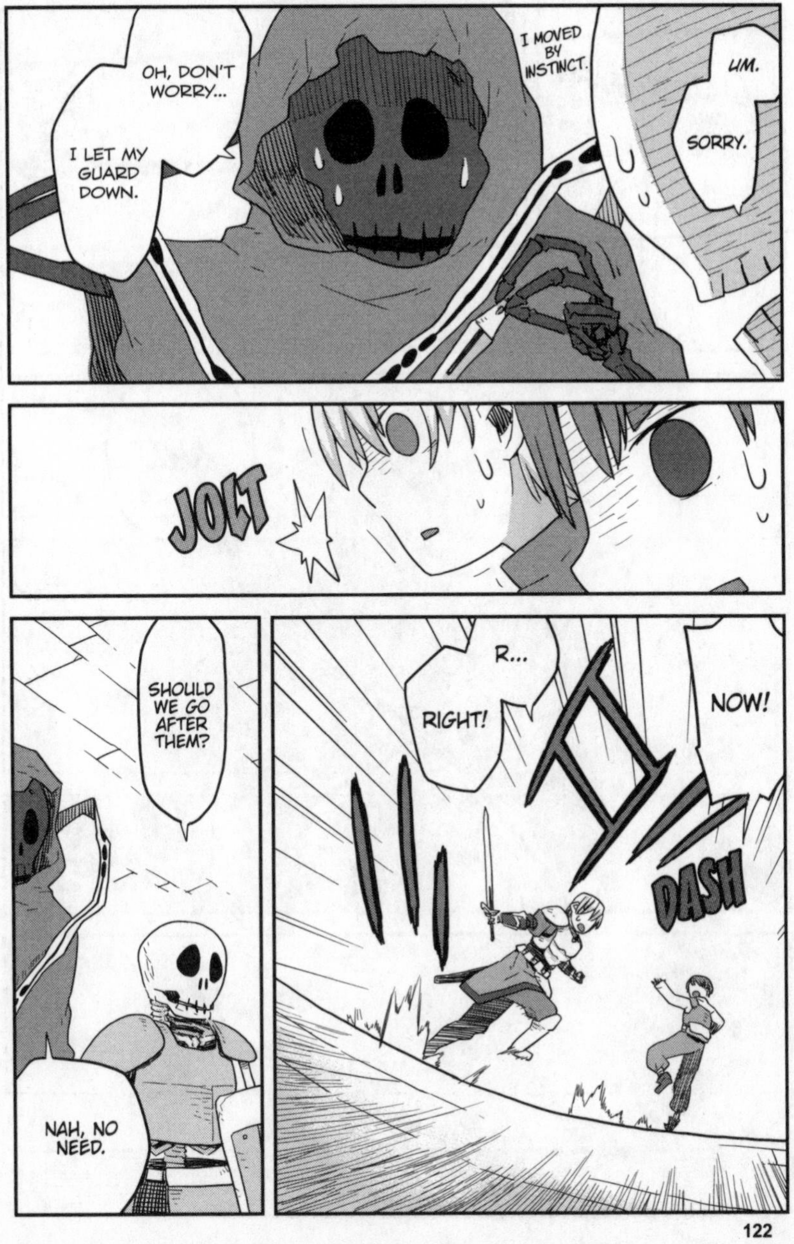
UM.
SORRY.
I MOVED BY INSTINCT.
OH, DON'T WORRY...
I LET MY GUARD DOWN.
JOLT
NOW!
R...
RIGHT!
HI
DASH
SHOULD WE GO AFTER THEM?
NAH, NO NEED.

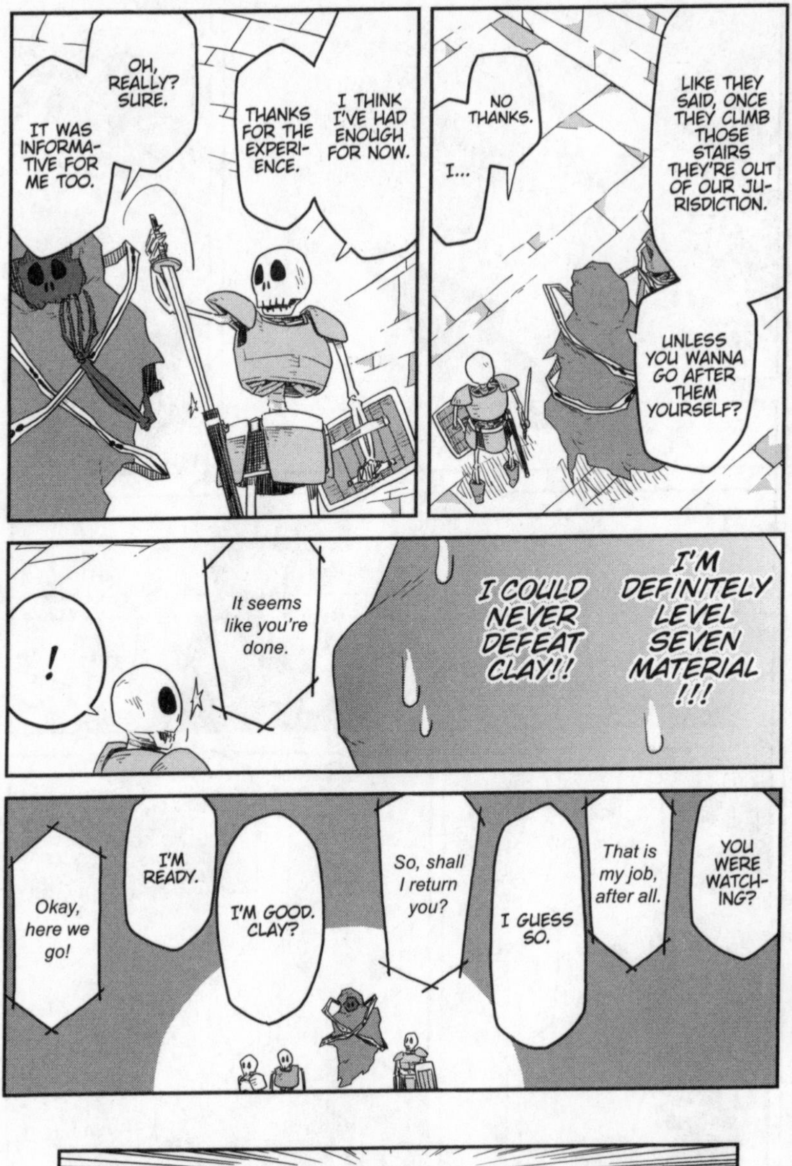
LIKE THEY SAID, ONCE THEY CLIMB THOSE STAIRS THEY'RE OUT OF OUR JURISDICTION.
UNLESS YOU WANNA GO AFTER THEM YOURSELF?
NO THANKS. I...
I THINK I'VE HAD ENOUGH FOR NOW.
THANKS FOR THE EXPERIENCE.
OH, REALLY? SURE.
IT WAS INFORMATIVE FOR ME TOO.
I'M DEFINITELY LEVEL SEVEN MATERIAL!!!
I COULD NEVER DEFEAT CLAY!!
It seems like you're done.
!
YOU WERE WATCHING?
That is my job, after all.
I GUESS SO.
So, shall I return you?
I'M GOOD. CLAY?
I'M READY.
Okay, here we go!

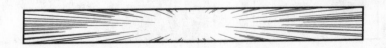

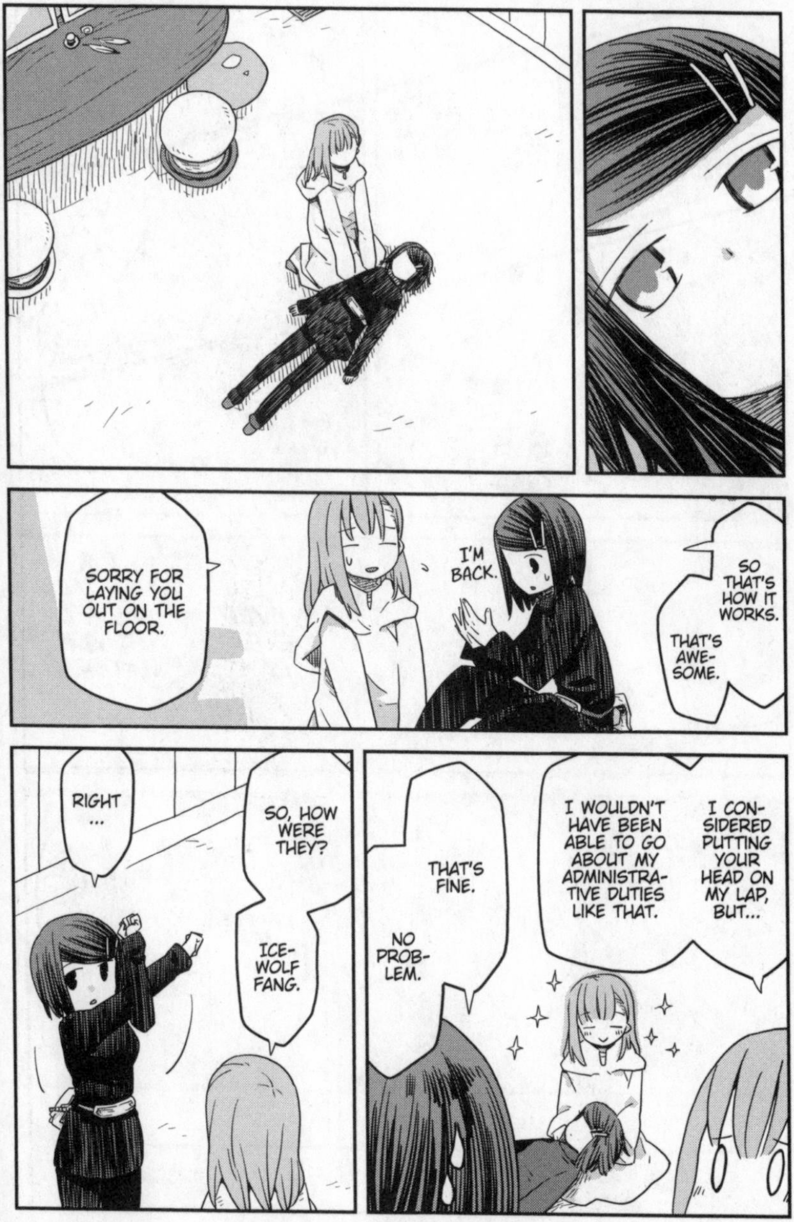
SO THAT'S HOW IT WORKS.
THAT'S AWESOME.
I'M BACK.
SORRY FOR LAYING YOU OUT ON THE FLOOR.
I CONSIDERED PUTTING YOUR HEAD ON MY LAP, BUT...
I WOULDN'T HAVE BEEN ABLE TO GO ABOUT MY ADMINISTRATIVE DUTIES LIKE THAT.
THAT'S FINE.
NO PROBLEM.
SO, HOW WERE THEY?
ICE-WOLF FANG.
RIGHT ...

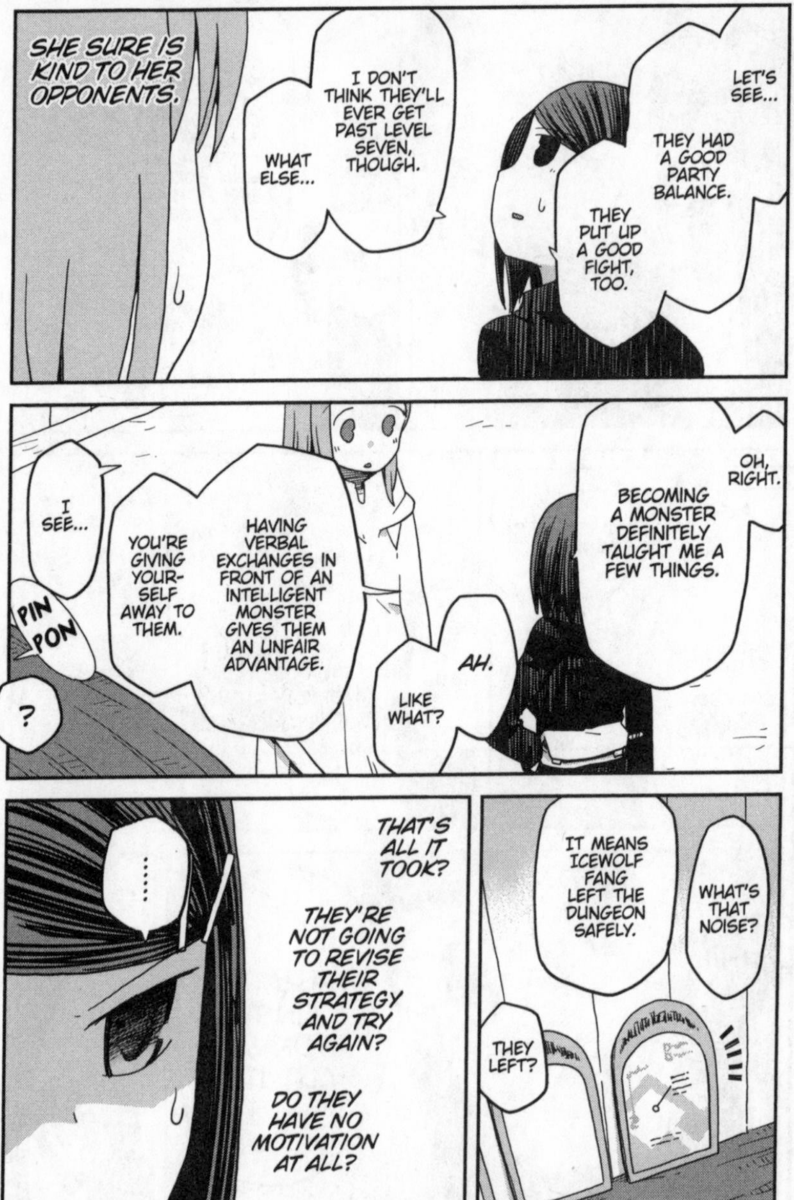
LET'S SEE...
THEY HAD A GOOD PARTY BALANCE.
THEY PUT UP A GOOD FIGHT, TOO.
I DON'T THINK THEY'LL EVER GET PAST LEVEL SEVEN, THOUGH.
WHAT ELSE...
SHE SURE IS KIND TO HER OPPONENTS.
OH, RIGHT.
BECOMING A MONSTER DEFINITELY TAUGHT ME A FEW THINGS.
AH.
LIKE WHAT?
HAVING VERBAL EXCHANGES IN FRONT OF AN INTELLIGENT MONSTER GIVES THEM AN UNFAIR ADVANTAGE.
YOU'RE GIVING YOUR-SELF AWAY TO THEM.
I SEE...
PIN PON
?
WHAT'S THAT NOISE?
IT MEANS ICEWOLF FANG LEFT THE DUNGEON SAFELY.
THEY LEFT?
THAT'S ALL IT TOOK?
......
THEY'RE NOT GOING TO REVISE THEIR STRATEGY AND TRY AGAIN?
DO THEY HAVE NO MOTIVATION AT ALL?

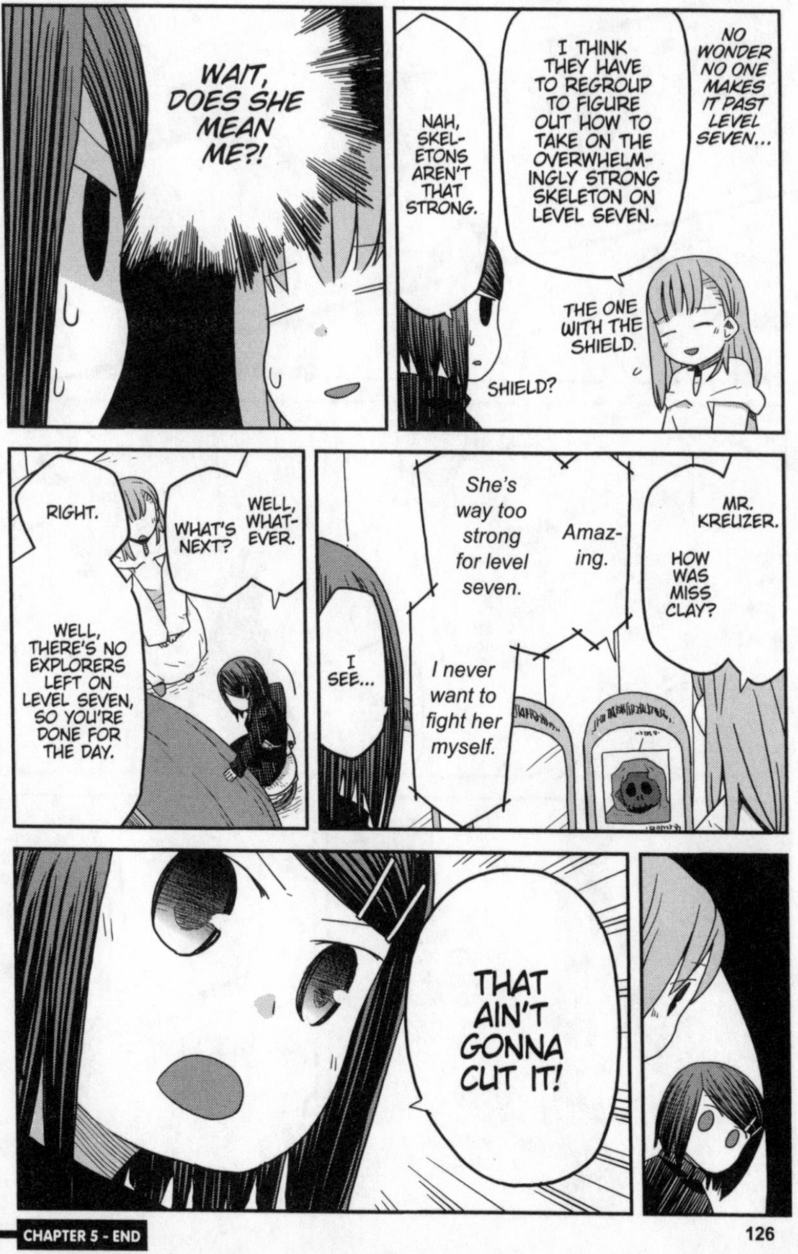
NO WONDER NO ONE MAKES IT PAST LEVEL SEVEN...
I THINK THEY HAVE TO REGROUP TO FIGURE OUT HOW TO TAKE ON THE OVERWHELMINGLY STRONG SKELETON ON LEVEL SEVEN.
NAH, SKELETONS AREN'T THAT STRONG.
THE ONE WITH THE SHIELD.
SHIELD?
WAIT, DOES SHE MEAN ME?!
MR. KREUZER.
HOW WAS MISS CLAY?
Amazing.
She's way too strong for level seven.
I never want to fight her myself.
I SEE...
WELL, WHATEVER.
WHAT'S NEXT?
RIGHT.
WELL, THERE'S NO EXPLORERS LEFT ON LEVEL SEVEN, SO YOU'RE DONE FOR THE DAY.
THAT AIN'T GONNA CUT IT!

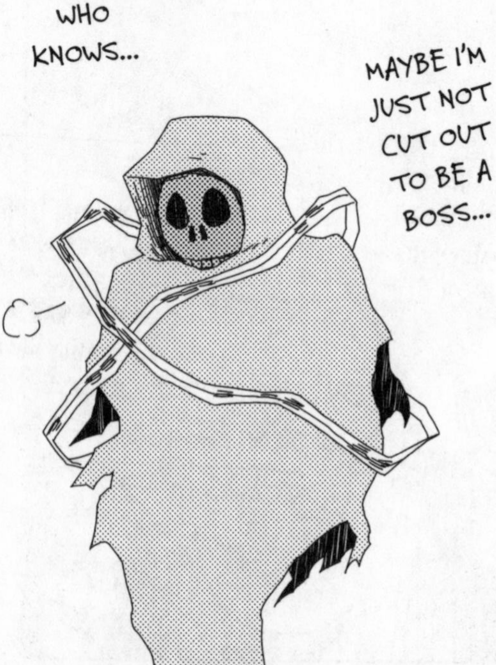
MAYBE I'M JUST NOT CUT OUT TO BE A BOSS...
WHO KNOWS...

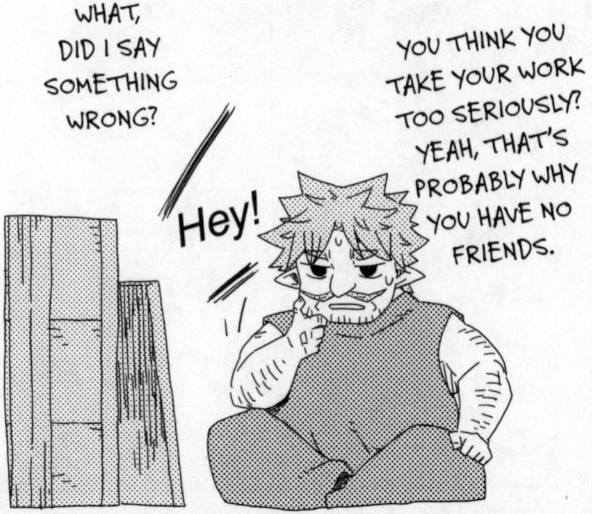
YOU THINK YOU TAKE YOUR WORK TOO SERIOUSLY? YEAH, THAT'S PROBABLY WHY YOU HAVE NO FRIENDS.
Hey!
WHAT, DID I SAY SOMETHING WRONG?

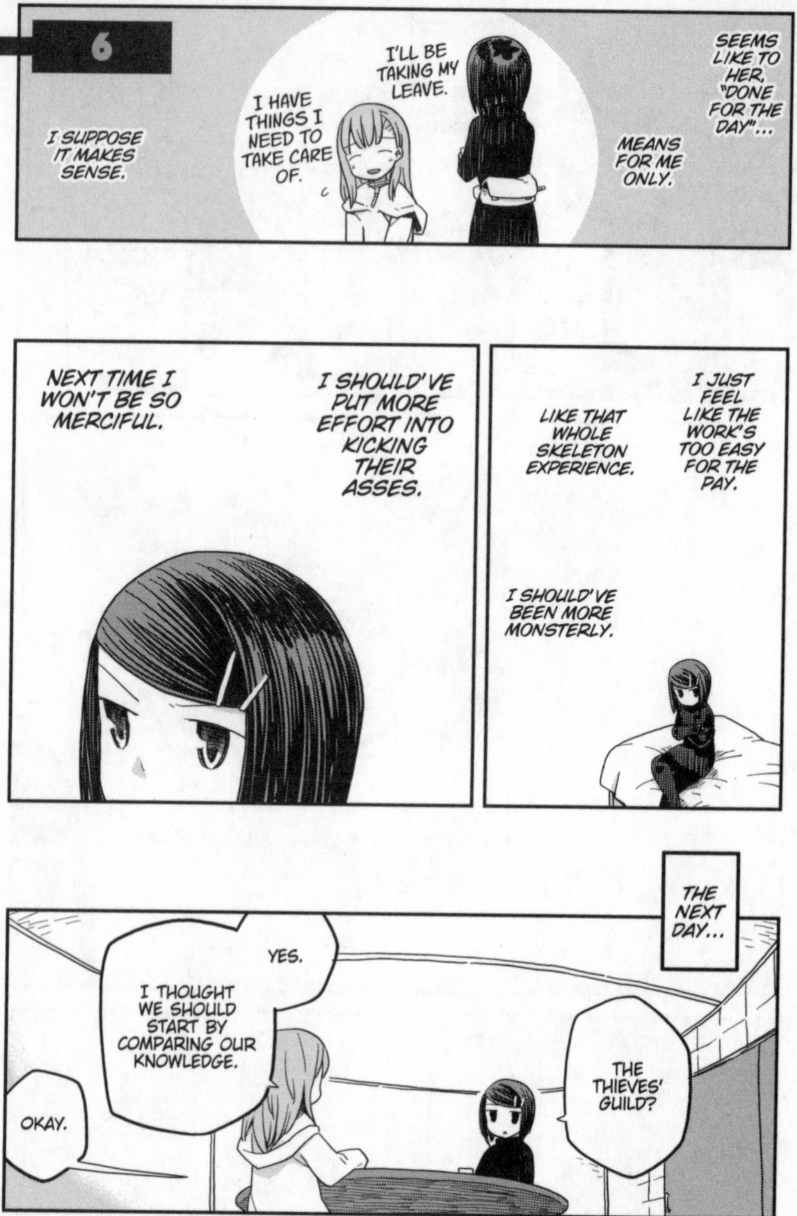
6
SEEMS LIKE TO HER, "DONE FOR THE DAY"...
MEANS FOR ME ONLY.
I'LL BE TAKING MY LEAVE.
I HAVE THINGS I NEED TO TAKE CARE OF.
I SUPPOSE IT MAKES SENSE.
I JUST FEEL LIKE THE WORK'S TOO EASY FOR THE PAY.
LIKE THAT WHOLE SKELETON EXPERIENCE.
I SHOULD'VE BEEN MORE MONSTERLY.
I SHOULD'VE PUT MORE EFFORT INTO KICKING THEIR ASSES.
NEXT TIME I WON'T BE SO MERCIFUL.
THE NEXT DAY...
THE THIEVES' GUILD?
YES.
I THOUGHT WE SHOULD START BY COMPARING OUR KNOWLEDGE.
OKAY.

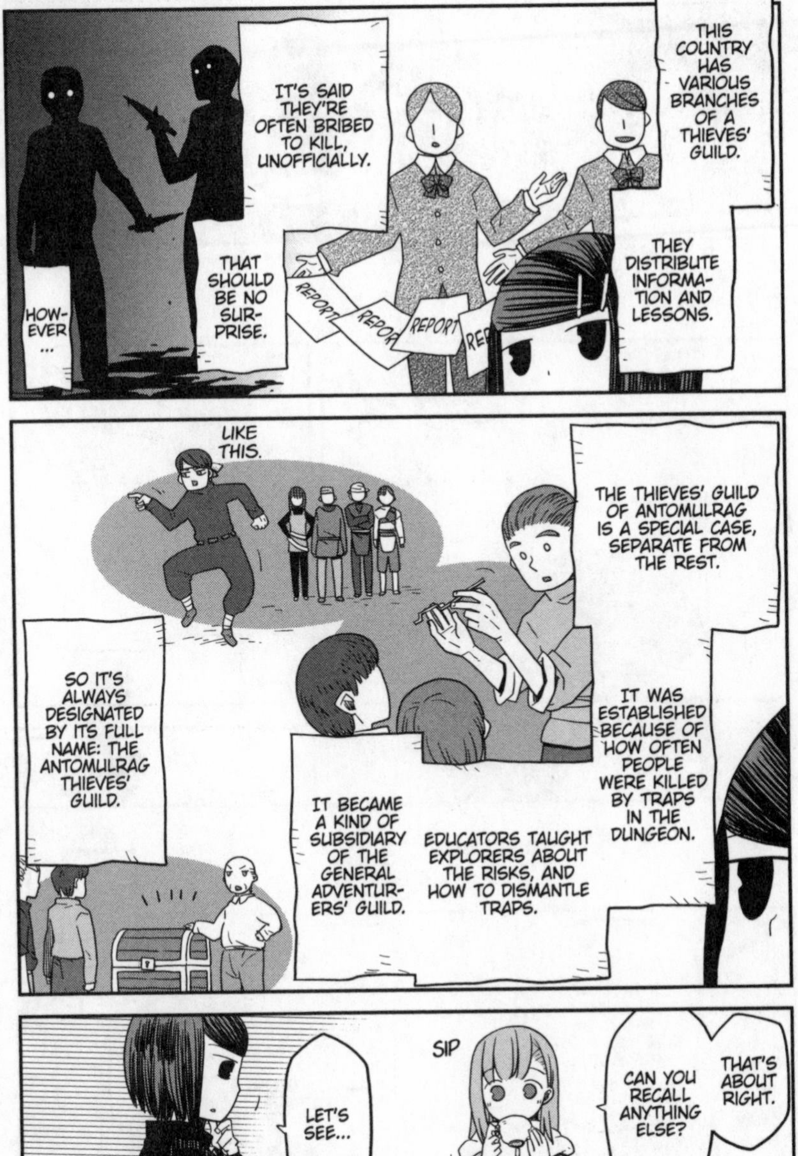
THIS COUNTRY HAS VARIOUS BRANCHES OF A THIEVES' GUILD.
THEY DISTRIBUTE INFORMATION AND LESSONS.
IT'S SAID THEY'RE OFTEN BRIBED TO KILL, UNOFFICIALLY.
REPORT
THAT SHOULD BE NO SURPRISE.
HOW-EVER ...
THE THIEVES' GUILD OF ANTOMULRAG IS A SPECIAL CASE, SEPARATE FROM THE REST.
LIKE THIS.
SO IT'S ALWAYS DESIGNATED BY ITS FULL NAME: THE ANTOMULRAG THIEVES' GUILD.
IT WAS ESTABLISHED BECAUSE OF HOW OFTEN PEOPLE WERE KILLED BY TRAPS IN THE DUNGEON.
EDUCATORS TAUGHT EXPLORERS ABOUT THE RISKS, AND HOW TO DISMANTLE TRAPS.
IT BECAME A KIND OF SUBSIDIARY OF THE GENERAL ADVENTURERS' GUILD.
THAT'S ABOUT RIGHT.
CAN YOU RECALL ANYTHING ELSE?
SIP
LET'S SEE...

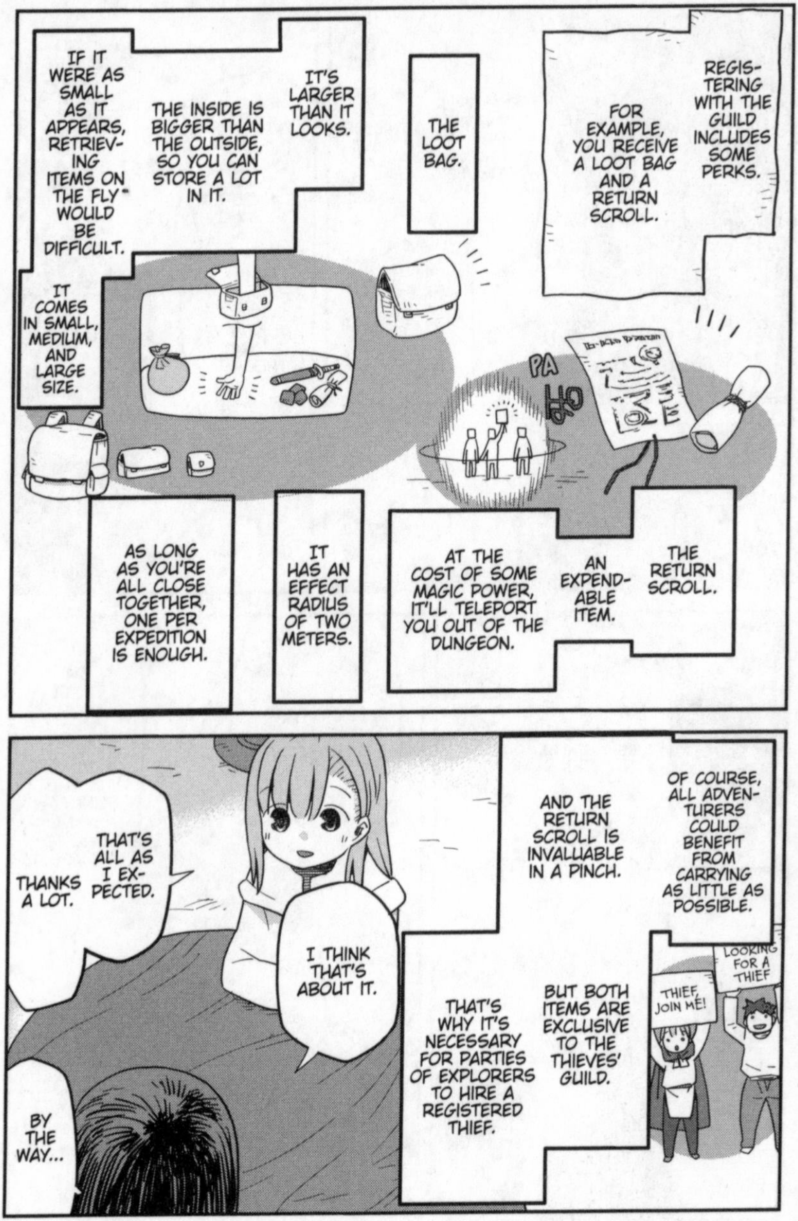
REGISTERING WITH THE GUILD INCLUDES SOME PERKS.
FOR EXAMPLE, YOU RECEIVE A LOOT BAG AND A RETURN SCROLL.
THE LOOT BAG.
IT'S LARGER THAN IT LOOKS.
THE INSIDE IS BIGGER THAN THE OUTSIDE, SO YOU CAN STORE A LOT IN IT.
IF IT WERE AS SMALL AS IT APPEARS, RETRIEVING ITEMS ON THE FLY WOULD BE DIFFICULT.
IT COMES IN SMALL, MEDIUM, AND LARGE SIZE.
PA
THE RETURN SCROLL.
AN EXPENDABLE ITEM.
AT THE COST OF SOME MAGIC POWER, IT'LL TELEPORT YOU OUT OF THE DUNGEON.
IT HAS AN EFFECT RADIUS OF TWO METERS.
AS LONG AS YOU'RE ALL CLOSE TOGETHER, ONE PER EXPEDITION IS ENOUGH.
OF COURSE, ALL ADVENTURERS COULD BENEFIT FROM CARRYING AS LITTLE AS POSSIBLE.
AND THE RETURN SCROLL IS INVALUABLE IN A PINCH.
LOOKING FOR A THIEF
THIEF, JOIN ME!
BUT BOTH ITEMS ARE EXCLUSIVE TO THE THIEVES' GUILD.
THAT'S WHY IT'S NECESSARY FOR PARTIES OF EXPLORERS TO HIRE A REGISTERED THIEF.
I THINK THAT'S ABOUT IT.
THAT'S ALL AS I EXPECTED.
THANKS A LOT.
BY THE WAY...

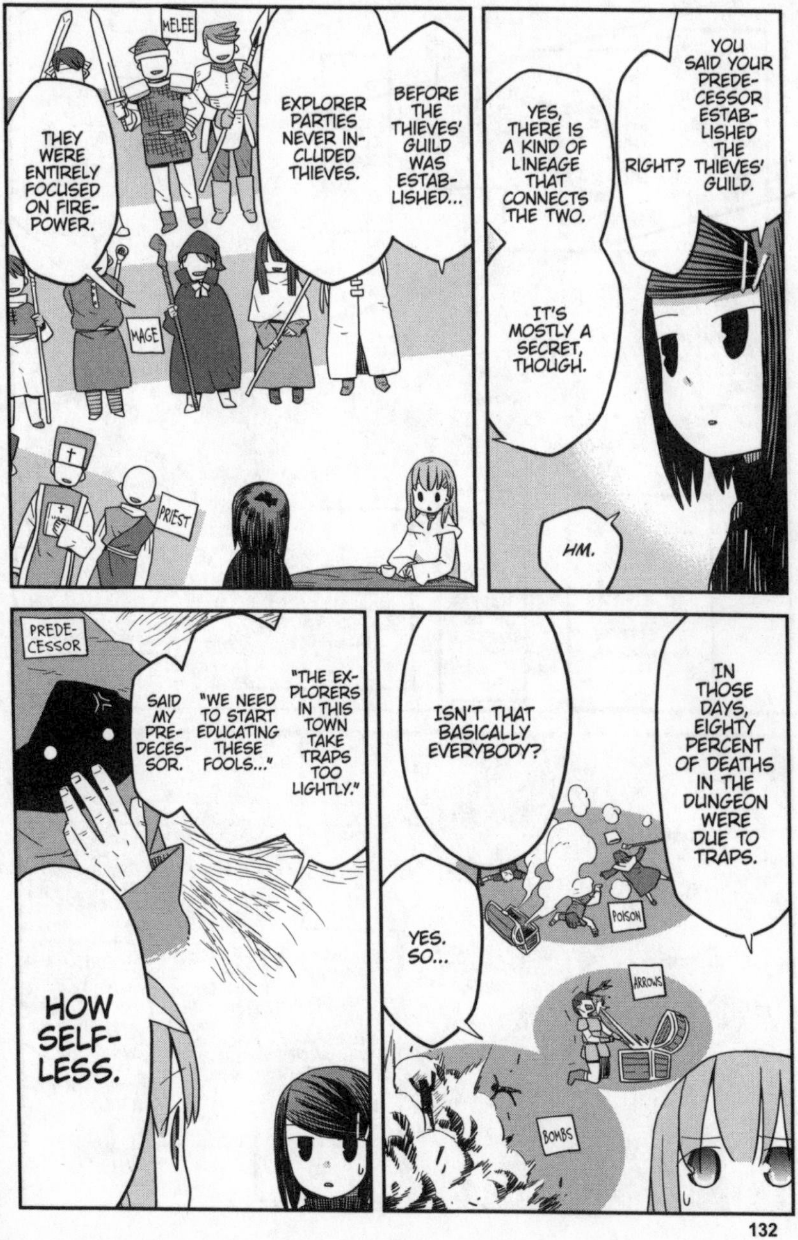

YOU SAID YOUR PREDECESSOR ESTABLISHED THE THIEVES' GUILD.
RIGHT?
YES, THERE IS A KIND OF LINEAGE THAT CONNECTS THE TWO.
IT'S MOSTLY A SECRET, THOUGH.
HM.
BEFORE THE THIEVES' GUILD WAS ESTABLISHED...
EXPLORER PARTIES NEVER INCLUDED THIEVES.
MELEE
THEY WERE ENTIRELY FOCUSED ON FIREPOWER.
MAGE
PRIEST
IN THOSE DAYS, EIGHTY PERCENT OF DEATHS IN THE DUNGEON WERE DUE TO TRAPS.
ISN'T THAT BASICALLY EVERYBODY?
POISON
YES. SO...
ARROWS
BOMBS
PREDECESSOR
"THE EXPLORERS IN THIS TOWN TAKE TRAPS TOO LIGHTLY."
"WE NEED TO START EDUCATING THESE FOOLS..."
SAID MY PREDECESSOR.
HOW SELFLESS.

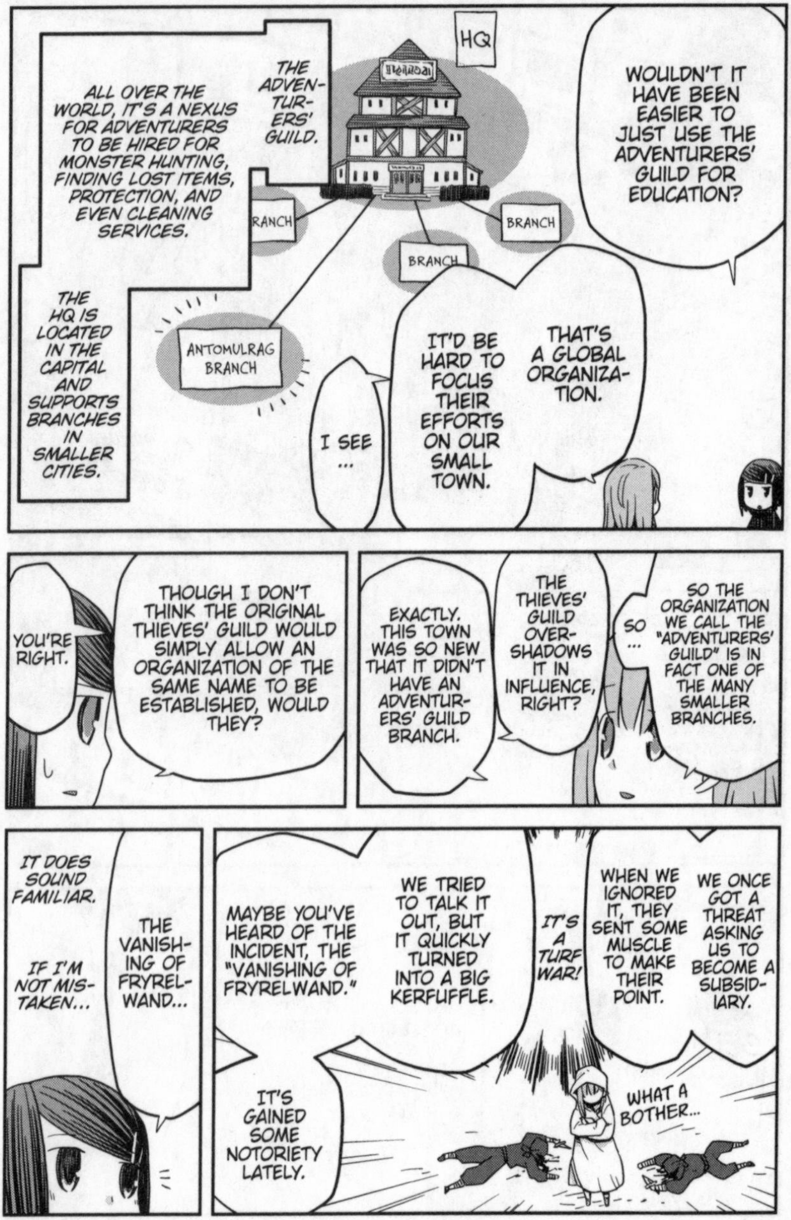
WOULDN'T IT HAVE BEEN EASIER TO JUST USE THE ADVENTURERS' GUILD FOR EDUCATION?
THAT'S A GLOBAL ORGANIZATION.
IT'D BE HARD TO FOCUS THEIR EFFORTS ON OUR SMALL TOWN.
I SEE ...
HQ
THE ADVENTURERS' GUILD.
ALL OVER THE WORLD, IT'S A NEXUS FOR ADVENTURERS TO BE HIRED FOR MONSTER HUNTING, FINDING LOST ITEMS, PROTECTION, AND EVEN CLEANING SERVICES.
BRANCH
BRANCH
BRANCH
ANTOMULRAG BRANCH
THE HQ IS LOCATED IN THE CAPITAL AND SUPPORTS BRANCHES IN SMALLER CITIES.
SO THE ORGANIZATION WE CALL THE "ADVENTURERS' GUILD" IS IN FACT ONE OF THE MANY SMALLER BRANCHES.
SO ...
THE THIEVES' GUILD OVERSHADOWS IT IN INFLUENCE, RIGHT?
EXACTLY. THIS TOWN WAS SO NEW THAT IT DIDN'T HAVE AN ADVENTURERS' GUILD BRANCH.
THOUGH I DON'T THINK THE ORIGINAL THIEVES' GUILD WOULD SIMPLY ALLOW AN ORGANIZATION OF THE SAME NAME TO BE ESTABLISHED, WOULD THEY?
YOU'RE RIGHT.
WE ONCE GOT A THREAT ASKING US TO BECOME A SUBSIDIARY.
WHEN WE IGNORED IT, THEY SENT SOME MUSCLE TO MAKE THEIR POINT.
IT'S A TURF WAR!
WE TRIED TO TALK IT OUT, BUT IT QUICKLY TURNED INTO A BIG KERFUFFLE.
MAYBE YOU'VE HEARD OF THE INCIDENT, THE "VANISHING OF FRYRELWAND."
WHAT A BOTHER...
IT'S GAINED SOME NOTORIETY LATELY.
THE VANISHING OF FRYRELWAND...
IT DOES SOUND FAMILIAR.
IF I'M NOT MISTAKEN...

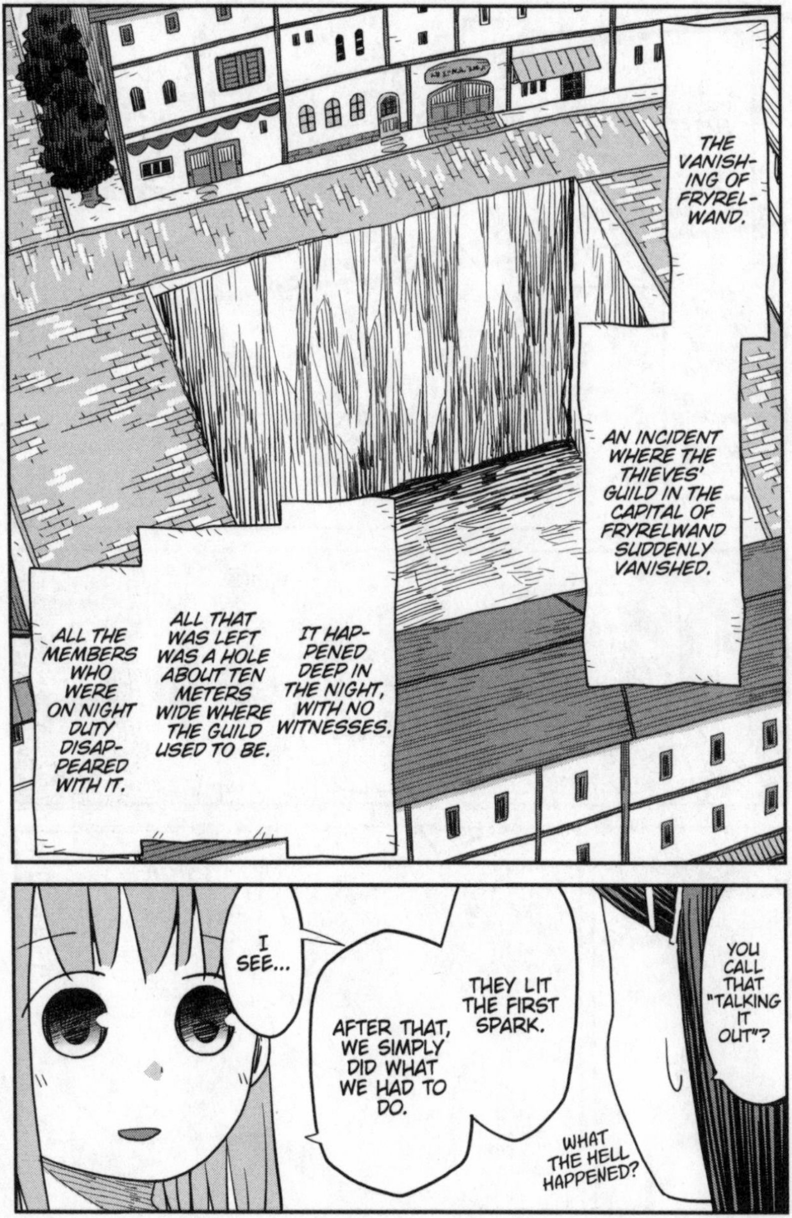
THE VANISHING OF FRYRELWAND.
AN INCIDENT WHERE THE THIEVES' GUILD IN THE CAPITAL OF FRYRELWAND SUDDENLY VANISHED.
IT HAPPENED DEEP IN THE NIGHT, WITH NO WITNESSES.
ALL THAT WAS LEFT WAS A HOLE ABOUT TEN METERS WIDE WHERE THE GUILD USED TO BE.
ALL THE MEMBERS WHO WERE ON NIGHT DUTY DISAPPEARED WITH IT.
YOU CALL THAT "TALKING IT OUT"?
WHAT THE HELL HAPPENED?
THEY LIT THE FIRST SPARK.
AFTER THAT, WE SIMPLY DID WHAT WE HAD TO DO.
I SEE...

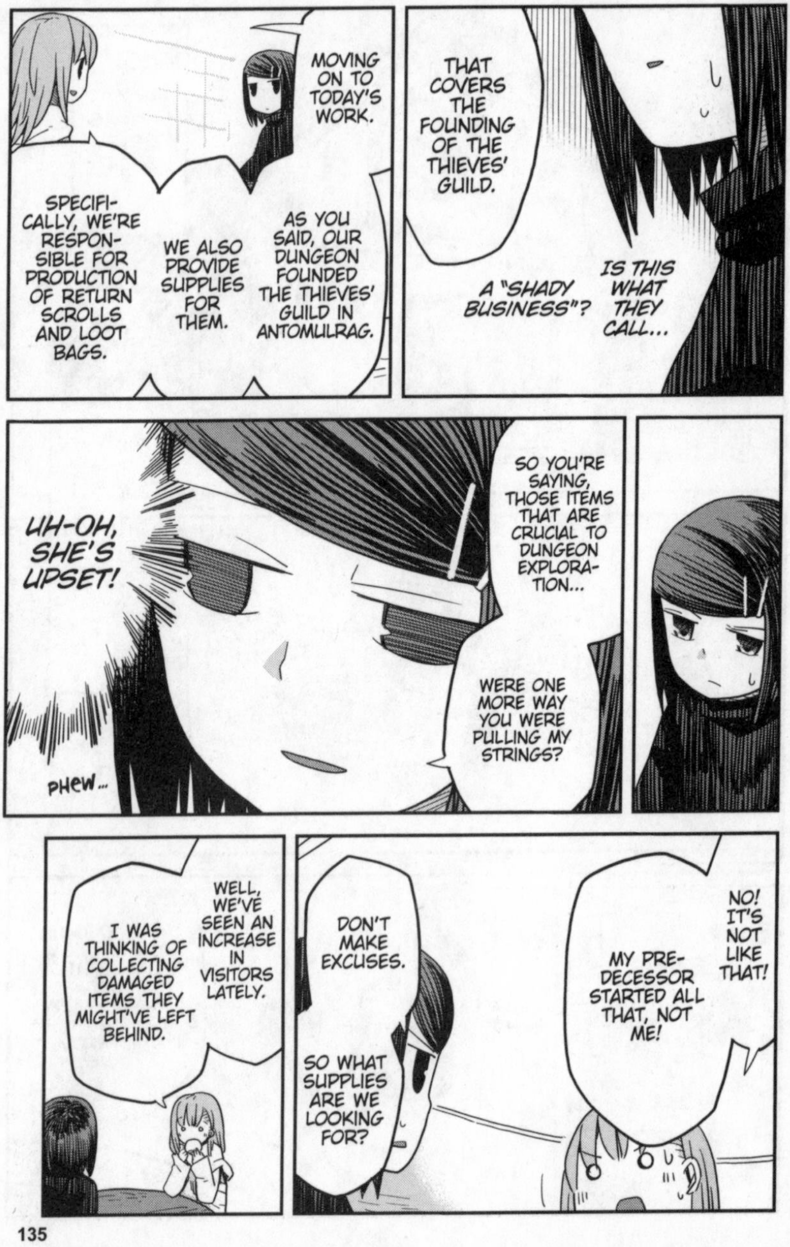
THAT COVERS THE FOUNDING OF THE THIEVES' GUILD.
IS THIS WHAT THEY CALL...
A "SHADY BUSINESS"?
MOVING ON TO TODAY'S WORK.
AS YOU SAID, OUR DUNGEON FOUNDED THE THIEVES' GUILD IN ANTOMULRAG.
WE ALSO PROVIDE SUPPLIES FOR THEM.
SPECIFI-CALLY, WE'RE RESPON-SIBLE FOR PRODUCTION OF RETURN SCROLLS AND LOOT BAGS.
SO YOU'RE SAYING, THOSE ITEMS THAT ARE CRUCIAL TO DUNGEON EXPLORA-TION...
WERE ONE MORE WAY YOU WERE PULLING MY STRINGS?
UH-OH, SHE'S UPSET!
PHEW...
NO! IT'S NOT LIKE THAT!
MY PRE-DECESSOR STARTED ALL THAT, NOT ME!
DON'T MAKE EXCUSES.
SO WHAT SUPPLIES ARE WE LOOKING FOR?
WELL, WE'VE SEEN AN INCREASE IN VISITORS LATELY.
I WAS THINKING OF COLLECTING DAMAGED ITEMS THEY MIGHT'VE LEFT BEHIND.

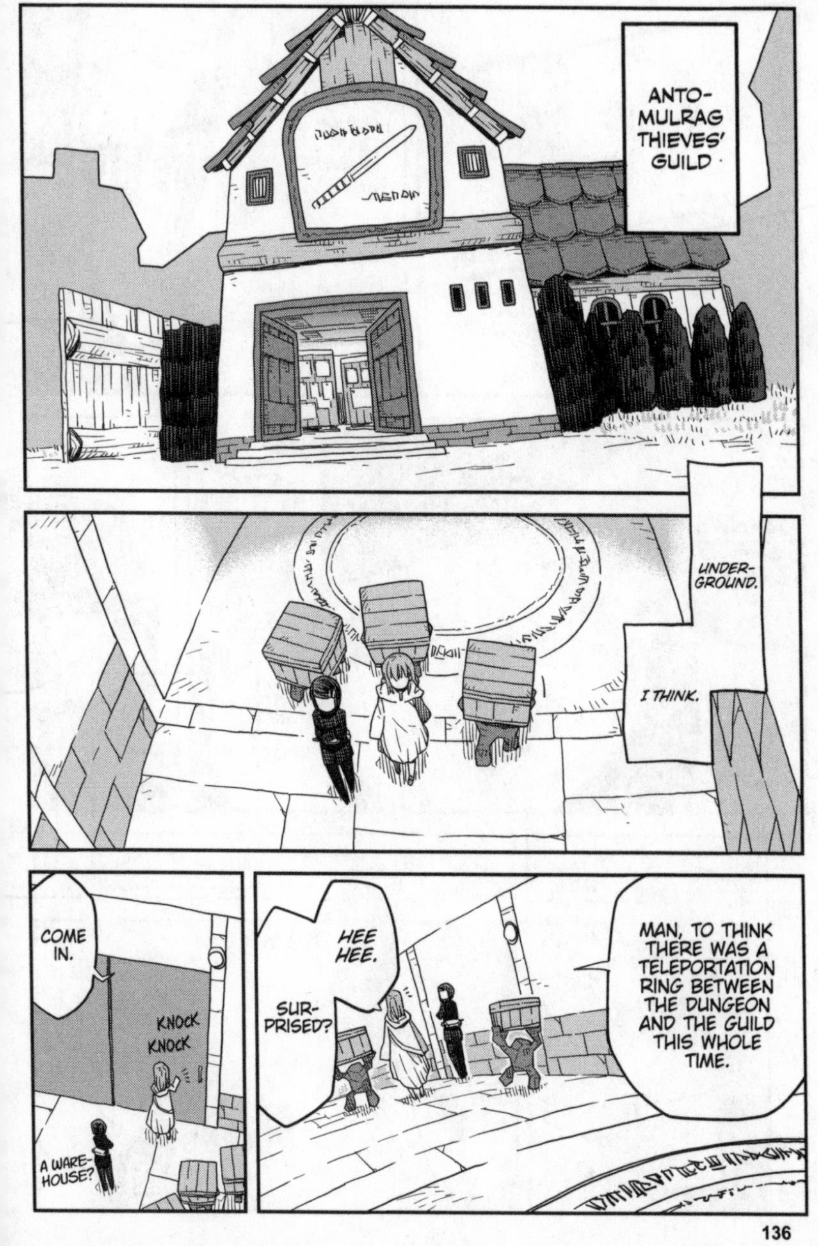
ANTO-MULRAG THIEVES' GUILD
UNDER-GROUND.
I THINK.
MAN, TO THINK THERE WAS A TELEPORTATION RING BETWEEN THE DUNGEON AND THE GUILD THIS WHOLE TIME.
HEE HEE.
SUR-PRISED?
COME IN.
KNOCK KNOCK
A WARE-HOUSE?

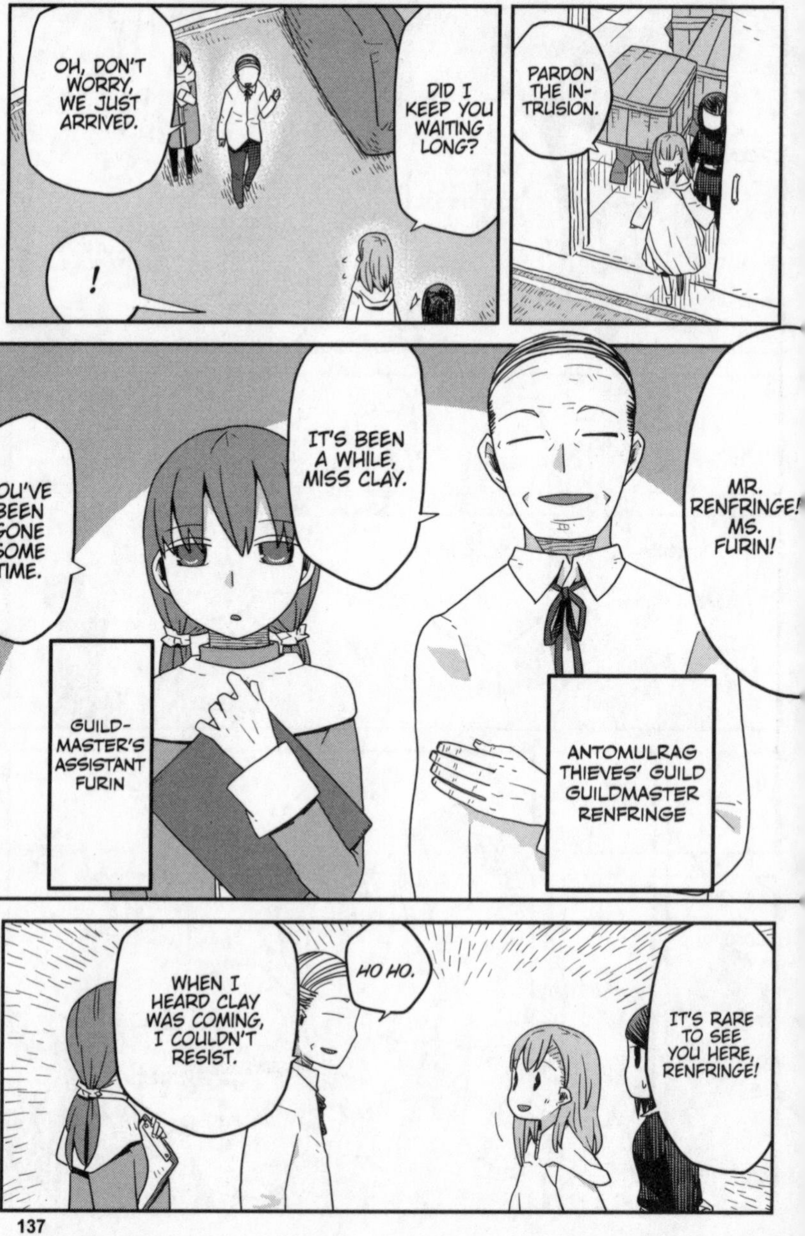
PARDON THE IN-TRUSION.
DID I KEEP YOU WAITING LONG?
OH, DON'T WORRY, WE JUST ARRIVED.
!
MR. RENFRINGE! MS. FURIN!
IT'S BEEN A WHILE, MISS CLAY.
YOU'VE BEEN GONE SOME TIME.
ANTOMULRAG THIEVES' GUILD GUILDMASTER RENFRINGE
GUILD-MASTER'S ASSISTANT FURIN
IT'S RARE TO SEE YOU HERE, RENFRINGE!
HO HO.
WHEN I HEARD CLAY WAS COMING, I COULDN'T RESIST.

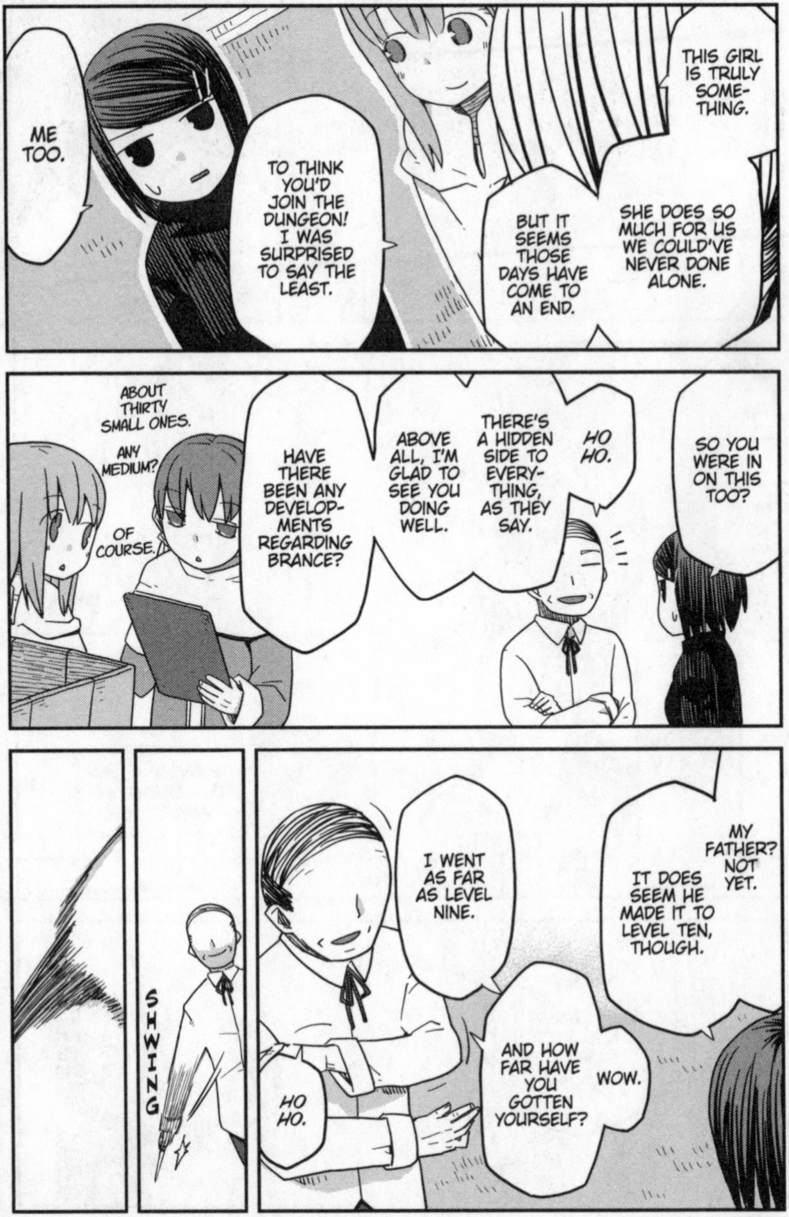
THIS GIRL IS TRULY SOME-THING.
SHE DOES SO MUCH FOR US WE COULD'VE NEVER DONE ALONE.
BUT IT SEEMS THOSE DAYS HAVE COME TO AN END.
TO THINK YOU'D JOIN THE DUNGEON! I WAS SURPRISED TO SAY THE LEAST.
ME TOO.
SO YOU WERE IN ON THIS TOO?
HO HO.
THERE'S A HIDDEN SIDE TO EVERY-THING, AS THEY SAY.
ABOVE ALL, I'M GLAD TO SEE YOU DOING WELL.
HAVE THERE BEEN ANY DEVELOP-MENTS REGARDING BRANCE?
ABOUT THIRTY SMALL ONES.
ANY MEDIUM?
OF COURSE.
MY FATHER? NOT YET.
IT DOES SEEM HE MADE IT TO LEVEL TEN, THOUGH.
I WENT AS FAR AS LEVEL NINE.
WOW.
AND HOW FAR HAVE YOU GOTTEN YOURSELF?
HO HO.
SHWING

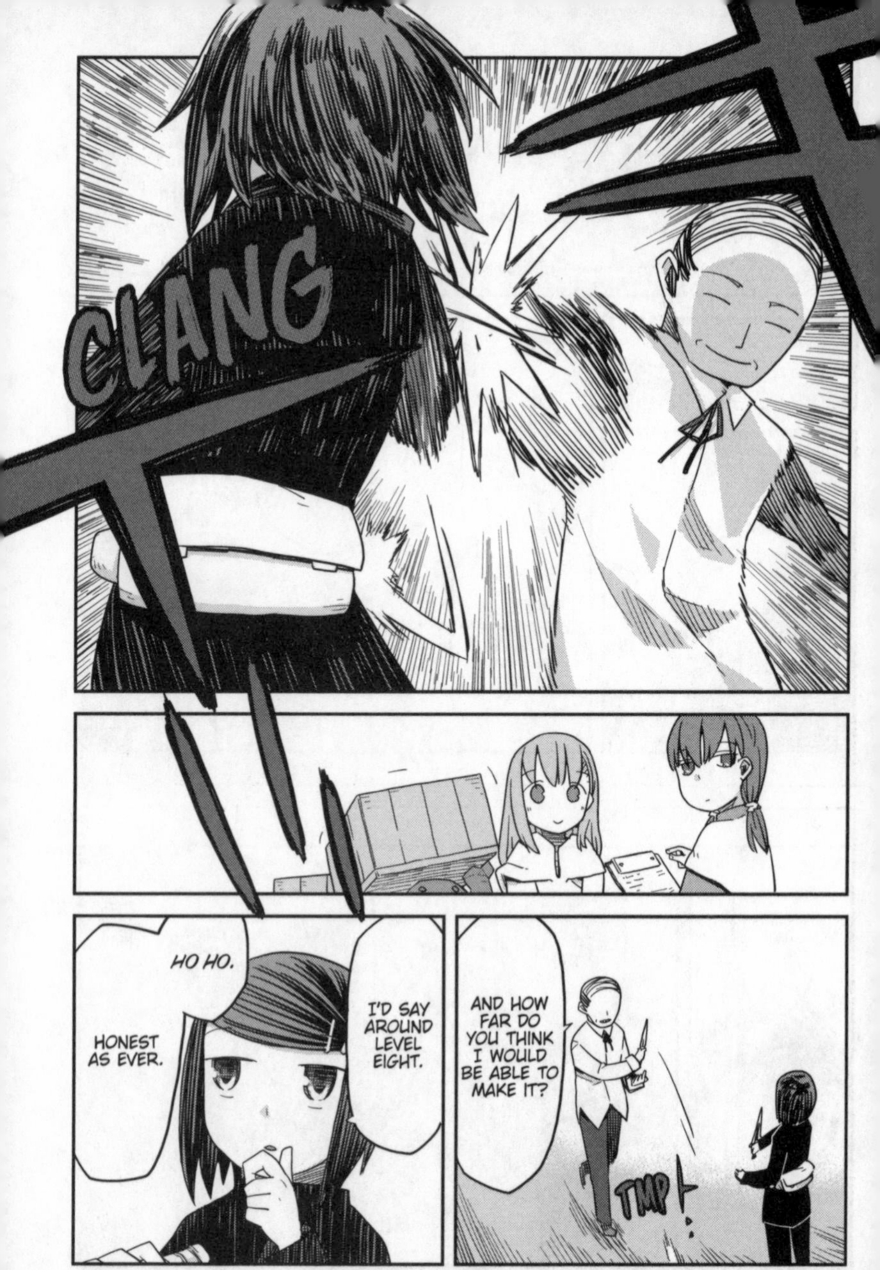
CLANG
AND HOW FAR DO YOU THINK I WOULD BE ABLE TO MAKE IT?
TMP
I'D SAY AROUND LEVEL EIGHT.
HO HO.
HONEST AS EVER.

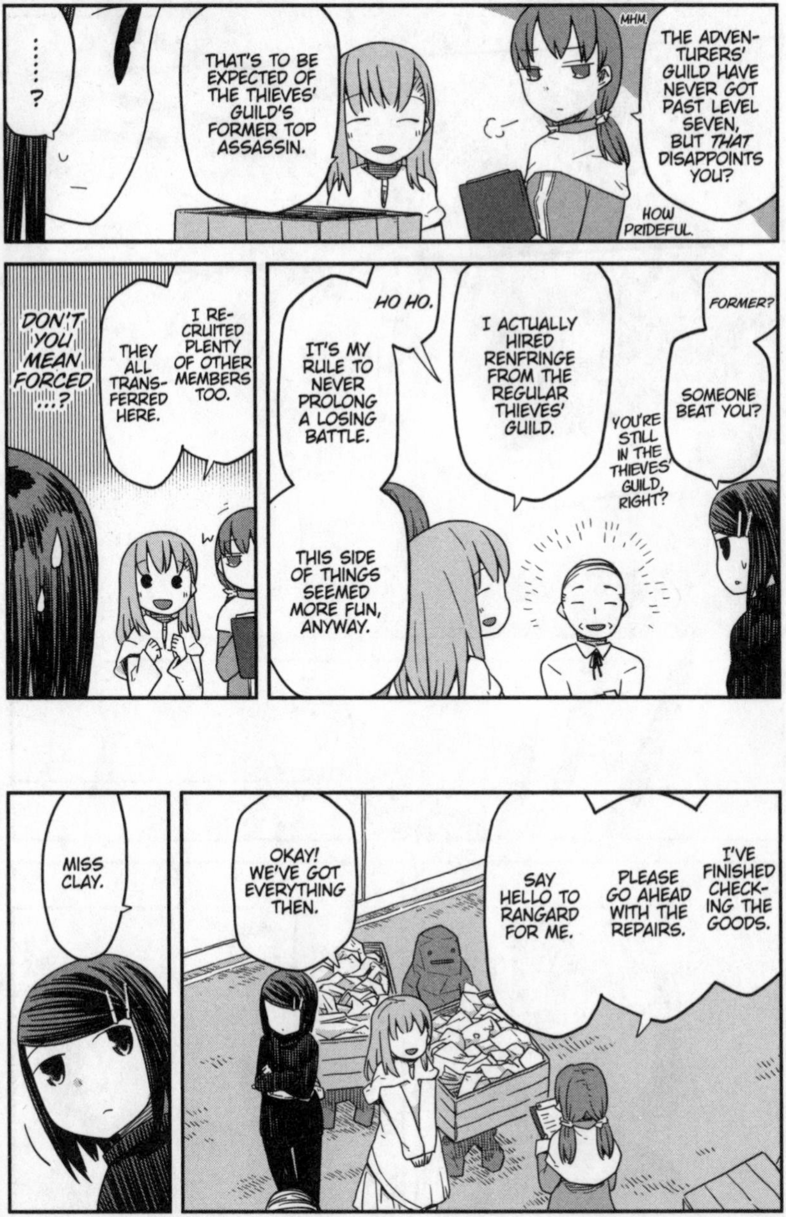
THE ADVEN-TURERS' GUILD HAVE NEVER GOT PAST LEVEL SEVEN, BUT *THAT* DISAPPOINTS YOU?
MHM.
HOW PRIDEFUL.
THAT'S TO BE EXPECTED OF THE THIEVES' GUILD'S FORMER TOP ASSASSIN.
......?
FORMER?
SOMEONE BEAT YOU?
YOU'RE STILL IN THE THIEVES' GUILD, RIGHT?
I ACTUALLY HIRED RENFRINGE FROM THE REGULAR THIEVES' GUILD.
HO HO.
IT'S MY RULE TO NEVER PROLONG A LOSING BATTLE.
THIS SIDE OF THINGS SEEMED MORE FUN, ANYWAY.
I RE-CRUITED PLENTY OF OTHER MEMBERS TOO.
THEY ALL TRANS-FERRED HERE.
DON'T YOU MEAN FORCED ...?
I'VE FINISHED CHECK-ING THE GOODS.
PLEASE GO AHEAD WITH THE REPAIRS.
SAY HELLO TO RANGARD FOR ME.
OKAY! WE'VE GOT EVERYTHING THEN.
MISS CLAY.

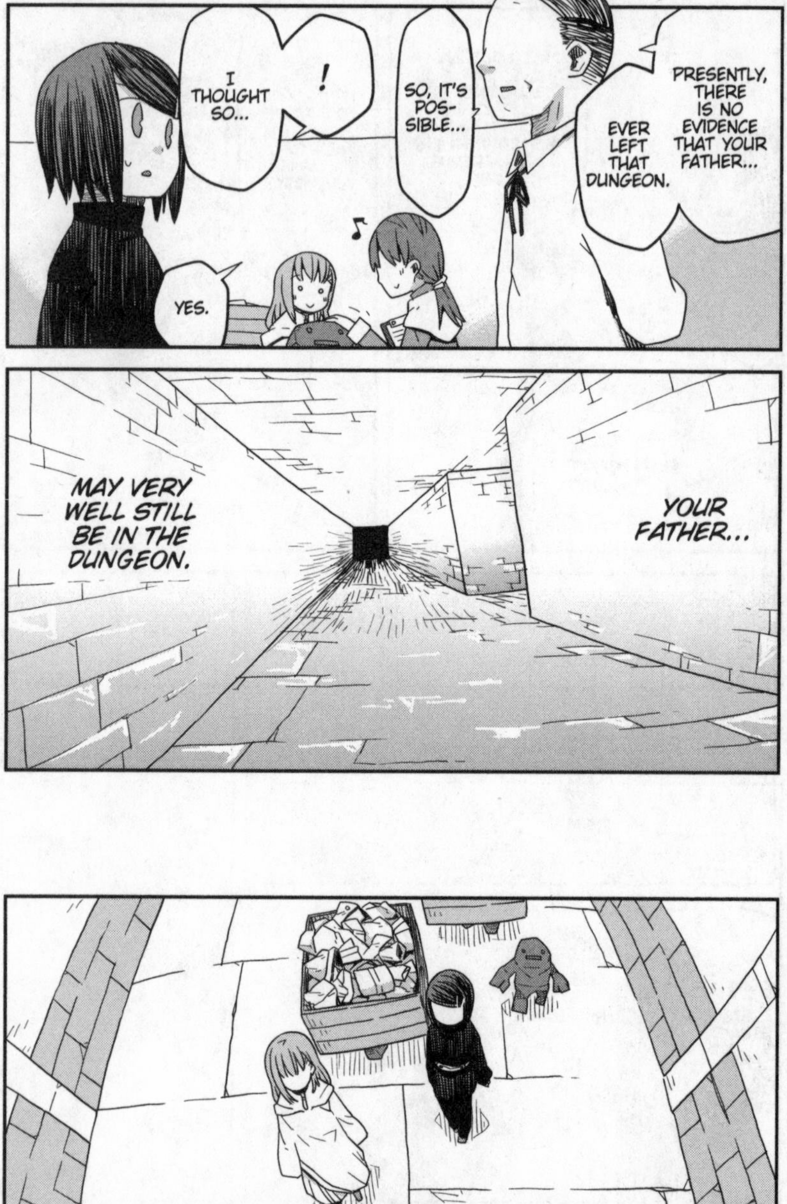
PRESENTLY, THERE IS NO EVIDENCE THAT YOUR FATHER...
EVER LEFT THAT DUNGEON.
SO, IT'S POS-SIBLE...
!
I THOUGHT SO...
YES.
YOUR FATHER...
MAY VERY WELL STILL BE IN THE DUNGEON.

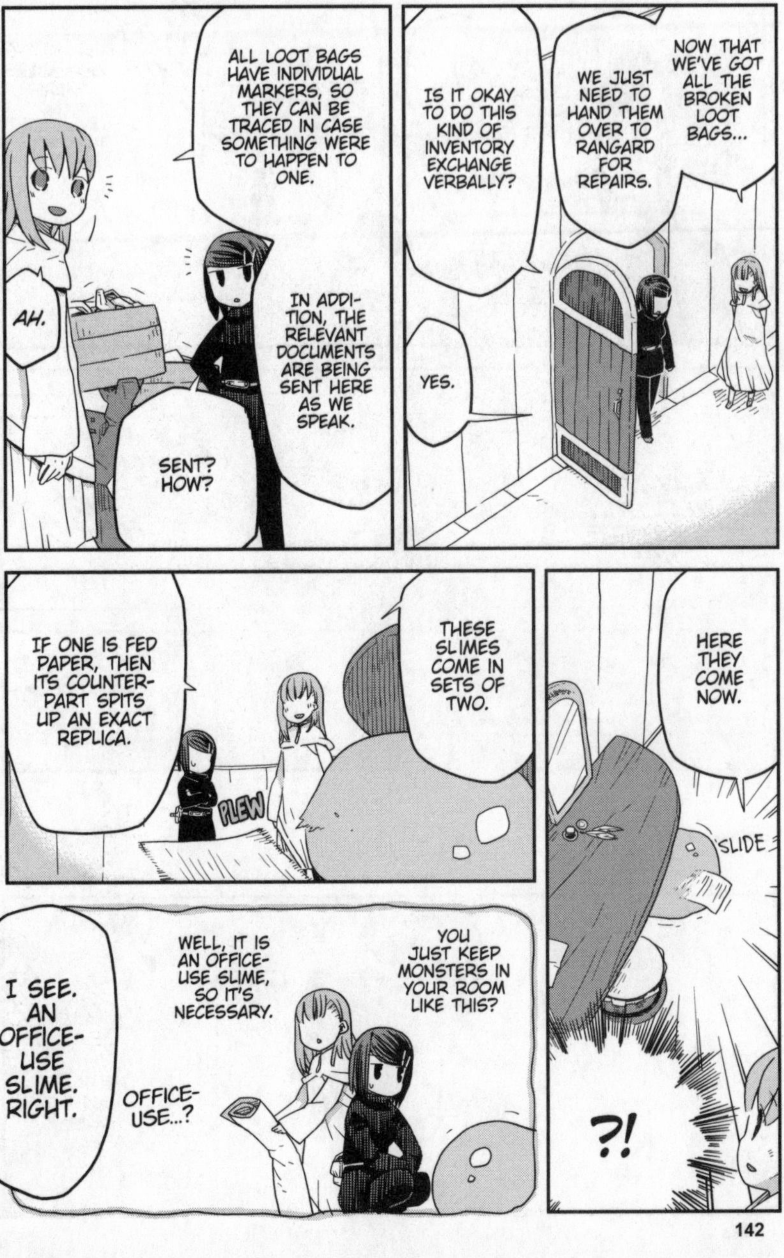
NOW THAT WE'VE GOT ALL THE BROKEN LOOT BAGS...
WE JUST NEED TO HAND THEM OVER TO RANGARD FOR REPAIRS.
IS IT OKAY TO DO THIS KIND OF INVENTORY EXCHANGE VERBALLY?
YES.
ALL LOOT BAGS HAVE INDIVIDUAL MARKERS, SO THEY CAN BE TRACED IN CASE SOMETHING WERE TO HAPPEN TO ONE.
IN ADDITION, THE RELEVANT DOCUMENTS ARE BEING SENT HERE AS WE SPEAK.
AH.
SENT? HOW?
HERE THEY COME NOW.
SLIDE
?!
THESE SLIMES COME IN SETS OF TWO.
IF ONE IS FED PAPER, THEN ITS COUNTERPART SPITS UP AN EXACT REPLICA.
PLEW
YOU JUST KEEP MONSTERS IN YOUR ROOM LIKE THIS?
WELL, IT IS AN OFFICE-USE SLIME, SO IT'S NECESSARY.
I SEE. AN OFFICE-USE SLIME. RIGHT.
OFFICE-USE...?

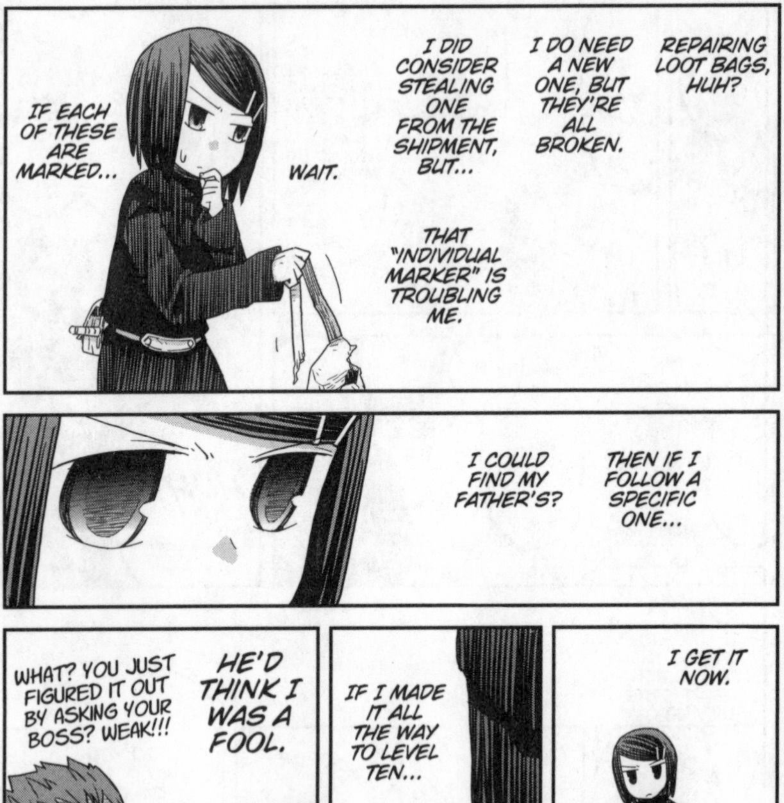
REPAIRING LOOT BAGS, HUH?
I DO NEED A NEW ONE, BUT THEY'RE ALL BROKEN.
I DID CONSIDER STEALING ONE FROM THE SHIPMENT, BUT...
THAT "INDIVIDUAL MARKER" IS TROUBLING ME.
WAIT.
IF EACH OF THESE ARE MARKED...
THEN IF I FOLLOW A SPECIFIC ONE...
I COULD FIND MY FATHER'S?
I GET IT NOW.
TOSS
MY FATHER DEFINITELY MADE IT TO LEVEL TEN.
HE MUST HAVE FOUGHT BELLE, TOO.
AND THEN...
IF I MADE IT ALL THE WAY TO LEVEL TEN...
AND JUST SETTLED IT ALL BY ASKING BELLE.
MY FATHER...
HE'D THINK I WAS A FOOL.
WHAT? YOU JUST FIGURED IT OUT BY ASKING YOUR BOSS? WEAK!!!
IS SOME- THING WRONG?

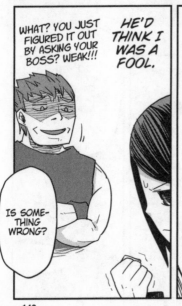

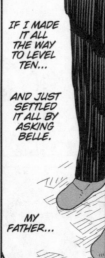

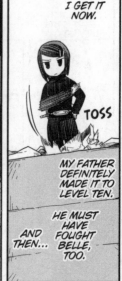

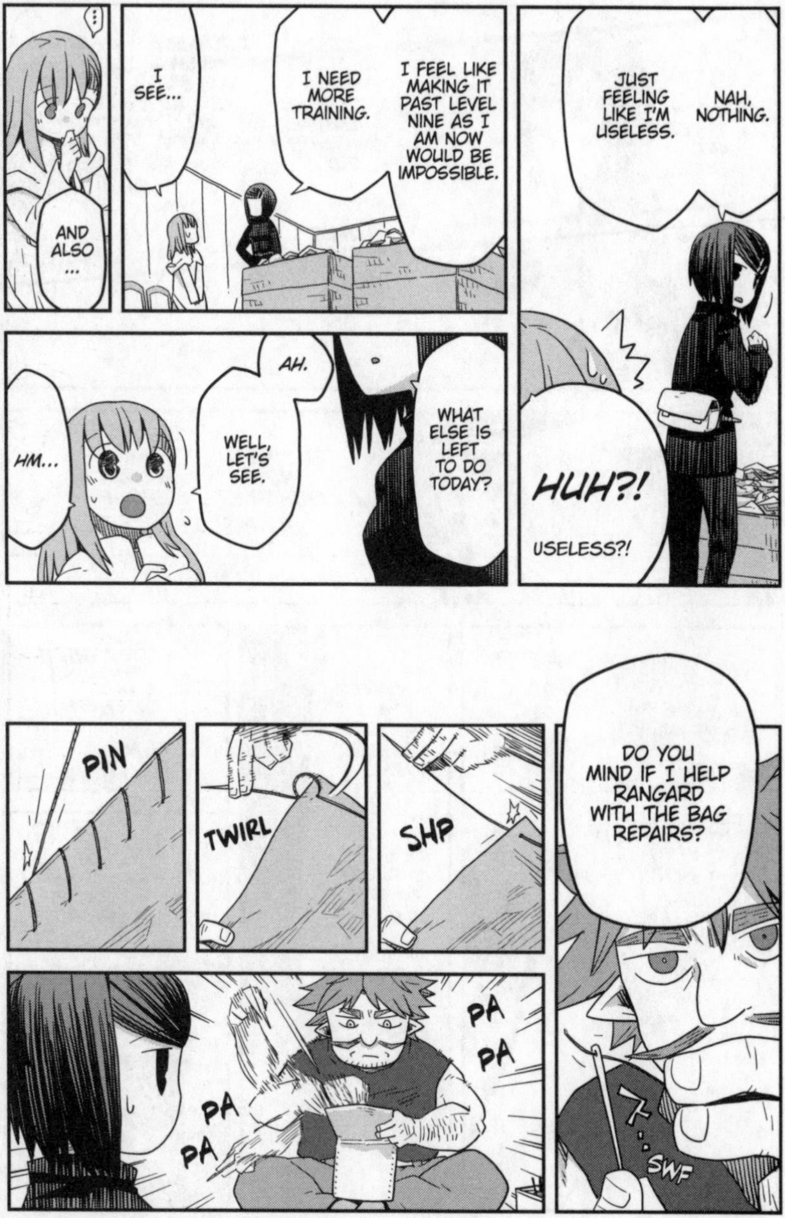
NAH, NOTHING.
JUST FEELING LIKE I'M USELESS.
HUH?!
USELESS?!
I FEEL LIKE MAKING IT PAST LEVEL NINE AS I AM NOW WOULD BE IMPOSSIBLE.
I NEED MORE TRAINING.
I SEE...
...
AND ALSO ...
WHAT ELSE IS LEFT TO DO TODAY?
AH.
WELL, LET'S SEE.
HM...
DO YOU MIND IF I HELP RANGARD WITH THE BAG REPAIRS?
SWF
SHP
TWIRL
PIN
PA
PA
PA
PA

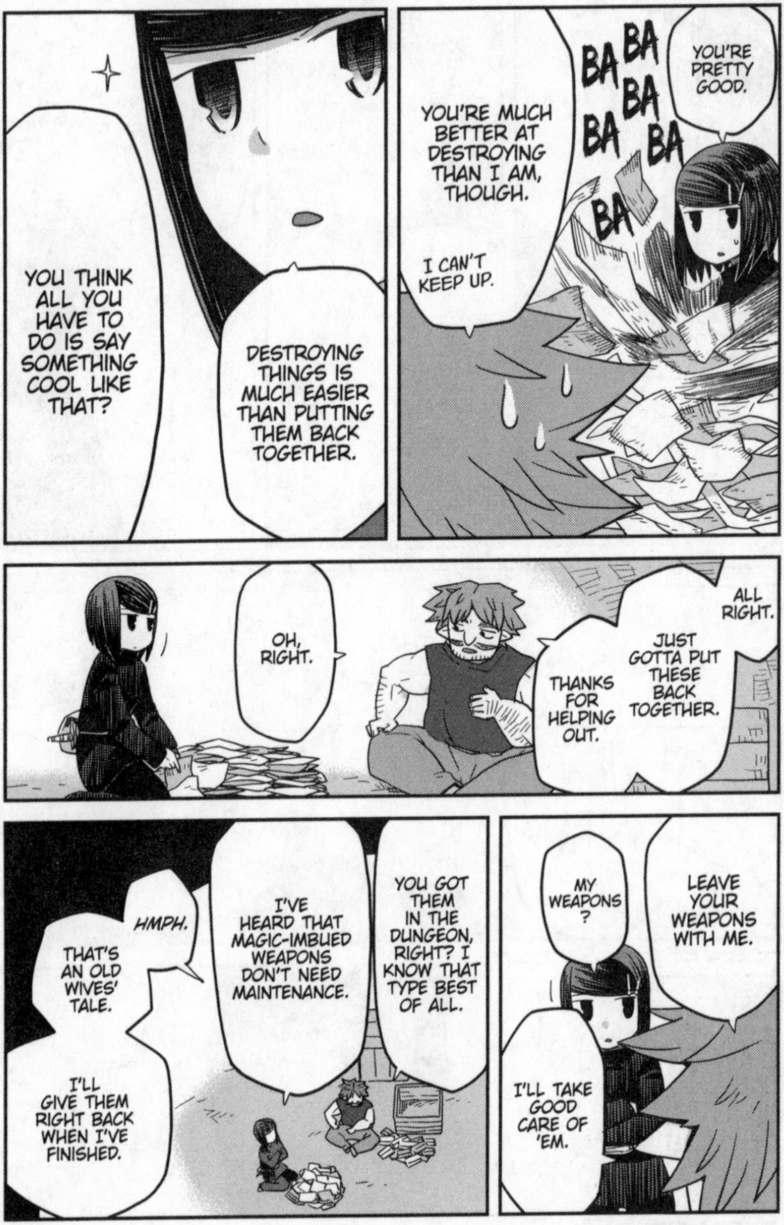
YOU'RE PRETTY GOOD.
BA BA BA BA BA BA
YOU'RE MUCH BETTER AT DESTROYING THAN I AM, THOUGH.
I CAN'T KEEP UP.
DESTROYING THINGS IS MUCH EASIER THAN PUTTING THEM BACK TOGETHER.
YOU THINK ALL YOU HAVE TO DO IS SAY SOMETHING COOL LIKE THAT?
ALL RIGHT.
JUST GOTTA PUT THESE BACK TOGETHER.
THANKS FOR HELPING OUT.
OH, RIGHT.
LEAVE YOUR WEAPONS WITH ME.
MY WEAPONS ?
I'LL TAKE GOOD CARE OF 'EM.
YOU GOT THEM IN THE DUNGEON, RIGHT? I KNOW THAT TYPE BEST OF ALL.
I'VE HEARD THAT MAGIC-IMBUED WEAPONS DON'T NEED MAINTENANCE.
HMPH.
THAT'S AN OLD WIVES' TALE.
I'LL GIVE THEM RIGHT BACK WHEN I'VE FINISHED.

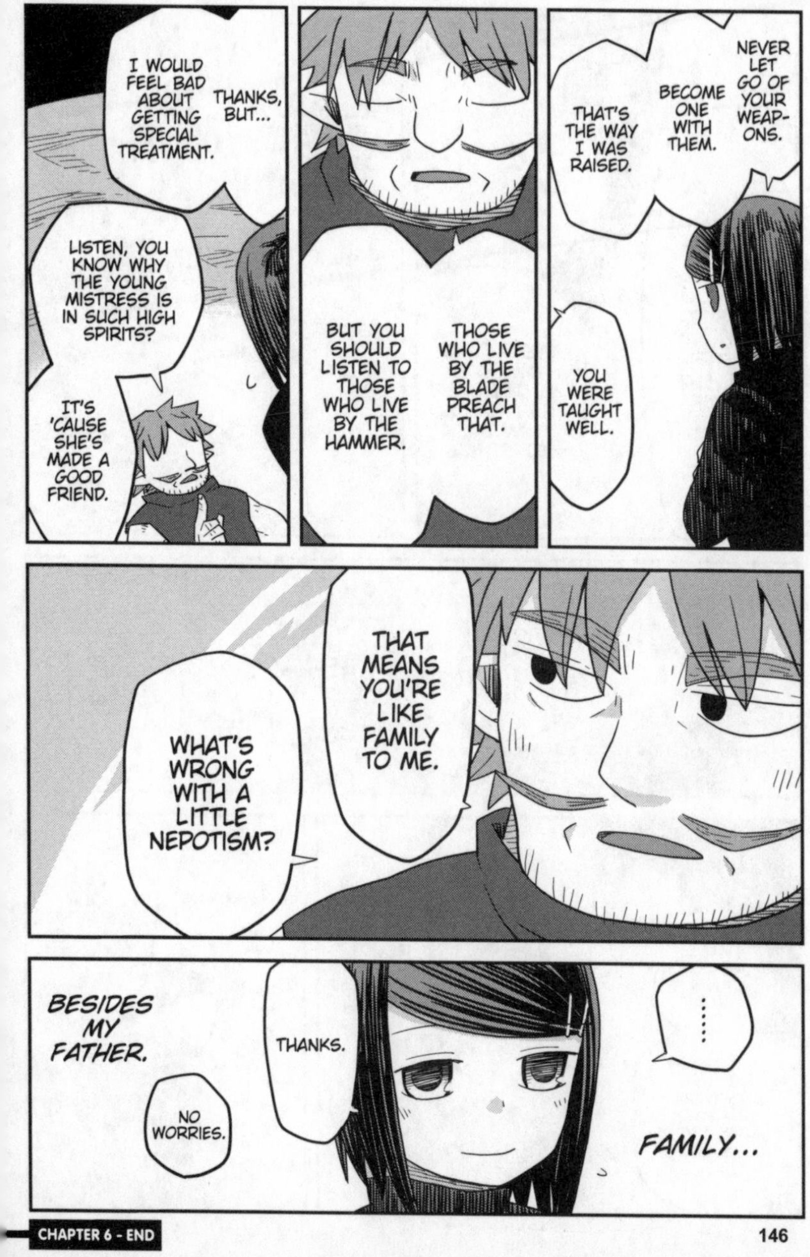
NEVER LET GO OF YOUR WEAPONS.
BECOME ONE WITH THEM.
THAT'S THE WAY I WAS RAISED.
YOU WERE TAUGHT WELL.
THOSE WHO LIVE BY THE BLADE PREACH THAT.
BUT YOU SHOULD LISTEN TO THOSE WHO LIVE BY THE HAMMER.
THANKS, BUT...
I WOULD FEEL BAD ABOUT GETTING SPECIAL TREATMENT.
LISTEN, YOU KNOW WHY THE YOUNG MISTRESS IS IN SUCH HIGH SPIRITS?
IT'S 'CAUSE SHE'S MADE A GOOD FRIEND.
THAT MEANS YOU'RE LIKE FAMILY TO ME.
WHAT'S WRONG WITH A LITTLE NEPOTISM?
......
THANKS.
NO WORRIES.
FAMILY...
BESIDES MY FATHER.

CHAPTER 6 - END

I MADE SUCH A FUSS ABOUT IT, BUT THIS THING'S BASICALLY PERFECT. THERE'S NOTHING THAT NEEDS TOUCHING UP AT ALL.
THAT GIRL IS AN UTTER PERFECTIONIST.

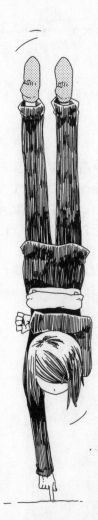

WHILE MY WEAPONS ARE IN THE SHOP...

I SHOULD WORK ON MY INNER BALANCE.

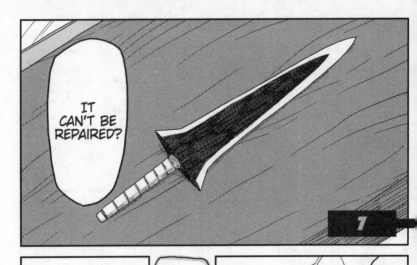

IT CAN'T BE REPAIRED?
NO.
OR, RATHER, THERE'S NO NEED.
NO NEED?
THERE'S A SECRET REASON WHY.
WOULD YOU LIKE TO KNOW?
UM.
I MEAN, YEAH ...
Weapons and their masters ...
......
need to be evenly matched in strength.
I WANT TO KNOW.
PLEASE TELL ME.
UNDER-STOOD.

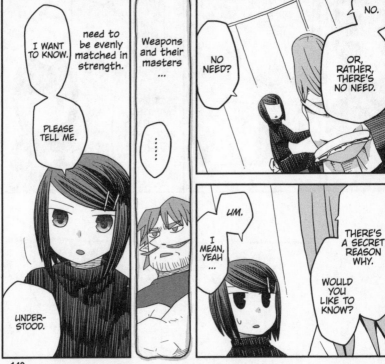

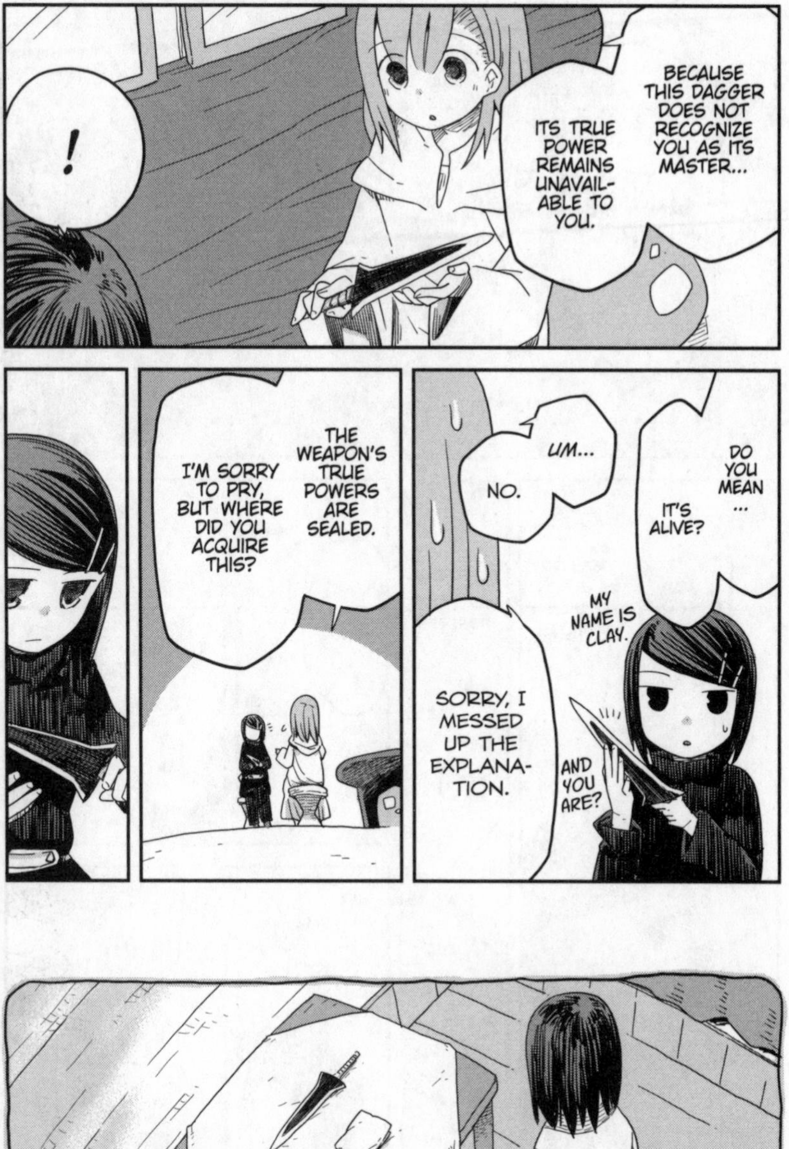
BECAUSE THIS DAGGER DOES NOT RECOGNIZE YOU AS ITS MASTER...
ITS TRUE POWER REMAINS UNAVAILABLE TO YOU.
!
DO YOU MEAN ...
IT'S ALIVE?
UM...
NO.
SORRY, I MESSED UP THE EXPLANATION.
MY NAME IS CLAY.
AND YOU ARE?
THE WEAPON'S TRUE POWERS ARE SEALED.
I'M SORRY TO PRY, BUT WHERE DID YOU ACQUIRE THIS?

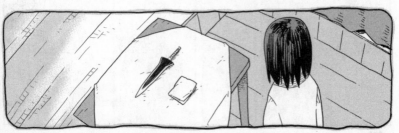

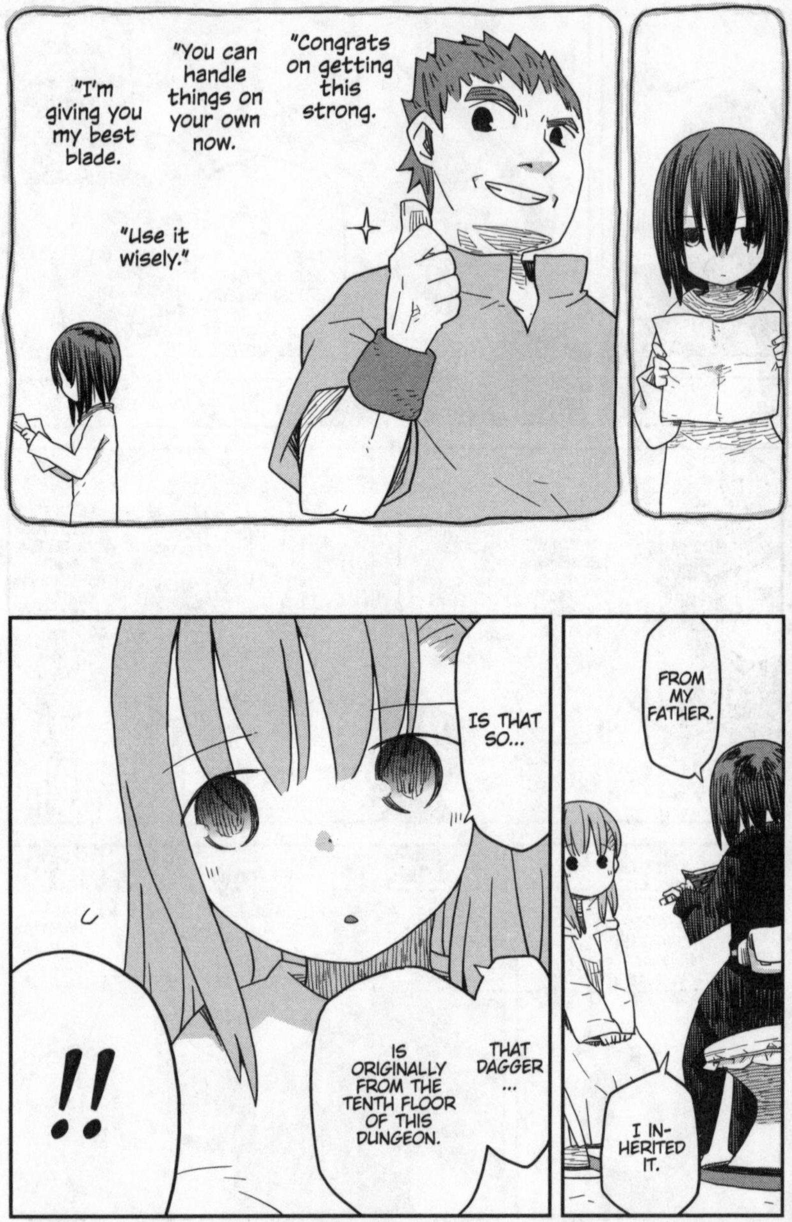
"Congrats on getting this strong.
"You can handle things on your own now.
"I'm giving you my best blade.
"Use it wisely."
FROM MY FATHER.
I IN-HERITED IT.
IS THAT SO...
THAT DAGGER ...
IS ORIGINALLY FROM THE TENTH FLOOR OF THIS DUNGEON.
!!

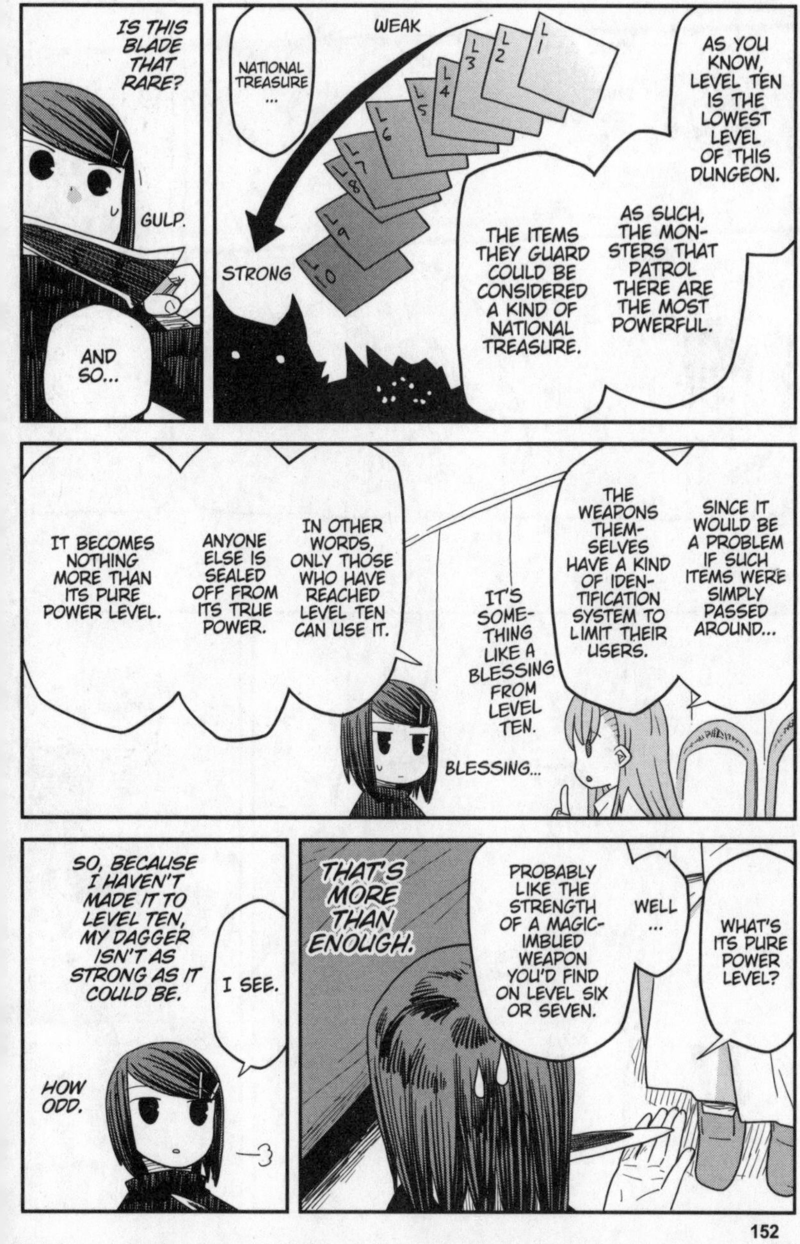
AS YOU KNOW, LEVEL TEN IS THE LOWEST LEVEL OF THIS DUNGEON.
AS SUCH, THE MONSTERS THAT PATROL THERE ARE THE MOST POWERFUL.
THE ITEMS THEY GUARD COULD BE CONSIDERED A KIND OF NATIONAL TREASURE.
WEAK
L1
L2
L3
L4
L5
L6
L7
L8
L9
L10
STRONG
NATIONAL TREASURE ...
IS THIS BLADE THAT RARE?
GULP.
AND SO...
SINCE IT WOULD BE A PROBLEM IF SUCH ITEMS WERE SIMPLY PASSED AROUND...
THE WEAPONS THEMSELVES HAVE A KIND OF IDENTIFICATION SYSTEM TO LIMIT THEIR USERS.
IT'S SOMETHING LIKE A BLESSING FROM LEVEL TEN.
BLESSING...
IN OTHER WORDS, ONLY THOSE WHO HAVE REACHED LEVEL TEN CAN USE IT.
ANYONE ELSE IS SEALED OFF FROM ITS TRUE POWER.
IT BECOMES NOTHING MORE THAN ITS PURE POWER LEVEL.
WHAT'S ITS PURE POWER LEVEL?
WELL ...
PROBABLY LIKE THE STRENGTH OF A MAGIC-IMBUED WEAPON YOU'D FIND ON LEVEL SIX OR SEVEN.
THAT'S MORE THAN ENOUGH.
SO, BECAUSE I HAVEN'T MADE IT TO LEVEL TEN, MY DAGGER ISN'T AS STRONG AS IT COULD BE.
I SEE.
HOW ODD.

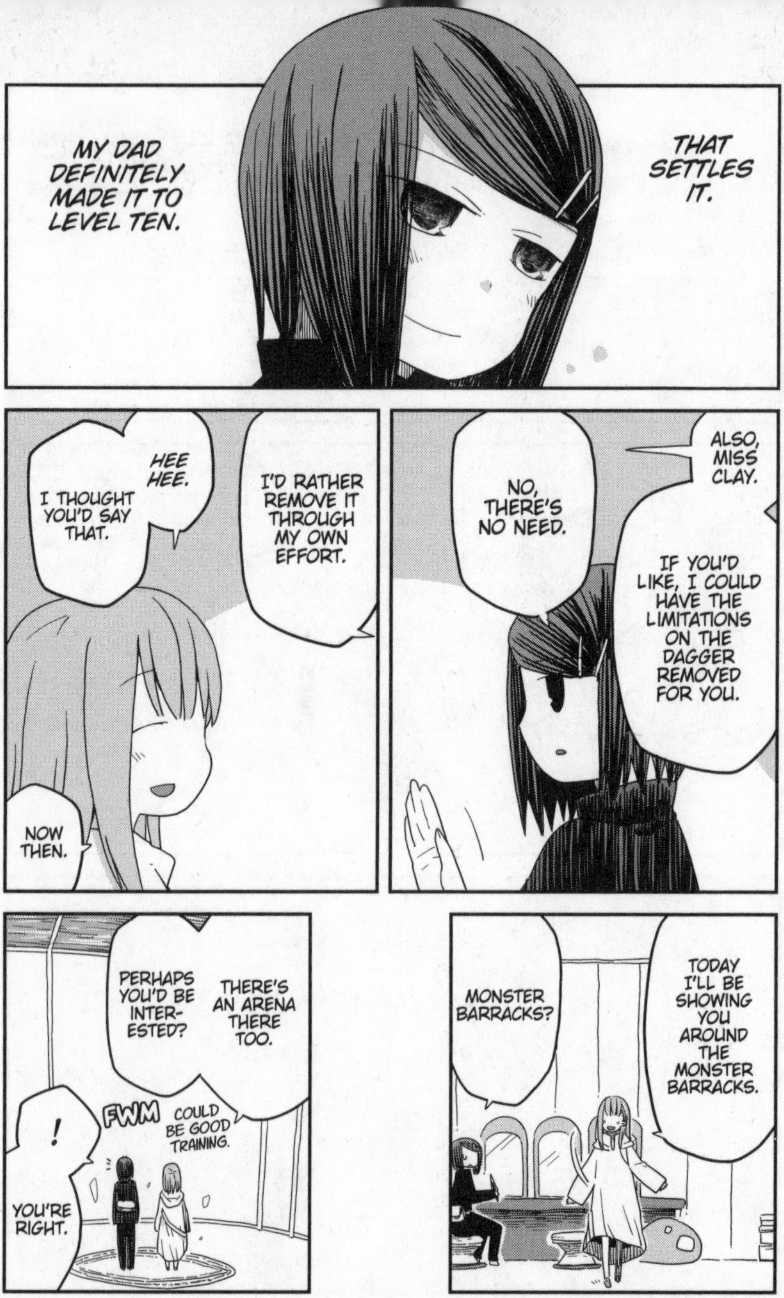
THAT SETTLES IT.
MY DAD DEFINITELY MADE IT TO LEVEL TEN.
ALSO, MISS CLAY.
IF YOU'D LIKE, I COULD HAVE THE LIMITATIONS ON THE DAGGER REMOVED FOR YOU.
NO, THERE'S NO NEED.
I'D RATHER REMOVE IT THROUGH MY OWN EFFORT.
HEE HEE.
I THOUGHT YOU'D SAY THAT.
NOW THEN.
TODAY I'LL BE SHOWING YOU AROUND THE MONSTER BARRACKS.
MONSTER BARRACKS?
THERE'S AN ARENA THERE TOO.
PERHAPS YOU'D BE INTER-ESTED?
FWM
COULD BE GOOD TRAINING.
!
YOU'RE RIGHT.

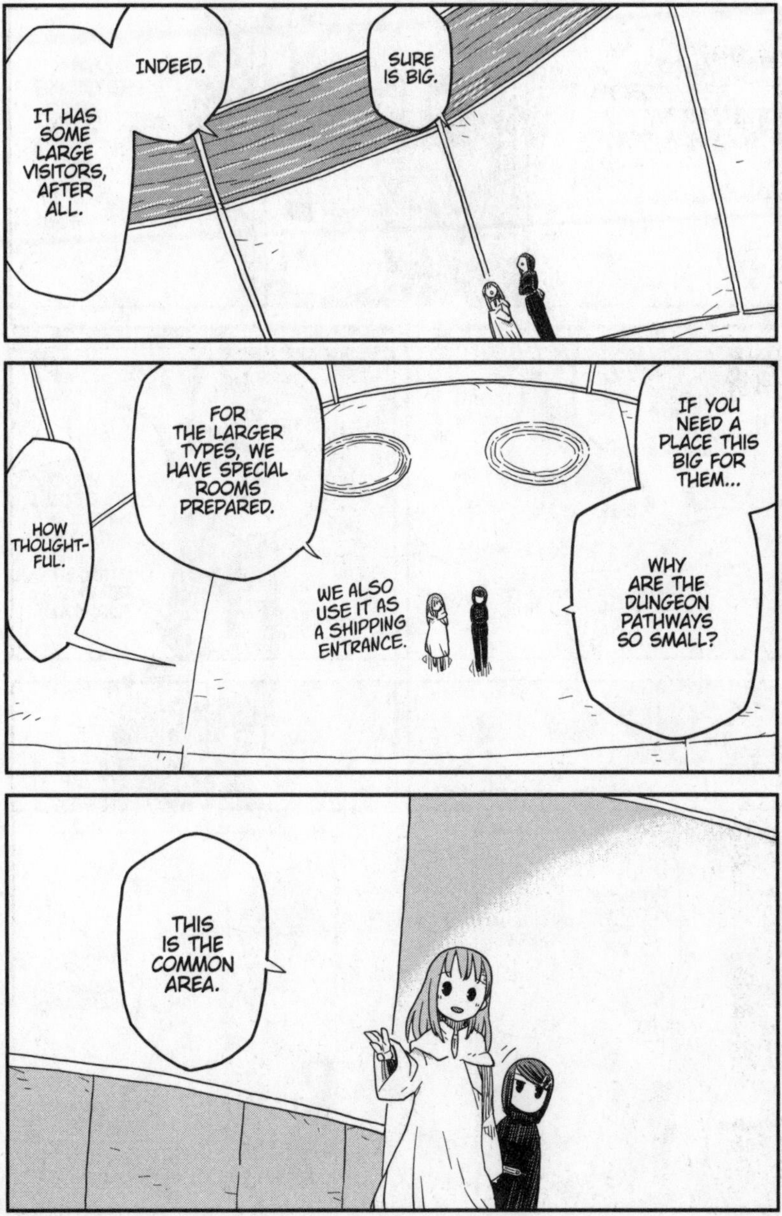
SURE IS BIG.
INDEED.
IT HAS SOME LARGE VISITORS, AFTER ALL.
IF YOU NEED A PLACE THIS BIG FOR THEM...
WHY ARE THE DUNGEON PATHWAYS SO SMALL?
WE ALSO USE IT AS A SHIPPING ENTRANCE.
FOR THE LARGER TYPES, WE HAVE SPECIAL ROOMS PREPARED.
HOW THOUGHTFUL.
THIS IS THE COMMON AREA.

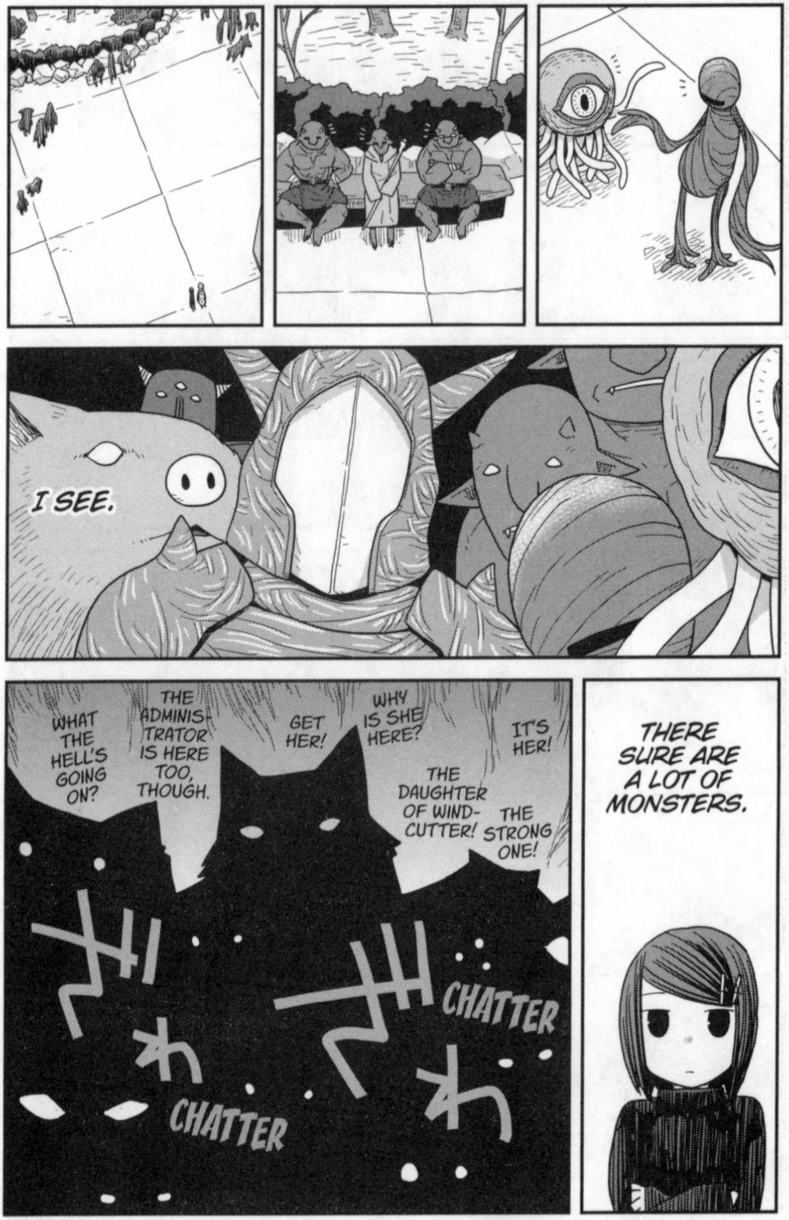
I SEE.
THERE SURE ARE A LOT OF MONSTERS.
IT'S HER!
THE STRONG ONE!
WHY IS SHE HERE?
THE DAUGHTER OF WIND-CUTTER!
GET HER!
THE ADMINISTRATOR IS HERE TOO, THOUGH.
WHAT THE HELL'S GOING ON?
ざわ
CHATTER
ざわ
CHATTER

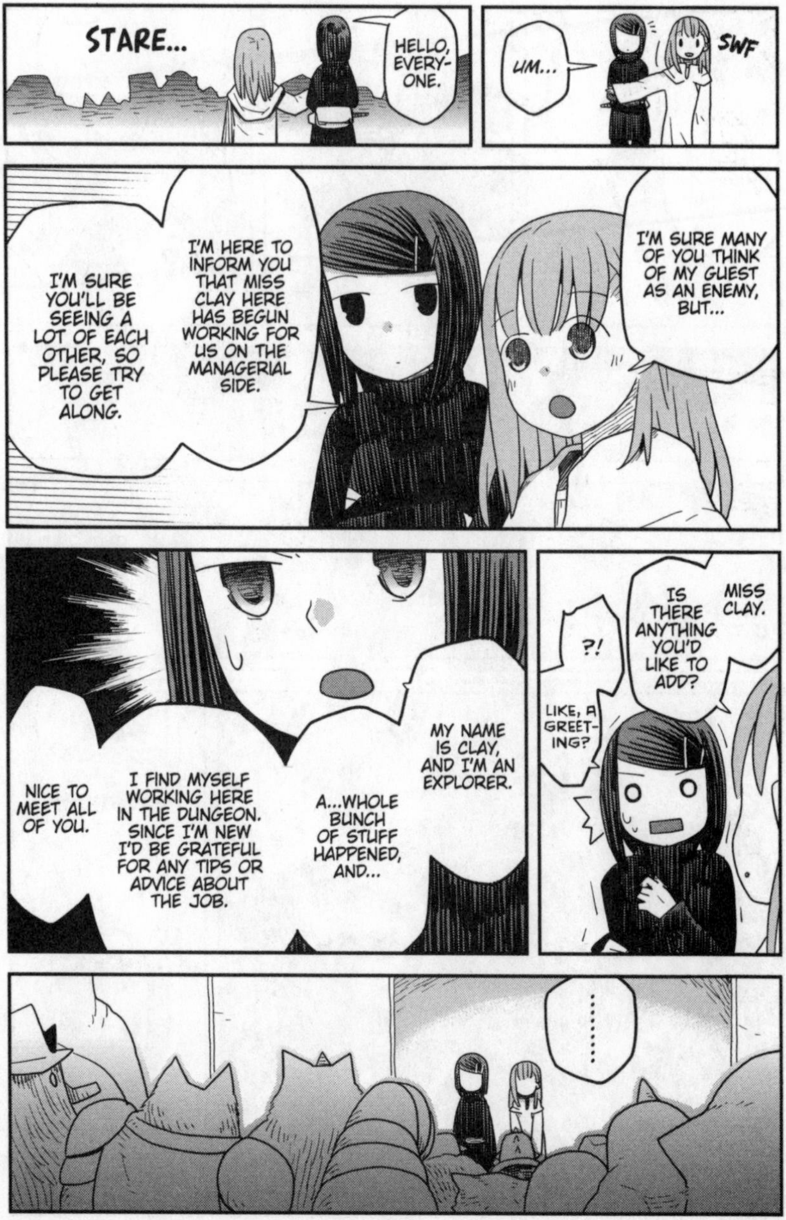
SWF
UM...
HELLO, EVERYONE.
STARE...
I'M SURE MANY OF YOU THINK OF MY GUEST AS AN ENEMY, BUT...
I'M HERE TO INFORM YOU THAT MISS CLAY HERE HAS BEGUN WORKING FOR US ON THE MANAGERIAL SIDE.
I'M SURE YOU'LL BE SEEING A LOT OF EACH OTHER, SO PLEASE TRY TO GET ALONG.
MISS CLAY.
IS THERE ANYTHING YOU'D LIKE TO ADD?
?!
LIKE, A GREETING?
MY NAME IS CLAY, AND I'M AN EXPLORER.
A...WHOLE BUNCH OF STUFF HAPPENED, AND...
I FIND MYSELF WORKING HERE IN THE DUNGEON. SINCE I'M NEW I'D BE GRATEFUL FOR ANY TIPS OR ADVICE ABOUT THE JOB.
NICE TO MEET ALL OF YOU.
......

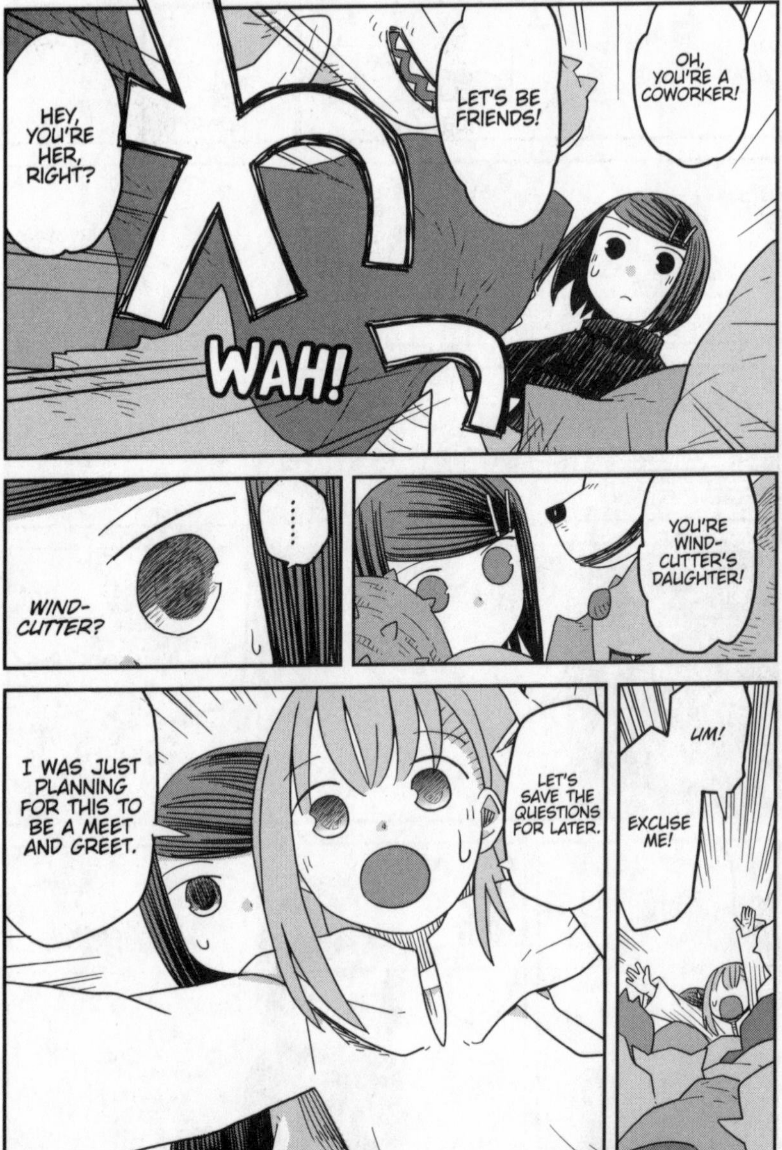
OH, YOU'RE A COWORKER!
LET'S BE FRIENDS!
HEY, YOU'RE HER, RIGHT?
WAH!
YOU'RE WIND-CUTTER'S DAUGHTER!
......
WIND-CUTTER?
UM!
EXCUSE ME!
LET'S SAVE THE QUESTIONS FOR LATER.
I WAS JUST PLANNING FOR THIS TO BE A MEET AND GREET.

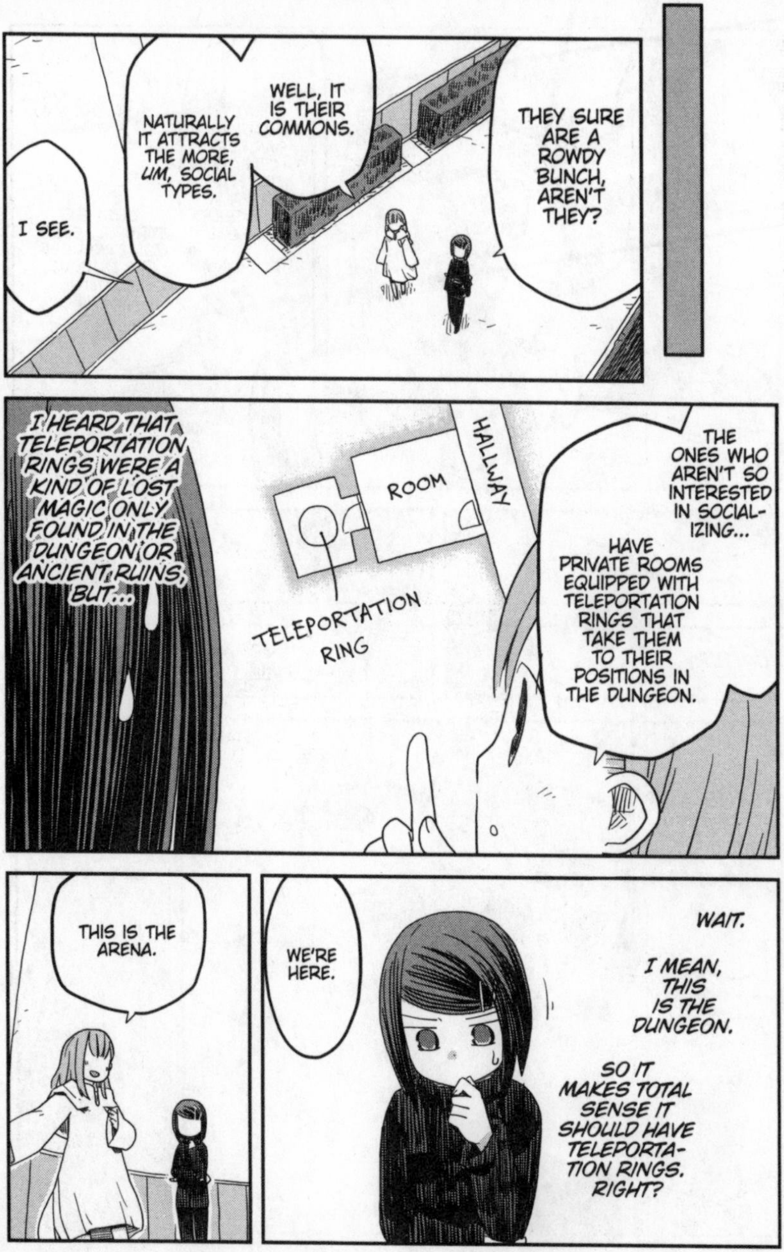
THEY SURE ARE A ROWDY BUNCH, AREN'T THEY?
WELL, IT IS THEIR COMMONS.
NATURALLY IT ATTRACTS THE MORE, UM, SOCIAL TYPES.
I SEE.
THE ONES WHO AREN'T SO INTERESTED IN SOCIAL-IZING...
HAVE PRIVATE ROOMS EQUIPPED WITH TELEPORTATION RINGS THAT TAKE THEM TO THEIR POSITIONS IN THE DUNGEON.
HALLWAY
ROOM
TELEPORTATION RING
I HEARD THAT TELEPORTATION RINGS WERE A KIND OF LOST MAGIC ONLY FOUND IN THE DUNGEON OR ANCIENT RUINS, BUT...
WAIT.
I MEAN, THIS IS THE DUNGEON.
SO IT MAKES TOTAL SENSE IT SHOULD HAVE TELEPORTA-TION RINGS. RIGHT?
WE'RE HERE.
THIS IS THE ARENA.

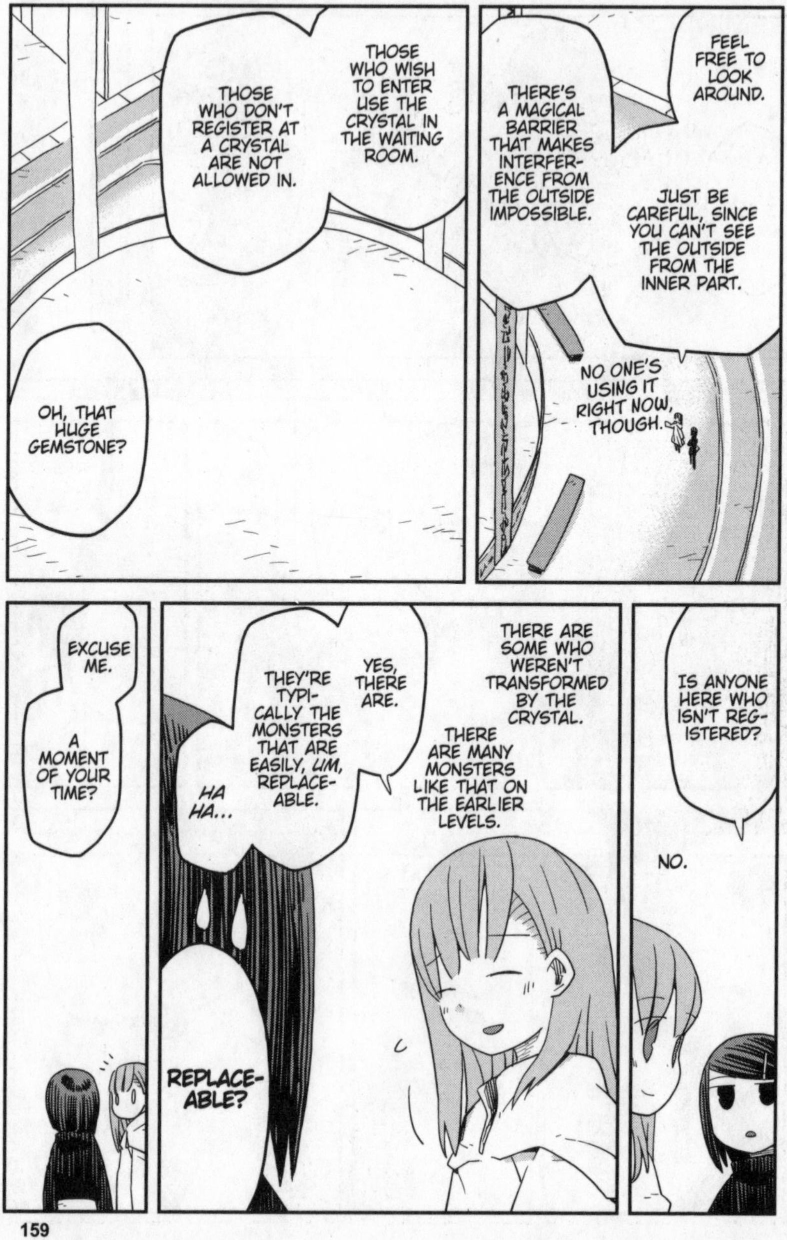
FEEL FREE TO LOOK AROUND.
THERE'S A MAGICAL BARRIER THAT MAKES INTERFERENCE FROM THE OUTSIDE IMPOSSIBLE.
JUST BE CAREFUL, SINCE YOU CAN'T SEE THE OUTSIDE FROM THE INNER PART.
NO ONE'S USING IT RIGHT NOW, THOUGH.
THOSE WHO WISH TO ENTER USE THE CRYSTAL IN THE WAITING ROOM.
THOSE WHO DON'T REGISTER AT A CRYSTAL ARE NOT ALLOWED IN.
OH, THAT HUGE GEMSTONE?
IS ANYONE HERE WHO ISN'T REGISTERED?
NO.
THERE ARE SOME WHO WEREN'T TRANSFORMED BY THE CRYSTAL.
YES, THERE ARE.
THERE ARE MANY MONSTERS LIKE THAT ON THE EARLIER LEVELS.
THEY'RE TYPICALLY THE MONSTERS THAT ARE EASILY, *UM,* REPLACEABLE.
HA HA...
REPLACEABLE?
EXCUSE ME.
A MOMENT OF YOUR TIME?

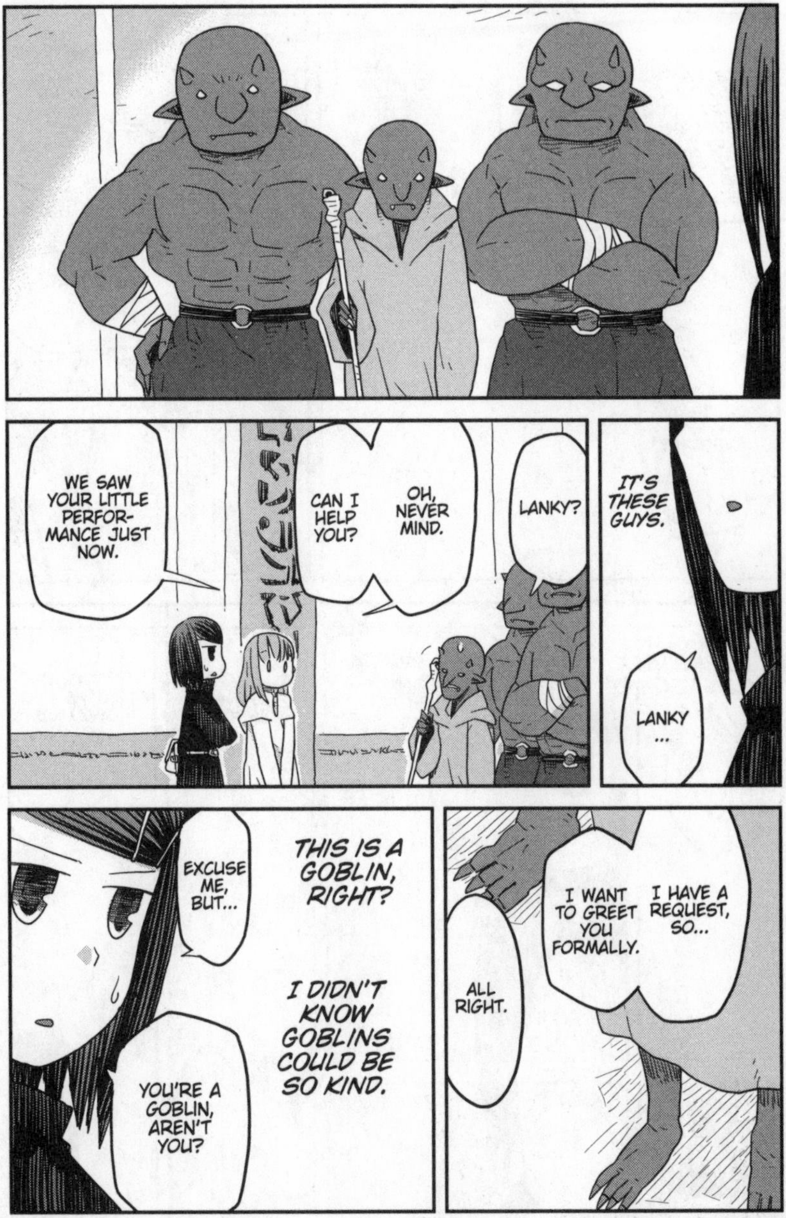
IT'S THESE GUYS.
LANKY ...
LANKY?
OH, NEVER MIND.
CAN I HELP YOU?
WE SAW YOUR LITTLE PERFORMANCE JUST NOW.
I HAVE A REQUEST, SO...
I WANT TO GREET YOU FORMALLY.
ALL RIGHT.
THIS IS A GOBLIN, RIGHT?
EXCUSE ME, BUT...
I DIDN'T KNOW GOBLINS COULD BE SO KIND.
YOU'RE A GOBLIN, AREN'T YOU?

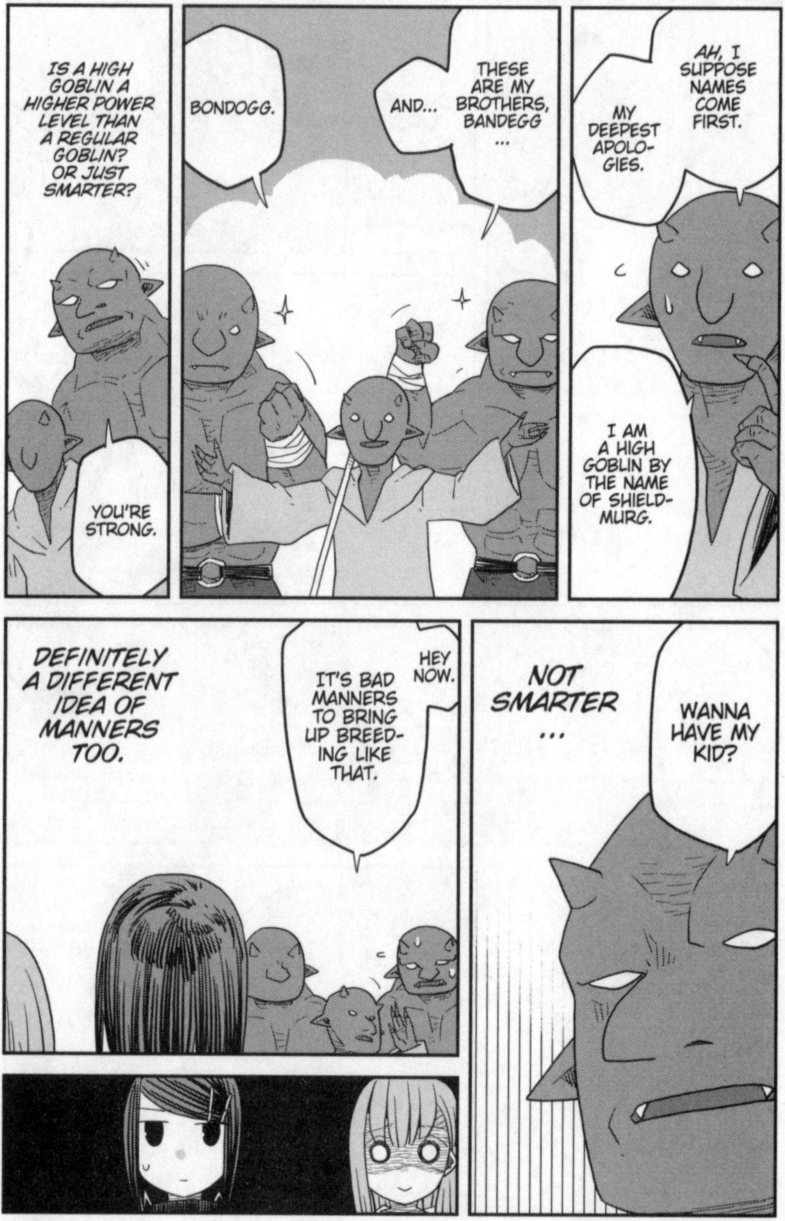
AH, I SUPPOSE NAMES COME FIRST.
MY DEEPEST APOLOGIES.
I AM A HIGH GOBLIN BY THE NAME OF SHIELD-MURG.
THESE ARE MY BROTHERS, BANDEGG ...
AND...
BONDOGG.
IS A HIGH GOBLIN A HIGHER POWER LEVEL THAN A REGULAR GOBLIN? OR JUST SMARTER?
YOU'RE STRONG.
WANNA HAVE MY KID?
NOT SMARTER ...
HEY NOW.
IT'S BAD MANNERS TO BRING UP BREED-ING LIKE THAT.
DEFINITELY A DIFFERENT IDEA OF MANNERS TOO.

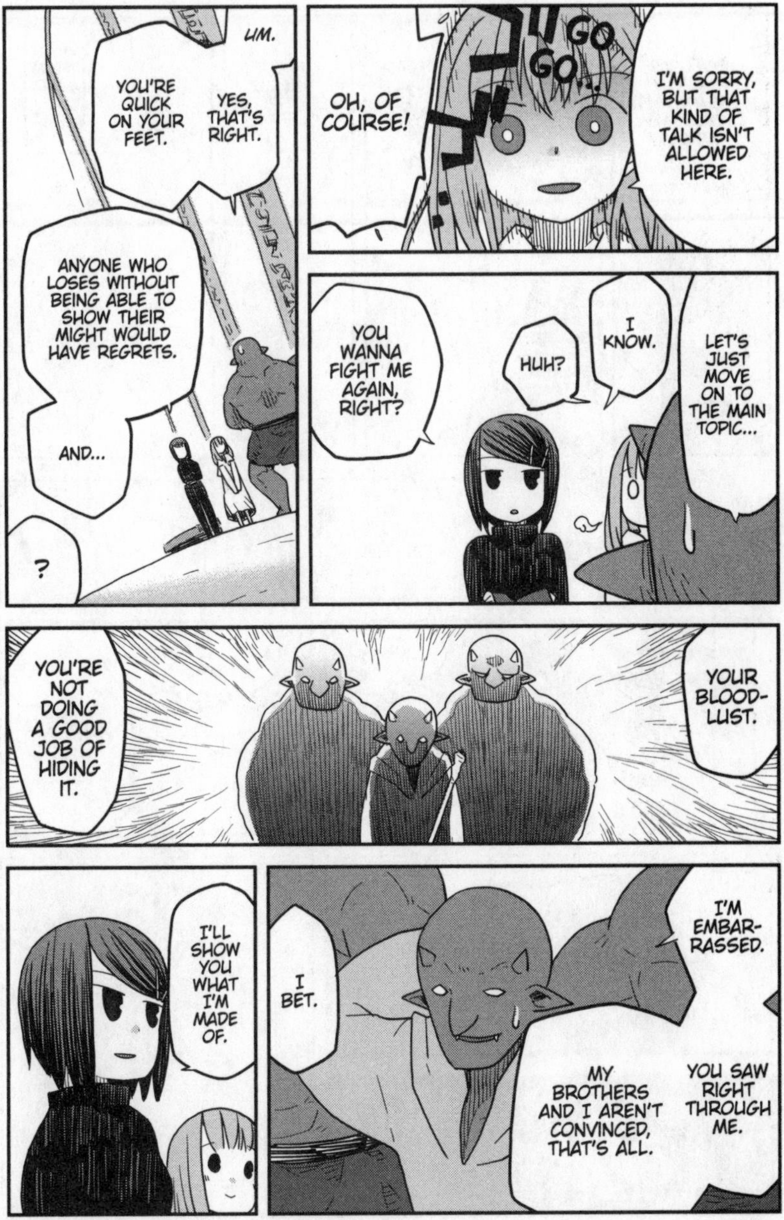
I'M SORRY, BUT THAT KIND OF TALK ISN'T ALLOWED HERE.
GO GO...
OH, OF COURSE!
LET'S JUST MOVE ON TO THE MAIN TOPIC...
I KNOW.
HUH?
YOU WANNA FIGHT ME AGAIN, RIGHT?
UM.
YES, THAT'S RIGHT.
YOU'RE QUICK ON YOUR FEET.
ANYONE WHO LOSES WITHOUT BEING ABLE TO SHOW THEIR MIGHT WOULD HAVE REGRETS.
AND...
?
YOUR BLOOD-LUST.
YOU'RE NOT DOING A GOOD JOB OF HIDING IT.
I'M EMBAR-RASSED.
YOU SAW RIGHT THROUGH ME.
MY BROTHERS AND I AREN'T CONVINCED, THAT'S ALL.
I BET.
I'LL SHOW YOU WHAT I'M MADE OF.

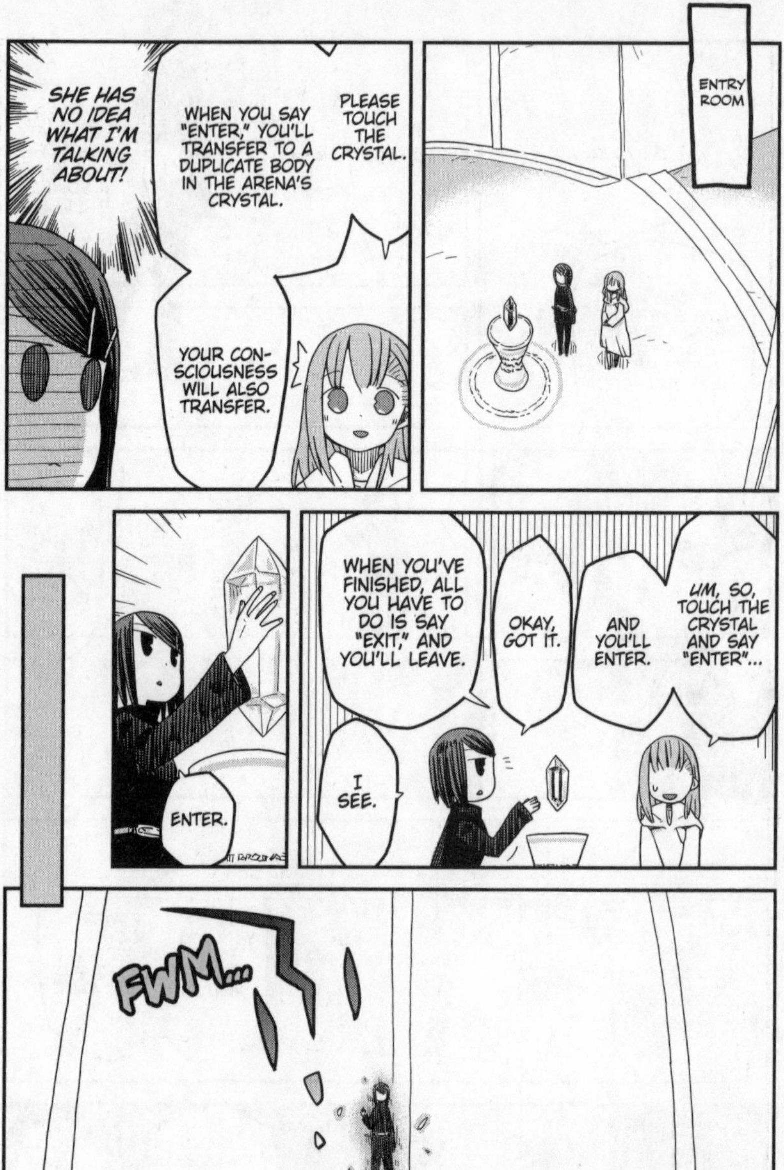
ENTRY ROOM
PLEASE TOUCH THE CRYSTAL.
WHEN YOU SAY "ENTER," YOU'LL TRANSFER TO A DUPLICATE BODY IN THE ARENA'S CRYSTAL.
YOUR CONSCIOUSNESS WILL ALSO TRANSFER.
SHE HAS NO IDEA WHAT I'M TALKING ABOUT!
UM, SO, TOUCH THE CRYSTAL AND SAY "ENTER"...
AND YOU'LL ENTER.
OKAY, GOT IT.
WHEN YOU'VE FINISHED, ALL YOU HAVE TO DO IS SAY "EXIT," AND YOU'LL LEAVE.
I SEE.
ENTER.
FWM...

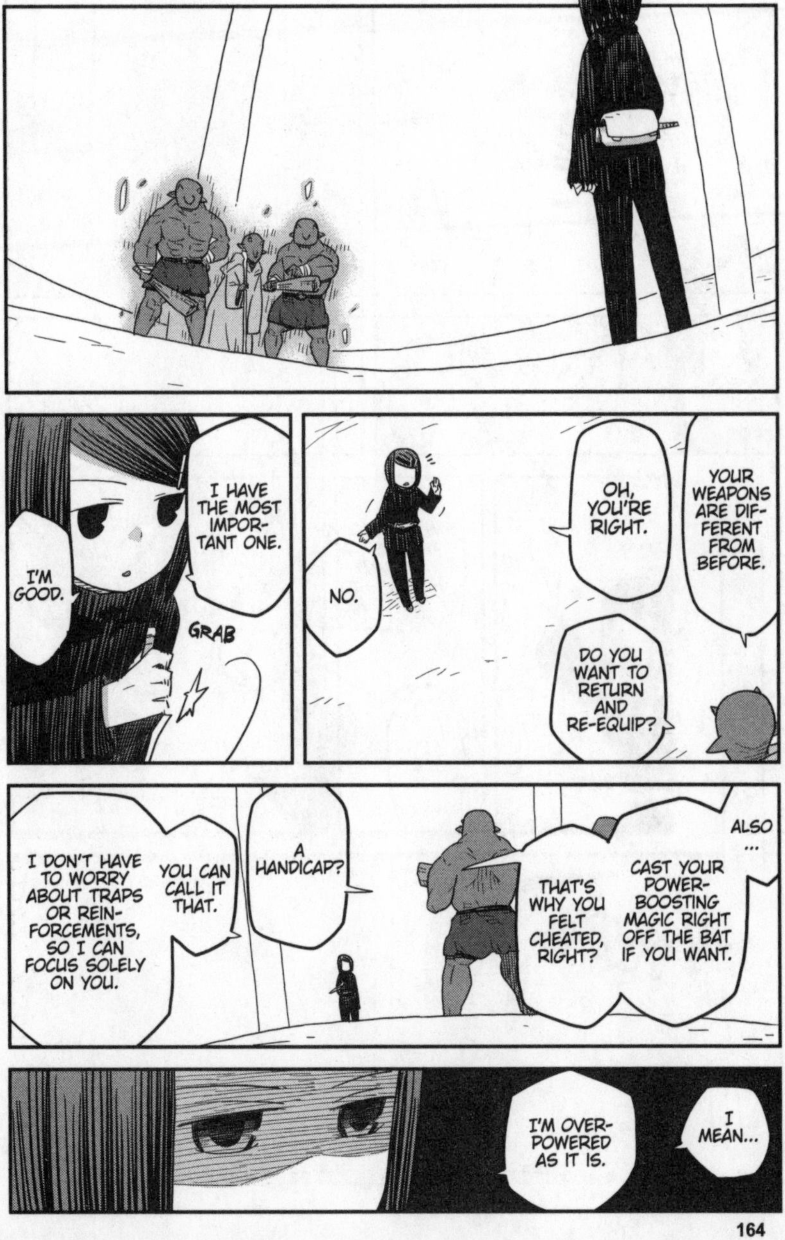
YOUR WEAPONS ARE DIFFERENT FROM BEFORE.
OH, YOU'RE RIGHT.
DO YOU WANT TO RETURN AND RE-EQUIP?
NO.
I HAVE THE MOST IMPORTANT ONE.
I'M GOOD.
GRAB
ALSO ...
CAST YOUR POWER-BOOSTING MAGIC RIGHT OFF THE BAT IF YOU WANT.
THAT'S WHY YOU FELT CHEATED, RIGHT?
A HANDICAP?
YOU CAN CALL IT THAT.
I DON'T HAVE TO WORRY ABOUT TRAPS OR REINFORCEMENTS, SO I CAN FOCUS SOLELY ON YOU.
I MEAN...
I'M OVERPOWERED AS IT IS.

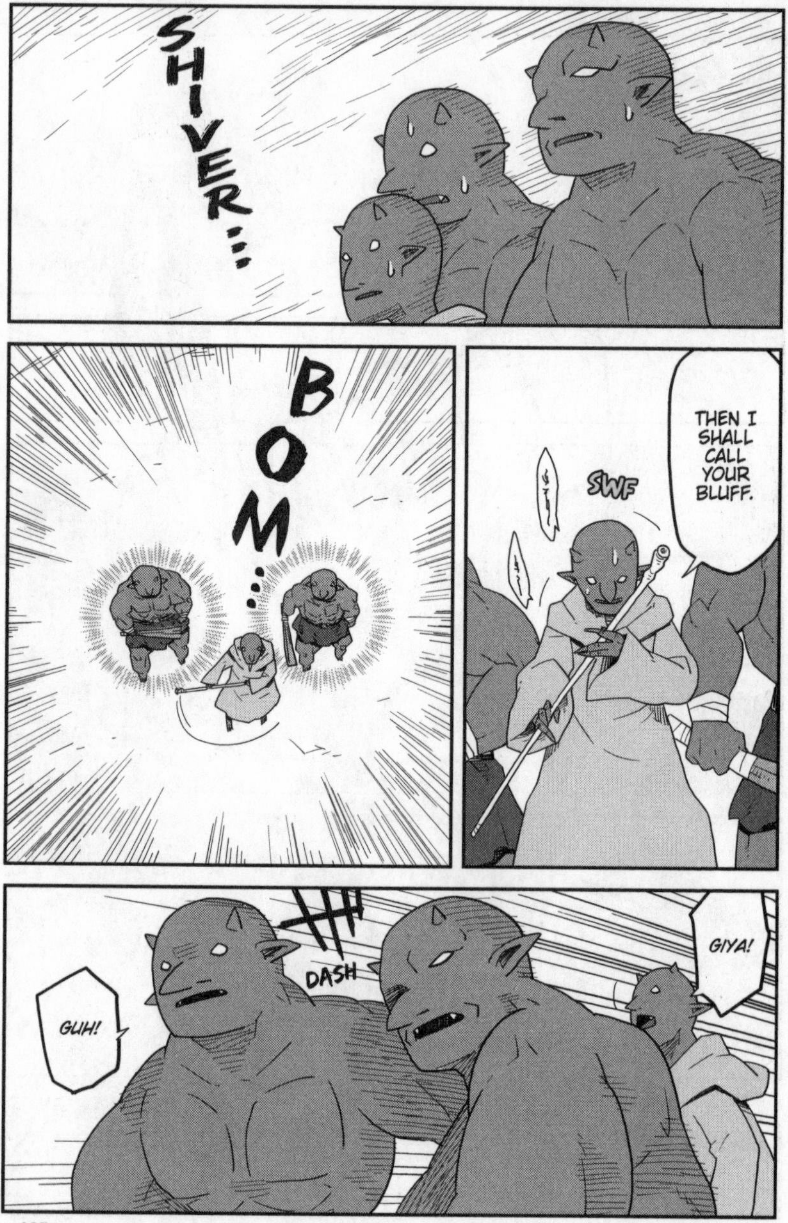
SHIVER...
THEN I SHALL CALL YOUR BLUFF.
SWF
BOM...
GIYA!
DASH
GUH!

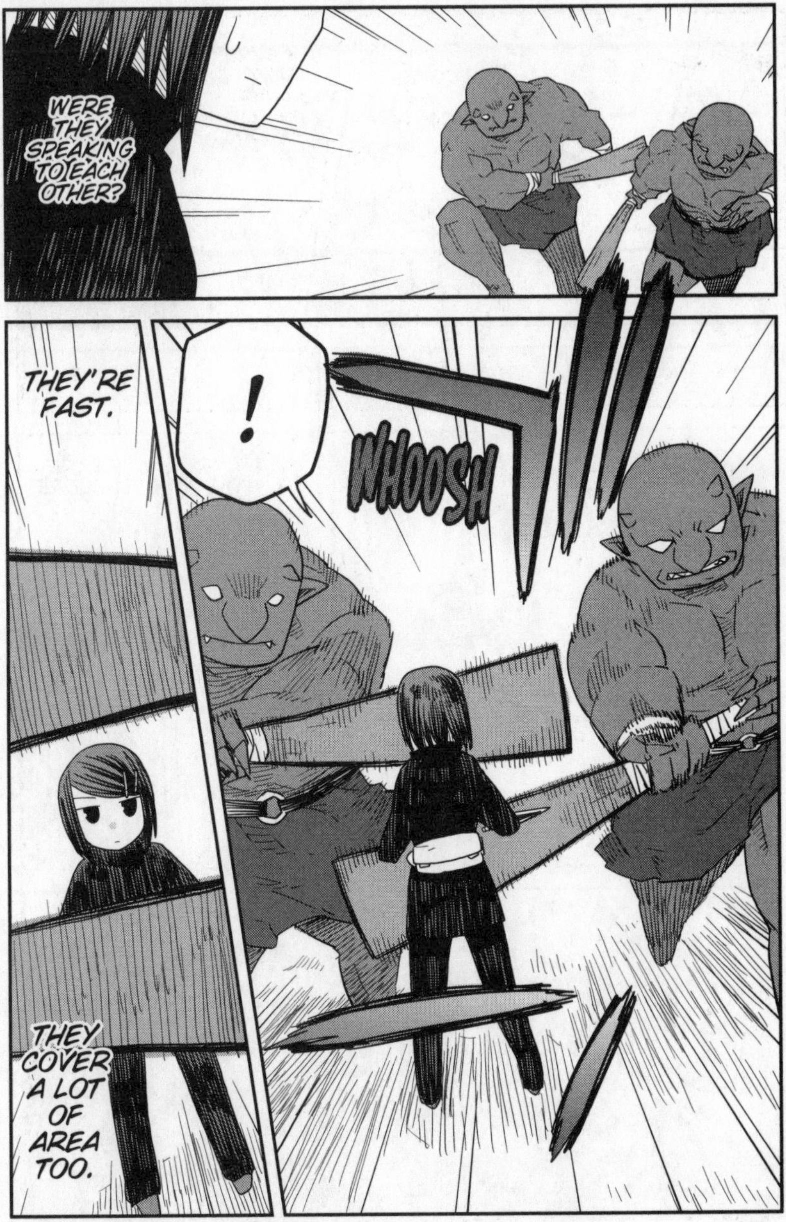
WERE THEY SPEAKING TO EACH OTHER?
!
WHOOSH
THEY'RE FAST.
THEY COVER A LOT OF AREA TOO.

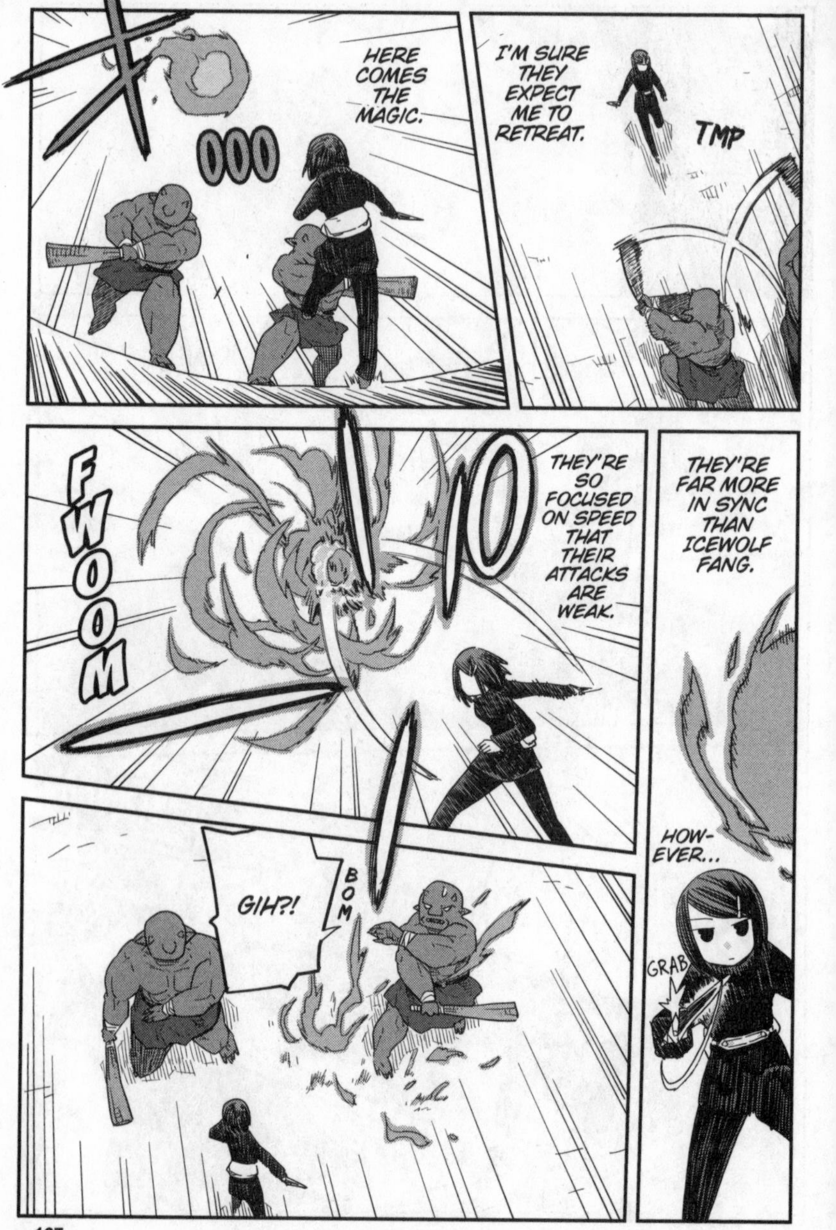
I'M SURE THEY EXPECT ME TO RETREAT.
TMP
HERE COMES THE MAGIC.
OOO
THEY'RE FAR MORE IN SYNC THAN ICEWOLF FANG.
HOW-EVER...
GRAB
FWOOM
THEY'RE SO FOCUSED ON SPEED THAT THEIR ATTACKS ARE WEAK.
BOM
GIH?!

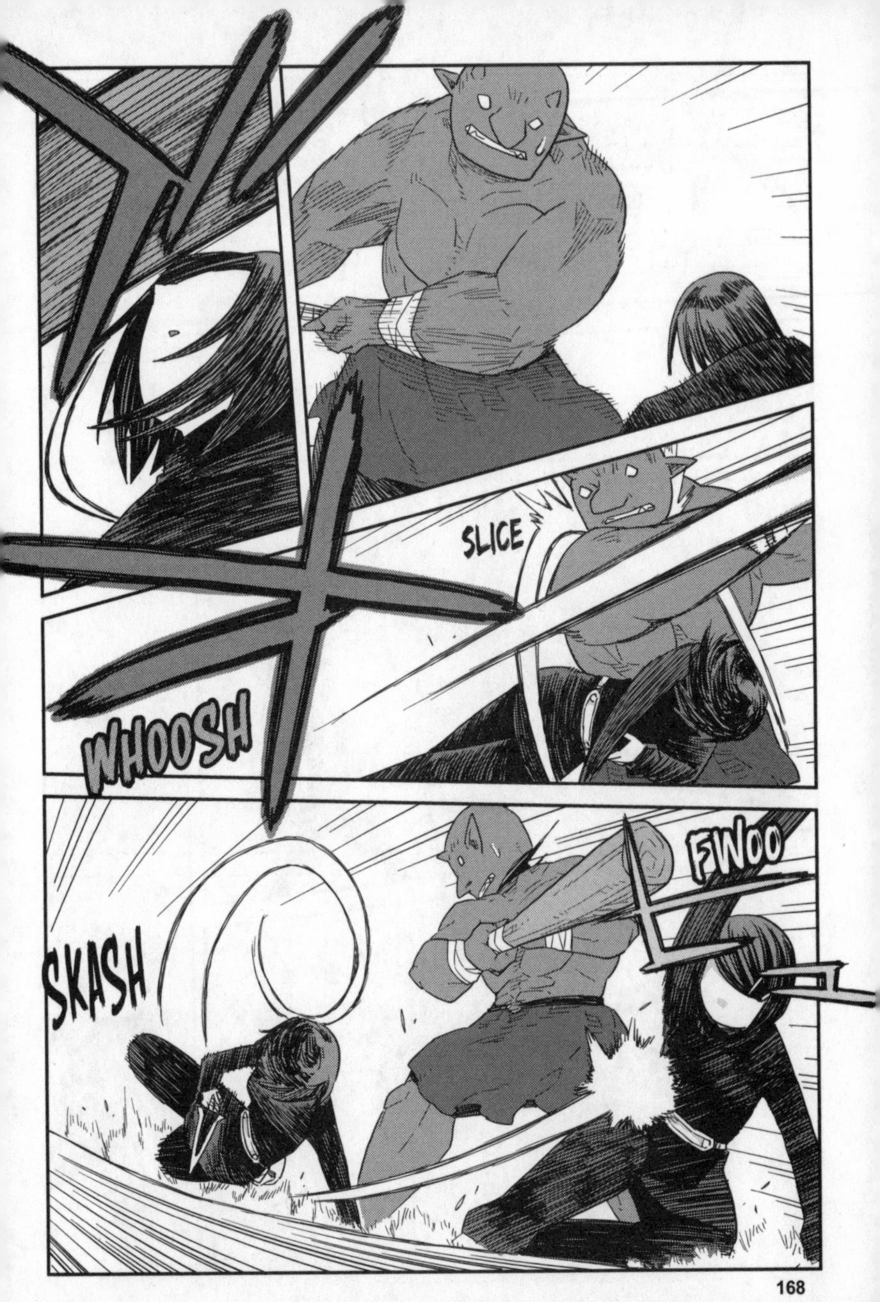
SLICE
WHOOSH
FWOO
SKASH

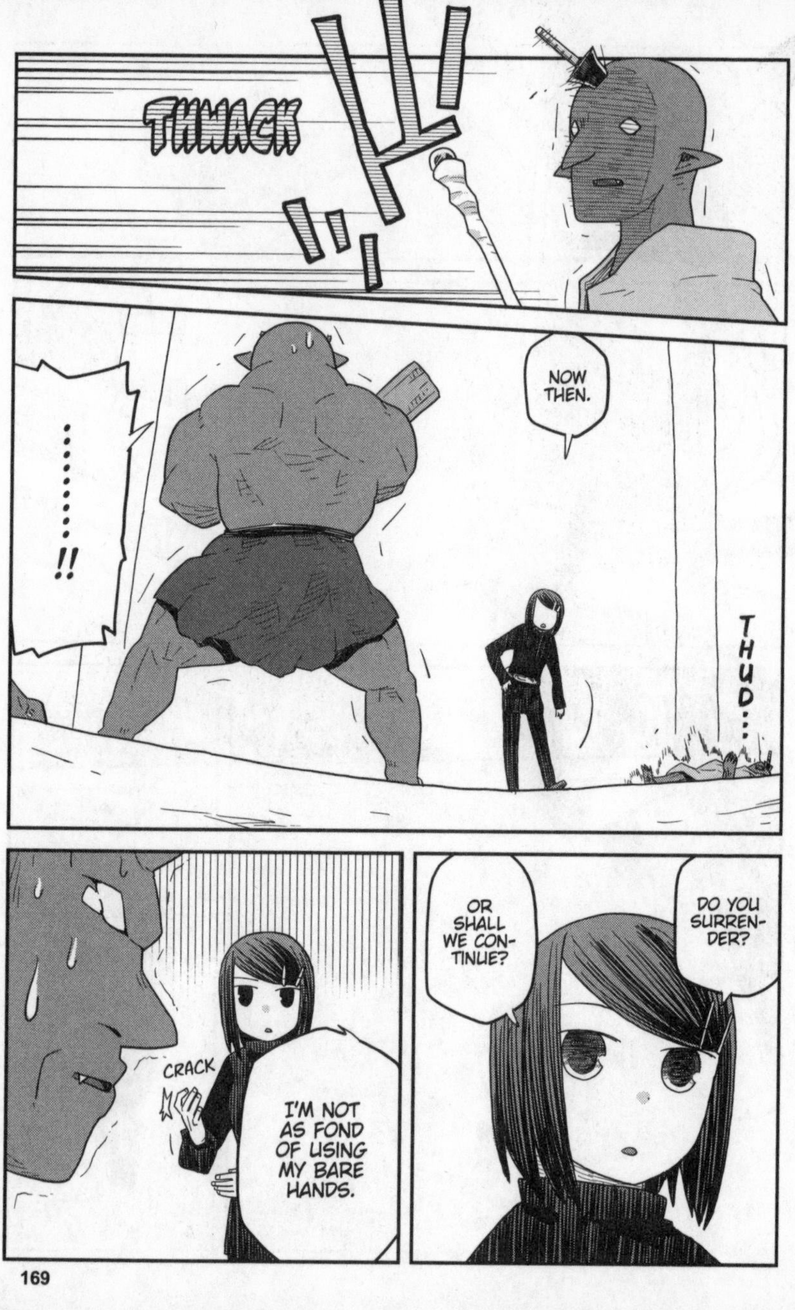
THWACK
NOW THEN.
THUD...
......!!
DO YOU SURRENDER?
OR SHALL WE CONTINUE?
CRACK
I'M NOT AS FOND OF USING MY BARE HANDS.

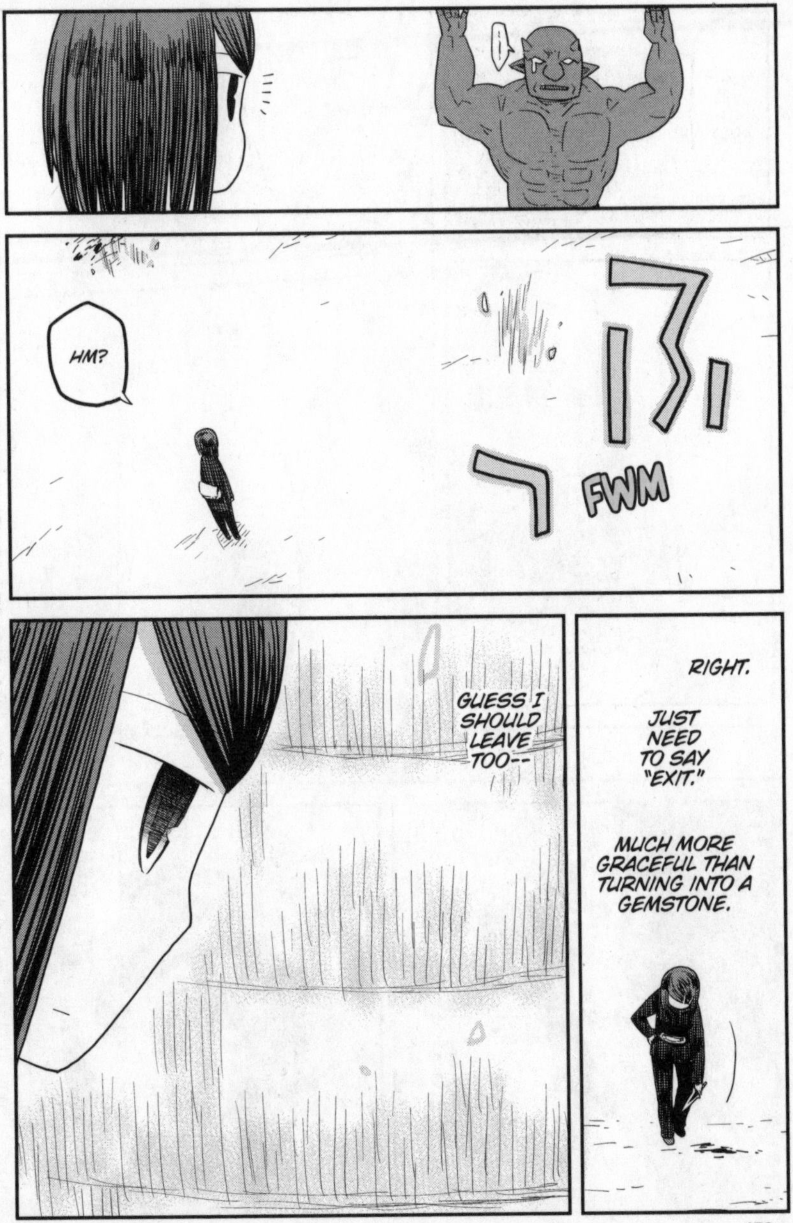
HM?
FWM
RIGHT.
JUST NEED TO SAY "EXIT."
MUCH MORE GRACEFUL THAN TURNING INTO A GEMSTONE.
GUESS I SHOULD LEAVE TOO--

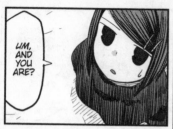

UM, AND YOU ARE?

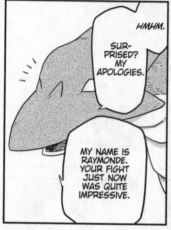

HMHM.

SURPRISED? MY APOLOGIES.

MY NAME IS RAYMONDE. YOUR FIGHT JUST NOW WAS QUITE IMPRESSIVE.

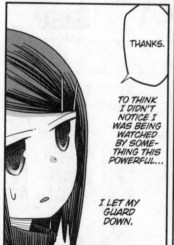

THANKS.

TO THINK I DIDN'T NOTICE I WAS BEING WATCHED BY SOMETHING THIS POWERFUL...

I LET MY GUARD DOWN.

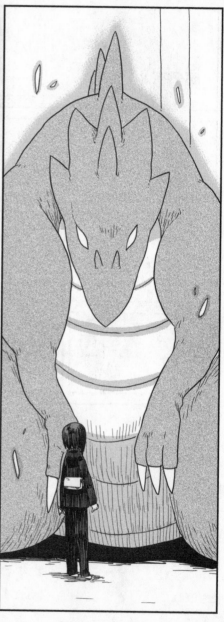

171

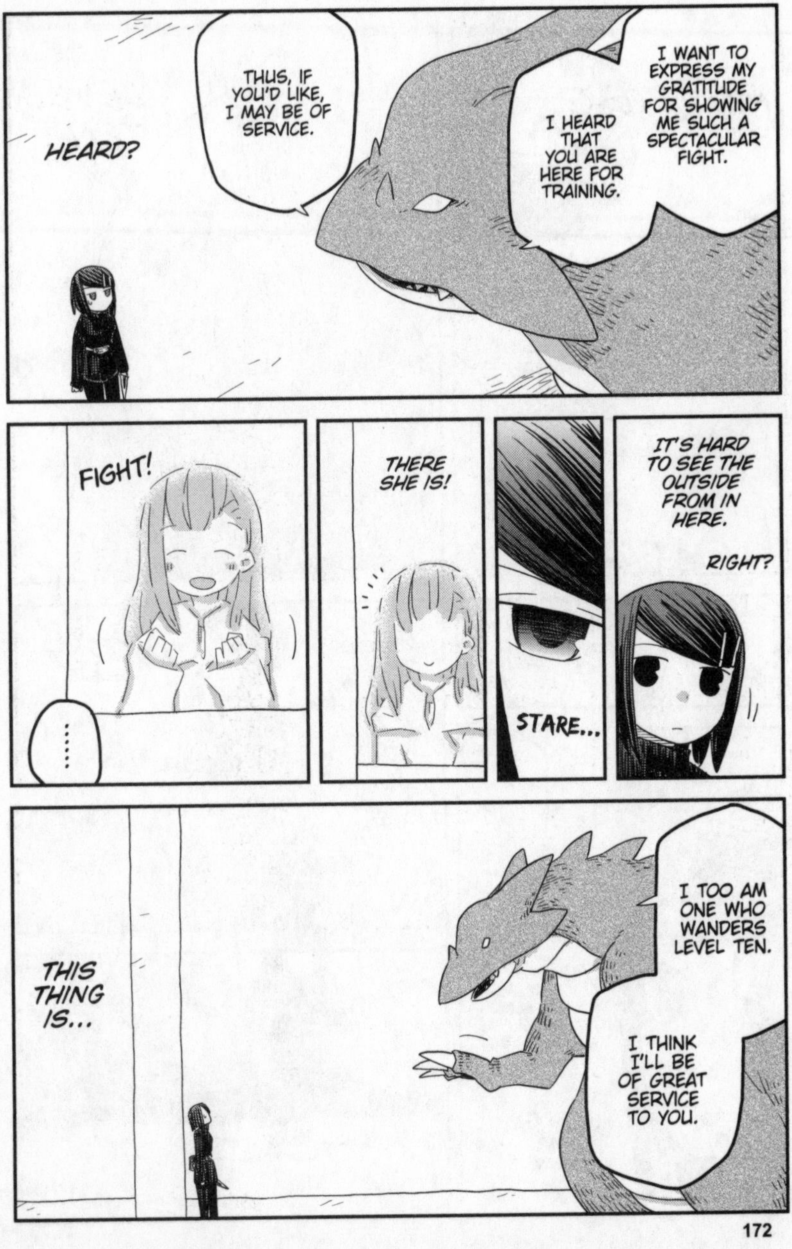
I WANT TO EXPRESS MY GRATITUDE FOR SHOWING ME SUCH A SPECTACULAR FIGHT.
I HEARD THAT YOU ARE HERE FOR TRAINING.
THUS, IF YOU'D LIKE, I MAY BE OF SERVICE.
HEARD?
IT'S HARD TO SEE THE OUTSIDE FROM IN HERE.
RIGHT?
STARE...
THERE SHE IS!
FIGHT!
......
I TOO AM ONE WHO WANDERS LEVEL TEN.
I THINK I'LL BE OF GREAT SERVICE TO YOU.
THIS THING IS...

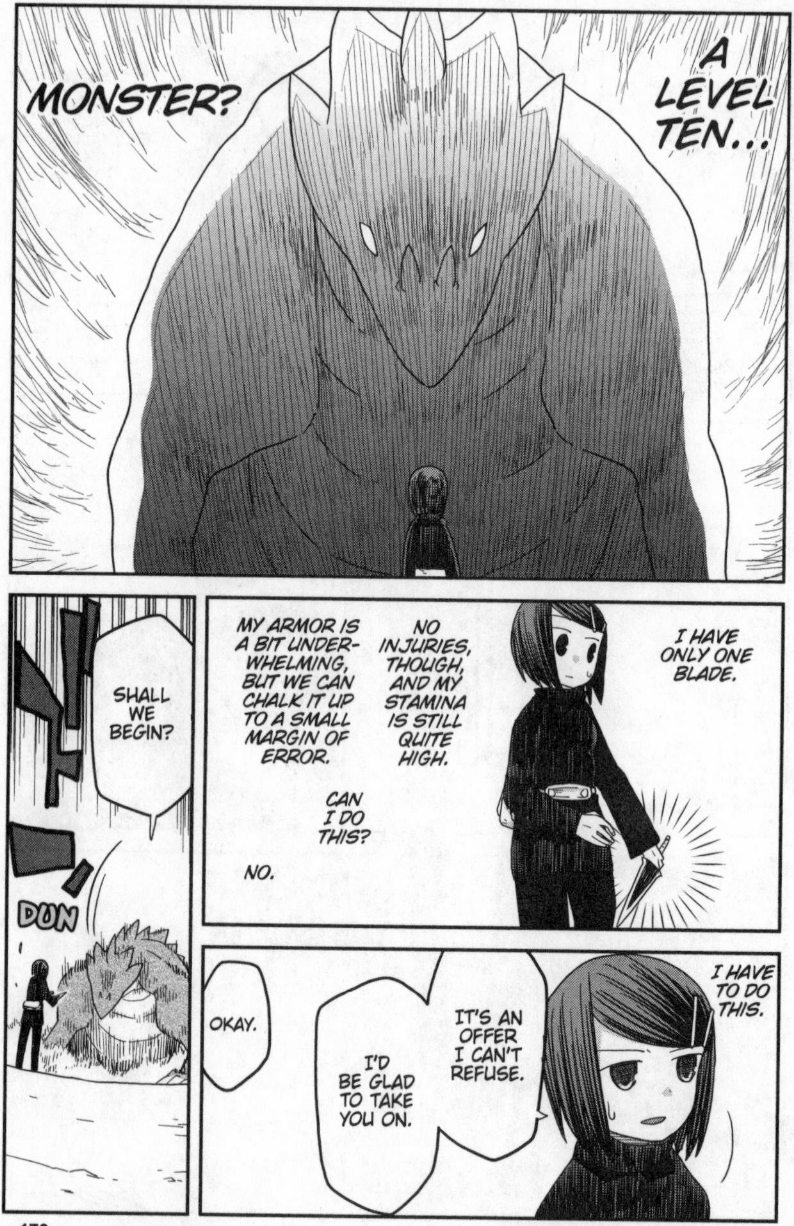
A LEVEL TEN...
MONSTER?
I HAVE ONLY ONE BLADE.
NO INJURIES, THOUGH, AND MY STAMINA IS STILL QUITE HIGH.
MY ARMOR IS A BIT UNDER-WHELMING, BUT WE CAN CHALK IT UP TO A SMALL MARGIN OF ERROR.
CAN I DO THIS?
NO.
I HAVE TO DO THIS.
IT'S AN OFFER I CAN'T REFUSE.
I'D BE GLAD TO TAKE YOU ON.
OKAY.
SHALL WE BEGIN?
DUN

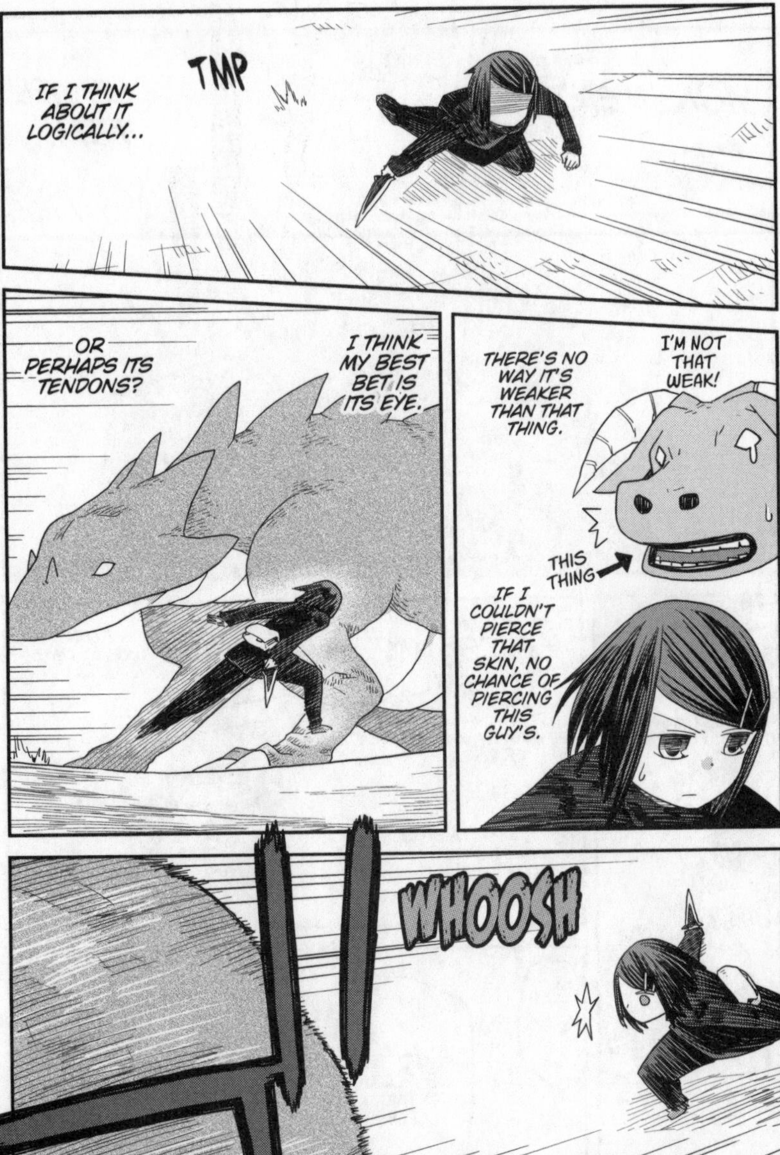
TMP
IF I THINK ABOUT IT LOGICALLY...
I'M NOT THAT WEAK!
THERE'S NO WAY IT'S WEAKER THAN THAT THING.
THIS THING
IF I COULDN'T PIERCE THAT SKIN, NO CHANCE OF PIERCING THIS GUY'S.
I THINK MY BEST BET IS ITS EYE.
OR PERHAPS ITS TENDONS?
WHOOSH

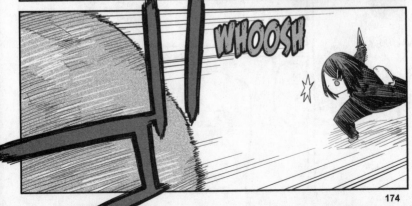

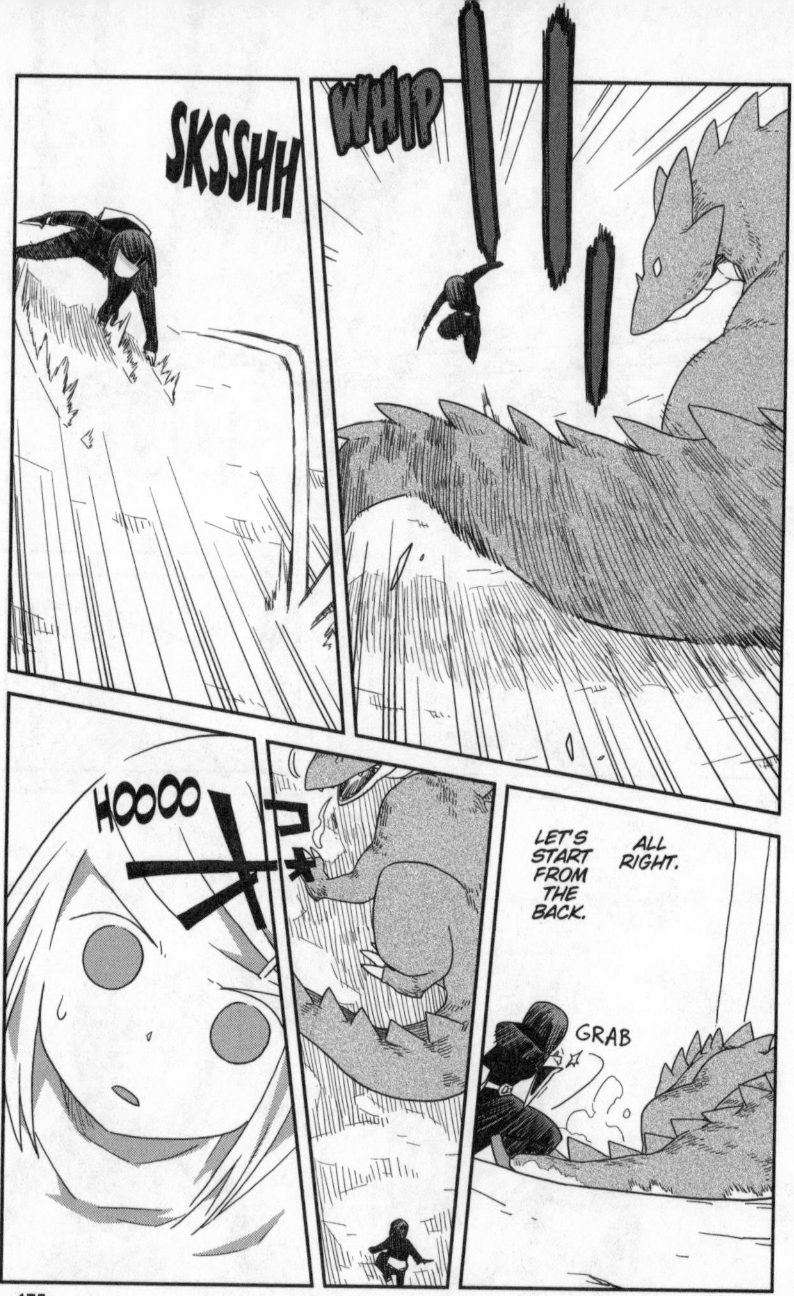
WHIP
SKSSHH
ALL RIGHT.
LET'S START FROM THE BACK.
GRAB
HOOOO

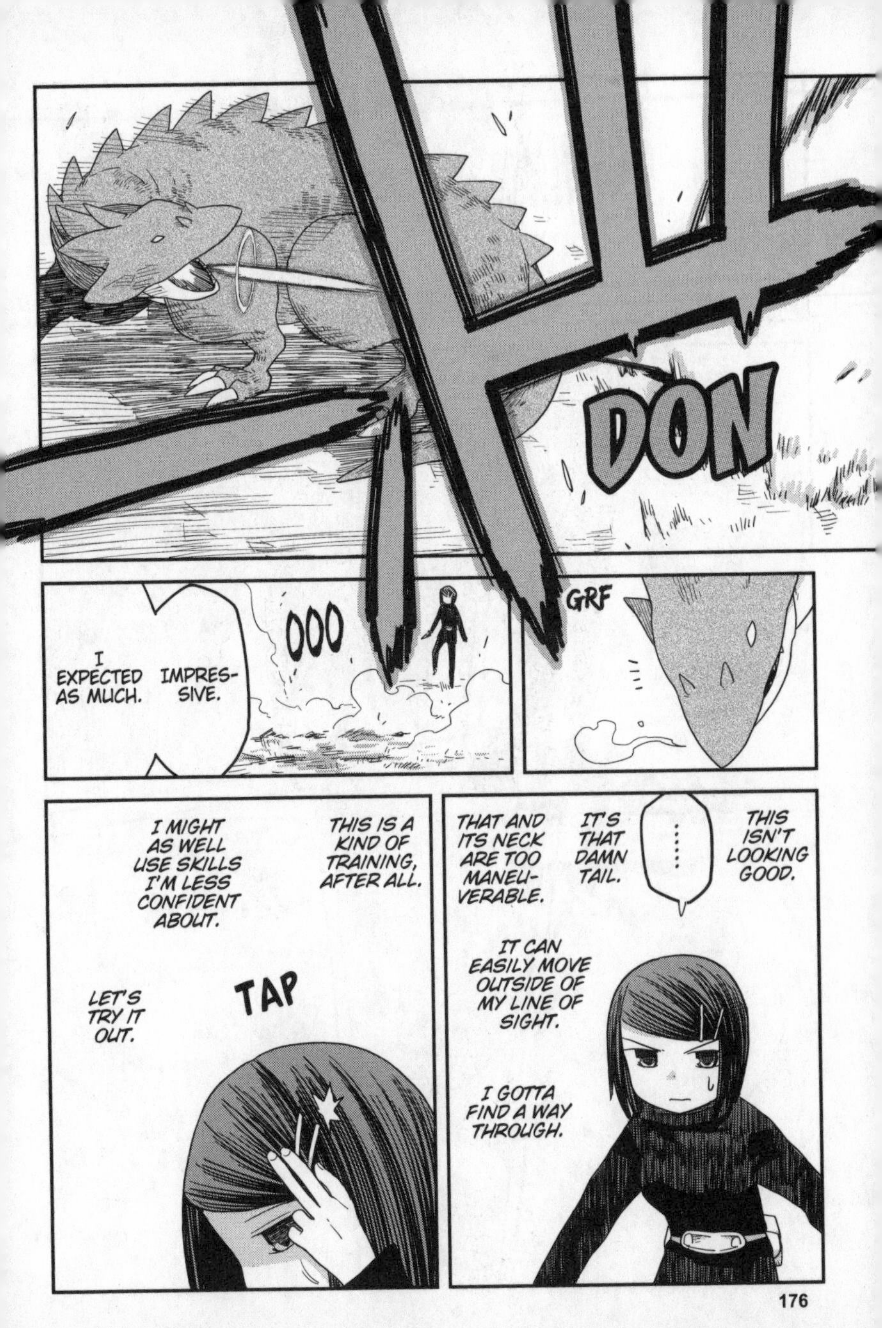
DON
GRF
OOO
IMPRES-SIVE.
I EXPECTED AS MUCH.
THIS ISN'T LOOKING GOOD.
......
IT'S THAT DAMN TAIL.
THAT AND ITS NECK ARE TOO MANEU-VERABLE.
IT CAN EASILY MOVE OUTSIDE OF MY LINE OF SIGHT.
I GOTTA FIND A WAY THROUGH.
THIS IS A KIND OF TRAINING, AFTER ALL.
I MIGHT AS WELL USE SKILLS I'M LESS CONFIDENT ABOUT.
TAP
LET'S TRY IT OUT.

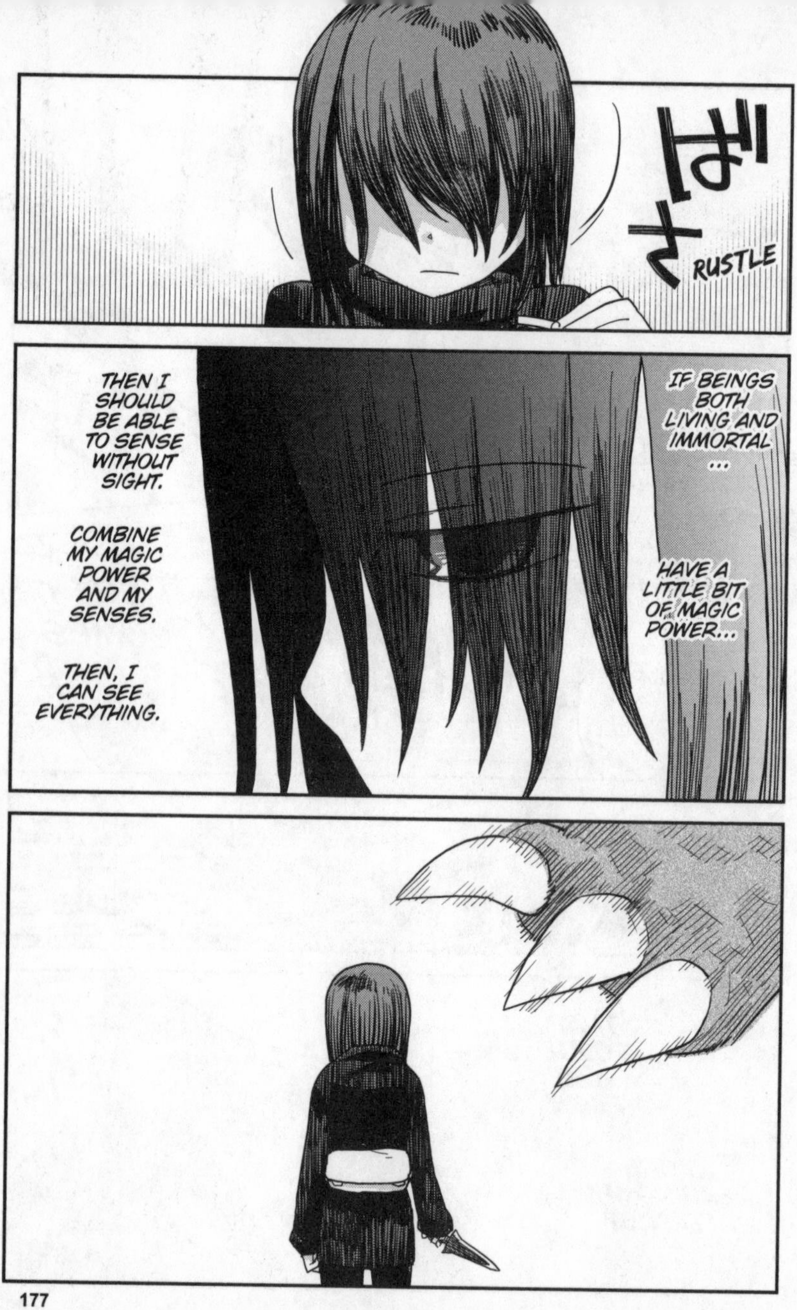
ばさ
RUSTLE
IF BEINGS BOTH LIVING AND IMMORTAL ...
HAVE A LITTLE BIT OF MAGIC POWER...
THEN I SHOULD BE ABLE TO SENSE WITHOUT SIGHT.
COMBINE MY MAGIC POWER AND MY SENSES.
THEN, I CAN SEE EVERYTHING.

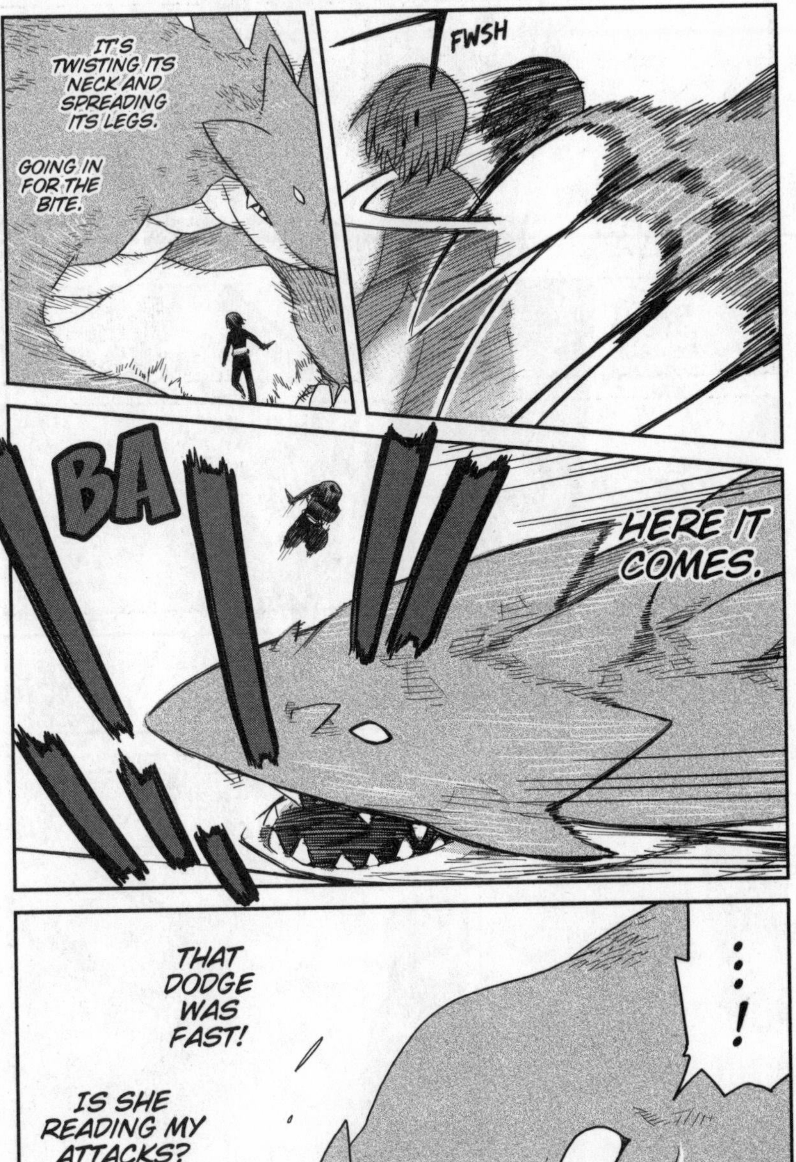
FWSH
IT'S TWISTING ITS NECK AND SPREADING ITS LEGS.
GOING IN FOR THE BITE.
HERE IT COMES.
BA
...!
THAT DODGE WAS FAST!
IS SHE READING MY ATTACKS?

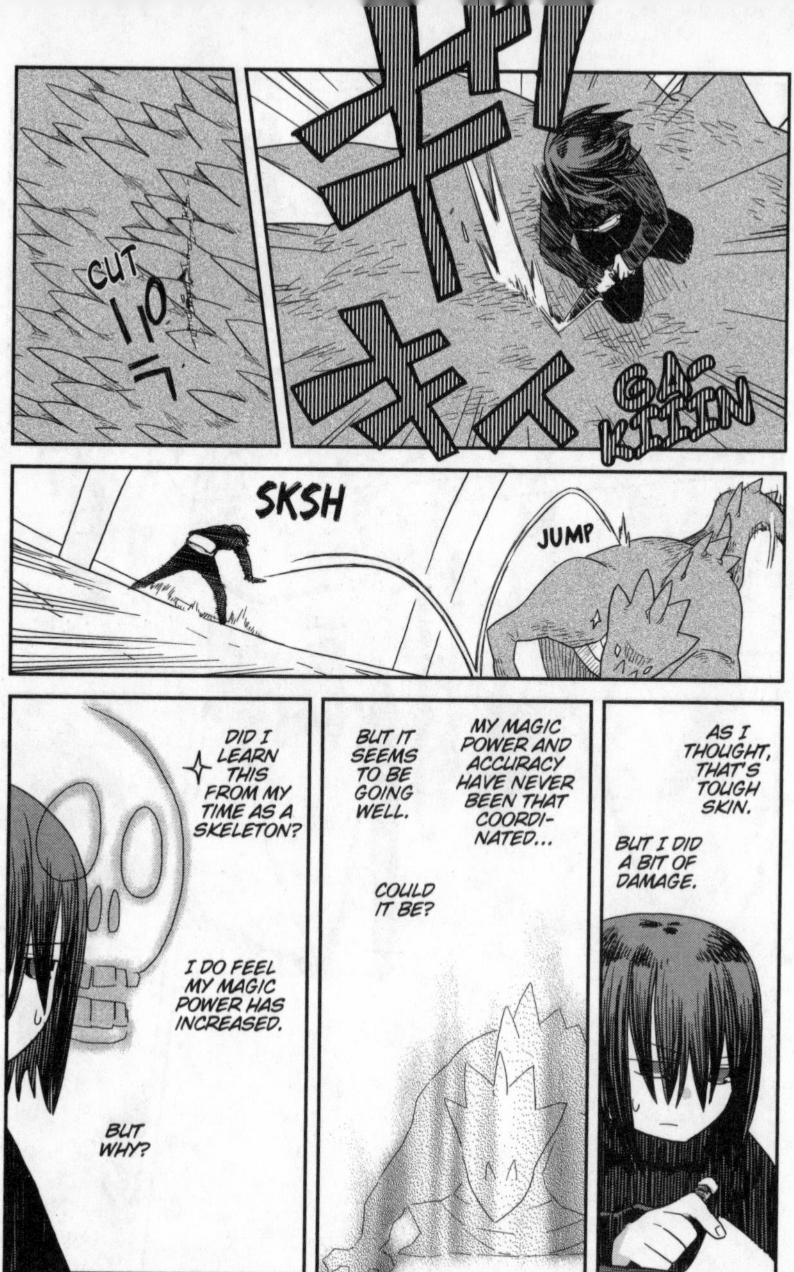
CUT
JUMP
SKSH
AS I THOUGHT, THAT'S TOUGH SKIN.
BUT I DID A BIT OF DAMAGE.
MY MAGIC POWER AND ACCURACY HAVE NEVER BEEN THAT COORDINATED...
BUT IT SEEMS TO BE GOING WELL.
COULD IT BE?
DID I LEARN THIS FROM MY TIME AS A SKELETON?
I DO FEEL MY MAGIC POWER HAS INCREASED.
BUT WHY?

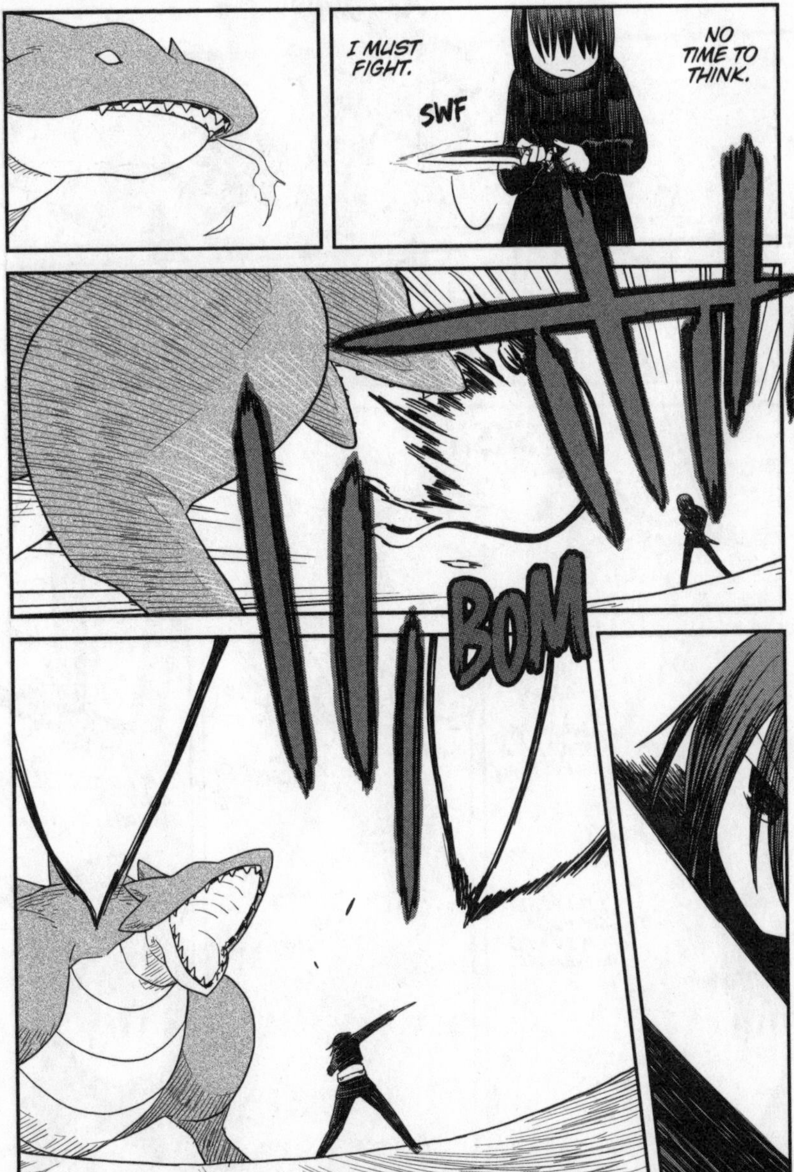
NO TIME TO THINK.
I MUST FIGHT.
SWF
BOM

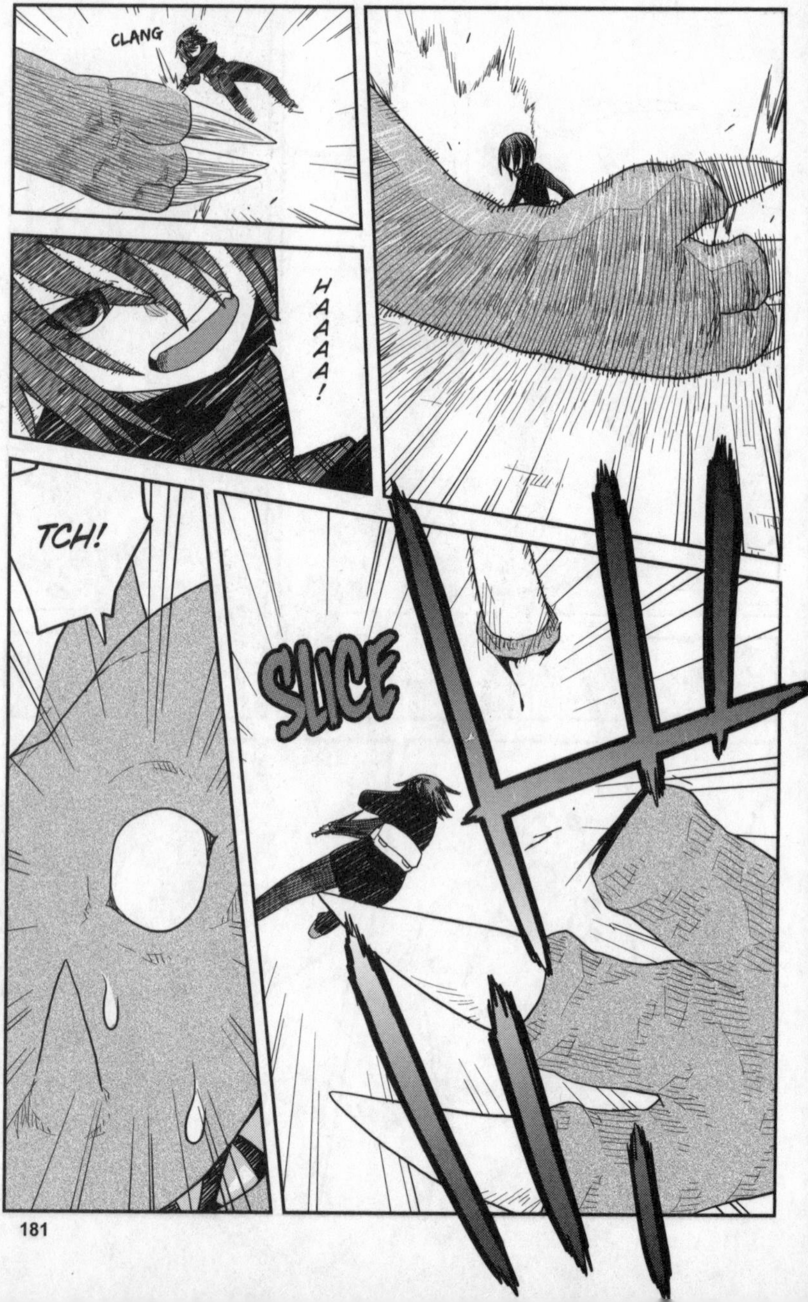
CLANG
HAAAAA!
SLICE
TCH!

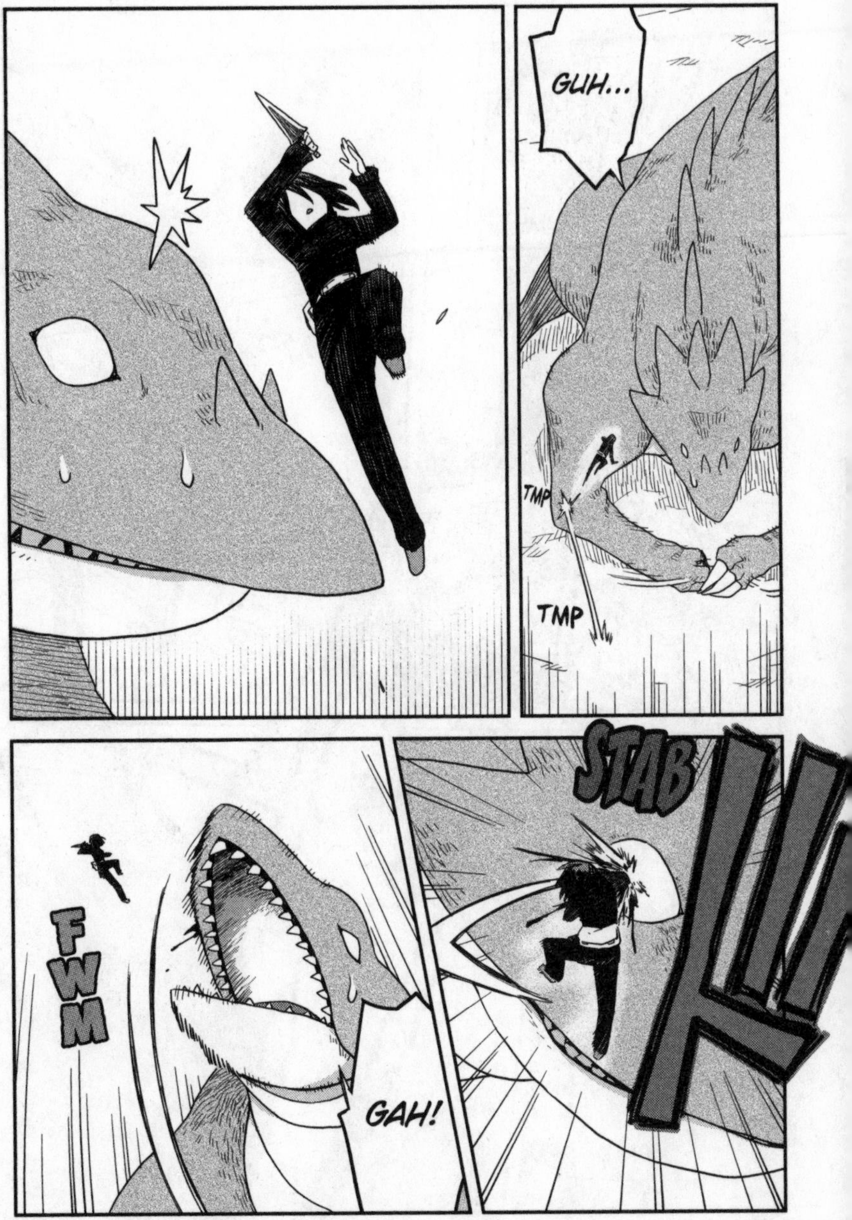
GUH...
TMP
TMP
STAB
FWM
GAH!

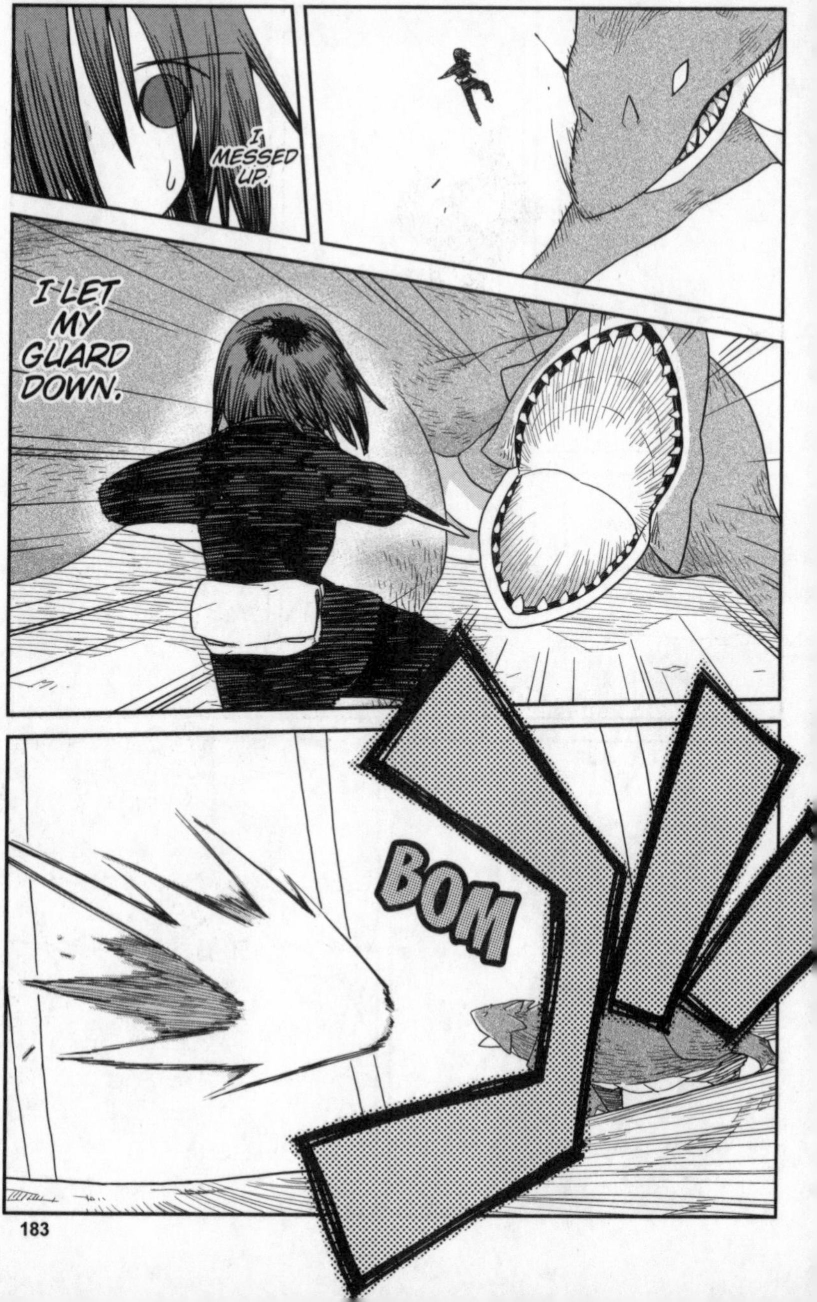
I MESSED UP.
I LET MY GUARD DOWN.
BOM

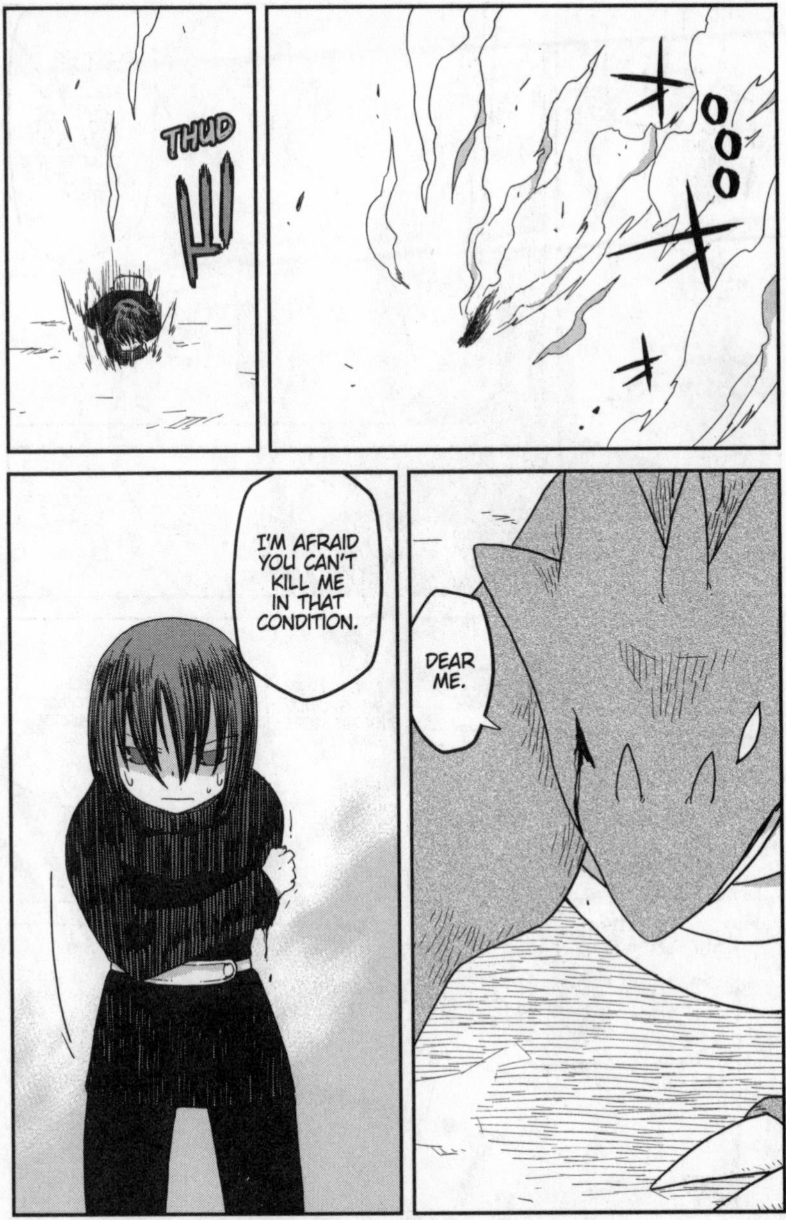
OOO
THUD
DEAR ME.
I'M AFRAID YOU CAN'T KILL ME IN THAT CONDITION.

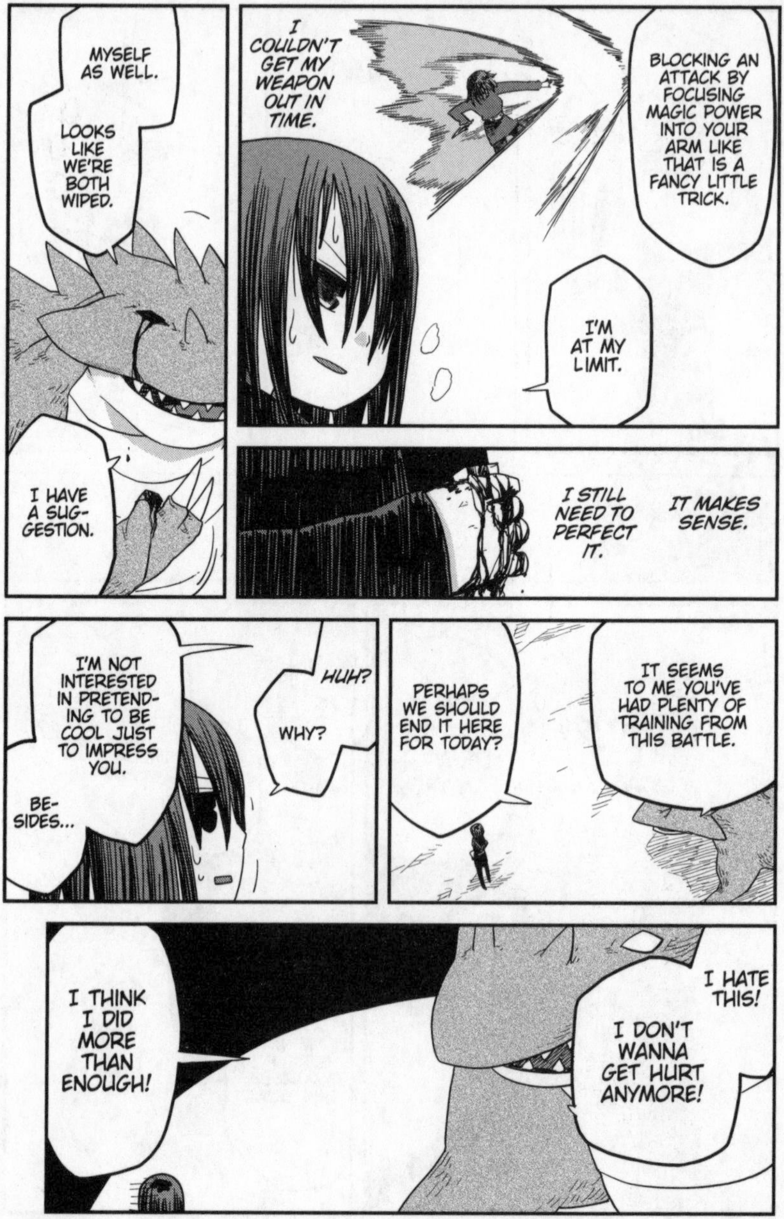
BLOCKING AN ATTACK BY FOCUSING MAGIC POWER INTO YOUR ARM LIKE THAT IS A FANCY LITTLE TRICK.
I COULDN'T GET MY WEAPON OUT IN TIME.
I'M AT MY LIMIT.
IT MAKES SENSE.
I STILL NEED TO PERFECT IT.
MYSELF AS WELL.
LOOKS LIKE WE'RE BOTH WIPED.
I HAVE A SUG-GESTION.
IT SEEMS TO ME YOU'VE HAD PLENTY OF TRAINING FROM THIS BATTLE.
PERHAPS WE SHOULD END IT HERE FOR TODAY?
HUH?
WHY?
I'M NOT INTERESTED IN PRETEND-ING TO BE COOL JUST TO IMPRESS YOU.
BE-SIDES...
I HATE THIS!
I DON'T WANNA GET HURT ANYMORE!
I THINK I DID MORE THAN ENOUGH!

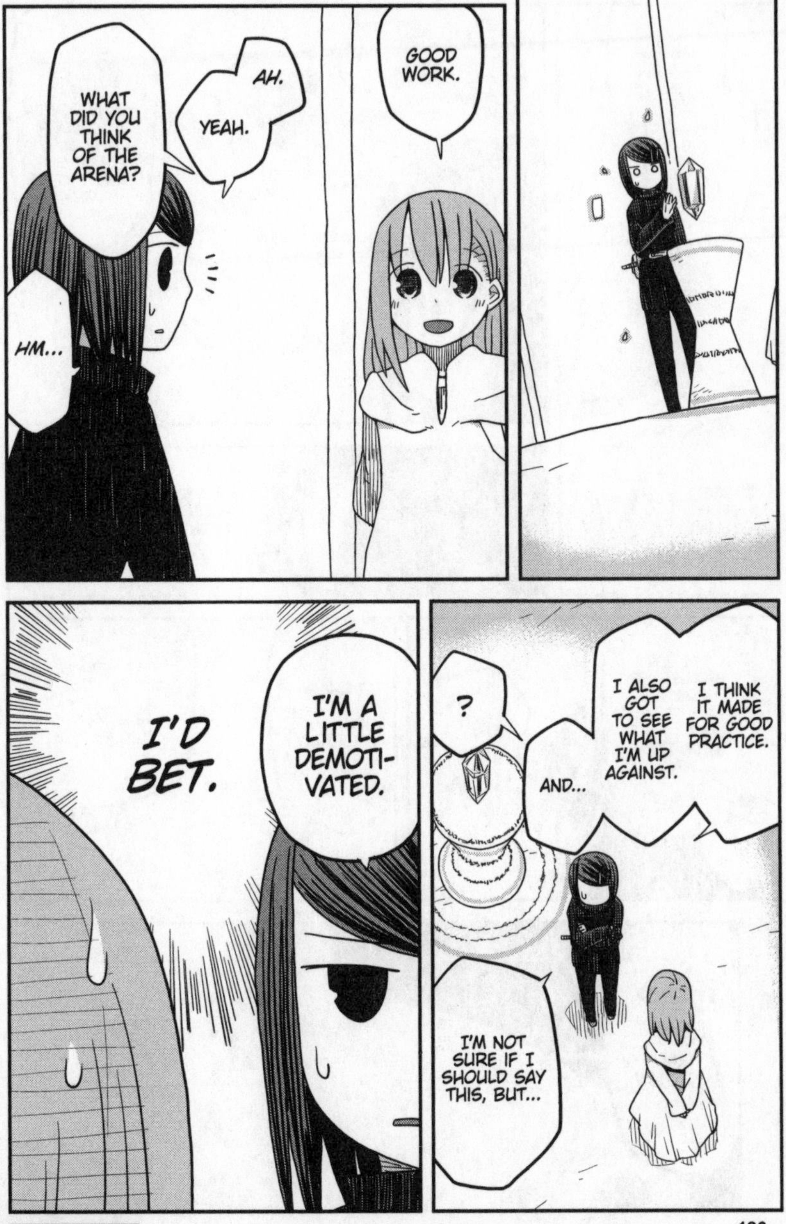
GOOD WORK.
AH.
YEAH.
WHAT DID YOU THINK OF THE ARENA?
HM...
I THINK IT MADE FOR GOOD PRACTICE.
I ALSO GOT TO SEE WHAT I'M UP AGAINST.
AND...
?
I'M NOT SURE IF I SHOULD SAY THIS, BUT...
I'M A LITTLE DEMOTI-VATED.
I'D BET.

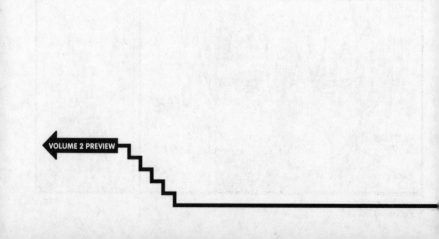

VOLUME 2 PREVIEW

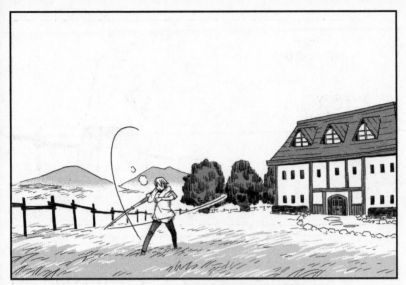

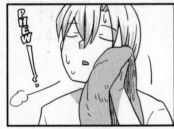

PHEW!

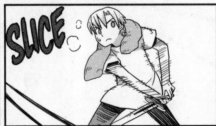

SLICE

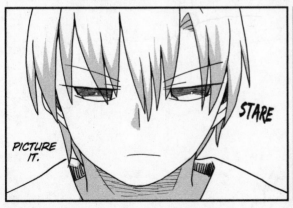

PICTURE IT.

STARE

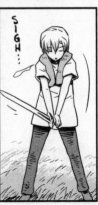

SIGH...

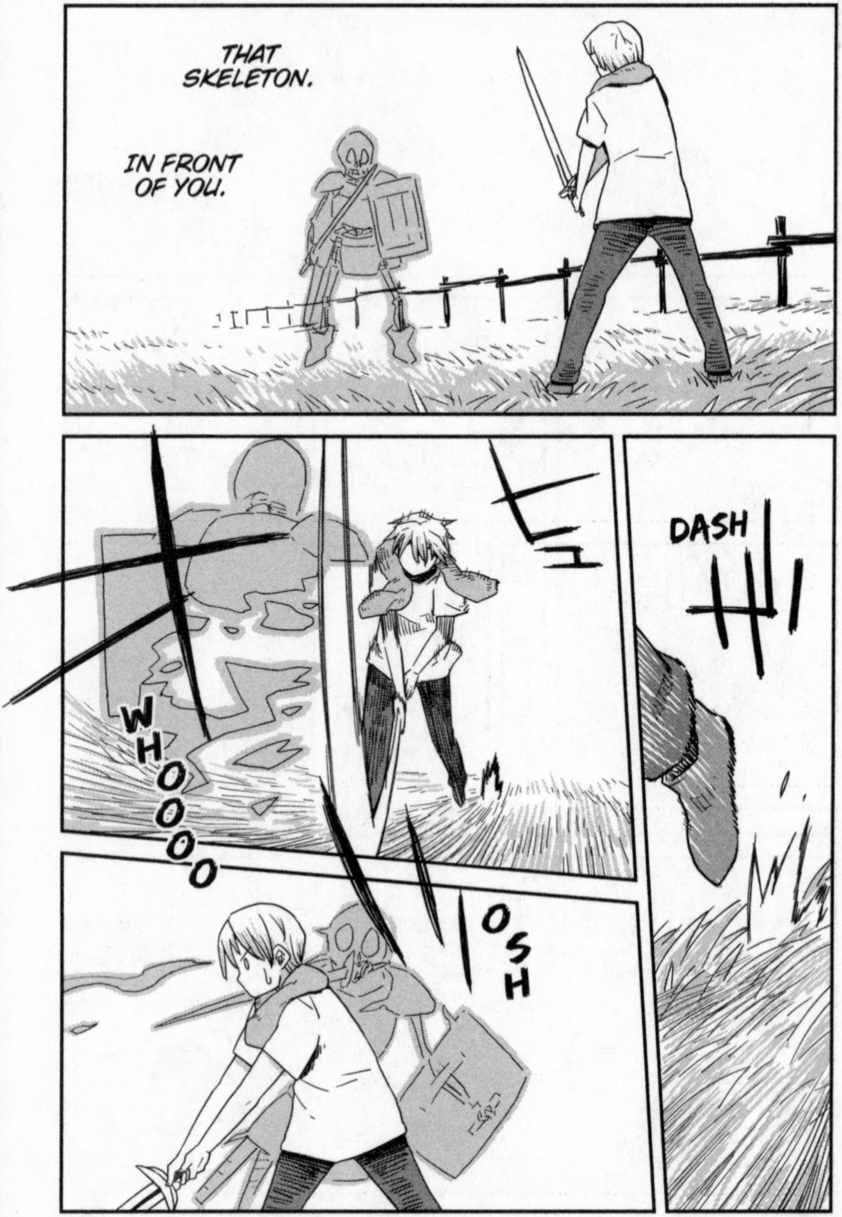

THAT SKELETON.
IN FRONT OF YOU.
DASH
WHOOOOO
OSH

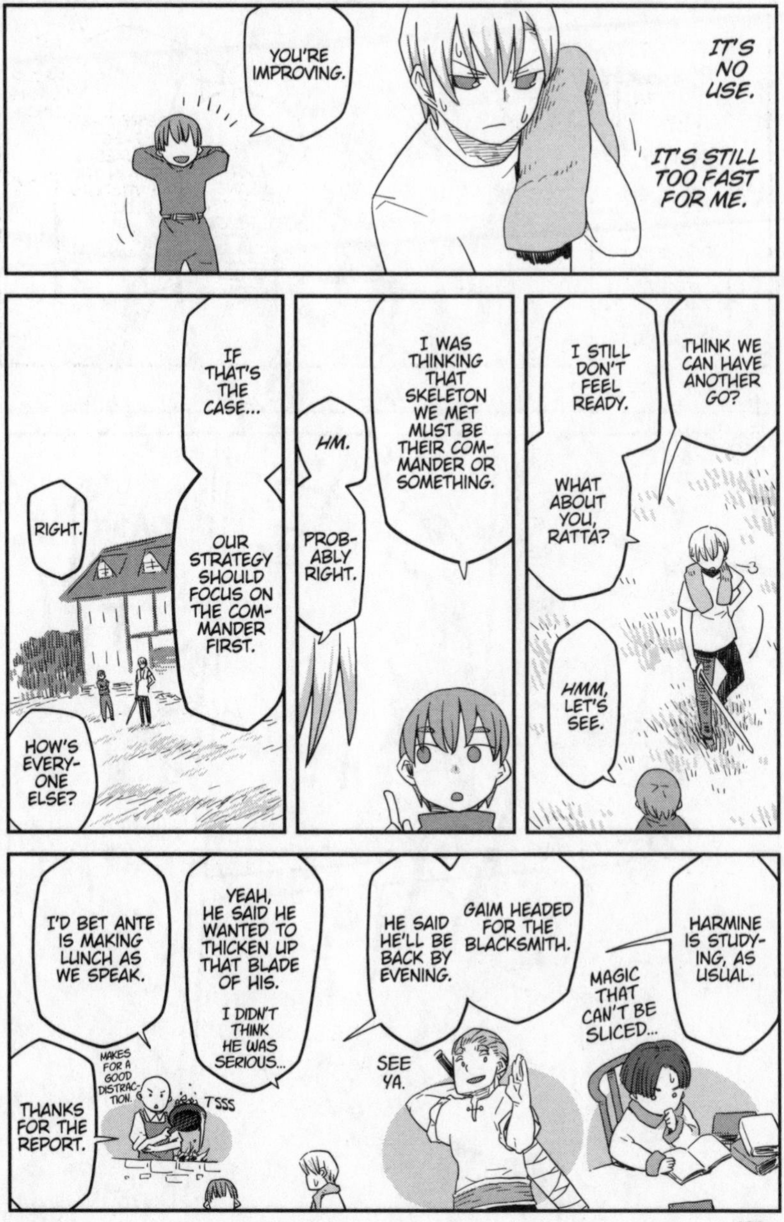
IT'S NO USE.
YOU'RE IMPROVING.
IT'S STILL TOO FAST FOR ME.
THINK WE CAN HAVE ANOTHER GO?
I STILL DON'T FEEL READY.
WHAT ABOUT YOU, RATTA?
HMM, LET'S SEE.
I WAS THINKING THAT SKELETON WE MET MUST BE THEIR COMMANDER OR SOMETHING.
HM.
PROBABLY RIGHT.
IF THAT'S THE CASE...
OUR STRATEGY SHOULD FOCUS ON THE COMMANDER FIRST.
RIGHT.
HOW'S EVERYONE ELSE?
HARMINE IS STUDYING, AS USUAL.
MAGIC THAT CAN'T BE SLICED...
GAIM HEADED FOR THE BLACKSMITH.
HE SAID HE'LL BE BACK BY EVENING.
SEE YA.
YEAH, HE SAID HE WANTED TO THICKEN UP THAT BLADE OF HIS.
I DIDN'T THINK HE WAS SERIOUS...
I'D BET ANTE IS MAKING LUNCH AS WE SPEAK.
MAKES FOR A GOOD DISTRACTION.
TSSS
THANKS FOR THE REPORT.

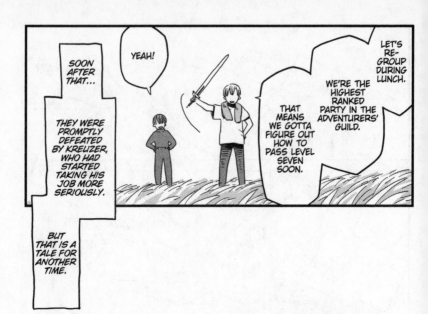

LET'S RE-GROUP DURING LUNCH.
WE'RE THE HIGHEST RANKED PARTY IN THE ADVENTURERS' GUILD.
THAT MEANS WE GOTTA FIGURE OUT HOW TO PASS LEVEL SEVEN SOON.
YEAH!
SOON AFTER THAT...
THEY WERE PROMPTLY DEFEATED BY KREUZER, WHO HAD STARTED TAKING HIS JOB MORE SERIOUSLY.
BUT THAT IS A TALE FOR ANOTHER TIME.

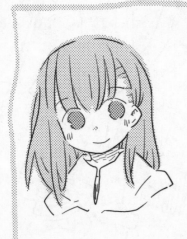

THANK YOU FOR
READING THIS FAR!

I HOPE TO SEE YOU
AGAIN FOR VOLUME 2!!

SPECIAL THANKS
BOSS - HORIE-SAMA
CHARACTER DESIGN -
NAKASO NEKO-SAMA
THANK YOU, THANK YOU!
SUI HUTAMI

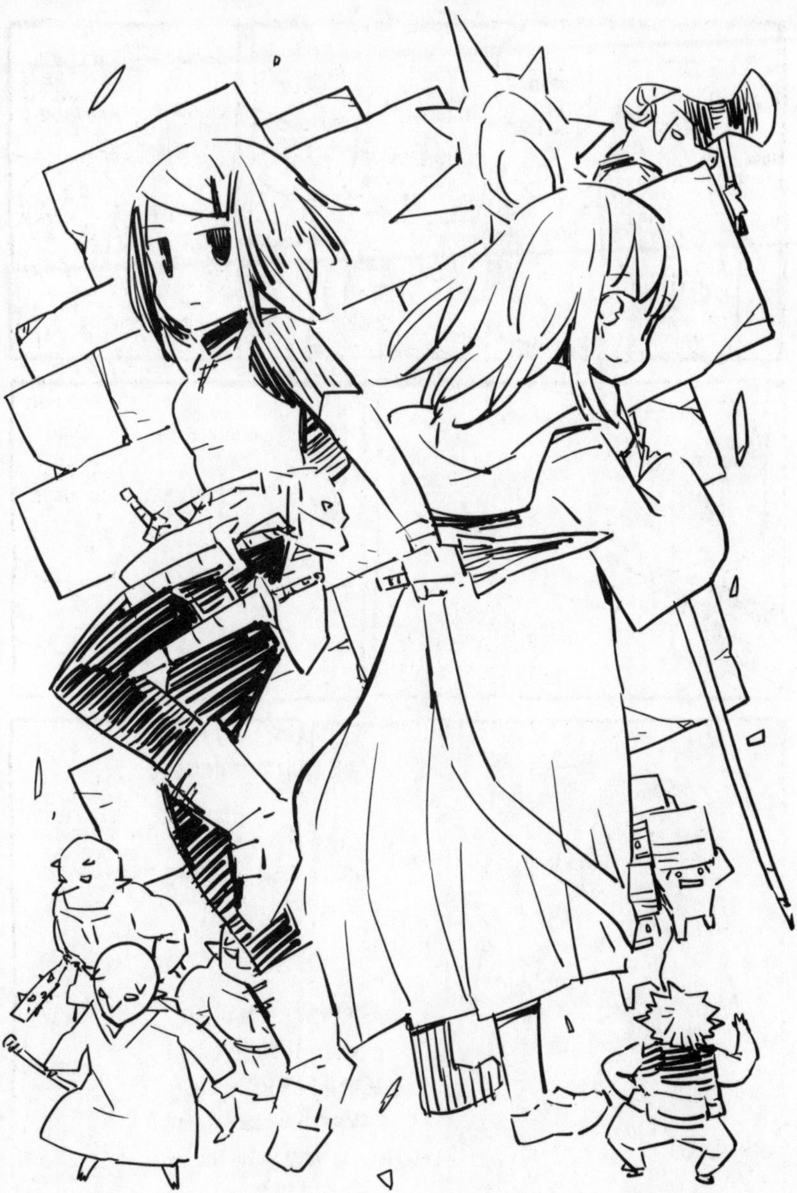

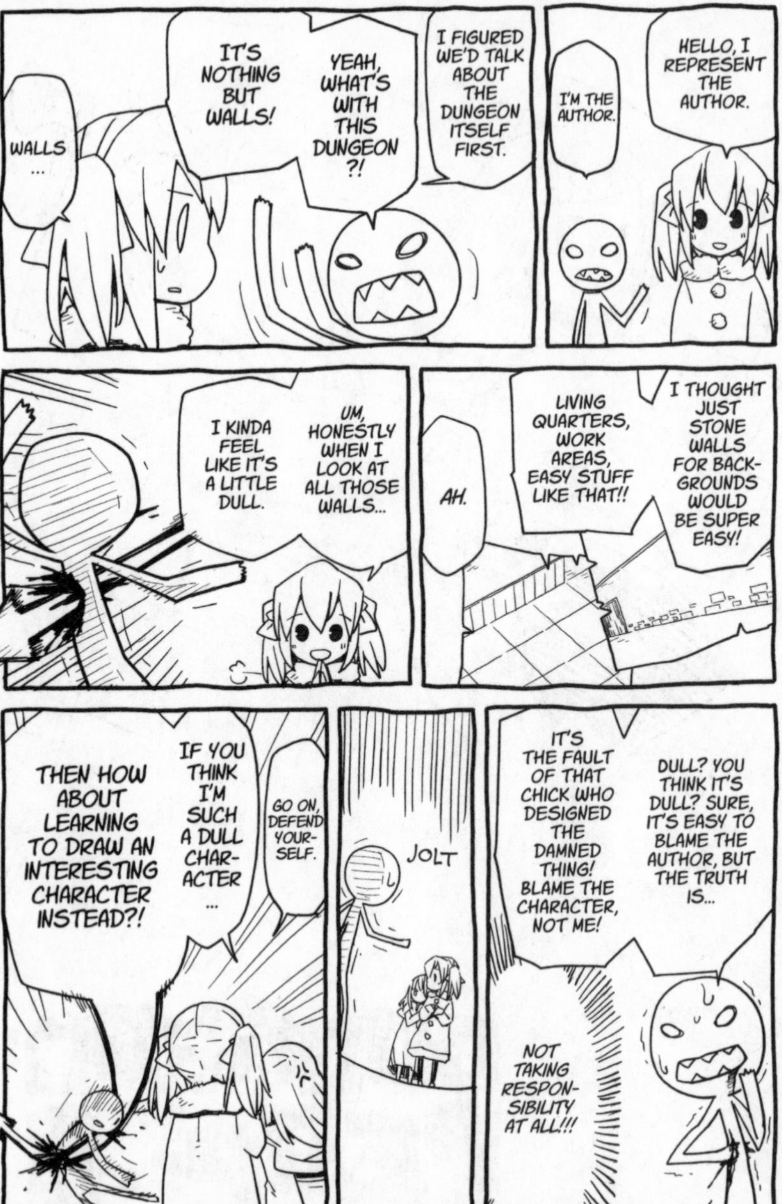
HELLO, I REPRESENT THE AUTHOR.
I'M THE AUTHOR.
I FIGURED WE'D TALK ABOUT THE DUNGEON ITSELF FIRST.
YEAH, WHAT'S WITH THIS DUNGEON?!
IT'S NOTHING BUT WALLS!
WALLS...
I THOUGHT JUST STONE WALLS FOR BACKGROUNDS WOULD BE SUPER EASY!
LIVING QUARTERS, WORK AREAS, EASY STUFF LIKE THAT!!
AH.
UM, HONESTLY WHEN I LOOK AT ALL THOSE WALLS...
I KINDA FEEL LIKE IT'S A LITTLE DULL.
DULL? YOU THINK IT'S DULL? SURE, IT'S EASY TO BLAME THE AUTHOR, BUT THE TRUTH IS...
IT'S THE FAULT OF THAT CHICK WHO DESIGNED THE DAMNED THING! BLAME THE CHARACTER, NOT ME!
NOT TAKING RESPONSIBILITY AT ALL!!!
JOLT
GO ON, DEFEND YOURSELF.
IF YOU THINK I'M SUCH A DULL CHARACTER...
THEN HOW ABOUT LEARNING TO DRAW AN INTERESTING CHARACTER INSTEAD?!

DUNGEON
PEOPLE

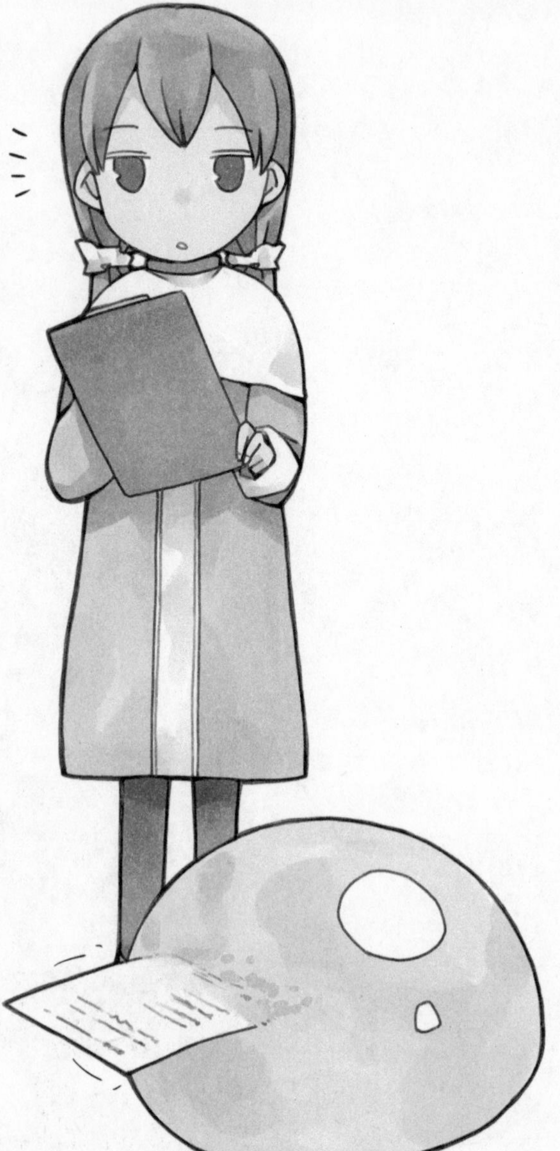

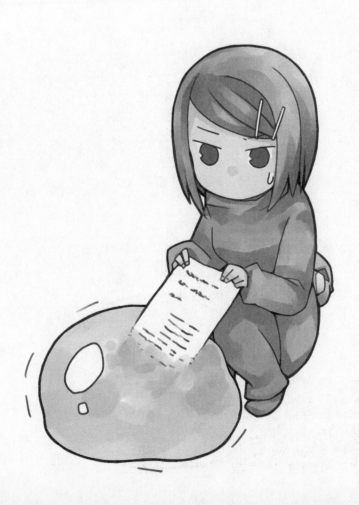

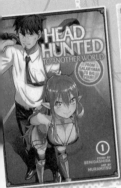
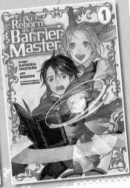
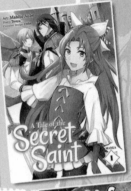
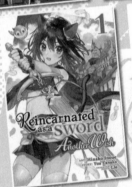
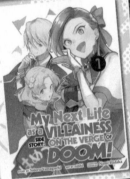
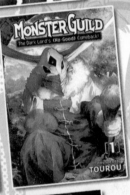
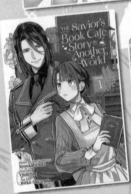

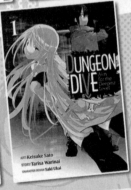

DUNGEON PEOPLE

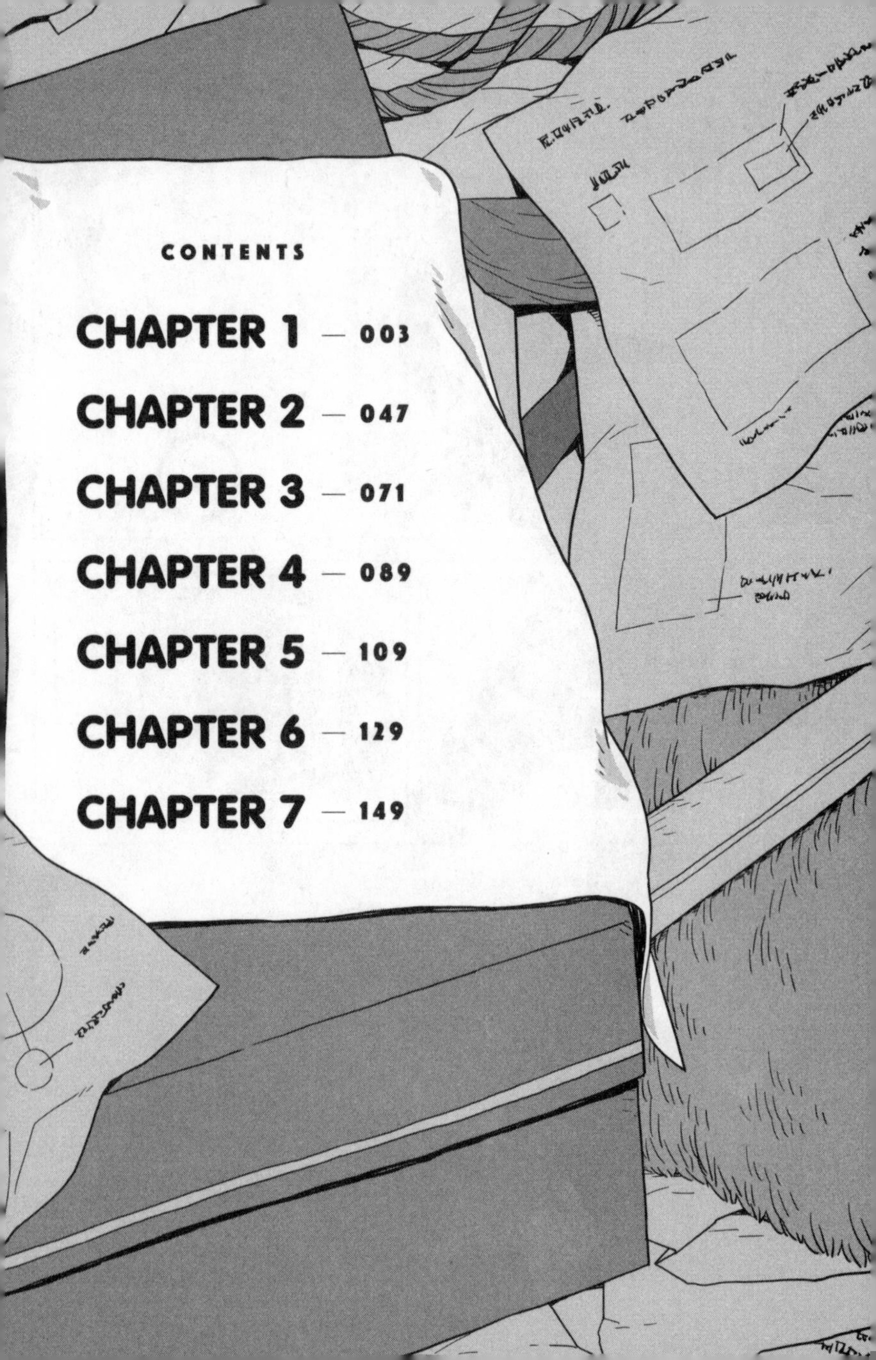

CONTENTS

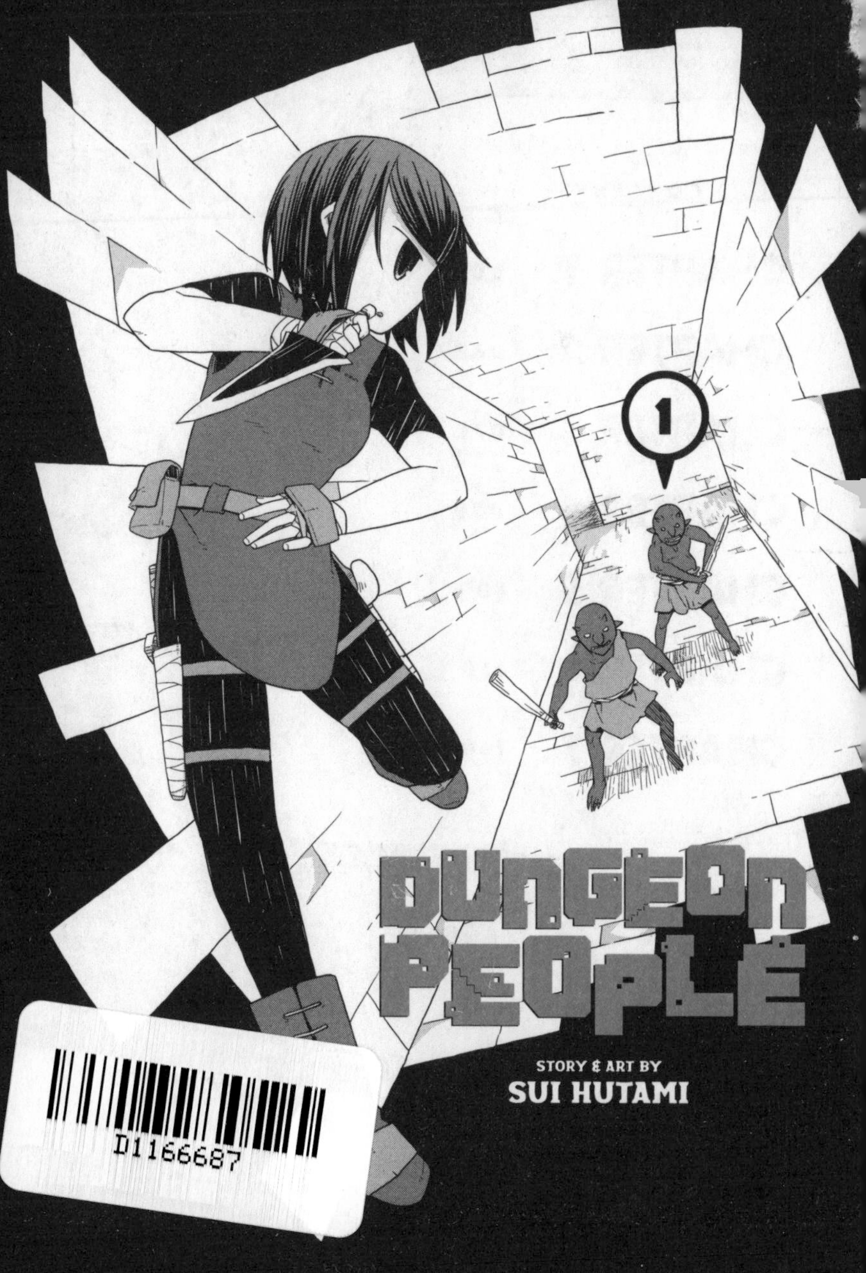

1

DUNGEON PEOPLE

STORY & ART BY
SUI HUTAMI